KNIGHT'S
FOODSERVICE
DICTIONARY

KNIGHT'S
FOODSERVICE
DICTIONARY

John B. Knight, Ed.D

Edited by

Charles A. Salter, Ph.D

A CBI BOOK

Published by Van Nostrand Reinhold Company

New York

A CBI book
(CBI is an imprint of Van Nostrand Reinhold Company Inc.)

Copyright (c) 1987 by Van Nostrand Reinhold Company Inc.
Library of Congress Catalog Card Number 84-27140
ISBN 0-442-24666-8

Printed in the United States of America
Designed by Joy Taylor

Van Nostrand Reinhold Company Inc.
115 Fifth Avenue
New York, New York 10003

Van Nostrand Reinhold Company Limited
Molly Millars Lane
Wokingham, Berkshire RG11 2PY, England

Van Nostrand Reinhold
480 La Trobe Street
Melbourne, Victoria 3000, Australia

Macmillan of Canada
Division of Canada Publishing Corporation
164 Commander Boulevard
Agincourt, Ontario M1S 3C7, Canada

16 15 14 13 12 11 10 9 8 7 6 5 4 3 2 1

Library of Congress Cataloging-in-Publication Data

Knight, John Barton, 1950-
  Knight's Foodservice dictionary.

  "A CBI book."
  1. Food service–Dictionaries. I. Salter, Charles A.,
1947- . II. Title. III. Title: Foodservice dictionary.
TX905.K65 1985 642'.03'21 84-27140
ISBN 0-442-24666-8

Preface

Knight's Foodservice Dictionary brings together for the first time definitions from all aspects of the foodservice industry: basic terms, basic ingredients, cost controls, culinary arts, foodservice equipment, management information systems, menu analysis and development, nutrition, sanitation and safety, service and merchandising, and bar management.

As with any new reference work, the author and editor have researched the field to provide the most current information. Unlike other texts, however, this dictionary is meant to be updated continually to reflect new trends and definitions. Should any reader feel a term is inappropriately defined or is misused, we would appreciate knowing about it. If the terminology of the vast foodservice industry is to be standardized, the opinions and comments of many will be valuable over the years. Therefore we welcome suggestions for new terms or expanded definitions from all concerned readers. Please write in care of the publishers.

We wish to thank and give credit to the following individuals, without whom this dictionary would not have been possible:

Bonnie Bruttig	Rajan Lai	Carol Pound
Steven Bruttig	Leah Lucas	Doris Ryan
Arlene Calhoun	Nicholas Naples	Carlota Salter
Mary Anne Duble	David Nelson	Walter Scott
Brigitte Fefer	Paula Nelson	Jeffrey Starrett
Emilie Gostanian	Normad Peckenpaugh	

A

ABAISSE—French; rolled-out pastry, a layer of biscuit, or thin bottom crust.

ABATEMENT—Cancellation of all or part of an expenditure.

ABATIS—French; giblets; edible viscera, e.g., heart, liver, and kidneys.

ABATTE—French; a thick, broad, double-edged knife used to flatten meat.

ABATTOIR—French; slaughterhouse.

ABSENTEEISM—Failure of employees to appear at work because of illness, transportation difficulties, or other reasons, on a normal workday.

ABSENTEEISM RATE—Index calculated by dividing the total number of all days of absenteeism (A) by the product of the average number of employees (E) and the total number of work days (T), times 100 percent. Thus the absenteeism rate (R) = (A/E × T) × 100%.

ABSOLUTE HUMIDITY—Total amount of water vapor (humidity) in a specified weight of air. Contrast **relative humidity.** Greatly affects comfort level of any given area.

ABSORB—To transfer an account or group of accounts into one or another group, thus eliminating the first one(s). Also, to take up fluid, as a sponge.

ABSORBENT PACKING—Packing materials, used when liquids are shipped, that will absorb fluids in the event of leakage.

ABSORPTIOMETER—Instrument that measures the relative amount of light absorbed by colored solutions. In general, the stronger the color, the less light is absorbed. The device is used to measure the strength of various nutrients present in a food solution. If the nutrient is colorless, a chemical can be added that will react with the nutrient to provide color.

ABSORPTION—Passage of digested nutrients through the walls of the intestines into the bloodstream.

ACCELERATED FREEZE-DRYING—Fast process of dehydration in which heat is applied to frozen foods to draw off the water.

ACCEPTANCE BUYING—Method used by large-volume buyers in which the vendor submits his products to a federal inspector, who ensures that they meet government specifications before final purchase is authorized.

ACCEPTANCE SAMPLING—Inspecting a representative amount of goods from a lot offered by a supplier or potential supplier to see if they are up to par.

ACCESS—The process of entering data in computer memory storage or of retrieving it from storage.

ACCESS TIME—Time necessary to transmit to or receive data from computer storage once the command is given.

ACCIDENT INCIDENCE RATE—Proportion of people in an organization who have an accident during a given time period. It is calculated by dividing the number of people who have had an accident by the total number of hours worked by the people in the organization, and then multiplying by a constant, such as 200,000.

ACCOMMODATION PURCHASE—Purchase made by an establishment on behalf of one of its employees or customers, perhaps to secure a larger discount or similar benefit.

ACCOMPANIMENT SALAD—Moderate-size salad served with the main course or as a separate course of the meal.

ACCOUNT—Record of additions and subtractions regarding a specific activity or business transaction; e.g., interest expenses or sales revenues.

ACCOUNTABILITY—Responsibility of employees to make periodic reports to their superiors, evidencing that they have been performing according to regulation.

ACCOUNTABLE—Having responsibility for performance, cash, or property.

ACCOUNTANT—Person with skills in accounting, the recording of business transactions.

ACCOUNT EXECUTIVE—Person in charge of an advertising agency's dealings with a client.

ACCOUNTING—Process of classifying, recording, and summarizing business transactions into useful reports.

ACCOUNTING CONTROL—Process of ensuring the accuracy of bookkeeping records.

ACCOUNTING PERIOD—Period of time covered in a standard business statement or report, e.g., one month or one year.

ACCOUNTING RECORDS—All the business records of an establishment, including original sources, such as invoices and vouchers, as well as secondary records, such as journals and ledgers.

ACCOUNT PAYABLE—Liability account in the ledger that records amounts owed to a creditor, e.g., to a supplier who has not yet been paid for goods delivered.

ACCOUNT RECEIVABLE—Asset account in the ledger that records money owed to the establishment, e.g., by customers with charge accounts.

ACCOUNT SHEETS—Lined pages in which transactions regarding a particular account can be entered, thus keeping them separate from those regarding any other account. Contrast **journal sheets.**

ACCRETION—Addition of money to any fund according to plan, e.g., payroll deductions, or interest earned and added to a pension fund balance.

ACCRUAL BASIS OF ACCOUNTING—Accounting method in which revenues and expenses are included in the period in which they are incurred, independent of the time when cash is received. Contrast **cash basis of accounting.**

ACCRUAL COSTING—Recording the expense of goods and services according to when they were used, regardless of when they were actually purchased.

ACCRUED ASSET—Amount of an asset that has been earned, but neither received nor past due. For example, earned interest on savings is an accrued asset until the interest is paid.

ACCRUED EXPENSE—Expense incurred in a present period but payable in a future period. For example, wages expense accrues during the pay period until payday, when it becomes an actual expense.

ACCRUED LIABILITY—Amount of a liability that has been incurred, but not yet paid. For example, interest on a loan becomes an accrued liability until it is paid.

ACCRUED REVENUE—Income earned in a present period, but not due to be received until a future one. For example, a charge account customer may be given 30 days to pay for services rendered by the establishment.

ACCUMULATED AUDIENCE—Total number of people who have been exposed to a given advertisement at least once.

ACCUMULATED DEPRECIATION—Total depreciation to date entered into a ledger account against a particular asset.

ACCUMULATED FOOD COST PERCENTAGE—**Food cost percentage** calculated on the basis of the total food costs and total food sales to date during a given accounting period.

ACEROLA—West Indian or Barbados cherry. This small fruit is the richest source of vitamin C known.

ACESCENCE—Vinegar smell of wine that has undergone aerobic bacterial spoilage, a trait desirable in small amounts in some ports and in some wood-aged red table wines.

ACETARY—Acidic fruit pulp.

ACETATE, ACTIVE—Compound formed during the metabolism of glucose and fat.

ACETIC ACID—One of the **fatty acids.** It is formed from alcohol and oxygen by the action of bacteria. See **acetobacter.** Also, the organic compound responsible for the distinctive taste and smell of vinegar.

ACETOBACTER—Type of bacteria that turns alcohol to **acetic acid;** thus it is used in the production of vinegar. If unchecked, it can ruin wine.

ACETOGLYCERIDES—Fat whose molecules, unlike the **triglycerides,** contain **acetic acid** in addition to **glycerol.** Since they are less greasy and melt at a lower temperature than triglycerides, they are often used in the production of shortening and other spreads.

ACETONE—One of the final biochemical products of the metabolism of **fatty acids.** Any excess that cannot be oxidized by the body shows up in the blood or urine.

ACETYLCHOLINE—One of the neurotransmitter chemicals in the body derived from dietary **choline.**

ACHLORHYDRIA—Lack of sufficient **hydrochloric acid** in the gastric juices required for proper digestion.

ACHRODEXTRIN—Type of **dextrin** formed during the conversion of starch to **maltose.**

ACHROMOTRICHIA—Loss of color in the hair caused by a deficiency of **pantothenic acid** or **para-aminobenzoic acid** (PABA).

ACID—Any compound with a pH below the neutral point of 7.0. Contrast **alkali.**

ACID-BASE BALANCE—The equilibrium in bodily fluids between **acids** and **bases**. Normal bodily fluids are slightly alkaline, or on the base side (above the neutral pH of 7.0). Since metabolism produces acids, bases must be ingested to maintain the proper balance.

ACID CALCIUM PHOSPHATE (ACP)—Also called calcium acid phosphate, this is the acid ingredient in baking powder. When mixed with dough, moistened, and heated, it causes the release of carbon dioxide gas, thereby making the dough rise.

ACID FOODS—Foods containing the minerals chlorine, phosphorous, or sulfur, that tend to lower the pH of bodily fluids when digested. Such foods include cheese, cereals, eggs, fish, and meat. Contrast **base-forming foods.**

ACIDITY, WINE—Tartness, sharpness, or sourness caused by fruit acids in the beverage.

ACID NUMBER—Measure of the rancidity of fat in food, thus indicating its state of deterioration.

ACIDOPHILUS THERAPY—Therapy for problems of digestion and elimination in which the person eats foods containing *Lactobacillus acidophilus* bacteria, the bacteria that produces lactic acid. The foods are primarily milk to which the bacteria have been added, or yogurt, in which the bacteria form the basic culture. Lactic acid bacteria normally exist in the intestines and aid in the digestion of the lactose in milk, but if they die (as from antibiotics) they can be replaced in this way.

ACIDOSIS—Lowering of the pH of bodily fluids due to an excess of acid. This excess may be attributable to a loss of bases as well as to an overabundance of acids themselves. Contrast **alkalosis.**

ACORN SQUASH—Small acorn-shaped vegetable with a furrowed dark-green rind.

ACQUISITION—Process of coming to own or control an asset.

ACQUISITION COST—Total expense incurred in coming to own or control an asset.

ACQUISITION DATE—See **date of acquisition.**

ACRALDEHYDE—Acrid substance produced by the glycerol component of fat when fats are overheated.

ACRODYNIA—Dermatitis caused by a dietary lack of vitamin B_6.

ACROLEIN—See **Acraldehyde.**

ACTIN—Protein comprising about 13 percent of total muscle protein.

ACTIVATORS—Substances required to activate enzymes so that they may perform their biochemical work. For example, chloride is required to activate saliva.

ACTIVE IMMUNITY—See **immunity, active.**

ACTIVE OXYGEN METHOD—**Swift stability test.**

ACTOMYOSIN—Protein, composed of **actin** and **myosin,** that is responsible for the contractile property of muscle.

ACTUAL FOOD COST—Amount spent for food during a certain period, regardless of how much was originally budgeted.

ACTUAL FOOD COST PERCENTAGE—Ratio of cost to sales, multiplied by 100 percent.

ACTUAL INVENTORY—Number of each food item on hand, as verified by a physical count.

ADDED VALUE—Increase in an item's selling price caused by additional costs incurred in the production, processing, transporting, or retailing of that item.

ADDITIONAL MARK-ON—Adding another increase in selling price to an item that already has at least one mark-on, or **markup.**

ADDITIVE, FOOD—Any material added to food, such as a preservative. Additives include emulsifiers, thickeners, flavors, curing agents, humectants, colors, vitamins, minerals, yeast, and bacterial inhibitors.

ADDRESS—Label, name, or number that indicates a particular location in computer memory.

ADENOSINE—Molecular combination of adenine and ribose

sugar. When combined further with mono-, di-, or triphosphate, it is important in energy transformations.

ADENOSINE DIPHOSPHATE (ADP)—Combination of **adenosine** and two **phosphate** groups of atoms. Energy is released when one of these phosphates is biochemically separated. Additional energy is stored when a third phosphate group is added to ADP.

ADENOSINE MONOPHOSPHATE (AMP)—Combination of **adenosine** and one phosphate group of atoms. Adding additional phosphates stores energy for later use in a living cell.

ADENOSINE TRIPHOSPHATE (ATP)—Combination of **adenosine** and three phosphate groups of atoms. ATP is the chemical molecule that stores energy within each living cell. Energy is released when phosphates are biochemically separated. Energy from digested food restores ATP.

ADIPOSE—Fat or fatty, as in **adipose tissue.**

ADIPOSE TISSUE—Tissue that stores fat. Women of normal weight are composed of 20–25 percent adipose tissue; men of normal weight, 15–20 percent. Obese people have a higher percentage.

ADJUSTED GROSS INCOME—Gross income minus business expenses, losses, and certain other specified deductions.

ADJUSTING JOURNAL ENTRY (AJE)—Entry in the journal or other business record to correct an error or make a change. For example, if a check bounces, an adjusting entry removes that amount from revenue.

ADJUSTMENT—Any change in the accounts produced by **adjusting entries.**

ADSORPTION—Process of a solid surface attracting and collecting molecules of a gas or liquid, e.g., activated charcoal collecting a gaseous odor is considered to have adsorbed it.

ADULTERATED—Condition of having filth, poisons, or other deleterious substances that make the material potentially dangerous for human consumption.

AD VALOREM TAX—Any tax calculated by taking a fixed percentage of the value of the item or property being taxed.

ADVANCE—Any partial or complete payment made for goods or services before they are delivered.

ADVERTISEMENT—Paid announcement in any of the mass media, designed to attract customers.

ADVERTISING ALLOWANCE—Money given by a producer to merchandisers for promotion of his products.

ADVERTISING REGISTER—See **standard advertising register.**

AEQUUM—Amount of food required to sustain normal body weight.

AERATED FLOUR—See **self-rising flour.**

AEROBES—Bacteria that can grow only when oxygen is present. Sterilizing and sealing foods in containers (as in canning) prevents aerobes from infecting the food.

AEROBIC—Any living organism that must have oxygen to survive and reproduce. Contrast **anaerobic.**

AFLATOXICOSIS—Disease resulting from ingesting food infested with **Aflatoxin.** It occurs most commonly among domestic animals (e.g., poultry, cows, pigs) who have eaten tainted feed. The toxins attack the liver, causing lesions, cancer, and often death.

AFLATOXIN—Toxin produced by the fungus **Aspergillus flavus,** which grows on grains, nuts, beans, and certain other foods if they have been kept in too moist an environment after harvesting. Ingesting it can cause **aflatoxicosis.**

AFTERTASTE—Lingering taste of a food or wine in the mouth after it has been swallowed; used particularly in reference to wine.

AGAR-AGAR—Product derived from certain forms of seaweed that forms a gel. It is used widely in the preparation of such foods as jelly and ice cream, and as a stabilizing ingredient as well.

AGATEWARE—Type of metal kitchenware with a porcelain-enamel lining that facilitates cleaning.

AGENCY SHOP—Arrangement by which all workers at an establishment holding union contracts are required to pay dues or fees to the union whether they join it formally or not.

AGEUSIA—Reduction in the sense of taste that may be caused by nerve damage from disease or trauma.

AGING, FLOUR—Addition of oxidizing agents (e.g., nitrogen trichloride) to flour, thus bleaching it and producing stronger dough.

AGING, MEAT—Keeping purchased meat in the storeroom at 34°–36° F for a few weeks to improve its flavor and tenderness. Aging also causes some shrinkage.

AGING, WINE—Gradual process, in which continuing oxidation in wine produces a smoother taste and bouquet.

AGLYCON—Any molecule that forms a **glycoside** when attached to a sugar molecule.

AGRICULTURAL MARKETING REPORTS—Reports published by the U.S. Department of Agriculture that quote price trends for agricultural products before these changes are reflected at the local level.

AIGUILLETTES—French; thin slices or small strips of cooked meat, usually poultry.

AIR GAP—Empty vertical distance between the point where water enters a plumbing fixture and the maximum level it rises inside that fixture. The air gap prevents **backflow.**

AIR LOCK—Closure that is tight enough to prevent the passage of air in or out of a container.

AJI, AGI—South American red-hot pepper used in spicy dishes.

A LA (AU, AUX)—French; literally means *to the.* In usage, however, it means *with, at,* or *in;* e.g., *à la moutarde,* with or in mustard; *au jus,* with natural juices.

A LA CARTE—French; idiom that means each menu item is

charged for separately; i.e., there are no package deals for a complete meal.

A L'ALLEMANDE—French; means German style.

A LA MODE—French; literally, "in the fashion of." Used with cake or pie to mean topped with ice cream. Other dishes may be so named if specially served, e.g., boeuf à la mode, braised larded beef served with a scoop of mashed potatoes.

ALANINE—One of the 22 amino acids that compose protein. Alanine is abundant, is found in most protein foods, and can be synthesized within the body.

ALBEDO—White fibrous mass along the inner peel of oranges and other citrus fruits. A rich source of **pectin.**

ALBUMEN—White of an egg. Also spelled **albumin.**

ALBUMIN—Any of a group of simple, water-soluble proteins that coagulate during cooking. The ovalbumin in egg white is an example. See **egg albumins.**

ALBUMIN/GLOBULIN RATIO (A/G RATIO)—Ratio of **albumin** to **globulin** in the blood. Any deviation from normal (about 1:82) may indicate a dietary or metabolic problem.

ALBUMIN INDEX—Ratio of the height of the egg white (albumin) to the width as the mass sits on a flat surface. The greater the height, the greater the index, and the greater the quality of the egg.

ALCOHOL—Result of yeast fermentation of carbohydrates, as in wine- and beer-making. It is the intoxicating ingredient in beer, wine, and liquors. Pure alcohol is colorless and flammable.

ALCOHOL, DENATURED—Alcohol to which noxious substances have been added to make it undrinkable; used for industrial purposes.

ALDEHYDES—Chemical byproducts resulting from acid, alcohol, and air being combined in alcoholic beverages.

AL DENTE—Italian; literally "to the teeth." Used to describe foods, such as vegetables and pasta, that are firm and chewy (i.e., slightly undercooked).

ALDOSTERONE—Hormone produced by the adrenal glands, which are instrumental in the regulation of salts and water in the urine.

ALDOXIME—Noncaloric artificial sweetener that is 450 times stronger than sucrose.

ALE—Bittersweet malt beverage.

ALGAE—Simple plant that grows in water (e.g., seaweed). Some forms are edible. Although now used mostly for cattle feed, algae may become a major source of human food in the future.

ALGINATE—Salt derivative of seaweed that can be used as a thickener or emulsifier in ice cream or other food products.

ALGORITHM—Step-by-step process for deriving the desired results or output from a certain computer input.

ALIMENTARY CANAL—The entire digestive tract, extending from the mouth to the large intestine.

ALIMENTARY PASTES—Pasta, macaroni, noodles, and related products made from dough.

ALIMENT DE SEVRAGE—French; baby-food mixture enriched with about 20 percent protein.

ALKALI—Any substance with a pH above the neutral point of 7.0; another term for **base.** Contrast **acid.**

ALKALINE RESERVE—Buffer substances in the bodily fluids that help maintain the normal pH balance.

ALKALOIDS—Organic nitrogen-containing molecules produced by plants that have strong effects when ingested. Alkaloids include both potent drugs (e.g., morphine) and poisons (e.g., strychnine).

ALKALOSIS—Rise of the pH of bodily fluid caused by an excess of basic (or alkaline) substances. This excess may occur through a loss of acids (e.g., from vomiting) as well as through an increased consumption of alkaline compounds. Contrast **acidosis.**

ALKANNET—Food additive derived from the plant *Alkanna tinctoria* that is used to color fats and cheeses.

ALLERGEN—Any substance (as from food or drink) that causes an allergic reaction in bodily tissues.

ALLERGY—An abnormal tissue or blood response to any substance near, on, or entering the body, as through eating.

ALLICIN—Chemical ingredient in garlic that gives it its characteristic flavor.

ALL-INCLUSIVE INCOME STATEMENT—Income statement based on all profit and loss figures for a specified accounting period. This statement gives a more accurate picture than a partial or adjusted income statement.

ALLOCATION—Direct assignment of indirect costs to a particular department so they can be accounted for.

ALLOLACTOSE—One of the group of sugar compounds. It is found in human milk.

ALLOTRIOPHAGY—Any unnatural craving for food.

ALLOWANCES—Hotel business term representing rebates and overcharges not known at the time of the transaction but adjusted at a subsequent date.

ALLOWANCES, SALES—See **sales allowances.**

ALLOXAN—Substance that can cause diabetes when ingested by damaging the portions of the pancreas (Isles of Langerhans) that produce insulin.

ALLOXAZINE—Molecule that is part of riboflavin, or vitamin B_2.

ALL-RISK—Type of insurance coverage; the establishment is covered against all perils not specifically excluded in the policy.

ALPHANUMERIC—Character set for computer usage that consists of the letters A through Z, numbers 0–9, space characters, and special characters including comma, dash, period, slash, and the like.

ALTERATIONS—Changes made in menu text after the type has been set. Such changes are expensive, except for the correction of printer's errors.

ALUM—Astringent compound used in some foods (e.g., pickles) as a preservative. Its use is restricted by law, as the compound is poisonous in large quantities.

ALUMINUM—Common mineral that appears only in traces in human tissue. No dietary requirement has been established for it.

ALVEOGRAPH—Procedure for measuring the protein quality of dough prior to baking. The pressure at which a bubble of dough bursts reveals its strength.

AMANDINE—Served with almonds; e.g., á l'amande, slivered almonds sautéed lightly in butter, often served over fish.

AMARANTH—Additive that gives a red coloring to food. Also called red dye #2, it was banned in 1976 by the Food and Drug Administration because it is carcinogenic.

AMBIENT HUMIDITY—Humidity in the air of a given space.

AMBIENT TEMPERATURE—Temperature of the air in a given area.

AMERICAN COCKROACH—Largest of the three principal varieties that infest foodservice establishments. They are about 1.5 inches long and of a reddish-brown color. See **cockroaches.**

AMERICAN GAS ASSOCIATION (AGA)—National association that, among other things, inspects equipment using natural gas as fuel (e.g., stoves, heaters) and issues its seal of approval only if the equipment meets national safety standards.

AMERICAN PLAN—Hotel payment plan that covers not only the room but also three meals a day. Contrast **European plan.**

AMERICAN PLAN, MODIFIED—See **modified American plan.**

AMERICAN SERVICE—Method of service in which food is

cooked in the kitchen, portioned onto individual plates by the cook, and served by the waiter. Contrast **Russian service.**

AMERICAN STANDARD CODE FOR INFORMATION IN-TERCHANGE (ASCII)—American Standard Association (ASA) computer coding system for data transfer.

AMINE—Any organic compound that contains nitrogen, e.g., amino acids.

AMINO ACID—Any of a group of 22 compounds that form protein in chemical combination; most can be synthesized by the human body. Each amino acid is composed of an **amine** and an acid group of atoms.

AMINO ACID OXIDASE—Substance that oxidizes amino acids into ketonic acids during the body's process of metabolism.

AMINO ACIDS, ANTIKETOGENIC—Amino acids that are converted during the body's process of metabolism into glucose, a rich source of energy.

AMINO ACIDS, ESSENTIAL—Eight amino acids that cannot be synthesized within the human body. Sufficient quantities must be obtained from the diet.

AMINO ACIDS, KETOGENIC—Amino acids that are converted during the body's process of metabolism into **ketone bodies.**

AMINO ACIDS, LIMITING—Essential amino acids least prevalent in a particular protein compared to what is required for a balanced diet. The limiting amino acid is used to calculate the **chemical score.**

AMINO ACIDS, NONESSENTIAL—Amino acids that can be synthesized within the human body if they are not obtained in the diet.

AMINOPEPTIDASE—Enzyme that helps the digestion of protein by splitting up the **polypeptide** chains of amino acids into **dipeptides.**

AMOEBA—Single-cell protozoan. Certain kinds, if contracted from impure drinking water or food, can cause **amoebic dysen-**

tery. It is usually transmitted from fecal matter on the unwashed hands of an infected person.

AMOEBIC DYSENTERY—Inflammation of the colon caused by one-celled organisms called *Entamoeba dysenteriae.* These amoeba are picked up by ingesting infected food or water. They cause intestinal cramps with alternating constipation and diarrhea. Left untreated, the amoeba can spread to other organs such as the liver and cause serious damage or death.

AMORTIZATION—Gradual reduction of any amount or sum over a long period. This occurs, for example, when paying off a loan or subtracting accumulating depreciation from an asset.

AMORTIZATION SCHEDULE—Table of dates and the amount to be amortized at each date.

AMPELOGRAPHY—Study and science of cultivating grapevines.

AMPHETAMINES—Stimulant drugs that depress the appetite and thus are widely used in weight reduction. Overuse can cause dangerous physical and psychological side effects.

AMYGDALIN—**Glucoside** found in almonds and cherry seeds. It can be hydrolyzed into glucose and other compounds.

AMYGDALINE—Similar in nature to the almond, as in smell or taste.

AMYLASES—Enzymes that digest starches and **glycogen** and break them down to **maltose.** They are found in saliva and pancreatic juices.

AMYLODYSPEPSIA—Inability to metabolize dietary starch into sugar.

AMYLOGRAPH—Measure of the thickness of dough during heating that reveals the ability of the flour to provide chemically the sugar required to "feed" the yeast.

AMYLOLYTIC—Referring to the hydrolysis or chemical breakdown of starch in food to its component simple sugars.

AMYLOPECTIN—One of the key components of starch, accounting for about three fourths of the total. Each molecule is composed of **glucosides.**

AMYLOSE—One of the components of starch, accounting for about one-fourth of the total. The molecules are composed of glucose.

ANABOLISM—Part of metabolism that involves chemical buildup or restructure.

ANAEROBES—Bacteria that can grow only when oxygen is absent. If not killed with heat, they can thrive within sealed cans, thus posing a serious health hazard.

ANAEROBIC—Any living organism that can survive and reproduce without free oxygen. Contrast **aerobic.**

ANALOG COMPUTER—Device that measures rather than counts, such as a household thermostat.

ANALYSIS SHEET—Columnar sheet on which expense items from the voucher register can be subclassified before being posted to the ledger.

ANCHOR—To use bolts, straps, or any other method to secure goods in their containers so they are not jostled during shipment.

ANEMIA—Insufficient supply of red blood cells usually caused by lack of iron. Taking iron supplements can help overcome the problem.

ANGELICA—Bright-green substance derived from the herb *Angelica archangelica;* used to flavor and color candies and liquors.

ANGIOSTRONGYLUS CANTONESIS—Nematode or roundworm parasite found in the Far East that is acquired by eating infected mollusks or prawns. It causes eosinophilic meningoencephalitis.

ANGLAISE, A L'—French; food cooked English style, usually denoting a simply prepared, ungarnished dish.

ANGOSTURA BITTERS—Reddish-brown aromatic bitters produced in Trinidad. Used primarily in making cocktails.

ANGULAR STOMATITIS—Splitting of the skin around the mouth into little ridges and valleys. It is symptomatic of **riboflavin** deficiency, although it can be caused by other diseases.

ANHYDRATED—Dehydrated; dried.

ANHYDROUS—Dry; compound that does not include liquid.

ANISEED—Licorice-flavored seed often sprinkled on cookies, cakes, fruit salads, and sweet bread; also frequently used in oriental and Italian dishes.

ANISEED OIL—Oil from the **aniseed.** It gives the licorice flavor to **anisette.**

ANNATTO—Food-coloring agent derived from the seeds of a Central American plant, frequently used to impart yellow color to cheese and butter. Also called bixin.

ANNUAL CLOSING—Posting closing entries in the ledger at the end of the fiscal year to close out the revenue and expense accounts.

ANNUITY—Monetary payments made at yearly or other fixed time intervals, e.g., pension payments to a retiree.

ANORECTIC DRUGS—Drugs such as **amphetamines** that suppress feelings of hunger. Overuse can be physically and psychologically dangerous.

ANOREXIA—Pathological loss of appetite caused by any one of several physical or psychological factors.

ANOSMIA—Any impairment of the sense of smell.

ANTABUSE—Drug that causes extreme nausea, vomiting, and headaches when alcohol is ingested. It is used to help alcoholics overcome their desire to drink.

ANTACID—Any base compound that acts as a buffer by neutralizing acid. It is often used to relieve stomach distress caused by acidity.

ANTHOCYANINS—Additives derived from flowers, fruits, and leaves used as food coloring. These additives can be dangerous in canned foods since they react with iron and tin.

ANTIBIOTIC—Drug such as penicillin that inhibits the growth of bacteria; used to preserve food and to fight disease. Antibiotics are also fed to meat-producing animals for greater yield; some experts believe this practice helps lead to the dangerous development of antibiotic-resistant strains of bacteria both in the animals and in humans.

ANTIBODY—Protein substance produced by the body's immune system to neutralize specific toxins.

ANTICAKING AGENT—Substance added to such powdered compounds as salt and sugar to prevent their caking with moisture, e.g., magnesium silicate in salt.

ANTICIPATED PROFIT—Profit that has not yet been realized but that an establishment has good reason to expect will be realized in the future. For example, once a sales contract has been signed, profit can be anticipated even before the contract has been completed.

ANTICIPATED RATE OF RETURN—Index indicating the relative worth of an asset that has been or might be purchased. It is calculated by dividing the average net income produced through the asset by the average value of the asset. The average value takes into consideration the years of useful life and the initial and final value after depreciation.

ANTICIPATED SALES—Expected number of sales of a given item for a given period (usually the next day). It is calculated by multiplying the customer forecast by the popularity index.

ANTIDOTE—Drug or other substance that will neutralize a poison or at least alleviate its effects.

ANTIENZYMES—Any substance that inhibits or neutralizes enzymes. For example, the stomach creates antienzymes to prevent its own digestion by gastric juices that contain enzymes.

ANTIFOAMING AGENTS—Substance such as octanol that reduces foaming in liquids by chemically reacting with the stabilizers therein.

ANTIGEN—Any foreign substance that, when introduced into the body (as with food), stimulates the immune system to produce an antibody to neutralize it.

ANTIMETABOLITE—Compound that is chemically similar to a metabolite (i.e., vitamin K or any other compound important in metabolism) but acts in opposition to it. Such compounds can inhibit the vegetative growth of bacteria, although they have little effect on spore germination.

ANTIMONY—Metal sometimes used to plate the surface of gray enamelware. High-acid foods such as sauerkraut can dissolve the metal and cause poisoning.

ANTIMYCOTIC—Any compound (e.g., calcium propionate) that inhibits the growth of molds.

ANTIOXIDANT—Any substance that slows down **oxidation.** Antioxidants include food preservatives, such as **BHT,** that retard the chemical breakdown of food materials.

ANTIPENETRANT—Chemical added to any substance (e.g., an adhesive) to retard the migration of that substance into another.

ANTIQUE FINISH—Paper covering for menus with a naturally rough appearance.

ANTISEPTIC—Any medicine or other substance that stops the growth of bacteria and other microorganisms.

ANTISIALAGOGUE—Any substance that inhibits the flow of saliva.

ANTISKID SHEET—Heavy cardboard sheets structured so that, placed between cartons or cases, they help prevent loads from shifting or sliding.

ANTISPATTERING AGENT—Compound such as lecithin that prevents the spattering of fats during frying by inhibiting the formation of water droplets.

ANTISTALING AGENT—Compound such as **sucrose stearate** that slows the process by which baked goods turn stale.

ANTIVITAMIN—Substance that interferes with the production or utilization of a vitamin.

ANURIA—Inability to produce urine; characteristic of poisoning by *Amanita phalloides* mushrooms.

APASTIA—Abnormal mental state involving the refusal to accept food.

APERITIF—French; wine or spirits served as an appetizer.

APHAGIA—Severe form of **anorexia** involving a complete refusal to eat.

APORINOSIS—General term for all diseases resulting from dietary deficiencies.

APORRHEGMA—Any toxic substance formed when bacteria decompose the amino acids of protein.

APOSIA—Loss of the feeling of thirst.

APOSITIA—An avoidance of food despite the presence of hunger.

APPEARANCE—In wines, a term referring to the clarity and color. Good appearance means the wine is free of cloudiness or suspended particles.

APPELLATION D'ORIGINE CONTROLEE—French; found on French fine-wine labels, indicating wine's origin and its legal right to the name signified.

APPERTIZATION—French; partial sterilization of food in which only safe microorganisms remain.

APPETIZER—Food or drink served to whet the appetite before the main course.

APPETIZER SALAD—Light small salad served to whet the appetite.

APPLE—Fleshy fruit about the size of a fist. There are over 200 varieties in the United States, including Delicious, McIntosh,

Rome Beauty, and Winesap. Apples may be eaten raw or cooked, or processed into juice or apple sauce. They remain fresh longer than most fruits.

APPLE CORER—Tube-shaped knife used to cut out cores from apples.

APPLICATION BULLETIN—Memo sent to computer dealers to inform them of changes that should or must be made to existing equipment, usually to improve its operation.

APPLICATION, COMPUTER—Problem or task to which a computer is applied.

APPLICATOR—Device fitted to a container of a product (e.g., a cleanser) so that the product can be dispensed where needed, thus reducing waste and the chance of contaminating something else.

APPLIED COST—Any cost that has been set aside in the accounting books as pertaining to a particular business activity.

APPLIED OVERHEAD—Overhead costs that have been allocated in the accounting books to a specific business activity.

APPORTIONMENT—Division of indirect costs among two or more departments so that they may be accounted for properly.

APPRAISE—To decide upon a selling price by evaluating the current value of an item in the marketplace.

APPRECIATION—Increase in the value of an asset as a function of time rather than improvement in the asset. For example, the value of goods in the storeroom appreciates as their market cost goes up.

APPROPRIATION OF NET INCOME—Distribution of the net income from the preceding accounting period.

APPROVED—Certified by a designated health authority to be in conformance with health and safety standards.

APRICOT—Small, round fruit with a yellowish-orange color, related to peaches and nectarines. They contain less sugar than most other fruits, and are eaten dried as well as fresh or canned.

AQUA VITA(E)—Italian or Latin for spirits, literally "water of life."

ARABICA—Columbian coffee plant producing fine quality beans. First discovered in Arabia, it is today considered the first in quality of the two varieties of arabica and **robusta.**

ARACHIDONIC ACID—One of the **essential fatty acids,** found only in animal fat. One of the **polyunsaturated fats.**

ARACHIN—One of the main proteins in peanuts.

ARACHIS OIL—Peanut oil.

ARBITRAGE—Simultaneous purchase and sale of an item in different markets to profit from the difference in price.

ARBITRATION—To settle differences between two parties, e.g., between a union and an establishment's management, by submitting both cases to a neutral outside party. Such a person is called the arbitrator.

ARCHITECTURE, COMPUTER—Design of some element of a computer system, including the hardware or engineering of the computer, the software or workings of the program itself, and the communications or design of the communication hardware and software (including control characters, message formats, and so on). All of these elements make up a computer's architecture.

ARGINASE—One of the enzymes involved in the conversion of amino acids to **urea,** which is excreted in the urine.

ARGININE—One of the nonessential amino acids in protein. Arginine is involved in the formation of **urea.**

ARGOL—Crude tartar formed during wine fermentation. It is used in the production of vinegar and tartaric acid.

ARIBOFLAVINOSIS—Syndrome caused by riboflavin (vitamin B_2) deficiency. Symptoms include red, swollen lips and tongue, and cracking of the skin around the mouth.

ARMENIAN BOLE—Ferric oxide, an additive used to color food.

AROMA—The part of a wine's odor or **nose** that is derived from the grape variety and yeast fermentation. See **bouquet.**

ARROWROOT—Food derived from the tubers of the plant *Maranta arundinacea.* Composed almost entirely of starch, it is useful in low-protein, low-salt diets. It is also used as a thickening agent in soups and gravies. Easily digested, arrowroot is useful for invalids and the aged.

ARSANILIC ACID—Chemical compound used to increase the growth of poultry.

ARSENIC—Highly toxic substance found in some weed killers and pesticides, as well as in certain fish, eggs, milk, cereals, and vegetables. Since it tends to be stored in bodily tissues, even small amounts, if ingested repeatedly, can become poisonous.

ARSENIC POISONING—Poisoning resulting from the ingestion of **arsenic.** Symptoms resulting from a single dose include abdominal cramps, vomiting, and diarrhea. Repeated small doses cause a variety of gastrointestinal complaints, scaling and pigmentation of the skin, and mental disturbances. Even small doses can be fatal.

ARTICHOKE—Globe or French artichokes are buds of a plant belonging to the thistle family. After being boiled, the leaves are pulled off, dipped into sauce, and the tender bottom portion eaten. The artichoke heart is the center bottom of the bud and is considered a delicacy. Jerusalem artichokes, also known as Girasole artichokes, are of the sunflower family and are tubers. They may be boiled or chilled raw to be eaten like celery.

ARTICLES OF INCORPORATION—Legal document required to establish a business corporation. It includes the name and address of the corporation and its founders, describes the type of stock issued, and details the nature of the business activities.

ASCARID—Nematode or roundworm parasite that dwells in the intestines.

ASCORBIC ACID—Vitamin C. As an **antioxidant,** it is used in foods to retard spoilage and to preserve the red color of fresh or preserved meats.

ASCORBIC ACID OXIDASE—Enzyme in plants that can destroy their Vitamin C (ascorbic acid) content. Plunging vegetables briefly into boiling water can prevent this loss during later cooking by inactivating the enzyme.

ASCORBIN STEARATE—Derivative of **ascorbic acid** and **stearic acid** that can be used as an **antioxidant.**

ASCORBYL PALMITATE—Derivative of **ascorbic acid** and **palmitic acid** that can be used to retard the staling process in baked goods.

ASEPSIS—Making something free of harmful microorganisms or contamination, i.e., making it aseptic.

ASEPTIC FILLING—Placing sterilized food in sterilized containers, to be sealed in such a way that bacteria cannot infest the food. See **asepsis.**

ASH—Minerals such as iron and phosphorus present in flour and other foods.

ASKING PRICE—Price at which the owner of an item offers to sell it.

ASPARTAME—Artificial sweetener that tastes much like table sugar (sucrose) but is 200 times sweeter. It is derived from the amino acids L-aspartic acid and L-phenylalanine.

ASPARTIC ACID—One of the nonessential **amino acids.**

ASPERGILLUS FLAVUS—Fungus that causes **aflatoxicosis.**

ASPIC—Method of arranging cold dishes that consists of placing slices of food into aspic jelly.

ASPIC MOLD—Vessel, usually made of metal and in a decorative shape, used to form gelatinous dishes called **aspics.**

AS PURCHASED (AP) WEIGHT—Weight of purchased meat or other goods purchased in bulk, including all unusable portions.

ASSEMBLER LANGUAGE—Manufacturer-supplied computer program that translates the programmer's instructions into machine language.

ASSESSED VALUE—Value of an asset as appraised by an expert; usually done for insurance or tax purposes.

ASSESSMENT—Government appraisal of the value of an establishment's property for tax purposes.

ASSET—Any item with a monetary value in the marketplace. It can be tangible, such as goods in the storeroom, or intangible, such as good will.

ASSIGNMENT—Transfer of legal ownership or interest in an asset to another party.

ASTAXANTHIN—Natural substance that causes the pink color in salmon.

"AS THEY FALL"—Buying meat in wholesale cuts, before trimming.

ASTRINGENCE—Pungent characteristic of certain **tannic wines** that causes drying and puckering sensations in the mouth.

ASYNCHRONOUS—Literally, nonsynchronized transmission. In electronic data communications, it means that characters may arrive at irregular intervals if they have a signal at the beginning and the end to inform the computer when to start and stop.

ATEBRINE—Common name for **quinocrine hydrochloride.**

ATHEROSCLEROSIS—Buildup of fatty deposits along the inner walls of arteries. It tends to decrease blood flow, increase blood pressure, and increase the chances of artery blockage, heart attacks, and other heart ailments. Many experts believe that excess cholesterol (or some other dietary element) creates the condition.

ATOM—Smallest particle of an element that is indivisible by chemical means.

ATROPHY—Wasting away of part or all of the body due to malnutrition, disease, or parasitic infection.

ATTACHMENT—Using legal means to obtain assets from a borrower when he cannot repay a debt.

ATTAINABLE COST—During budget formulation, any realistic estimate of the amount of future costs.

ATTELET—French; small skewer with an ornamental top on which certain garnishes are threaded to decorate hot or cold dishes served in a grand style.

ATTENDANCE BONUS—Bonus given to an employee as an incentive for perfect attendance or minimal use of sick time. The incentive may be some combination of money, recognition, and time off.

ATTEREAUX—French; skewers. The term refers to alternating food pieces on a skewer. Attereaux differ from **brochettes** in that they are usually coated in batter and deep fried in fat.

ATTRITION—Formation of dust particles resulting from a substance's subjection to friction, sharp blows, or heat, which causes a reduction in size. Attrition may also refer to any gradual reduction, as in an establishment's labor force.

ATWATER FACTORS—Numbers that indicate the number of kilocalories of energy provided for bodily use by each gram of a given food. For example, the number for carbohydrates is four.

AU BEURRE—French; cooked in or with butter sauce or browned butter.

AU BLEU—French; literally, "to the blue." A cooking method in which a live fish is stunned, not killed, with a sharp blow to the head, then quickly cleaned and cooked in white wine or vinegar. The flesh turns slightly blue.

AUDIENCE—People who have read, heard, or seen a given advertisement in any of the mass media.

AUDIENCE ACCUMULATION—Addition of more people to the total of those who are exposed to an ad with each repetition of it.

AUDIENCE PROFILE—List of the traits, such as age, education, and income, that describe the audience exposed to a particular ad in a given media outlet.

AUDITING—Systematic investigation of the business records of an establishment to ascertain their accuracy; usually performed by an accountant.

AU FOUR—French; baked in the oven.

AU GRAS—French; cooked in fat or a rich meat gravy.

AU GRATIN—French; food covered with a sauce and baked with a browned crumb topping of bread and/or cheese, e.g., potatoes au gratin.

AU JUS—French; roasted food served only with its own natural juices.

AU LAIT—French; served with added milk.

AU MAIGRE—French; served without meat.

AU NATUREL—French; cooked plainly or served raw.

AURANTIAMARIN—Natural **glucoside** responsible for part of the flavor of the bitter orange.

AUREOMYCIN—Antibiotic sometimes used as a food preservative and as a means of increasing meat yield by stimulating animal growth.

AUTHORIZED SIGNATURE—Signature of the person responsible for validating the order or payment on requisitions, checks, or similar forms involving expenses. The purpose is to prevent unauthorized use of funds.

AUTOCLAVE—High-pressure steam vessel or pressure cooker that cooks food and kills bacteria. It is used in the canning industry to sterilize food in hermetically sealed cans.

AUTOLYSIS—Breakdown of tissues brought about by naturally present enzymes after the death of the organism. For example, hanging game leads to autolysis of connective tissue, thus tenderizing the meat.

AUTOMATED BAR—System that dispenses liquor automatically

when a sales check is inserted. The machine keeps track of the number of each type of drink sold, the selling price, and so on. Since only the manager has access to the liquor room, this system helps prevent fraud and theft without close supervision. However, it is expensive.

AUTOMATIC CHANGE COMPUTER—Electronic device that compares the bill to the amount offered by the customer and computes the change due back to him.

AUTOMATIC KITCHEN THERMOSTAT—Device that senses the temperature in ovens or other cooking units and turns off the heat when a selected temperature has been reached. The device saves energy and helps prevent overcooking of food.

AUTOMATIC KITCHEN TIMER—Device that turns off ovens or other cooking units after a selected amount of time has elapsed. They not only help conserve energy but also can prevent food from being overcooked.

AUTOMATIC PRICE LOOKUP—Feature of electronic registers, in which they are programmed to give the price of a given item automatically. It is especially useful when prices change frequently, as during promotional price cuts and "happy hours."

AUTOMATIC REINSTATEMENT—Automatic continuation of insurance coverage after a claim has been submitted for a recently incurred loss.

AUTOMATIC TAX CALCULATION—Feature of electronic registers, in which they are programmed to compute sales tax automatically.

AUX CROUTONS—French; food, usually soup, served with a garnish of butter-sautéed bread cubes, the croutons.

AUXILIARY MEMORY—Extra memory, in contrast to a main memory, on an electronic data processing device.

AUXILIARY STORAGE—Additional storage, in contrast to the main memory of a computer.

AVAILABLE BALANCE—Number of goods on hand and available for customers' orders.

AVAILABLE NUTRIENTS—Nutrients in a food that can be freed by the digestive system and used by the body. In contrast, some nutrients are chemically unavailable in certain circumstances, e.g., **biotin** when combined with **avidin.**

AVENALIN—Part of the protein in oats that is soluble in salt solution but not in water.

AVENIN—Part of the protein in oats that is soluble in acid or alkaline solutions but not in water or salt solutions.

AVERAGE BEVERAGE INVENTORY—Average dollar value of the beverage inventory for a given period.

AVERAGE CHECK—Total sales for a given period divided by the number of guests served.

AVERAGE COST—Total cost of a set of items divided by the total number of items. Such a calculation becomes useful when subgroups of the stock of a particular item cost different amounts.

AVERAGE COVER—**Average check.**

AVERAGE EXPOSURE—Average number of times that a given audience has been exposed to a given ad.

AVERAGE GROSS PROFIT PER COVER—Index that is calculated by dividing the total gross profit on all items served that day by the total number of covers. See **gross profit per item.**

AVERAGE INVENTORY—The average dollar value of inventory for a given period.

AVERAGE LIFE—The expected number of years before a depreciable asset loses its value, e.g., five or seven years for an office typewriter.

AVERAGE NUMBER OF SALES PER HOUR—Measure of business success calculated by dividing the total number of sales during a given period (e.g., a normal business day) by the number of hours in that period.

AVERAGE SALES PER SEAT—Measure of business success

calculated by dividing the total sales in a given period by the number of seats in the establishment available for customer use.

AVERAGE UNIT COST—Measure of item cost calculated by dividing the total cost of a collection of a given item by the number of those items in that collection. This averages out cost fluctuations due to different suppliers, seasons, discounts, and so on.

AVIDIN—Protein in raw egg whites that makes **biotin** nutritionally unavailable. Cooking the eggs prevents this.

AVITAMINOSIS—Disease resulting from the lack of one or more vitamins.

AVOCADO—Pear-shaped fruit with pulpy flesh and a large pit, also known as the alligator pear. It is peeled, then sliced or cubed for salads, or puréed and seasoned for dips. Now widely grown in California.

AZASERINE—Derivative of the amino acid serine that interferes with serine's metabolism.

AZO DYES—Group of strongly colored compounds, some of which are used as food additives.

B

BABA MOLD—Metal vessel of decorative design used to shape and cook babas.

BABCOCK TEST—Means of measuring the fat content of milk.

BACILLARY DYSENTERY—**Shigellosis.**

BACILLI—Rod-shaped bacteria. Contrast **cocci** and **spirilla.**

BACILLUS CEREUS—Spore-bearing bacteria most commonly

found in rice. The spores may survive cooking and reproduce as the food cools. The resulting bacteria can cause infection, the symptoms of which include vomiting and diarrhea.

BACKFLOW—Flow of fluids from an unsanitary source (e.g., sewage) into a supply system of purified water. See **air gap.**

BACKGROUND PROCESSING—Computer processing of low-priority work during off-peak hours. The processing may be interrupted should the need arise.

BACKING UP—Printing on the second side of a sheet of paper that has been printed on the first side, as in menu production.

BACK OF THE HOUSE—Employee work areas in a foodservice establishment, e.g., the kitchen, storeroom, and so on. Contrast **front of the house.**

BACK ORDER (BO)—To ship merchandise as it becomes available if it has been ordered before then. The supplier will mark the item on the invoice as a back order and ship it as soon as it comes into stock.

BACK-SHELF BROILER—Similar to the heavy-duty broiler but smaller. It usually sits over the back of a range to which it is attached and is used for such functions as browning casseroles, melting cheese, or broiling short orders. Also called a salamander.

BACK SIPHONAGE—**Backflow.**

BACK SPITTLE—Long-handled wooden spatula or shovel used in baking to move dishes around in the oven.

BACON DISH—Dish with a cover meant to keep cooked bacon warm.

BACTERIA—One-celled microscopic organisms of the monera kingdom (neither plant nor animal). Some species spoil food or cause disease; others aid in food production or digestion.

BACTERIAL COUNT—Approximate number of bacteria present in a food sample as indicated by laboratory tests.

BACTERIAL GROWTH—Four-stage process in the development and decline of a bacterial colony. See **lag phase, log phase, stationary phase,** and **decline phase.**

BACTERICIDE—Chemical compound that can kill active bacteria; it may not necessarily kill bacteria dormant in spore form.

BACTERIOLOGIST—Scientist trained in the study of bacteria, who is able to identify microorganisms and recommend ways to deal with them.

BACTERIOPHAGE—Any virus that attacks and destroys bacteria. Both beneficial and harmful bacteria can be lost by its action.

BACTERIOSTAT—Any chemical compound that only inhibits the growth of bacteria but that may not destroy them. Contrast **bactericide.**

BACTOFUGATION—Use of a centrifuge to remove bacteria from milk.

BAD DEBT—An account receivable that was not paid when due and there is reason to believe that it will not be paid.

BAIL—Carrying handle, usually made of wire, that is attached to a container.

BAIN-MARIE—Any vessel half-filled with hot water in which pots of sauces, soups, or other materials may be held hot or gently cooked. Steam tables or double boilers may also serve the same purpose.

BAIT—Food containing insecticide or rodenticide that is left out where insects or rodents will find it. Baits should be carefully placed so that they will not be eaten by humans or pets.

BAKE PAN—Large rectangular shallow pan without cover used for oven baking.

BAKE PAN, STRAIGHT-SIDED—Oblong pan with medium-high walls and two loop handles used to bake puddings, apples, rolls, and so on.

BAKER'S DOZEN—Thirteen, i.e., a regular dozen plus a bonus of one.

BAKER'S YEAST—Yeast used to leaven dough rather than produce alcohol. The scientific name is S. *cerevisiae.*

BAKING—Cooking in an oven with indirect heat. Confusingly, also called **roasting** when applied to meats, nuts, and certain fruits and vegetables.

BAKING ADDITIVE—Any substance added to improve the texture, appearance, or yeast activity in baked goods.

BAKING AMMONIA—Leavening agent that emits carbon dioxide and ammonia when moistened and then heated.

BAKING POWDER—Powdered mixture containing sodium bicarbonate and an acidic substance, e.g., tartaric acid. When mixed with dough, moistened, and heated, carbon dioxide gas is released, thus making the mixture rise.

BALANCE—Difference in a given account between total debits (which increase assets or expenses) and total credits (which decrease assets or expenses).

BALANCED BUDGET—Budget in which the total expected revenues for a given period matches the total expected expenses.

BALANCE, DIETARY—Relationship between nutrient intake and loss. A negative balance means the body loses more than it takes in, while a positive balance means the body loses less than it takes in, thus retaining the remainder for use.

BALANCE SHEET—Financial statement produced at the end of an accounting period that shows the assets and liabilities of the establishment at that time. The categories of the statement balance out so that total assets equal total liabilities plus owner's equity.

BALANCE, WINE—Wine components such as acidity and sweetness, oak and varietal flavors, combine in harmony so that no one is dominant in the overall taste.

BALLOTINE—French; boned stuffed fish, fowl, game or meat rolled into a bundle.

BALTHAZAR—Extra-large champagne bottle that holds 16 regular bottles, or 416 ounces.

BAMBOO SHOOTS—Young bamboo-plant sprouts, often used in Chinese cuisine.

BANANA—Long tropical fruit with characteristic yellow skin, which is peeled. Raw, they may be eaten whole, sliced over cereal or in fruit mixtures, split lengthwise for ice cream specials, and so on. They may also be cooked, e.g., mashed for use in baking.

BANANA FIG—Sun-dried banana slice to which no sulfur dioxide has been added as a preservative. The pieces are dark and sticky, resembling figs in appearance.

BANANA SQUASH—Type of winter squash with a tapered end; it is shaped much like a banana.

BANDS—Plastic or metal strips wrapped around a package or carton, pulled tight, and sealed.

BANKRUPTCY—The state of being considered legally insolvent, i.e., unable to pay one's debts.

BANQUET BILLING FORM—Form similar to an ordinary sales check, but expanded to include all the information required to bill a group for an entire banquet. Details include the contract number, the name and address of the group served, and the number of people present.

BANQUET BOOK—Business record in which are entered all tentative and confirmed banquet bookings.

BANQUET CONTRACT FORM—Form on which are recorded the basic details for a banquet as listed in the daily banquet diary, and the menu and cost per person. It is signed by the representative of the group booking the banquet.

BANQUET GUARANTEE—Minimum number of people from a given group expected to attend a banquet. This is the minimum number of meals the group must pay for even if fewer people show up. The guarantee protects an establishment from losing money in overproduction.

BANQUET LIQUOR CONTROL—Form on which can be listed all the types of liquor served at a particular banquet, the amount of each, and the total sales.

BANQUET PORTION CONTROL FORM—Form that lists the number of servings issued and the number of guests served by each waiter, to make sure the numbers match.

BANQUET PRICING TABLE—Table of entrees and **makeup menus** that can be ordered for banquets, along with the price for each entree and makeup combination.

BANQUET REQUISITION AND RETURN REPORT—Form used to control liquor sales at a banquet by noting the amount of each type of liquor issued, the amount returned, the net sold, and the total sales.

BANQUET SALES CHECK—**Banquet/billing form.**

BANQUET SALES CONTROL—Special procedures required for banquets since they differ from normal daily service in most establishments. See **daily banquet diary, banquet contract form,** and **weekly banquet sheet.**

BANQUET SERVICE—The **American, French,** or **Russian** styles of service, or a combination of these services, organized so that every table is served at the same time.

BARBECUE—Method of cooking under or over direct heat, like broiling. It differs from broiling in that a highly seasoned sauce with a tomato base is used to baste the food or is served with it.

BARD—To wrap thin slices of fat, bacon, or salt pork around poultry, fish, or game before roasting in order to protect the delicate food and keep it moist while cooking.

BARFOED'S TEST—Test for the presence of **monosaccharides** in a substance. If they are present, a red precipitate forms when copper acetate and acetic acid are added.

BAR LE DUC—Piquant-tasting red currant jam.

BARLEY—Grain used in soups and as a cooked cereal. It also

furnishes malt for beers and ales and is used with other grains in the making of whiskey.

BARLEY, PEARL—Polished barley, typically used in cooking.

BARM—**Yeast.**

BARREL—Small cask of varying capacity used as a container for brandy, oil, vinegar, wine, and so on. In France it is usually 72 liters (19.75 U.S. gal.); in Britain a barrel of wine is 115 liters (31 U.S. gal.).

BAR REQUISITION FORM—Form used by bartenders to request bottles from the storeroom.

BAR/RESTAURANT TERMINAL—Point-of-sale data processing terminal used for recording sales and payments in a bar or restaurant with the capability of recording sales at a different terminal from that at which payment is made.

BARRIER MATERIAL—Any type of coating, cover, or packaging designed to keep foreign matter out of the product inside a package and to keep the product from leaking out.

BAR SPOON—Spoon used to stir cocktails. It has a long handle and a small bowl.

BARTENDER'S SHAKER—Container for liquids resembling a Thermos. The cocktail ingredients are added separately, often with ice, the lid is put on, and the container is shaken to mix the contents. The drink is then strained into a serving glass.

BARTER—Payment for goods or services purchased with other goods or services rather than money.

BASAL METABOLIC RATE (BMR)—Rate at which energy is used to sustain life when the body is completely at rest. It is affected by age, sex, weight, and thyroid hormones. The average rate is approximately 1,700 kcal each day.

BASE—Any compound with a pH above the neutral point of 7.0. Also called **alkali.** Contrast **acid.**

BASE-FORMING FOODS—Foods containing the minerals calcium, potassium, sodium, and magnesium. They tend to raise the pH of bodily fluids when digested. Such foods include fruit, milk, and vegetables.

BASE PERIOD—Period of time chosen for comparison with another period. For example, one year's income can be compared with that of ten years ago; the earlier period is the base period.

BASE PRICE METHOD—Establishment of a menu price by noting how much the average customer spends (e.g., $7.00). The manager decides which items can earn the desired level of profit when offered for about that price.

BASIC—Acronym for the Beginner's All-Purpose Symbolic Instruction Code, a computer programming language. The language can be learned easily and is often used in processing business data.

BASIC SEVEN FOODS—Division of foods into seven groups, each of which should be included in the diet every day. The groups are green and yellow vegetables, fruits, potatoes and related vegetables, milk products, meat and eggs, cereal products, and margarine or butter.

BASIS OF ACCOUNTING—Accounting method chosen by an establishment, usually either the **accrual method** or the **cash basis method.**

BASIS WEIGHT—Weight of a **ream** of a certain grade and size of paper. The heavier the basis weight, the thicker the paper.

BASKET PURCHASE—**Lump-sum purchase.**

BASKETWEAVE TUBE—Nozzle for a pastry-decorating bag or syringe whose opening has one straight side for making smooth, wide icing stripes, and one serrated side for making ribbed stripes.

BASTE—To moisten food with melted fat, meat drippings, stock, water, or a sauce while cooking in order to improve flavor and to prevent scorching or drying.

BASTER—Ladle or cup used to pour fat or other liquid over cooking food. See **baste.**

BASTING BRUSH—Brush used to spread fat or some other liquid over a dish being cooked.

BATCH—Specific number of items being processed, tested, or sold together.

BATCH PROCESSING—Computer processing of different groups of data in sequence rather than handling them individually.

BATF—Abbreviation for the U.S. Treasury Department's Bureau of Alcohol, Tobacco, and Firearms.

BATTEN—To seal doors, especially of vehicles transporting supplies, to keep the elements, dust, and other contaminants away from the products inside.

BATTER—Flour and liquid mixture that can be stirred and poured, as for waffles and cakes. Mixed with other ingredients, it can be used to coat foods before deep frying.

BAUD—A measure of speed in electronic data transmission equivalent to one bit per second.

BAUME—A table that provides the **specific gravity** for liquids other than water, specifically salt solutions.

BDELYGMIA—Extreme aversion to food.

BE—Abbreviation for the degrees in a **Baumé table.**

BEAN CURD—Another name for **tofu.**

BEANS AND LEGUMES—Leguminous plants of many varieties. The seeds and young pods are eaten as vegetables while the mature seeds are dried and eaten as a starch. Beans are an excellent source of protein and vitamin B. The following is a list of the seven basic categories.

Black-eye beans: Tiny off-white beans with a black "eye" in the center. They come from a tropical leguminous plant. Often called "peas," they are popular in the United States, particularly the South.

Broad beans: Another term for fava bean, a light-green bean. It is popular in Europe and grows well in cool climates.

Common beans: Includes both shell and snap beans. The most common varieties of shell beans for drying include yellow eye, pintos, red kidneys, small white navy, bit whites, pinks, and great northerns. Snap beans include green beans and wax beans.

Garbanzos: Also known as chickpeas, these are round with a nutty flavor. They are especially popular in Asia and in the Mediterranean.

Lima beans: These are similar to **common beans** and are of the haricot variety. There are two types, the baby lima and the large lima. Lima beans originated in South America.

Mung beans: Sprouting bean popular in Asia.

Scarlet runner: Closely related to common beans, their seeds are dried and sold as Oregon limas or butternut beans.

Soybean: The most important legume in the world by virtue of its versatility and nutritional content. It is very high in protein and is used to produce cooking oil, flour, and milk. It is also used for nonfood products, such as plastics and adhesives. The soybean has been a staple in China for thousands of years.

BEAN SPROUTS—Young shoots of the Chinese mung bean. Tiny, tender, and green, these are used in the preparation of Oriental dishes and sometimes as toppings for salads.

BEAT—To stir and mix vigorously, often incorporating a lot of air, to bring about a smooth texture. The result is light and fluffy.

BEEF—Meat from steers, heifers, cows, stags, and bulls that are over one year old. The best beef comes from steers that are castrated when young and fattened on grain. Quality beef is bright red in color with firm, fine-grained, well-marbled flesh. Grades of beef in descending order of quality are: prime, choice, good, standard, and commercial. Prime is rarely sold in consumer retail stores. Wholesale cuts of beef are the rump, loin, flank, short loin, plate, rib, brisket, chuck, and shank. A whole of beef is divided into four quarters—a left and right forequarter and a left and right hindquarter. The forequarter contains the chuck, rib, short plate, brisket, and foreshank. The hindquarter includes the short loin, sirloin, round, tip, and flank. The following is a description of the major wholesale and more common cuts of beef.

Baron of beef: An extra-large cut that includes part of the ribs and both sirloins. It is traditionally served at Christmas.

Brisket: Cut from the breast, including parts of five ribs and part of the shoulder. It is an economical cut that should be cooked a long time to make it tender.

Chuck: Portion of the forequarter remaining after the removal of the foreshank, brisket, short plate, and rib. Chuck also includes clod, the beef just above the blade bone that is suitable only for stewing.

Flank: The fleshy part between the ribs and the hip. The flank steak, a flat muscle embedded in the inside of the udder end of the flank, is obtained from this cut.

Loin: Portion of the hindquarter remaining after the removal of the round, flank, hanging tender, kidney knob, and excess fat. Sirloin steak comes from the loin. T-bone steak, porterhouse steak, shell steak, club steak, and top loin steak come from the tenderloin.

Rib: Portion of the forequarter remaining after the removal of the crosscut chuck and short plate. It contains part of the seven ribs, sixth to twelfth inclusive, the section of the backbone attached to the ribs, and the tip of the blade bone. The standing rib roast, rib steak, boneless rib steak, Delmonico steak, and rib-eye roast come from this cut.

Round: Portion of the hindquarter remaining after the removal of the untrimmed loin. Tender, expensive cuts come from the round, including the top round, side of round, round steak, and bottom round.

Rump: Portion between the loin and the round. This is an economical cut.

Shank: Portion from the upper or sometimes lower part of the leg. It is an economical cut.

Short loin: Anterior portion of the full loin where the loin eye and tenderloin are located. Filet mignon comes from the short loin.

Short plate: The portion of the forequarter immediately below the primal rib, yielding both the short ribs and boiling or ground meat.

Sirloin tip: Part of the hindquarter, also known as the knuckle.

BEEF, BABY—Meat that has come from a beef animal just moving out of the age range for calves (about 14 to 52 weeks old). See **beef.**

BEEF, DRIED—Beef soaked in brine, smoked, and dried. Sliced thin or flaked, it may be used in sandwiches or mixed with a cream sauce and served as chipped beef over toast, rice, or mashed potatoes.

BEEF TEA—Extract made by stewing beef in water for two to three hours. It is used to stimulate the appetite and the secretions of digestive glands.

BEER—Alcoholic beverage of amber color brewed from malted cereal, grain, hops, and water. Fermentation gives the beverage its carbonated effervescence. The five main types include lager, ale, bock beer, porter, and stout. The last three are progressively darker, heavier, richer, and sweeter than lager and ale.

Bock: Brewed from barley, roasted malt, wheat, and hops, resulting in a rich, dark carbonated alcoholic beverage.

Dark: Brewed with roasted malt, resulting in a rich, dark beverage.

Draft: Tapped directly from the keg. The result is fuller taste than most canned or bottled beer. It is often served in a frosty mug.

Lager: Light, with a sparkle and effervescence resembling carbonated beverages. Lager is pale gold in color and dry.

BEESTINGS—Milk provided by cows for a few days after calving. It is higher in protein and antibodies than usual milk.

BEETS, STRAWBERRY—Small red beets often pickled or used in salads as a vegetable garnish.

BEET SUGAR—Sucrose derived from the sugar beet. See **sugar.**

BEETURIA—Condition occurring in about 12 percent of the

population, in which the pigment betanin from red beets is not broken down during digestion and thus turns the urine red.

BEGINNING INVENTORY—Inventory at the beginning of a given time period.

BELL PEPPER—Also known as capsicum or sweet pepper. A common American type is the large apple-shaped green pepper, often eaten fresh in salads or baked in casseroles. There are also yellow and red bell peppers, some hot-tasting rather than sweet.

BELT CONVEYOR—Flight-type dishwashing unit with a continuous belt allowing dishes, pots, pans, and other large units to be placed directly on the belt, thus eliminating the need for racks.

BENCH—Placing dough to rest after **punching.**

BENCHMARK—Basic point of comparison with which to evaluate future results in marketing or sales.

BENEDICT'S TEST—Test to reveal the presence and the rough amount of **reducing sugar.**

BENZIDINE TEST—Test to indicate the presence of blood in a sample. Benzidine and other substances are added, and if blood is present the sample turns blue or green.

BENZOIC ACID (BENZOATE)—Chemical derivative of benzene sometimes used as a food preservative because it kills microorganisms.

BERIBERI—Disease caused by insufficient thiamine (vitamin B_1). Symptoms include swelling in various body parts or emaciation, mental confusion, and disturbance of heart function. Sufficient thiamine cures or prevents this disease.

BERMUDA ONION—Large onion with a brown skin and a mild flavor. Also called Spanish onion.

BERRY—Generic name for all fruits that contain seeds embedded in the pulp. The term includes tomatoes as well as blackberries, raspberries, and the like.

BETA-OXIDATION—One of the chemical sequences involved in the metabolism of **fatty acids.**

BETEL LEAVES—Leaves from the vine *piper betel*. They are chewed because of the stimulating effect of the chemicals (arecoline and guvacoline) they contain.

BETTER BUSINESS BUREAU (BBB)—Organization that monitors the advertising and other business practices of the companies and proprietorships in its area to protect the public.

BEURRE—French; butter.

BEVERAGE COST—Cost to an establishment of a beverage that is in turn sold to a customer.

BEVERAGE COST PERCENTAGE—Ratio of beverage cost to beverage sales, multiplied by 100 percent.

BEVERAGE INVENTORY CONTROL FORM—Form used to record beverage receipts, issues, and the balance on hand.

BEVERAGE INVENTORY TURNOVER—Ratio of total beverage costs for that month to the **average beverage inventory.**

BEVERAGE PURCHASE REQUEST—Form used by the bar manager to inform the purchasing agent of the type and number of beverages to purchase.

BEVERAGE REQUISITION FORM—Form used by the bar or other department to order liquor, wine, or beer from the liquor storeroom.

BEVERAGE SALES AND COST REPORT—Form on which income from beverage sales and the cost of the beverages sold are recorded.

BEZOAR—Any solid lump of undigested matter. Failure to chew high-fiber foods sufficiently (e.g., vegetable fibers) can create these. They can cause serious intestinal blockage.

BHA—Abbreviation for **butylated hydroxyanisole,** an antioxidant food additive.

BHT—Abbreviation for **butylated hydroxytoluene,** an antioxidant food additive.

BID—An offer to buy something from its owner.

BILE—Fluid produced by the liver and stored in the gall bladder. Bile aids in fat digestion.

BILE SALTS—Chemicals in bile fluid that play a role in fat digestion.

BILIRUBIN—Pigmented compound in bile formed by the breakdown of **hemoglobin** and excreted in the feces.

BILL—Statement listing the goods or services that have been delivered and the charges due.

BILLBOARD—Outdoor advertisement, usually large and mounted high on posts.

BILL OF LADING (B/L)—Contractual statement issued by a carrier acknowledging receipt of the goods and promising delivery to a specified point.

BILL OF SALE—Written agreement transferring the ownership of goods from one person to the other in return for payment.

BINARY—Base-two number system that uses the numbers 0 and 1 to form all numbers and letters in computer processing.

BINARY CODED DECIMAL (BCD)—A computer method for representing decimal digits as 4-bit binary numbers, e.g., 0000=0, 0001=1, etc.

BIN CARD—Used to record a running balance of the number of an item in inventory.

BIND—Using a substance to make food materials adhere together, e.g., eggs to bind flour and sugar in baking, gelatin to bind mixed fruits.

BINDING—Way in which the cover and sheets of a menu are held together. See **pamphlet stitching, saddle stitching, side stitching, and perfect binding.**

BINNING—Storage of wines for aging in bins within a cellar.

BIOCYTIN—One of the forms of vitamin H (**biotin**) that must be **hydrolyzed** before it can be used.

BIOLOGICAL OXYGEN DEMAND (BOD)—Amount of oxygen used up in a substance (e.g., milk). Since microbes use oxygen, the BOD reveals how contaminated a substance is.

BIOLOGICAL VALUE (BV)—Numerical scale that indicates what percent of the protein of a given food will be retained in the body. Usually animal proteins have a higher BV than vegetable protein. For example, the BV of eggs is 95, while that of peanuts is only 45.

BIOTIN—One of the B-complex vitamins, which is sometimes called vitamin H. Good food sources include vegetables, cereals, nuts, and organ meats. Biotin is important in metabolic processes such as fat synthesis. The **avidin** in raw egg whites renders this vitamin useless.

BIOTIN DEFICIENCY DISEASE—Caused by lack of **biotin.** It is rare because the vitamin can be synthesized by the body's intestinal bacteria. Substances that kill bacteria can inhibit this process, however. Symptoms include dermatitis, depression, anorexia, anemia, and nausea.

BIRCH BEER—Carbonated soft drink made from sap from the black birch tree.

BISCUIT CUTTER—Light metal or plastic frame used to cut individual biscuits out of rolled dough.

BISCUITWARE—Porcelain that has been fired once but has not yet been glazed.

BISMARK FILLER—Long nozzle used with a decorating bag or syringe with a round opening to pipe fillings into pastries.

BISYNC (BSC)—Literally, binary synchronous communication discipline. The term refers to a particular type of synchronous communication using certain control characters to format data, respond to messages, and so on.

BIT—Short form of binary digit, referring to the fact that computers are based on binary number systems that require only a zero and a one (0 and 1) to represent all numbers and letters. Bits allow for fast processing by the use of an opening in a computer card or by two different levels of voltage in magnetic devices.

BITOT'S SPOTS—Small plaques formed on the surface of the eye caused by vitamin A deficiency.

BITTER CHOCOLATE—Chocolate containing only 5–20 percent sugar that is used in baking rather than eaten plain. Also called baker's chocolate.

BITTERS—Various compounds such as calumba and quinine that stimulate the taste buds and enhance the appetite. In cocktail-making, the term refers to a reddish-brown spirit with a bitter taste used to flavor mixed drinks. See **angostura bitters.**

BIURET TEST—Chemical test for the presence of protein.

BIVALVE—Shellfish creature with two valves, seen as a hinged shell, e.g., clam, oyster, scallop.

BIXIN—Another name for **annatto,** the food-coloring agent for butter and cheese.

BLACK PN—Food-coloring additive; not particularly stable.

BLACKSTRAP MOLASSES—Unrefined, dark, thick syrup produced in the process of refining sugar.

BLACK TEA—Tea that is fully fermented. Contrast **green tea.**

BLACK TENSION INDICATOR—Device on a meat saw used in conjunction with a tension control adjuster to achieve the proper tension in the saw blade.

BLANCH—To plunge a food item into boiling water for a short time. Usually a step preliminary to further cooking by another method.

BLAND DIET—Any diet that minimizes fiber, strong spices, and other potential digestive and intestinal irritants. Such diets are most often used in cases of intestinal distress.

BLANK-CHECK PURCHASE—To order an item without checking the cost. Since the establishment is obligated to pay whatever the vendor charges, only reputable vendors should be relied on in this way.

BLANKET—Rubber sheet used in **offset lithography** that transfers ink from the printing plate to the menu paper.

BLAST FREEZER—Freezer cold enough (about −20°F) to freeze foods with great speed, as opposed to normal freezers designed to keep foods already frozen.

BLAZER—Flaming drink; traditionally served in the winter.

BLEACHING—Chemical removal of color from a food substance.

BLEEDING BREAD—Bright-red stain that speeds quickly through bread due to infestation by the bacteria *B. prodigiosus*.

BLEND—To mix two or more ingredients together completely into one.

BLENDER—Machine consisting of a vessel that sits on top of an electric motor, which drives a pair of whirling blades that are built into the bottom of the vessel. The spinning blades chop, purée, blend, and emulsify liquids and soft foods. The blender is very useful in the bar for mixing drinks.

BLENDING SPIRITS—Mixing various similar spirits to produce a uniform combination of higher quality and complexity than any one ingredient.

BLIND—Cooking pie or tart without a filling.

BLIND RECEIVING—Receiving goods when the quantity, quality, weight, and price are omitted from the invoice. The goods must be checked with the packing slip on delivery.

BLOCK SCRAPER—Wooden-handled brush with chisel-pointed bristles of strong spring steel used to clean butcher blocks.

BLOND—Method of braising in which the product to be cooked is not browned first.

BLOND ROUX—**Roux** cooked slowly until a fawn color is obtained.

BLOOD CELLS, RED—Common name for erythrocytes, the cells that transport oxygen from the lungs to the body's tissues. They are red due to the action of hemoglobin, a substance that contains iron. Sufficient iron in the diet is required for the production of these cells, each one of which lives only about four months.

BLOOD CELLS, WHITE—Common name for leucocytes, the cells that destroy invading microorganisms by producing the antibodies that fight disease.

BLOOD ORANGE—Sweet orange with a tight skin. The pulp and juice are a dark red color.

BLOOD POISONING—Common name for **septicemia.**

BLOOD SUGAR—**Glucose** concentration in the blood.

BLOOM—Whitish substance that forms on the surface of chocolate during storage. It is caused by chemical changes in the fat content.

BLOOM GELOMETER—Device to measure the firmness of jellies, breads, marshmallows, and the like by measuring the force required to push a half-inch plunger four millimeters into the food.

BLOTTER—Informal record of business transactions entered as they occur, without processing or classifying of any kind. Entries can later be transferred to more formal records.

BLOWER-DRYER—Device attached to the discharge end of a dish machine that consists of a stainless steel chamber five feet long through which the dishes pass as they are dried by blasts of hot air.

BLOWUP—An enlargement, as of a photograph or drawing for a menu.

BLUEBERRY—Native American berry that grows on bushes. The fruit is blue or black, small and round, with tiny soft seeds. The genus is *Vaccinia.* Blueberries are often eaten fresh, in jellies or syrups, or in baked products such as muffins.

BLUE VALUE OF STARCH—Measure of the amount of amylose, or soluble starch, present in a food. It is so named because the amylose turns blue upon contact with iodine in a laboratory test.

BOAR—Sexually mature male swine; may be wild or domesticated.

BOARD, SPECIAL FOOD—Sanitary paperboard made to package oily or moist food. Unless it is torn or ruptured, it will not leak.

BODONI TYPEFACE—Modern style of type suitable for printing menus. See **Roman type.**

BODY, SALAD—Main ingredients of a salad, from which it usually gets its name.

BODY TYPE—Type used to print the main text of the menu, as opposed to the headings.

BODY, WINE—Refers to the richness of wine flavor; for example, a thin wine has less body than a full wine.

BOGUS PAPER—Paper passed off as high-grade menu stock that is actually made of recycled or otherwise inferior materials.

BOILING—Method of cooking by immersion of food in water or some liquid brought to the boiling point. Preferred for tough meats because of its tenderizing effect. However, a certain portion of vitamins, particularly the B-complex, are destroyed this way.

BOILING POINT OF WATER—At standard atmospheric pressure, water boils at 212°F (100°C).

BOLDFACE TYPE—Style of type for menus in which each letter is thick and dark, providing added emphasis. See **special type.**

BOLIVIAN HEMORRHAGIC FEVER—Disease caused by the **Machupo virus** and spread by rodents. Symptoms include sudden fever, nausea, vomiting, bleeding, and shock.

BOLUS—Mass of chewed food contained in a single swallow.

BOM—Abbreviation for beginning of month, when a new set of business records is usually begun.

BOMB CALORIMETER—Device that measures the amount of energy, or calories, in a portion of food by burning it and measuring the amount of heat produced.

BOMBE MOLD—Metal vessel used to shape ice cream for a dessert of molded ice cream called a bombe. The classic bombe was spherical, but modern bombe molds are cone-shaped.

BONDED WAREHOUSE—Warehouse for spirits or wines that is supervised by the government.

BOND, IN—Spirit or wine held under government supervision, or "in bond," because appropriate duty and taxes have not yet been paid.

BOND PAPER—Good-quality paper that is stronger and more durable than most. It is commonly used for letters and other business purposes. See **paper types.**

BONE—Skeleton of an animal's body. Bone is 95 percent composed of calcium compounds. Of that, calcium phosphate accounts for 85 percent and calcium carbonate for 10 percent. Calcium in the diet is critically important for bone formation.

BONE BROTH—Soup prepared by boiling chopped bones. However, very little calcium is liberated in this way.

BONE CHINA—Porcelain made from a mixture that includes the ash of animal bones.

BONE GLASS—Glass that includes bone ash in its makeup, which gives it a milky-white appearance.

BONE MEAL—Ground animal bones. Added to human or animal food, it provides a rich source of calcium.

BONING KNIFE—Stout knife with narrow pointed blade about six inches long used for separating flesh from bone.

BONUS—Any kind of extra payment made to an employee in addition to his regular salary. Bonuses are usually given as a reward for superior performance.

BOOKING—Reservation, by an individual or organization, of a

portion of an establishment's facilities for his or its use, as for banquets or meetings.

BOOKING DEPOSIT—Cash down payment to confirm a reservation for a banquet or other function. The deposit is applied toward the charges an organization or party will incur.

BOOK INVENTORY—Balance calculated by adding all purchases to the previous amount on hand and subtracting all issues, according to the business record. Contrast **physical inventory.**

BOOKKEEPER—Person who maintains the ledger and other business books of an establishment.

BOOK OF ACCOUNT—Any journal, ledger, or other book in an establishment's accounting system.

BOOK OF FINAL ENTRY—Ledger or other business record to which transactions are posted or transferred from their original entries.

BOOK OF ORIGINAL ENTRY—Journal, cashbook, or other business record in which transactions are formally entered for the first time. Earlier informal records such as check stubs are considered only supporting documents.

BOOK PAPER—Type of paper commonly used in books. Because it is cheaper than **text paper,** it is often used for menus. The heavier weights are perfectly suitable for this purpose. See **paper types.**

BOOK VALUE—Value of items of property as shown in the accounts (books) of the business owning them.

BOOSTER WATER HEATER—Device that heats water to the 180° F recommended for the final rinse cycle of the dishwashing machine. There are two basic types: small, compact tanks that instantaneously supply the 180° F rinse, and storage models with tanks that hold up to 25 gallons.

BOOT—To start up a computer system from scratch.

BORD-DE-PLAT—French; small utensil used to prevent spilling over the border of the plate when serving a food with sauce.

BORDURE—French; mashed potato or rice border used to surround and decorate hot foods.

BORIC ACID—Chemical once used as a food preservative. It is no longer used for this purpose because it builds to toxic levels in the body when repeatedly eaten.

BORON—Basic component of **boric acid,** which can be dangerous to eat.

BOTRYTIS—Mold that grows on the surface of certain grapes, shrivelling the grapes, concentrating both sugar and flavor, and resulting in wines that are uniquely aromatic, intensely flavored, sweet and luscious. Botrytis is known as the "noble rot." It is characteristic of the production of such wines as Johannisberg Riesling, Sauvignon Blanc, and Sémillon.

BOTTLE BUSTER—Machine that crushes empty bottles, thereby greatly reducing the volume of waste.

BOTTLED IN BOND—In America, the term indicates a straight 100 proof whiskey that is four or more years old and is bottled under government supervision because the taxes have not yet been paid on it. In Canada, it may be only three years old.

BOTTLE FOR BOTTLE—The practice of turning in the old, empty bottle of catsup, vinegar, and so on, to prove that a new one is needed.

BOTTLE LABEL—Gummed label, often numbered and dated, that can be placed on liquor bottles in lieu of **bottle stamping.**

BOTTLE STAMPING—Stamping the establishment's seal on all liquor bottles issued from the storeroom to ensure that only authorized merchandise is sold on the premises.

BOTTOM LINER—Extra or reinforced layer on the inside bottom of packing containers used to provide more support and cushioning for the product within.

BOTULINUM—Toxin in infected food caused by the bacteria

Clostridium botulinum. It is one of the most toxic substances known.

BOTULISM—Rare but extremely dangerous form of food poisoning caused by the anaerobic bacteria *Clostridium botulinam.* Since the spores are difficult to kill and thrive without oxygen, infected canned goods present the greatest potential threat.

BOUQUET—That portion of a wine's odor that develops after it is bottled and, with the wine's aroma, completes what is known as the **nose** of the wine. See **aroma.**

BOUQUET GARNI—French; herbs and seasonings, including parsley, garlic clove, peppercorn, thyme, and bay leaf, tied together between two celery stalks or bundled in knotted cheesecloth, and used to flavor sauces and soups.

BOURBONAL—Ethylvanillin, an artificial vanilla-flavoring additive.

BOYSENBERRY—Large berry with a blackberry shape but a purple color. It was developed from a hybrid of blackberries and raspberries in the early 1920's by Rudolph Boysen, hence its name.

BPI—Abbreviation for bits per inch, meaning a measure of the density of digital data on a magnetic tape or other recording device.

BRADYPHAGIA—To eat abnormally slowly.

BRAINS—Organ or variety meat consisting of the cerebral cortex, the brains, of any species, but usually the cow. They may be battered and deep fried, sauteed, or scrambled with eggs. Either way, brains are rich in protein and extremely high in cholesterol. They are not very popular in the United States.

BRAISE—Method of cooking in which vegetables or meat are prepared by first browning or searing in a small amount of fat, then cooking in a small amount of liquid, such as water, stock, juice, or meat drippings, that produces steam and keeps the meat soft.

BRAISING PAN—Large rectangular pan with a tight lid used to braise meat.

BRAN—Outer husk of wheat grains, separated from flour during the milling process. It can be processed into cereal or ground into flour for whole wheat bread and is a rich source of fiber.

BRAND—Product(s) of one manufacturer that can be identified and distinguished from similar goods produced by its competitors.

BRAND IMAGE—Overall impression of a specific brand of a product as perceived by consumers.

BRANDING GRIDDLE—Cooking surface with a tilted, ribbed exterior. The ribs give food a grilled appearance, and excess fat is drained off through the grooves.

BRANDY SNIFTER—Bar glass with a short stem and large bulbous bowl designed to maximize enjoyment of the brandy aroma. It can hold six to twelve ounces, but usually no more than two ounces of brandy is served in it.

BRAZIER—Heavy, round shallow pot with loop handles that holds burning coals; it is used for searing, braising, or stewing. Capacity is commonly between twelve to twenty-eight quarts.

BREAD—Staple of life, made by baking dough that has been raised with yeast. There are a tremendous number of varieties based on different additional ingredients, shapes, and sizes. Among them: buttermilk, corn, cracked wheat, oatmeal, oat, potato, pumpernickel, sourdough, stoneground, white, wheat-free, and wholewheat bread. To bread a food item is to coat it with breadcrumbs prior to cooking.

BREAD AND BUTTER PLATE—Small flat plate, usually five or six inches in diameter. In a dinner place setting, it is placed about one inch above the fork tips.

BREAD FRUIT—Sweet, starchy, green, round fruit that is similar to bread when baked. Grown mostly in the South Pacific.

BREAD KNIFE—Long-bladed knife with serrated edge; used to cut bread.

BREAKER—Buyer of meat in great bulk, often whole carcasses, who then prepares cuts for wholesale purchase.

BREAKEVEN POINT—Sales volume at which revenues and expenses exactly equal each other. Above this point is increasing profit; below it is increasing loss.

BREAK KEY—Key on the computer keyboard that usually causes the system to **boot** when it is pressed.

BREATHING PACKAGE—Package with seals loose enough (deliberately or accidentally) to permit air to move in and out with changes in the surrounding temperature and atmospheric pressure.

BREED—A wine's character or brand of excellence.

BREW—To make a beverage by fermenting vegetable matter (e.g., hops, barley, and malt) in water, as in beer production, or by heating it in water so that the essential ingredients leach out, as in making coffee or tea.

BREWER'S GRAINS—High-protein residue left after brewing beer; used in animal feed.

BREWER'S YEAST—High-protein yeast used in brewing beer to ferment cereal grains; used as a nutritional supplement.

BRISK FLAVOR—A taste with a zestful, stimulating quality.

BRISTOL BOARD—Heavy, cardboardlike paper at least 0.006 of an inch thick; used for menu covers.

BRITISH THERMAL UNIT (BTU)—Standard unit of heat; one BTU equals the heat required to raise the temperature of one pound of water by 1°F.

BRIX—Graduated scale that measures the percentage of sugar in syrups.

BROCCOLI—Green vegetable of Italian origin. It is a type of cauliflower and is high in vitamin C. It is served boiled or steamed with butter or Hollandaise sauce.

BROCHETTE—Skewer used for broiling pieces of meat, fish, or poultry, which are often alternated with green pepper slices, mushrooms, onions, and tomatoes.

BROILER—Piece of equipment that cooks food mainly by radiant heat supplied by charcoal, coke, heated ceramic, gas flame, or electric heating element. It usually cooks one side at a time, although some models cook both sides at once.

BROILING—Method of cooking whereby the food is exposed to intense direct heat, as under a broiler flame or over a charcoal fire. Meat juices quickly evaporate on the surface, but leave most of the vitamins in the meat, although some B-complex vitamins are lost.

BROMELAIN—Enzyme from pineapple juice used to tenderize meat.

BROMINATED OILS—Various oils used to stabilize the emulsions of flavoring additives in soft drinks. Excessive consumption may be harmful because the oil's residues build up in the body's fatty tissues.

BROUILLI—French; in cognac making, the middle distillate of about 24 to 32 percent alcohol collected for the second distillation.

BROWNING, ENZYMATIC—Browning of fruits and vegetables (e.g., apples) when they are exposed to air. The reaction is caused by the oxidation of the **phenol** compounds in the foods. The use of an acid, e.g., lemon juice or vinegar, will halt or slow down the process.

BROWNING, NONENZYMATIC—Browning of food during cooking or storage caused by the chemical reactions between proteins and sugars. It results in some loss of the nutrient lysine.

BROWN RICE—Whole-grain rice from which only the hull and a small amount of the bran have been removed. It is unpolished, contains more nutrients, and takes longer to cook than white rice.

BROWN STOCK—Thin liquid rendered from simmering roasted

beef and veal bones in water with vegetables and seasonings for six to eight hours.

BRUCELLAE—Bacteria that cause undulant fever or **brucellosis.**

BRUCELLOSIS—Disease caused by ingesting milk containing **Brucellae** bacteria or handling infected animals such as goats, swine, and cattle. Symptoms include loss of appetite, chills, fever, and weakness.

BRUN—French; method of braising in which the meat is first browned by searing.

BRUSSELS SPROUTS—Small vegetable, one inch or less in diameter, which resembles a miniature cabbage. It originated near Brussels, Belgium. The scientific name is *Brassica oleracea gemmifera.*

BRUT—French; dry, used for the driest type of champagne.

BTU—Abbreviation for **British Thermal Unit.**

BTU-KCAL CONVERSION—One BTU equals 0.252 *kcal* or calories.

BTU-KWH CONVERSION—It takes 3,412 **BTUs** of energy to equal one kilowatt-hour (KWH) of electricity.

BUDDING—Type of asexual reproduction in which a new organism grows out of an old one, much like a budding limb of a bush. Yeasts typically reproduce this way.

BUDGET—Estimate of future expenses and revenues that helps an establishment plan ahead and control future operations.

BUDGET PERIOD—Time period encompassed by a budget, usually one year.

BUFFALO CHOPPER—See **food chopper, bowl type.**

BUFFERED TERMINAL—Computer terminal with a specialized memory that holds input from the keyboard until a transmit key is pressed, in order to synchronize more efficiently the data rate between two storage or data-handling units.

BUFFERS—Compounds, such as protein, that resist pH changes in a solution by neutralizing excess acids or **bases.**

BUFFET—Display of assorted ready-to-eat foods, sometimes offered through self-service; similar to a **smorgasbord.**

BUFFET RUSSE—French; buffet of assorted Russian foods, such as caviar and blini.

BUFFET SERVICE—Service method in which platters of food are spread out on a table and guests pick up plates and serve themselves.

BUG—Fault in computer programming that may be difficult to detect, in that it is usually an error in logic that may not be noticeable until later in the program.

BULB BASTER—Kitchen utensil resembling a large eye dropper that works in the same way. It is used to baste meats with gravy or any other liquid.

BULGE PACKING—Deliberate overfilling of a crate of perishable produce so that when the lid is attached it bulges in the middle. The purpose is to prevent shifting during transport. Contrast **loose packing.**

BULGUR—Precooked and prepared wheat; recognized as the most ancient type of processed food; also known as cracked wheat. A Middle Eastern staple.

BULK—Measure of menu paper thickness.

BUNDLING—Combining a group of small packages together to form a larger unit.

BUNDT PAN—Baking pan with scalloped edges and a tube in the center to provide a decorative shape to the cake or other item baked in it.

BUNT—Group of fungi that infest wheat.

BURDEN—Indirect factory costs that contribute to the cost of an item purchased there.

BUS CART—Wheeled rack used to stack and transport soiled tableware.

BUSINESS CYCLE—Period of time in which sales or other business goes through a series of stages, e.g., from prosperity to below average, to average, and back to above average.

BUSINESS-INTERRUPTION INSURANCE—Insurance that protects an establishment against lost income if its business activities are interrupted by a specified cause, such as fire or flood.

BUTCHERING AND COOKING TEST FORM—Form on which a meat item is listed along with its raw weight, the weight after trimming, the weight after cooking, and the original cost per pound. The cost per net ounce of salable product can then be calculated.

BUTCHER KNIFE—Heavy knife with a curved pointed blade, used mainly for breaking down whole carcasses of meat.

BUTCHER TEST CARD—Form on which the butcher or cook can evaluate different cuts of meat by entering the original weight of each, the loss from trimming and cooking, the remaining salable meat, and its realistic cost per pound.

BUTT—Cask with a standard volume of 132 gallons, used to ship sherry.

BUTTER KNIFE—Small table knife with a flat blade used to pick up butter and spread it on bread, rolls, and so on.

BUTTERMILK—Liquid remaining after butter has been churned; contains no butterfat. Also, a cultured milk treated with certain bacteria.

BUTTERNUT—Large kernel or nut from the white walnut tree.

BUTTERNUT SQUASH—Type of winter squash that is slender and long. The skin is hard and yellow-brown, hence the name.

BUTYLATED HYDROXYANISOLE (BHA)—Antioxidant used to preserve baked goods, since heat does not destroy it.

BUTYLATED HYDROXYTOLUENE (BHT)—Antioxidant used to preserve foods containing fats.

BUTYRIC ACID—One of the **fatty acids,** appearing mainly in butterfat.

BUY AND HOLD—Method by which an establishment purchases large quantities of products in season, in plentiful supply, or priced low for any other reason, and then stores them till needed. Spoilage and storage costs, however, might reduce the savings in purchase price.

BUYER—Person responsible for making decisions regarding quality, amount, price, potential profit to be gained from commodities to be purchased, and ultimately customer satisfaction.

BUYERS' MARKET—Condition of the marketplace in which supply exceeds demand, buyers therefore have more options, and prices are generally lower. The opposite of **sellers' market.**

BYPRODUCT—Secondary item produced incidentally to the main product, e.g., butchering prime ribs might result in some hamburger as a byproduct. It is desirable since additional revenues may result.

BYTE—Unit of computer data equaling eight **bits** in sequence that together designate one **alphanumeric** character.

C

CABARET—Restaurant that sells liquor and offers live entertainment.

CABBAGE—Vegetable resembling a smooth and firm head of lettuce; it may be red or white rather than green. Cabbages belong to the family **cruciferae.**

CABERNET—Wine grape often used for French Bordeaux wines and red California wines.

CACAO—Liqueur used in sweet and creamy cocktails. Also the tropical bean from the cacao tree from which chocolate and cocoa are produced.

CACHEXIA—Severe malnutrition related to chronic disease.

CADAVERINE—One of the **ptomaine** food poisons; a derivative of the amino acid lysine.

CADMIUM—Metal compound used to plate some kitchen utensils, such as ice trays. Acid foods or drinks stored in such containers may dissolve some of the cadmium. The metal is poisonous if ingested in more than minute amounts, causing severe stomach pains, vomiting, and diarrhea within minutes.

CAERULOPLASMIN—Another spelling of **ceruloplasmin.**

CAFE—French; numerous meanings, including, literally, coffee, the place where it is served or a coffeehouse, or an eating spot that serves alcoholic beverages.

CAFFEINE—Stimulant drug found in coffee, tea, and certain beverages such as colas. It increases the heart rate, raises blood pressure, and diminishes the awareness of fatigue. It is often considered undesirable and is forbidden in certain diets.

CAFFEOL—Natural oil responsible for the odor and taste of coffee.

CAISSE—French; oblong container not more than 2.5 inches in diameter used to hold hot food. It may be of crockery, paper, or dough. A caisse with a handle is called a **cassolette.**

CAKE COVER—Any sort of cover used to protect cake and help preserve it.

CAKE RACK—A frame supporting a wire or thin rod grid used for holding a cake as it cools.

CAKE STAND—A round platform on a pedestal used to hold a cake as it is being decorated. Ornamental cake stands are also used for displaying the finished cake.

CALCIFEROL—**Vitamin D$_2$.**

CALCITONIN—Thyroid hormone that helps control the level of **calcium** in the blood and hence the retention of **calcium** in the bones.

CALCIUM—An essential mineral required for proper formation

of bones and teeth. Sources include milk products, certain dark-green vegetables such as broccoli, and small-boned fish such as sardines. Vitamin D aids in the body's absorption of calcium.

CALCULUS—Stones formed from chemicals within the body, e.g., kidney stones, gallstones.

CALENDERING—Pressing menu paper between rollers to change its surface, e.g., to make it smoother or more glossy.

CALENDULA—A plant, the petals of which may be used to decorate salads and to give aroma to fish, meats, or soups. They may also be used to make a yellow dye. Also known as pot marigold.

CALF—Beef carcass of a cow from 14 to 52 weeks old.

CALIPER—Thickness of an individual piece of menu paper, as measured in thousandths of an inch.

CALL LIQUOR—Liquor a customer requests by name, e.g., a specific brand or type of bourbon. Call liquors usually cost more than so-called **bar liquors.**

CALORIE—Unit expressing the amount of energy produced by food when it is used by the body, e.g., fat offers nine calories per gram, protein and carbohydrates offer four calories per gram.

CALORIES, EMPTY—Calories derived from food that supply only energy and no necessary nutrients, e.g., pure carbohydrates such as sugar.

CALORIMETER—See **bomb calorimeter.**

CALORIMETRY, INDIRECT—Measurement of a person's energy use by the amount of oxygen consumed by the body while releasing energy.

CALTROPS—Group of plants such as water chestnuts that have pointed fruit or flowers. In Asia, the outer skin of caltrops is often infected with the parasite **Fasciolopsis buski.**

CAMPAIGN—Series of advertisements presented in one or more media according to a predetermined schedule.

CAMPDEN PROCESS—Use of sodium bisulphite additives to preserve food.

CAMPDEN TABLETS—Sodium bisulphite tablets for use in the **Campden process.**

CANADIAN BACON—Lean loin (hogback) of pork that has been trimmed, pressed, and smoked. It is closer in flavor and appearance to ham than to American bacon, which is cut from side-meat and served in strips.

CANADIAN SERVICE—Variation of **English service,** in which no waiter is used. The host or hostess apportions the food and then passes a plate to each guest.

CAN AND BOTTLE DISPOSAL—Machine that takes all sizes and shapes of empty cans and bottles, crushes and breaks them, and deposits them in a waste container.

CANAPE—Eye-appealing appetizers made of crackers or shaped slices of toast spread with a flavorful paste.

CAN CUTTING TEST—**Canned food test.**

CANDLE—To examine eggs in front of a high-intensity light to assess their quality and freshness. Originally done before a candle, hence the name.

CANDY—To cook fruit or vegetables in syrup, drain and then dry them. Sweet potatoes and yams are candied by first boiling, then glazing them in a thick syrup; they are customarily served hot in the glaze.

CANNED FOOD TEST—Weighing the food content of a can (minus the package and liquid) to verify the net weight stated on the label. Also called can cutting tests.

CANNED PROGRAMS—Commonly used computer programs available for purchase from manufacturers.

CANNER GRADE—Lowest of eight grades of meat. The quality is too poor for whole cuts but the grade is used in processing lunch meat. See **meat grading.**

CANNER'S ALKALI—Chemical mixture of sodium carbonate and sodium hydroxide used to remove fruit peels prior to canning.

CANNING, ASEPTIC—Sterilization of food prior to sealing it into cans by cooking at 300–350°F for a few seconds.

CANTALOUP(E)—Melon with a juicy, sweet, orange flesh and a ribbed or netted rind. Served chilled for breakfast or as an appetizer.

CANTHAXANTHIN—Red pigment added to animal diets to provide color to the meat they produce.

CAN WASHER—Device used to clean and sanitize garbage cans by pressure-spraying them with water and steam.

CAP, RESEALABLE—Any lid to a container that continues to provide an adequate seal after opening and may be reused.

CAPACITY COST—Costs of the establishment, or any department therein, when operating at full capacity. Contrast **program cost.**

CAPERS—Green buds from a Mediterranean bush that are pickled and used to flavor and garnish a variety of foods and dishes.

CAPITAL—Amount of money invested in an establishment by its owners.

CAPITAL GAINS—Increase in value of an item of property over the purchase price that accrues during the time a person or business owns the property. Items regularly offered for sale as part of the business operation are excluded.

CAPRIC ACID—One of the fatty acids found in animal butter.

CAPROIC ACID—Liquid glyceride or fat found in such foods as milk and some vegetable oils.

CAPRYLIC ACID—One of the saturated fatty acids in butter and fat.

CAPSICUM—Pods from a tropical plant used to make paprika if mild or cayenne pepper if hot. Used whole, they are called chilis in Mexican cooking.

CAPSULE—Metal or plastic protector for the cork in spirit or wine bottles.

CAPTION—An advertisement's title or heading.

CAPTIVE FOODSERVICE OPERATION—Organization serving food to customers who have nowhere else to eat, e.g., those in prisons and hospitals.

CARAFE—Container in which wine or coffee is often served.

CARAFE, COFFEE—Glass or stainless-steel vessel with a ten-cup capacity used to hold and serve coffee. On drip coffee machines, the beverage drips into the carafe as it is brewed.

CARAFE, WINE—Cylindrical glass vessel with a flared top used to serve wine. Wine carafes range in size from one tenth of a liter to a full liter.

CARAFON—French; any small carafe or decanter.

CARAMELIZATION—Production of a caramel color and flavor in a sweet by burning the sugar at a temperature above its melting point.

CARAMELIZE—To cook sugar over low heat until it is brown; used for both flavoring and coloring.

CARAWAY—Small, brown, crescent-shaped seeds used in some cheese and rye bread. The taste is between anise and fennel.

CARBOHYDRASES—Group of enzymes involved in the metabolism of simple carbohydrates.

CARBOHYDRATES—Compounds within the body that are sources of energy. They are manufactured by plants and are obtained for use from the diet. All break down in the body to the simple sugar glucose. Excess carbohydrates are converted in the liver to fat.

CARBOHYDRATES, AVAILABLE—Carbohydrates such as starch and sugar that can be digested and used by the body.

CARBOHYDRATES, UNAVAILABLE—Carbohydrates such as cellulose and pectin that cannot be digested by the human body, and therefore provide no nutrients, although they can serve the function of providing fiber.

CARBONATED BEVERAGE DISPENSER—Device that keeps

carbonated beverages cold and dispenses them into glasses. It may dispense from containers of premixed drinks or it may mix the flavored syrup and carbonated water at the time the drink is dispensed. The amount of syrup used and the degree of carbonization should be adjustable.

CARBON DIOXIDE—Gas produced by yeast during leavening and fermentation.

CARBOXYLASE—Enzyme that can chemically remove carbon dioxide from other compounds.

CARBOXYMETHYLCELLULOSE—Cellulose derivative used to help stabilize ice cream and jellies. Since it is indigestible, it is nonnutritive and adds no calories.

CARBOXYPEPTIDASE—Pancreatic enzyme that helps digest protein.

CARCASE—Another spelling of carcass, which is a dead body, as of a butchered animal.

CARCINOGEN—Any substance that can cause cancer. Some food additives—preservatives, dyes—were found to be carcinogens and their use discontinued, e.g., cyclamate and red dye # 2.

CARCINOGENIC—Having the property of causing cancer.

CARD—Sheet of paperboard inserted in some packages to help them retain their shape.

CARDOON—Plant of the globe artichoke family that has edible stalks.

CARD RATE—Basic charge for advertising with a particular outlet in a given medium.

CARMOISINE—Red food-coloring additive.

CAROB—Produced from the edible pods of a Mediterranean evergreen. The taste is similar to chocolate and it is often used as a chocolate substitute. The seeds were once used as a standard of weight (hence the term *carats* for gems). Also called St. John's bread.

CAROTENAL—Substance added to chicken diets. It is deposited in the egg yolks, and deepens the yellow color.

CAROTENE—Natural red pigment in carrots and certain other vegetables. It is converted in the body to vitamin A. Carotene can also be used as a food-coloring additive.

CAROTENOIDS—Class of compounds, e.g., annatto extract, used to color foods and drugs yellow or red. The name is derived from **carotene.** Carotenoids can be converted to vitamin A in the body.

CARRAGEENAN—Additive used as an emulsifier, clarifier, and thickener in many foods and beverages. It is derived from seaweed and Irish moss.

CARRAGHEEN MOSS—Another name for *Chondrus crispus,* a North Atlantic kelp used to produce gelatin and **carrageenan.**

CARRIAGE TRAY—The part of a food slicer that holds the product being sliced. It slides back and forth, moving the product across the spinning blade. Some slicers have motorized automatic carriage trays, while on simple models they are pushed by hand.

CARRIER—An individual infected with a disease that can be spread to others, although he or she shows no sign of the disease.

CARRIER, COMMON—See **common carrier.**

CARROT—Root vegetable with a conical shape and an orange color. Carrots are rich sources of **carotene,** which the body converts into vitamin A. They can be eaten raw, cooked alone, added to stews, and so on.

CARR-PRICE REACTION—Chemical test for the presence of vitamin A in a substance.

CARRYING VALUE—Net value of any property owned by an establishment, as recorded in the business records.

CARRYOUT SALES TOTAL—Total dollar value of all sales of food and beverages purchased in a given period to be taken off the premises and consumed later. Contrast with **inside sales total.**

CARRYOVER FOOD—Foods available for use that were prepared earlier.

CARTE DU JOUR—French; a daily menu or bill of fare.

CARTILAGE—Dense elastic connective tissue in the body, made up largely of protein. Soft in the embryo, most of it becomes hardened into bone during growth through the body's use of calcium.

CASABA MELON—Large oval melon with whitish pulp and yellow rind; sweet and juicy.

CASEIN—Milk protein. When coagulated by **rennet,** its fermentation is the origin of cheese.

CASEIN, IODINATED—A molecule, containing both **casein** and iodine, that acts on the body like thyroid hormone.

CASH BAR—Bar at a party or other private function at which guests must pay for their own drinks.

CASH BASIS—Accounting method in which revenues and expenses are recorded when actually received or paid, rather than when accrued, as in the **accrual basis.** No attempt is made to match revenues and expenses in determining income.

CASHBOOK—Business record in which cash receipts and payments are initially entered in the order they occur.

CASH COLLECTION—Payment of the bill, either with cash or a credit card, to the cashier directly or through the server.

CASH DISCOUNT—Amount of the purchase price (usually 2 percent) that can be saved if the bill is paid within a specified period (e.g., 10 days) before it becomes finally due (e.g., 30 days). Discounts may also be given for buying in large quantities.

CASH EQUIVALENT—Money value of goods or services provided in a business transaction.

CASH FLOW—Business term; referring (1) to the sum of the

profit in a given period and depreciation, and (2) to the tracing of items of cash expense or revenue in the accounting books from their first to their final entries.

CASHIER—Person whose job it is to receive payments from customers, including cash, credit card charges, charges to rooms, and so on.

CASHIER'S AND CHECKER'S RESTAURANT REPORT— Form on which all the cashiers at the end of a shift can report their receipts.

CASH ON DELIVERY (COD)—When the buyer pays for goods (and often the shipping charge) with cash at the time of delivery to an establishment.

CASH RECEIPTS JOURNAL—Business record in which cash amounts are listed in the order of their receipt.

CASH REMITTANCE—Payment by a customer in cash as opposed to payment by credit card or other charge account.

CASH STATEMENT—Form that lists the opening cash balance at the beginning of a period, the amounts received, the amounts disbursed, and the closing balance at the end of the period.

CASK—Large barrel or container, used in the development or aging and shipping of spirits and wines.

CASSE—French; a chemical imbalance, clouding, or precipitation of wines caused by excess iron, air, protein, or copper.

CASSEROLE—Cooking utensil, usually round or oval; with one or two handles. It may be made of copper, aluminum, terracotta, porcelain, glass, or enamelled cast iron. Food may be served as well as cooked in a casserole.

CASSEROLE RUSSE—French; a small pot with a single long handle resembling the modern American saucepan.

CASSETTE—Device used to program, store, and retrieve information on tape or to transfer data between different computers.

CASSOLETTE—Small flameproof dish of porcelain, glass, or

metal in which hot hors d'oeuvres, small entrees, or certain desserts are served. See **caisse.**

CASTOR OIL—Derivative of the castor-oil bean that, when hydrolyzed in the small intestine, acts as a laxative by irritating the intestinal lining.

CATABOLISM—Chemical breakdown by the body of complex substances to simpler ones; part of the metabolic process.

CATALASE—Protein enzyme that catabolizes hydrogen peroxide into water and simple oxygen.

CATALYST—Any substance that accelerates the chemical reaction occurring in other substances without itself undergoing any permanent change.

CATHARTIC—Synonym for purgative, any strongly laxative substance.

CATHEPSINS—Group of enzymes stored within animal cells that serve to catabolize proteins.

CATHODE RAY TUBE (CRT)—Display screen of a computer terminal, similar to a small television screen, on which figures and characters can be displayed by an electron beam.

CATSUP OR KETCHUP—Sauce of tomatoes, usually commercially prepared, served as a seasoned condiment with certain meats, fried potatoes, and other foods.

CAUL—Enclosing membrane, from mammals, that can be used as sausage casing. Also a plant stem.

CAUSTIC—Any strongly acid or alkaline chemical that is corrosive and can destroy living tissue.

CAVIAR—Salted roe (eggs) of salmon, sturgeon, or certain other fish, served ice-cold as a spread for crackers and often accompanied by minced onions and finely chopped hard-cooked eggs. Imported Russian black caviar is the most expensive; the cheaper red caviar is the most widely used.

CAYENNE PEPPER—Red seasoning produced by grinding the "hottest" capsicum pods into pepper. See **capsicum.**

CCD—Abbreviation for charged coupled device, another designation for a memory chip used for the storage of information.

CEILING PRICE—Maximum price for a given product as set by law or some other authority.

CELERIAC—Vegetable of the celery family, with a root or bulb that is similar to a turnip. It is either boiled and served hot, creamed, or scalloped, or cold, sliced in salads.

CELERY—Low-calorie green vegetable that grows in stalks. When fresh, it has a crisp feel and tangy flavor. It may be eaten raw, as in hors d'oeuvre, or cooked, as in soups. It is often used as a flavoring agent in stocks, casseroles, and the like.

CELERY SEED—Seeds of **celery.** They can be used as a food flavoring, particularly when ground and mixed with salt (celery salt).

CELIAC DISEASE—Disease characterized by severe reactions (diarrhea, appetite loss, growth retardation) to wheat gluten in the diet. A gluten-free diet is the only cure. Also spelled coeliac disease.

CELLAR—Warehouse in which spirits or wines are stored. It should be kept damp and at 50–54° F.

CELLOBIOSE—Basic molecules of **cellulose,** each composed of two molecules of glucose chemically combined in such a way that humans cannot digest it.

CELLOPHANE NOODLE—Thin, transparent noodle often used in oriental dishes.

CELLULASE—Enzyme required to digest **cellulose.** Humans do not have it, though some lower animals do.

CELLULOSE—Main **polysaccharide** in plants. Each molecule consists of chains of **glucose** molecules.

CELSIUS—Scale for measuring temperature. The freezing point is arbitrarily set at 0°; the boiling point at 100°. The distance between these two points is divided into 100 equal degrees.

CELSIUS-FAHRENHEIT CONVERSION—$°F = \frac{9}{5} (°C) + 32°$.

CENTRALIZED SERVICE—Trays are prepared in the serving section of the main kitchen and dispatched from there. Contrast with **decentralized service.**

CENTRAL PROCESSING UNIT (CPU)—Area of computers where arithmetic logic functions and instructions are handled.

CENTRAL PURCHASING—One office controls all of the major purchasing of all the different food and drink outlets for a single establishment or chain of establishments. Central purchasing makes possible greater discounts because of the larger volume bought in this way, increased quality control, and less duplication of effort.

CENTRIFUGE—Machine that spins rapidly and exerts forces much greater than gravity on the fluids contained therein. This action makes the heavier components separate out quite quickly.

CEPHALINS—**Phospholipids** important in the formation of nerve tissue.

CERTO—Type of fruit pectin that allows jams and jellies to be produced under brief boiling periods, resulting in greater yields and greater fresh-fruit flavor than those made by long-boiling methods.

CERULOPLASMIN—Protein in the blood that transports copper. When there is not enough ceruloplasmin, copper can become deposited in the tissues and unavailable for the body's use. Since copper is required for the formation of **hemoglobin,** a deficiency may cause anemia.

CESTODE—Group of parasitic flatworms, such as beef, pork, and fish tapeworms.

CHAFING DISH—Shallow metal pan heated by flame or electricity, used for cooking or holding hot foods at tableside in the dining room or on the buffet table.

CHAMBRER—French; to bring a red wine gradually to room temperature (65°-68°F), usually overnight.

CHANGING MENU—Menu that is changed as often as needed

to suit the tastes of an establishment's clientele. Contrast **fixed menu, combination menu,** and **cyclical menu.**

CHANNEL—Device connecting input/output/memory units to each other, or to a path along which electrical transmission occurs between two or more stations.

CHAPTALIZATION—Improvement of wine by adding more sugar to the juice before fermentation.

CHARACTER—A digit, letter, or special symbol; term used in printing.

CHARCOAL—Used to purify fluids by absorbing impurities. Charcoal may also be used as a cooking fuel, especially for grilling meats and fish.

CHARCUTERIE—French; prepared meats that are ready to eat, particularly pork products like sausage. Also, an establishment that specializes in pork products.

CHARD, SWISS—Plant of the beet family whose leaves may be used fresh for salads or cooked.

CHARGE SALES CHECK—Payment of a sales check not in cash but rather by the customer's charging it to his or her hotel room or to a credit card.

CHARHEARTH BROILER—Broiler in which food is cooked on a grid over a bed of hot coals or ceramic material heated by gas or electricity. Juices and fat from the food being cooked drip down and flame up to impart a characteristic charbroiled flavor. Also called underfired broiler.

CHARLOTTE MOLD—Large round mold used to make baked or chilled charlotte desserts. Its sides are tapered to aid in removal of the finished product.

CHARM PRICE—Price ending with an odd cents value, e.g., $1.99 or $1.95. It is thought to attract customers.

CHARRED OAK CASK—Wine cask with its interior charred to enhance distilled spirits stored in it. The charcoal absorbs impurities and mellows the liquor, while at the same time imparting a yellow color.

CHASSE ROYALE—French; decorative dishes made with wild game.

CHAYOTE—Pear-shaped squash grown in Central America. It has one large seed at the center, and the rind is covered with short hairs.

CHECK AVERAGE—Average amount of money spent per guest at a single meal.

CHECKING—**Crazing.**

CHECK NUMBER ISSUE CONTROL FORM—Form identifying which waiter or waitress was issued which pad of blank sales checks. If checks turn up missing, the person responsible can be identified.

CHECK POCKETING—Occurs when a dishonest waiter or waitress pockets both the check and the customer payment instead of turning them in. Numbering checks and controlling their issue can prevent this.

CHECK PRINTER—Device in a cash register that prints out the sales receipt as the cashier enters the figures.

CHECK REGISTER—A business journal that records information on every check issued.

CHECK WEIGH—To weigh a package on a scale to make sure it contains as much as it should.

CHEESE—Dairy product made by separating the milk curds from the whey. Cheese was originally made to preserve excess milk but is now a popular and nourishing protein food produced in virtually all countries of the world. Any listing of cheese cannot be exhaustive. What follows are some of the better-known cheeses of the world.

Altenburger: Soft goat's milk cheese from central Germany. Altenburger has a very strong flavor.

Banon: Goat's milk cheese made in the Marseilles area of France.

Bel Paese: Very mild cow's milk cheese from Italy.

Bierkase: In Germany, a term for a small, round cheese dropped into beer to dissolve before drinking.

Bleu d'Auvergne: Cow's milk blue cheese from central France.

Bleu de Bresse: Small, rich cheese, similar to Gorgonzola; made near Lyon in France.

Boursin: French cheese flavored with garlic and chopped herbs.

Brick: Semisoft American-made cheese with a mild flavor.

Brie: Soft cow's milk cheese with a white rind; made in Melun, Coulommiers, and Meaux in France.

Cabecou: Round, flat goat's milk cheese made in the Landes district south of Bordeaux in France.

Caerphilly: White, crumbly, easily digested cheese made in the Clamorgan area of England.

Camembert: Soft, whole-milk cheese from Camembert, France.

Chabichou: Goat's milk cheese made near Poiters in France.

Cheddar: Hard whole-milk yellow-orange cheese originally from Somerset, England, but now produced in Scotland, Canada, Australia, New Zealand, and the United States.

Cheshire: Hard, salty cow's milk cheese first produced in Cheshire and said to be the oldest of English cheeses.

Chevreton: Strong goat's milk cheese from France. Chevreton has a hard rind and a soft, runny interior.

Colby: American-made cheese similar to cheddar but more moist.

Coon: American-made, crumbly, dark-brown cheddar with a tangy flavor. Coon is cured in a different manner than regular cheddar.

Cottage cheese: Bland unripened cheese with white soft curds.

Cream Cheese: White, soft, rich, and creamy uncured cheese made of cream and whole milk.

Danablu: Creamy, salty, blue-veined cheese from Denmark.

Danbo: **Samsoe** family cheese with a nutty, sweet flavor; made in Denmark.

Derby: A mild, pale cheddar similar to double gloucester; made in England.

Edam: Mild, wax-covered cheese made in North Holland.

Elbo: Mild Danish cheese of the **samsoe** family.

Emmentaler: Hard swiss cheese named after the Emme Valley. Emmentaler is made from whole or part-skim milk.

Feta: Soft, spicy cheese from Greece; made from ewe's milk.

Fontainbleau: Triple cream cheese made in the Ile-de-France.

Fontina: Yellow, semisoft ewe's milk cheese made in the Piedmont region of Italy.

Gammelost: Potent sour-milk cheese from Norway.

Géromé: Munsterlike cheese originally made in the Strasbourg region of France.

Gjetost: Norwegian cheese made from cow and goat milk. The cheese has a moldy flavor that is an acquired taste.

Gloucester: Cheddarlike mellow cheese from the Gloucester area of England.

Gorgonzola: Salty, strong, crumbly ewe's milk cheese with blue veins; made in the Milan area of Italy.

Gouda: Mild, Edamlike cheese made in Southern Holland.

Gruyère: Creamy, firm cheese from the Gruyère valley in Switzerland.

Havarti: Mild, bland cheese from Denmark.

Herve: Soft limburger type of cheese from Belgium.

Kasseri: Hard ewe's milk cheese from Greece.

Le Cantral: Hard, yellow, cow's milk cheese from France.

Limburger: Very strong semisoft cheese made in Liège Province of Belgium and in Germany.

Livarot: Soft, pasty cheese from a small town in the Calvados region of France.

Mascarpone: Soft, fresh cream cheese made in the Lombardy region of Italy.

Minnesota Blue: An American copy of Roquefort cheese made from cow's milk.

Mont d'Or: Munsterlike cheese made east of Lyons near Switzerland.

Monterey Jack: A cheddar made without coloring in Monterey County, California.

Morbier: A hard cheese made in the French Alps.

Mozzarella: A mild buffalo's milk cheese made in Italy.

Munster: Fatty, semihard cow's milk cheese made in the Alsace region of France.

Neufchâtel: Very white, tube-shaped skim or whole milk cheese made in France.

Oka: Mild-flavored cheese similar to Port Salut. It is made by trappist monks in Quebec, Canada.

Parmesan: Hard, yellow grating cheese from the Parma region in Italy.

Pecorino: A hard, aromatic grating cheese made in Italy from ewe's milk.

Petit Suisse: Soft, fluffy dessert cheese made in France.

Picodou: Soft goat's milk cheese made in the Haute Savoie region of France.

Pineapple: Hard cheddar cheese molded into a pineapple shape; originally made in Connecticut.

Pont L'Evêque: Semihard fermented cheese from the Calvados region of France.

Port Salut: Creamy, yellow whole-milk cheese originally made by trappist monks near the Laval region of France.

Provolone: Smoky, semihard cheese from Italy.

Ricotta: Soft white cheese similar to cottage cheese; made in Italy.

Roquefort: Pungent blue-veined cheese made from ewe's milk in the Saint-Affrique district of France.

Saint-Marcellin: Soft, slightly salty cheese made in the Savoie district of France.

Sainte-Maure: Soft, creamy goat's milk cheese made in the Touraine region of France.

Samsoe: Cheddarlike, nutty cheese from Denmark.

Schabzigei: Pungent grating cheese also known as sapsago; made in Switzerland.

Stilton: Strong blue-veined cheese from England.

Tilsiter: Port Salut-type of cheese with small holes; made on the borders of Lithuania in Germany.

Tybo: Very mild cheese of the **samsoe** family; made in Denmark.

Vacherin: Soft, runny cheese made in France and Switzerland.

Vendôme: Hard ewe's milk cheese made in the Loire Valley in France.

CHEESE CLOTH—Loosely woven cotton cloth used to drain or filter foods, as when pressing milk curds in cheese production.

CHEESE FOOD—Similar to processed cheese but contains less cheese and fat and more milk and whey solids.

CHEESE HOOP—Large cylinder or hoop, usually of wood, used to hold milk curds during cheese manufacture.

CHEESE PRESS—Machine used to press milk curds during cheese production.

CHEESE, PROCESSED—Blend of shredded cheeses, pasteurized and processed with added emulsifiers.

CHEF BANQUET CONTROL FORM—Form on which the chef or other responsible person enters the number of meals actually served at a given banquet, as well as the date and room used for the event.

CHEF DE RANG—Chef of rank or the principal waiter in the French restaurant system.

CHEF'S SLICER—Knife with a pointed blade about 12 inches long, used to carve cooked meats when a point may be needed to get around bones.

CHEILOSIS—One of the symptoms of **riboflavin** deficiency disease; characterized by red, swollen, and cracked lips.

CHEMICAL CAPONIZATION—Feminization of a male chicken by implanting female sex hormones. The result is greater yield and more tender meat.

CHEMICAL ICE—Ice that contains chemical preservatives to inhibit deterioration of food.

CHEMICAL RESISTANCE—Ability of a material to be exposed to chemicals and still resist corrosion and moisture.

CHEMICAL SANITIZERS—Chemical compounds containing chlorine, iodine, or quarternary ammonia that can quickly kill enough bacteria to make a food contact surface safe for further use.

CHEMICAL SCORE—Measure of the relative nutritional value of proteins. The higher the score, the more prevalent the **limiting amino acid.**

CHEMISE—French; "jacketed" or wrapped, e.g., potatoes with their skins or a food with a thin coating of aspic jelly.

CHERIMOYA—Subtropical fruit with white flesh within a green, scaly exterior. The fruit is large and may weigh as much as 16 pounds. It has a pineapplelike flavor.

CHERRY TOMATO—Small red or yellow tomato, slightly larger than a cherry.

CHEVIOT PAPER—Menu paper in which most of the fibers have the same light color but are intertwined with a few highly colored fibers.

CHICKEN HALIBUT—Young halibut weighing from two to about ten pounds. See **fish.**

CHICLE—Gummy derivative from the *Achras sapota* tree used in chewing gum.

CHICORY ROOT—Powdered root of the *Cichorium* plant, used as a common coffee additive.

CHILI PEPPERS—Hot, pungent capsicum pods of a variety of types. The most popular chili peppers are listed below.
Anaheim or *California green chilis:* Chilis that are five to eight inches long and two inches in diameter, tapering to a point. Anaheim chilis are bright, shiny green when fresh and range in flavor from mild to mildly hot.
Ancho: The ancho looks similar to an ordinary **bell pepper** and can be as sweet or considerably hotter. They redden and sweeten with maturity. When dried, the ancho turns a dark red.
Armenian yellow wax: Mild yellow pepper similar in shape to the **Anaheim** chili.

Bell pepper: Mild, sweet flavored, bell-shaped peppers that ripen from green to red.

Chili verde: General term for the immature or green form of various peppers.

Chile negro: Very hot, richly flavored pepper.

Chipotle: Dried, wrinkled, brick-red pepper with a very hot flavor. These peppers are mature, smoked **jalapeños.**

Fresno: Conically shaped chili about two inches long and one inch in diameter. This chili is much hotter than the Anaheim chili. It is bright green when fresh and turns from orange to red as it matures.

Guajillo: Slender, bright-red, smooth-skinned chili.

Jalapeño: The fresh pepper is dark green and about two and a half inches long. These are very hot peppers.

Mulato: When fresh, the mulato looks similar to the **ancho** though larger. The mulato ripens to a chocolate brown and is quite pungent.

Pasilla: Long, thin pepper that is very hot. It is about seven to twelve inches long and one and a half inches in diameter. It is dark green when immature, and ripens to dark brown.

Poblano: Mexican term for green **ancho** or **mulato** chilis.

Serrano: Extremely hot little cylindrical pepper about one and a half inches long and a half inch in diameter. When fresh, they are a rich, waxy green. They change from orange to red as they ripen.

CHILLPROOFING—Preventing haze formation in beer when it is chilled by the use of additives such as tannic acid.

CHINA CAP STRAINER—Sturdy, cone-shaped metal strainer with a long handle, and a hook to allow it to be hung across the top of a pot. It is used to strain sauces and soft foods by forcing them through with a small wooden roller.

CHINE—Saddle cut of meat, which includes some of the backbone and its attached flesh.

CHINESE CABBAGE—Vegetable with a long, green, lettucelike head. Also known as celery cabbage.

CHINOIS—French; **china cap strainer.**

CHIP—Small integrated circuit of silicon that enables minicomputers to function.

CHITIN—Indigestible hard shell that surrounds crustaceans such as shrimp.

CHIVES—Onion-family plant with slender hollow stems that are minced and used as flavoring in salads, soups, vegetables, and so on.

CHLORELLA—Edible and nutritious algae that can be cultivated on a wide scale.

CHLORIDE ION—Each is one half of a sodium chloride (table salt) molecule. These ions are essential for proper nerve function and for maintaining the body's ionic and fluid balance. The chemical symbol is CL−.

CHLORINE—Extremely pungent poisonous element used in small amounts to kill bacteria and to purify water. It can damage lungs and skin and should be handled with extreme care.

CHLORINE DIOXIDE—Bleaching agent used to age and improve bread.

CHLORITIZER—Dishwashing machine that automatically injects a chlorine sanitizer into the rinse cycle, thereby eliminating the need for 180°F water to sanitize the dishes.

CHLOROPHYLL—Chemical that accounts for the green color of living plants. It is essential to photosynthesis, in which it absorbs the sunlight converted to energy by plants.

CHLOROPHYLLIDE—Chemical from chlorophyll that leaches out of some vegetables during cooking and imparts a green color to the water.

CHOCOLATE LIQUID OR LIQUOR—Liquid that results when the meat of the cocoa bean is ground. It contains about 53 percent cocoa butter, and is the basic material of all chocolate and cocoa products.

CHOICE GRADE—Second highest of eight grades of meat. See

meat grading. It is the grade most often purchased by individual consumers.

CHOLAGOGUE—Drug that controls the release of bile from the gall bladder.

CHOLECALCIFEROL—Vitamin D₃.

CHOLERETIC—Any agent that stimulates bile secretion.

CHOLESTEROL—Steroid alcohol found in high concentration in organ meats, egg yolks, and saturated fats (see **fatty acids, saturated**). It appears as a waxy or soapy crystalline substance. Though it is found naturally in the body and is necessary for life, ingesting too much has been linked with heart ailments and circulatory problems.

CHOLINE—Essential nutrient required by the body to produce **acetylcholine**. It is important in building and maintaining cell structure.

CHONDROITIN—**Polysaccharide** found in cartilage and bone.

CHONDRUS CRISPUS—Edible red seaweed from which **carrageenan** is derived.

CHOPPER—Machine used primarily for grinding or chopping meat. It may be a self-contained unit or an attachment to a vertical mixer. See **food grinder.**

CHOPPING—Cutting food into small (quarter-inch), medium (half-inch), or large (three-quarters to one inch) pieces with a knife or other cutting utensil.

CHOPSTICKS—Eating utensils from the orient. They are long and thin, somewhat less than a foot long, and usually made of wood. A pair of them is held in one hand and used as tongs, with the rounded ends pinching up food.

CHOUX PASTRY—Pastry used for cream puffs and éclairs.

CHROMATIC PAPER—Menu paper composed of a variety of mixed colors, which gives it a mottled appearance.

CHROMATOGRAPHY—Technique for analyzing the nutrients

or other components in a substance by noting their different reactions to a series of standardized test stimuli.

CHURN—To stir cream into butter by making its fat globules stick together. Also, the device for doing so.

CHUTE ATTACHMENT—Tubular device that fits on the carriage tray of a food slicer to hold items such as carrots or celery for slicing.

CHUTNEY—Relish of seasoned chopped fruit or vegetables or both, served with a variety of meat dishes.

CHYLE—Milky form of lymph containing emulsified fat.

CHYLOMICRON—Microscopic fat in **chyle.**

CHYME—Partly digested food in the stomach.

CHYMOTRYPSIN—One of the enzymes in pancreatic fluid that help digest protein.

CIBOPHOBIA—Extreme aversion to food, to the point of phobia.

CIDER—Juice of apples served as a beverage, used for producing vinegar or made into **apple brandy** or **apple jack.** It may also be fermented into a sweet and fruity, straw-colored, sparkling or still wine.

CIMETER—Knife with a curved, pointed blade used for making accurate cuts, as in cutting steaks. Also called a steak knife.

CIRCULATION—In advertising, the average number of copies distributed of one issue of a given periodical.

CIRRHOSIS—Potentially fatal disease of the liver, often caused by excessive alcohol intake. The liver, which metabolizes fats, protein, carbohydrates, and alcohol, progressively loses its ability to function as its cells are gradually replaced with fat and connective tissue.

CISSA—Abnormal desire for food.

CITRIC ACID—Acid commonly found in citrus fruits; used as a food additive for flavoring purposes.

CITRIC ACID CYCLE—Final step in the oxidation of carbohydrates, fats, and protein in the human body's metabolism.

CITRON—Yellow, semitropical, thick-skinned fruit, larger than a lemon, but less acid. The rind is candied and used in fruit cakes and the like.

CITROXANTHIN—Yellowish pigment found in orange peel.

CITRULLINE—Amino acid not directly derived from food, formed in the body during metabolism.

CLABBER—Milk that has been soured almost to the point where the curds separate from the whey. It may be eaten flavored or plain.

CLAM KNIFE—Knife with a flat blade and sharp edge used to open clams.

CLARIFICATION—Use of a filter, centrifuge, or any other means to clear suspended particles out of a fluid.

CLARIFYING AGENTS—Substances that remove impurities, either by chemically attacking the impurity or by reacting with it to form a precipitate that drops to the bottom. Gelatin and egg white are commonly used for this purpose in wine making.

CLARKE DEGREES—Numerical scale indicating the hardness of water.

CLASS A FIRE—Fire in an ordinary combustible solid such as cloth, paper, or wood. Foam or water extinguishers are suitable.

CLASS B FIRE—Fire in a flammable gas or liquid such as oil or grease. Carbon dioxide or foam extinguishers can be used.

CLASS C FIRE—Fire involving live electrical equipment. An extinguishing agent that conducts electricity (e.g., water), cannot be used unless the power is cut off first. Otherwise, only carbon dioxide or multipurpose dry chemical extinguishers are suitable.

CLASS COST BASIS—Dividing all menu items into a small number of classes (e.g., meats, vegetables) and then totaling the costs to an establishment for each class. This can simplify accounting.

CLASS D FIRE—Fire in a combustible metallic element such as magnesium or potassium; more likely to occur at a chemical plant than a food service establishment. A multipurpose dry chemical extinguisher is suitable.

CLASSIFICATION OF ACCOUNTS—List of accounts grouped into categories such as assets or expenses, along with descriptions of each.

CLASSIFICATION OF FIRES—Four categories defining the type of fire that relates to the type of extinguisher that should be used. See **class A, B, C,** and **D fire.**

CLASSIFIED ADVERTISING—Small ads in a specific section of a periodical, often in the back, put into categories according to the type of product or service offered. Since a large number of ads are usually clustered together, any one may attract little attention. Contrast with **display advertising.**

CLASSIFIED GROWTHS—Bordeaux wines noted according to merit in the years 1855, 1953, and 1959. During those years, certain wines were classified with quality groupings and these ratings still hold today, in most cases.

CLEAN-IN-PLACE—Cleaning food-contact surfaces within pieces of equipment by circulating a sanitizing solution over them. This method is used when removal of the parts involved is difficult, as in beverage dispensers.

CLEAR SOUP SPOON—Tablespoon with a rather large oval bowl used to eat clear, thin soups.

CLEAVER—Instrument with a wide, square, heavy blade used to chop through small bone and cartilage, as when cutting pork chops.

CLIP-ON—Menu addendum that is affixed to the front of the menu with a clip. It usually contains a message about daily specials.

CLISSE—French; a small tray used to drain cheese.

CLOCHE, SOUS—French; dish served under a bell or domed cover.

CLONORCHIASIS—Disease caused by the parasite *Clonorchis sinensis*, which invades the bile ducts in humans who have eaten improperly cooked fish. Symptoms include fever, inflammation of the liver, abdominal pain and diarrhea.

CLONORCHIS SINENSIS—Asian liver fluke that can cause **Clonorchiasis** in humans.

CLOSE (OR CLOSING) THE BOOKS—To transfer the net of revenue and expenses accounts, at the end of an accounting period, to retained earnings or another asset or liability account.

CLOSED SYSTEM FOR CONVENIENCE FOODS—Foodservice operation that makes convenience foods for its own use rather than buying from or selling to the outside.

CLOSING ENTRIES—Entries in the records that close out the expense and revenue accounts for the period and transfer their balances to an asset account such as retained earnings.

CLOSING INVENTORY—Amount of goods on hand at the end of a given accounting period.

CLOSTRIDIA—Genus of bacteria that can cause food poisoning. It is the most heat-resistant and requires high temperatures for complete food sterilization.

CLOSTRIDIUM BOTULINUM—**Anaerobic** bacteria responsible for **botulism.**

CLOSTRIDIUM PERFRINGENS—**Anaerobic** bacteria of the **bacilli** type that can infect food and cause food poisoning.

CLOSURE PACKAGE—Any kind of sealing device on a container.

CLOTH FILTER—Food filter made of cloth.

CLOUDING—Loss of clarity in a liquid. Also, the precipitation of the tannins in tea.

CLUB SODA—Distilled, carbonated water, to which minerals have been added.

CMOS—Abbreviation for complementary metal oxide semiconductor. Another computer device used as a memory component; its power demand is low.

COACERVATION—Clotting of the **amylopectin** in bread. It may account for its staling.

COAGULATION—Conversion of proteins from a relatively fluid state to a more solid one, as happens when eggs are cooked.

COATED PAPER—Menu paper that has been surfaced with any of a variety of finishes, e.g., glossy and water resistant. See **paper types.**

COATING—Dusting food lightly with plain or seasoned flour, dipping it in an egg mixture, and covering it with bread crumbs prior to frying or baking; dipping food in a batter; coating food with sauce.

COBALAMIN—Vitamin B_{12}.

COBALT—Mineral that appears in trace amounts in various nutrients (e.g., in vitamin B_{12} molecules). In excess, it can be poisonous.

COBOL—The acronym for common business oriented language, a computer programming language designed for business applications.

COCCI—Bacteria that are spherical in shape. Contrast **bacilli.** See also **diplococci, staphylococci,** and **streptococci.**

COCHINEAL—Red coloring additive derived from the female insects of *Coccus cacti.*

COCHYLIS—A disease that attacks grapes.

COCKLE FINISH—Rippled appearance in a sheet of menu paper created by shrinking during drying.

COCKROACHES—Three principal varieties infest foodservice establishments: the **American cockroach, German cockroach,** and **oriental cockroach.** All can carry pathogens such as **salmonella** bacteria and polio viruses.

COCKTAIL—Alcoholic beverage usually served iced, often with a garnish, in small glasses. Also, nonalcoholic food item such as shrimp, crab, oysters, clams, fruit cup, fish, fruit or vegetable juice. Both types may be served alone or, most often, preceding a meal.

COCKTAIL GLASS—Bar glass with a short stem and wide-topped shallow bowl holding three to six ounces.

COCKTAIL NAPKIN—Small paper napkin used as an underliner for beverage glasses. Also called beverage napkin.

COCKTAIL STRAINER—Perforated disk or spoon that fits over a cocktail shaker or glass, allowing the drink to filter through but leaving the fruit or other solid ingredients behind.

COCKTAIL TRAY—Small circular tray, often cork-lined, used to carry beverages.

COCOA—Chocolate that has had some of its oil removed.

COCOA BEANS—Ground and roasted, these beans are the source of all chocolate. The beans come from the pods of the cocoa tree, mainly grown in West Africa and Latin America.

COCOA BUTTER—Yellowish-white vegetable fat removed from **chocolate liquid** under high pressure.

COCOA POWDER—Solid that remains after cocoa butter has been removed from the chocolate liquid. Treated with potassium, it becomes soluble and can be used in cooking.

COCONUT—Hard-shelled fruit of the coco palm tree. The fruit contains a white fluid called coconut milk that is used in some blended drinks. The meat is usually shredded and used fresh or dried in dessert preparations.

COCOTTE—French; utensil of glass, earthenware, or metal, also called a **casserole,** in which food may be both cooked and served.

CODDLE—To cook something in water whose temperature is maintained just below 212°F, the boiling point.

CODE—Set of rules that allow a computer to be programmed.

CODING TAPE—Colored plastic tape, with the date of receipt or other marks, attached to a package for later identification.

COELIAC DISEASE—See **celiac disease.**

COENZYMES—Nonprotein compounds that chemically assist enzymes during **catalysis.** Since most coenzyme molecules contain one of several different vitamins, they depend on appropriate dietary intake for their proper functioning.

COFACTOR—Nonprotein chemical required for an enzyme, which is protein, to function.

COFFEE—Popular beverage made from roasted beans of the coffee plant; the darker the roast, the stronger the taste. It can be made by any of four methods: boiling, dripping, percolating, and with a vacuum maker. See **arabica** and **robusta.**

COFFEE, DRIP—Coffee-brewing method whereby boiling water is poured over finely ground coffee held in a filter, allowing the fresh brew to "drip" into the serving container below.

COFFEE, FRENCH—Strong coffee made of one-fourth roasted chicory and three-fourths coffee beans.

COFFEE GRINDER—Machine that grinds coffee beans to the desired consistency for brewing. It may be a self-contained unit or an attachment to a vertical mixer.

COFFEE MAKER, ONE-HALF GALLON AUTOMATIC—Machine that brews coffee automatically by spraying a regulated amount of hot water over a filter basket holding ground coffee. The coffee is collected below in half-gallon steel or glass carafes that are kept warm on ceramic-coated warmer plates.

COFFEE MAKER, TWIN URN TYPE—Large stainless-steel jacketed machine with two chambers or urns for brewing and holding coffee and a reservoir in which water for coffee and tea making is heated to 205°F, and stored. The reservoir surrounds the coffee urn compartments to keep them hot. When a start button is pushed, the correct amount of hot water is pumped from the reservoir and sprayed over the ground coffee in filter baskets from where it drips into the urn. Coffee is drawn off from the bottom of each urn through a spigot.

COFFEE MAKER, VACUUM TYPE—Device with two bowls,

one on top of the other. The bottom bowl holds the water to be heated, and the top bowl holds the ground coffee and a filter. When the water is heated, it is forced through a tube into the upper bowl, where it mixes with the coffee grinds and extracts the flavor. When the unit is removed from the heat, the coffee filters back down into the lower bowl.

COFFEE, PERCOLATED—Method of coffee preparation in which boiling water is continually siphoned over ground coffee.

COFFEE URN BRUSH—Special brush with a long wooden handle made to clear the interior of a coffee urn.

COFFEE URN, STEAM-JACKETED—Large urn that makes 20 to 150 gallons of coffee at a time by pumping hot water over ground coffee and filtering.

COLA—Any carbonated soft drink derived from cola nuts, basically containing caffeine, sugar or sweetener, and caramel coloring.

COLANDER—Perforated bowl on a stand used to drain liquids from solid foods.

COLD CRACKING—Cracks in a packaging material caused by storage at low temperatures.

COLD ROOM—Refrigerated room used to store perishable foods.

COLD STABILIZATION—Wine clarification technique in which the temperature of the wine is lowered to 25°F–30°F for one to three weeks.

"COLD STORE" BACTERIA—Psychrophilic bacteria that can grow at temperatures down to 13°F and are not killed even at much lower temperatures. They are a problem in the cold storage of food.

COLIFORM BACTERIA—Beneficial **aerobic** bacteria that are normally found in the human gastrointestinal tract, where among other things they ferment the sugar lactose. Outside an individual's intestinal tract, as when they are found in food, milk, or water, they are an indication of contamination and are themselves a contaminant.

COLLAGEN—Solid protein found in bone, skin, and tendons that is transformed by boiling into gelatin.

COLLARD GREENS—Cabbagelike green leaves of the collard plant; used primarily in the Southern United States as a vegetable.

COLLATERAL—Any property, e.g., building or equipment, put up by a borrower as security for a loan or other debt.

COLLATING—Gathering the printed menu sheets or signatures in the proper order prior to binding.

COLLOID—Small particles of one substance dispersed and suspended in another substance, e.g., oil and vinegar when shaken together. Both substances may be gases, liquids, or solids.

COLLOP—Thinly sliced meat, e.g., bacon, or vegetable.

COLLUSION—When two or more employees or suppliers conspire together to defraud an establishment.

COLON—Final segment of the large intestine.

COLONNE—Cylindrical instrument used to core apples or to cut vegetables into column shapes.

COLONY—Large mass of bacteria, yeast, or other microorganisms that have grown densely in a solid medium.

COLOR ADDED—Mandatory information that appears on labels for fruit that has been artificially colored to improve the appearance of the outer skin.

COLOR FASTNESS—Ability of a menu paper to retain its color when used and abused, e.g., moistened and exposed to light.

COLORIMETER—Device used to measure the amount of various substances present in a solution by noting the depth of color they produce after reacting with certain test compounds.

COLOR, WINE—Refers to the "right" color for each wine. Red

wines should correctly be violet to amber, rosé distinctly pink, and white wines gold, yellow, or straw colored.

COLUMNAR JOURNAL SHEET—**Journal sheets** arranged in columns.

COLUMN INCH—Basic unit of advertising space in a printed medium. It is one column wide and one inch deep.

COLUMN STACK—Positioning cases of goods in single vertical columns. Such a stack is less stable than an interlocked pile, as in bricks in a wall.

COMBINATION BUY—The purchase of advertising from two or more outlets under the same ownership.

COMBINATION MENU—Menu in which highly popular items are repeated each day while other items are changed on a cyclical or irregular basis. Combines the best elements of the **fixed menu** and **cyclical menu.**

COMMAND—Code or combination of letters, numbers, or words that a computer system must recognize in order to know what to do next.

COMMERCIAL GRADE—The fifth highest of eight grades of meat. See **meat grading.**

COMMERCIAL IMPRESSIONS—Total audience for all the ads of a given advertiser including both the **accumulated audience** and the **duplicated audience.**

COMMERCIAL PANELS—Walls of packages on which information or messages are printed.

COMMERCIAL PAPER—Banking term; refers to negotiable business papers limited to short-term use.

COMMINUTED—Crushed and finely ground whole fruit (e.g., orange) used to make fruit drinks.

COMMIS DE RANG—French; assistant waiter.

COMMODITY—Goods or tangible items of value.

COMMON CARRIER—One who transports people or goods as a

business. In foodservice, it is anyone who picks up goods from a supplier and transports them to a buyer. En route, he is responsible for damage or loss due to accident or negligence on his part.

COMMON TOWEL—Single towel in the washroom to be used by more than one person, a practice prohibited for foodservice employees. The more hygienic practice is to use throwaway paper towels or hot-air drying devices.

COMMUNICABLE—The ability to spread from one person to another by contact or through the air, a trait of many diseases.

COMPACTOR—Machine that reduces the volume of waste by compressing it to a small fraction of its original size. Some models may be used only for dry waste, while others handle any type. The typical compactor consists of a charge box with a hopper into which the trash is fed. A hydraulically or pneumatically operated ram compacts the trash into an accumulation container, a heavy-duty plastic bag, or wax-lined box, which is then removed and disposed of.

COMPARISON SHOPPING—Comparing the differences in quality and price of the same item as offered by different suppliers, to find the best price for the desired level of quality.

COMPATIBILITY—Computer's ability to interchange or adapt with different computers from the same manufacturer or others.

COMPENSATING BALANCE—Stipulation by banks that a certain portion of a loan or a certain amount in a checking account be kept on deposit to help defray expenses.

COMPENSATORY TIME—Hours or days off given to an employee to make up for overtime work already performed. It avoids the payment of overtime, which is usually at a higher rate.

COMPETITIVE BID—Purchasing method in which sellers are invited to submit their prices in writing. Normally the supplier who offers the lowest-priced goods that meet the purchaser's specifications is chosen.

COMPETITIVE INFORMATION—Information about revenue

and expenses among establishment's competitors in the market-place. This is needed to gauge the degree of an operation's success.

COMPETITIVE STAGE OF ADVERTISING—Second stage of advertising; designed to make the public aware of the distinctive qualities or superiority of an establishment or product over its competitors. See **pioneering stage** and **retentive stage.**

COMPILER—Computer program translating another programming language into the computer's own code or language.

COMPLEMENTARY PRODUCTS—Two or more different products made from the same materials, e.g., flour, or by the same procedures, e.g., baking.

COMPLETE PROTEIN—Protein containing all the essential amino acids. See **amino acids, essential.**

COMPOTIER—French; deep dish of china or crystal set on a raised base, used to present fruits, compotes, or preserves.

COMPOUND INTEREST—Interest on the sum of an original principal and the accrued interest.

COMPRESSOR—Motor-driven device in a refrigeration unit that pumps the expanded gas from the evaporator and compresses it before sending it to the condenser for cooling.

COMPTROLLER—**Controller.**

COMPUTER—Electronic machine having the ability to manipulate and make computations on data quickly, resulting in processed output.

CONALBUMIN—One of the egg-white proteins. If eggs come in contact with iron, this protein reacts to form a pink color.

CONDENSED MILK—Milk with some of its water content removed and sugar added.

CONDENSED TYPE—Any printing type with reduced space between **characters,** which are usually narrow as well. Contrast **expanded type.**

CONDENSER, DISHWASHER—Device on some dishwasher

models that cools and removes the moisture from the exhaust air before returning it to the dish room. The water used for cooling the air becomes heated in the process and may be returned for use in the prewash tank or discharged into the general hot-water system.

CONDENSER—Section of a refrigeration unit in which hot gas from the compressor is cooled and condensed by air or water. Also called heat exchanger.

CONDIMENT—Any sauce and seasoning such as mayonnaise, ketchup, mustard, and steak sauce, that is usually added by the diner at the table.

CONDIMENT SET—Tableware consisting of two or more small bottles set in a decorative carrier of metal, wood, or pottery, for holding oil, vinegar, or other **condiments.**

CONDITIONING OF MEAT—The natural process that occurs after the death of an animal, in which the **glycogen** in the meat is converted to **lactic acid;** it tends to improve the quality and add to the meat's preservation.

CONDUCTION—Movement of heat through solid matter, as it spreads from one molecule to the next. See also **convection** and **radiation.**

CONFIGURATION—Total layout or design of all the equipment in a computer system.

CONFORMATION—Shape and form of a cut of meat. One of the three characteristics checked in **meat grading.**

CONGIES—Water left after boiling rice; contains many of the vitamins leached out during cooking.

CONIDENDRIN—An antioxidant preservative.

CONIDIUM—Spore by which certain fungi reproduce asexually.

CONNECTIVE TISSUE—Collagen and elastin that hold muscle fibers together. The more connective tissue, the tougher the meat.

CONSECUTIVE NUMBER RECORD—Printed form listing the

numbers of all the checks that have been issued to waiters and waitresses. As checks are turned in, they can be crossed off. Missing checks are immediately obvious.

CONSIGNMENT—Goods shipped now to be paid for as sold. The receiver may buy the goods later, store, sell, or dispose of them in some other way.

CONSOLIDATED FINANCIAL STATEMENT—The combination of financial statements from two or more establishments into one overall record.

CONSUMER GOODS—Items used by the purchaser to satisfy personal needs such as food and clothing. Contrast **producer goods.**

CONSUMER PANEL—Area on back of a package in which instructions, warnings, or other information is printed for the benefit of the individual consumer.

CONTACT INSECTICIDE—An insect-killing substance that kills by contact and penetration, i.e., the insect need not ingest it. It is safe for use in kitchens if it is handled properly.

CONTAINER INVENTORY—Inventory of empty soft-drink bottles and other containers on which deposits have been paid.

CONTAMINATION—Infiltration of impurities into a product.

CONTAMINATION, FOOD—Presence of harmful organisms (such as bacteria) or other materials (such as poisons) in food.

CONTINGENT PROFIT—Profit that may or may not be realized in the future, depending upon future events. All budgeted or estimated profits are contingent until realized.

CONTINUOUS AUDIT—Checking the business books throughout the fiscal period to catch and correct mistakes early, rather than waiting till the end of the period.

CONTINUOUS BROILER—Broiler in which food is loaded on a conveyor and cooked on both sides as it travels to the unloading position.

CONTINUOUS INVENTORY—Taking inventory of at least

some items each day (usually when stocks of those are low) and comparing the number on hand with the number listed in the books to catch discrepancies early, rather than waiting to count all items at the end of a period.

CONTRACT PRICE—Price at which goods will be sold according to a binding contract. The price may be fixed or adjustable, depending upon conditions cited in the contract.

CONTRIBUTION MARGIN—Net difference between sales income and direct costs. Also called marginal income.

CONTROL—Process of making the activities of an establishment conform to the manager's plan for the establishment.

CONTROL CYCLE—Period during which food-cost percentage goals are set, actual costs and revenues are calculated, and the two compared to evaluate the degree of success.

CONTROLLER—Chief accountant of an organization. Also called comptroller.

CONVECTION—Movement of heat in a liquid or gas based on the principle that hotter portions of a substance expand and rise through colder ones. See also **oven, conduction,** and **radiation.**

CONVECTION OVEN—Oven in which heated air is circulated evenly by a fan throughout the cavity, thus allowing faster cooking of greater quantities of food than with a conventional oven. Also called forced convection oven.

CONVECTION STEAMER—Equipment that cooks food with steam at normal pressure. The steam is circulated within the cooking compartment so that cooking is rapid and even. The compartment can hold three 12″ × 20″ × 2.5″ pans.

CONVENIENCE CLOSURE—Any package seal that can be opened by hand, with no need for tools.

CONVENIENCE FOODS—Any food that has been prepared before packaging to save later time and/or effort.

CONVENIENCE STOCK—Manufactured base for stock, often used when needed bones or necessary staff is not available.

CONVERSATIONAL MODE—Communication with a computer through a terminal where the next command to be given by the operator is dependent on feedback from the computer.

CONVERT—To develop raw materials into an intermediate or finished product; also, to exchange one type of property for another.

CONVERTED RICE—Parboiled rice made through a patented method.

CONVERTIBLE REFRIGERATION SYSTEM—Frozen-food storage cabinet that can hold foods at 0°F or be converted to a 40°F refrigerator by operation of a manual selector switch.

COOKIE CUTTER—A die, usually with a decorative shape, that can be used to punch out cookies from a roll of dough.

COOKIE PRESS—Hollow cylinder that can be used to shape cookies. It is filled with dough that is pressed out through the opening in the other end, which can be fitted with variously shaped attachments.

COOKIE SHEET—Baking pan consisting of a flat metal sheet, either with no sides or slightly elevated edges. It often has a no-stick coating.

COOKIE TURNER—Small, broad spatula with an offset blade used to lift and turn small items.

COOKING LOSS—Reduction in size and weight of a food (e.g., steak) during cooking. Most of the loss is from evaporated water or juices that drip off; some nutrients are lost as well.

COOKING, TRIM, AND BUTCHERING TESTS—Tests carried out on meat or fish to determine which brand gives the most net yield for the best price.

COOK-N-HOLD OVEN—Oven that cooks food for a predetermined amount of time at a selected temperature and then automatically switches to a suitable holding temperature.

COOPERAGE—Cask. Also, the production and repair of casks or barrels.

COOPERATIVE ADVERTISING—Advertising in a local market that is paid for both by a local establishment, such as a franchise, and also the national manufacturer or distributor.

CO-OP PURCHASING—The system in which several similar establishments form a group and submit joint purchase orders in order to take advantage of large-quantity discounts. They divide the goods upon receipt. Contrast **open market purchasing.**

COPPER—Metallic element, traces of which are present in the human body in certain enzymes and in the blood. Some copper in the diet is necessary but toxic levels can be reached quickly. The metal itself is also used in the manufacture of some cooking utensils because it is a good conductor and spreads heat evenly and rapidly throughout the vessel walls.

COPY, ADVERTISING—Written text to be used in advertising.

COPYFITTING—Calculating, in advance of menu printing, the type size and spacing that must be used to make a given passage fit a certain area on the page. See **copy measurement.**

COPY MARK-UP—Using a colored pen or pencil to add instructions on manuscript **copy** sent to the typesetter.

COPY MEASUREMENT—A count of the total number of characters (letters, numbers, and spaces) in a menu passage to be printed. If the passage is typed, the calculation can be done easily by measuring the total length of all lines in inches and multiplying by 10 for pica type or by 12 for elite type.

COPY, MENU—See **menu copy.**

COQUETIER—French; egg cup used for holding boiled eggs in an upright position when served in their shells.

COQUILLES—French; scallops, scallop shells, or shell-shaped dishes.

CORDIAL—Liqueur, produced by mixing or redistilling neutral spirits with flowers, fruits, herbs, juices, plants, roots, or seeds. They are usually sweet and are often served after dessert.

CORDON BLEU—French; literally "blue ribbon." Renowned

French cooking school where many famous recipes were created.

CORE MEMORY—Computer memory capacity wired directly into the circuitry of the central processor so it can be accessed without any mechanical or operator intervention.

CORI CYCLE—Chemical sequence in which **lactic acid** is converted to **glycogen** by the liver.

CORI ESTER—One of the intermediate chemical stages in the metabolism of glucose.

CORK—Spongy bark from the cork oak used in making stoppers for bottles.

CORKAGE—Fee charged in a restaurant for opening a bottle of wine and serving it to a customer.

CORKSCREW—Device for removing a cork from a wine bottle. The simplest type has a spiral wire with a pointed end that is inserted in the cork. Then the handle end is pressed and rotated, driving the wire in, as a screw into wood. There are also many more complicated versions.

CORKY WINE—Wine with an unpleasant odor imparted by a bad cork.

CORN—Staple crop. Ears contain yellow or white kernels. It is available fresh, canned, or frozen, and is used to produce hominy, grits, and corn meal. Pressed, the oil from the germ is used for cooking, as salad oil, or in margarine production. Other byproducts include cornstarch and corn syrup.

CORN SYRUP—**Glucose** syrup derived from corn. It may also include **maltose** or other sugars.

COROLLARY COST—Cost that arises because it is related to another cost. For example, energy costs might go up if an additional oven is purchased.

CORONARY THROMBOSIS—Condition in which a blood clot blocks part of the artery feeding blood to the heart. A diet high in **saturated fats** and **cholesterol** has been linked to this condition.

CORPORATION—An organization formed under state law for the purpose of conducting business. Legally it is considered and treated as a person or single entity. This organization differs from a sole proprietorship and from a partnership in a number of significant legal ways, e.g., regarding taxes. One major difference is that a corporation can issue stock and the legal liability of its owners is limited to the amount they invest. See **articles of incorporation.**

CORRECT—To counteract an unwanted flavor in food by seasoning with its opposite; to neutralize.

COST—Amount required to be paid in cash or other remuneration in return for delivered goods or services.

COST ABSORPTION—Entering a cost as a business expense in one's own accounts rather than passing it on to the consumer.

COST ACCOUNTING—Subfield of accounting that focuses on costs or expenses and analyzing cost trends in an effort to lower costs.

COST ACCOUNTS—Accounts in a ledger pertaining to expenses or costs.

COST AND FREIGHT (C & F)—The price of an item includes the cost and freight charges to a foreign port. However, it does not include transportation from the port.

COST-BENEFIT ANALYSIS—Calculation of the different costs that would have alternative benefits, so that the best combination of costs and benefits can be selected.

COST CONTROLS—System by which managers collect information on costs so they can make sensible decisions that affect them. However, costs can never be completely controlled.

COST FACTOR—Ratio of the user's cost for meat (U) to the supplier's price (S). The user's cost is that involved in meat preparation, e.g., butchering. When the supplier's price changes, the cost factor (C) can be used to estimate the user's new cost. Thus $C = U/S$ and $U = C \times S$.

COST FRACTION—Portion of a total expense attributable to one item or part thereof. For example, the cost fraction for one egg is 1/144 times the cost of a gross of eggs.

COST, INSURANCE, AND FREIGHT (CIF)—Term indicating that a sale price includes cost, insurance, and freight up to delivery at a foreign port but no further.

COST OF GOODS PURCHASED—Total cost of goods that have been acquired, including purchase price, transportation, storage, and other factors.

COST OF SALES—Cost to an establishment for the goods sold to the customers.

COST PERIOD—Period chosen for an analysis of the costs incurred during that time, e.g., four weeks or a quarter-year.

COST PER THOUSAND (CPM)—Basic unit of advertising prices. It is the cost for each 1,000 people reached in broadcast advertising or each 1,000 copies distributed in print advertising.

COST-PLUS PRICING—Deciding on a selling price by adding a set fee or a set percentage of the costs to the actual costs.

COST-PLUS PURCHASING—System in which an establishment contracts to buy all of certain items, e.g., food, from a given supplier and agrees to pay the supplier's costs plus a set percentage as mark-up. Contrast with **open market purchasing.**

COST-REDUCTION PROGRAMS—Use of managers in a continual search to lower costs by finding cheaper materials, increasing productivity, saving on labor costs, and so on.

COST STANDARD—Desired estimated cost for a menu item or other product, to which actual costs are compared later for control purposes.

COST UNIT—Any unit to which costs are assigned for accounting purposes, e.g., to a menu item or class of items.

COTTON FIBER CONTENT PAPER—Menu paper in which a certain percentage of the cellulose fibers is derived from cotton as opposed to wood pulp.

COUNTER DISHWASHER—Smallest type of dishwashing unit available. It comes in either 24- or 20-inch models, both of which fit on top of the counter.

COUNTER GUARD—Glass or plastic shield at approximately face level separating customers from unwrapped food on display at salad bars or cafeterias. It prevents customers from coughing, sneezing, or otherwise breathing pathogens onto the food. Also called a sneeze guard.

COUNTER PAN—Shallow-walled, rectangular, stainless-steel pan with a wide rim made to fit in steam-table openings. It may be used both to cook and to hold foods in steam tables. The standard full size is 12 × 20 inches wide and 2.5 to 6 inches deep. It also comes in a half, third, quarter, or eighth of the standard size. Also called hotel pan, service pan, steam-table insert.

COUNTER REFRIGERATION—Units in the service area that hold chilled items to be served, such as salads, desserts, or juices. Items may rest on ice or directly on refrigeration plates.

COUNTER SERVICE—Method of service in which guests sit at a counter, behind which the waitress or waiter stands. Service is usually faster than at tables.

COUNTERTOP BROILER—Small broiler of the Charhearth or heavy-duty type mounted on top of a table or counter. Useful for short-order or cafeteria-line work.

COUPLER—Device fitted on the tip of a cake-decorating bag or syringe, that both holds the tube in place and allows tubes to be changed easily without emptying the bag each time.

COURT BOUILLON—Rich fish stock.

COUVERT—French; cover or place setting.

COVER—One seat at an establishment or one customer. Five covers per waiter means a maximum of five customers per waiter at any given time. Also, the guest's place setting at the dinner table including plates, silverware, glasses, and napkin.

COVER CHARGE—Set fee paid in night clubs and restaurants for seating, independent of charges for food or drink.

COVER FORECAST—**Customer forecast.**

COVER PAPER—Type of heavy, thick, and attractive paper used on the outside of many menus, not only because it bears up to frequent handling but also because it adds to the overall appearance. See **paper types.**

COVER PER MAN-HOUR—Index of employee productivity calculated by dividing the total number of meals served in a given period by the total number of employee man hours for the serving.

CPS—Abbreviation for characters per second, or the speed at which text is produced by printers.

CRANBERRY—Small red berries that grow in bushes, mostly in New England wetlands. They have a very tart flavor and are used mainly in juice or sauce production.

CRAZING—Formation of fine cracks on or in a plastic or glass surface (as in a container), often caused by excess heat. See **thermal stress cracking.**

CREAM DISPENSER—Insulated vessel that holds one to three quarts of cream, which are dispensed into portions by a hand pump. Larger units may be refrigerated.

CREAMER—Small pitcher of metal or china used on the dinner table to serve cream for coffee.

CREAMING—Blending of two ingredients until soft and creamy, such as sugar and shortening in cake preparation.

CREAMING QUALITY—Ability of fats to absorb air when mixed.

CREAM OF TARTAR—Another name for potassium hydrogen tartrate, one of the compounds in baking powder.

CREAM SOUP SPOON—Spoon with a round, deep bowl, used to eat thick soups.

CREATINE—Compound derived from acetic acid that is involved in energy release during muscular activity.

CREATININE—Metabolic waste product. A derivative of **creatine,** the amount of both compounds present indicates the quality of meat extract because it is proportional to the amount of protein present.

CRECY—Literally, a town in France. In cooking, à la Crécy means a dish with carrots, particularly glazed ones.

CREDIT—Accounting entry that serves to decrease an asset or expense account, or to increase a liability or revenue account. The opposite of **debit.**

CREDIT LINE—**Line of credit.**

CREDIT MEMORANDUM—Form signed by the delivery driver when the goods delivered were not accepted and must be returned. This form proves that the customer is due a credit invoice.

CREDITOR—Any person or organization to which one owes a debt.

CREDIT SALE—Delivery of goods to a customer in return for a promise to pay later, as verified by the customer's signature on a credit slip.

CREME FRAICHE—French; a very thickened sour cream.

CREPES—French; thin large pancakes filled with various ingredients and served as an appetizer, main dish, or dessert.

CRISPING—Chilling salad greens in ice water to make them firm and crisp.

CRITICAL MOISTURE CONTENT—The level of moisture in a food substance at which it deteriorates to the point of becoming unusable, e.g., crackers left exposed in a humid kitchen may become inedible.

CROOKNECK SQUASH—A squash with a long, curved neck

resembling a goose's. The yellow skin is rough and warty looking.

CROP—To cut out portions of a photograph or copy either to make it fit the menu better or improve the overall appearance.

CROSS-CONNECTION—Accidental connection between a system of pipes containing drinkable water and another set containing possible contamination.

CROSS-CONTAMINATION—When a person or piece of equipment transfers contaminants from one food to another.

CROWN PACK—**Bulge packing.**

CROWN SIZE—A particular paper used for menus. Each sheet measures 15 × 20 inches (38.1 × 50.8 cm). See **paper sizes.**

CRU—French; literally, growth. Used in connection with wines to mean vineyard.

CRUCIFERAE—Family of related vegetables, including broccoli, Brussels sprouts, cabbage, and cauliflower. Research suggests that the **phenols** present in these vegetables help the body resist cancer.

CRUET STAND—Table set consisting of bottles or jars for oil and vinegar set in a stand. Also called castor set.

CRUMBER—Instrument used by the waiter or waitress to remove crumbs from the dinner table prior to serving dessert. Some are simple scooping devices, and others are made like miniature carpet sweepers.

CRUST—The deposit produced by certain red wines, especially vintage ports that have been long in bottles. Also, the hard outer layer of a baked product, such as bread.

CRUSTACEAN—Shellfish with crustlike shell including crab, crayfish (or crawfish), lobster, and shrimp.

CRYOVAC AGING—Process in which meat is placed in an airtight, moisture- and vapor-proof wrap and held under refrigeration.

CRYPTOXANTHIN—Yellow compound responsible for the color of corn and some other vegetables.

CUCUMBER—Cylindrical green vegetable that may be eaten raw. It is also the usual source of pickles. The different types vary in length from about one to twenty inches. The scientific name is *Cucumis sativus*.

CULINAIRE—French; denoting the art of cooking.

CULL—To screen a group of items in order to remove the defective or substandard ones.

CURDLING—Process whereby eggs, sweet cream, or milk separate into protein and liquid fractions when combined with acids such as those found in sour cream or lemons.

CURDS—Globs of clotted protein resulting from the reaction of rennet in fresh milk.

CURE—To salt and dry or smoke meats in order to change the taste or preserve them.

CURED—Dried or smoked meat or fish. See **cure**.

CURL—Amount of curvature in a sheet of menu paper. Curvature can warp the paper's edges.

CURRANT—Small berry excellent for jellies when fresh or as seedless raisins when dried.

CURRENT-ASSET CYCLE—Time needed for sales to accumulate up to the same dollar value as the **current assets** account.

CURRENT ASSETS—Cash or other goods that can be readily converted into cash. Contrast **fixed assets.**

CURRENT COST—Any operating cost of an establishment.

CURRENT LIABILITIES—Amounts owed that are payable within a year or within a business cycle.

CURRENT MARKET PRICE—Going rate (cost) of a given product in the marketplace. For some items, the price can change daily or even more frequently.

CURRENT PRICE—Selling price at the actual time of sale.

CURRENT RATIO—An index of the financial health of an establishment. It is calculated by dividing current assets by current liabilities.

CURRY POWDER—Aromatic seeds and ground spices blended to give flavor to stews and soups, often served with rice. Indian in origin.

CUSTARD POWDER—Cornstarch with added color and flavor.

CUSTOMER FORECAST—Prediction of the total number of customers who will patronize an establishment on a given day or for a given meal. It is based on average attendance in the past for that day of the week, the expected weather, and unusual events such as holidays. Also called cover forecast.

CUSTOMER'S LEDGER—Business record with a separate account for each major customer.

CUSTOMS INVOICE—Invoice describing goods imported into this country. It must accompany the goods through the customs inspection upon entry.

CUT—Any type of photoengraving used in letterpress printing for menus.

CUT IN—To blend shortening into a mix of ingredients, as in pastry production. The term refers to a particular method of doing so, namely by repeatedly slicing with one or two knives. A blender may be used instead.

CUTOFF DATE—Date on which both receiving and shipping are halted briefly so that an accurate inventory can be taken of goods on the premises.

CUTTER GRADE—Second lowest meat grade out of eight grades. See **meat grading.** The quality is too low to use as a whole roast but it can be processed into lunch meat.

CUTTING BOARD—Flat surface on which food may be cut or chopped. Cutting boards were once almost exclusively made of hard wood. Modern boards may be of lucite or thermoplastic, are more resistant to cutting and gouging, and are more easily sanitized.

CUVEE—French; a blend of wines.

CYANIDE—Lethal poison, small quantities of which appear in certain foods such as apple seeds and black cherries. Some silver polishes also contain it and must therefore be used carefully.

CYANOCOBALAMIN—One of the active forms of **vitamin B$_{12}$**.

CYANOGENIC—Containing significant amounts of **cyanide,** e.g., apple seeds.

CYANOSIS—Bluish tint to the skin or mucous membranes caused by anemia or any other condition that results in insufficient oxygen in the blood.

CYCLAMATE—Artificial sweetener that has no calories but is 30 times sweeter than sugar. Its use was banned by the FDA but recent research has failed to confirm that it is carcinogenic.

CYCLICAL MENU—Menu that lists different meals each day for a given period, e.g., 30 days. After that time, the same menu list is used again for the next period.

CYCLITOLS—Group of compounds known as cyclic sugars (e.g., tetritol).

CYMLING—White summer squash shaped like a flat disk.

CYST—Sac into which a parasite encapsulates itself when it goes into an inactive state. The sac insulates it against damage caused by heat or cold.

CYSTEINE—One of the nonessential amino acids that contain sulfur. It is used in biochemical and nutrition research, and as a reducing agent in bread dough.

CYSTICERCUS—Tapeworm larva cyst often called a **bladderworm.**

CYSTINE—One of the nonessential amino acids that contain sulfur. Each molecule is composed of two **cysteine** molecules.

CYTOCHROME—Natural pigment found in almost all living cells; chemically involved in oxidation.

CYTOLYSIS—Process of destroying living cells.

CYTOLYTIC—Having the ability to dissolve or otherwise destroy living cells.

CYTOPLASM—That part of a cell's protoplasm that surrounds the nucleus.

CYTOSINE—One of the **pyrimidines** that appear in DNA; involved in heredity.

CYTOTOXIC—Property of being poisonous to living cells.

D

DAIKON—Japanese large white radish with a milder flavor than the usual American variety.

DAILY BANQUET COST SHEET—Form used for banquets to calculate the food cost percentage by recording the total costs and total sales for each.

DAILY BANQUET DIARY—Record of all pertinent information concerning upcoming banquets, either tentative or confirmed. Some of the items to include are date, time, estimated number of attendees, and the dining room(s) to be used.

DAILY FOOD COST—Dollar value of all food used by an establishment in a given day; the sum of direct purchases and storeroom issues.

DAILY FOOD PRODUCTION WORKSHEET—Form used to estimate the quantity of each item required to meet the next day's anticipated sales. The quantity required is calculated by multiplying the anticipated sales by the portion size.

DAILY FOOD RECEIVING REPORT—Form summarizing all

the food deliveries to an establishment for that day; it includes the supply source, the description of the items, and the cost.

DAILY LIQUOR RECEIVING AND ISSUES REPORT—Form listing suppliers and the dollar value of goods received from each that day, as well as the total purchases accumulated in the period so far. The amounts issued to the bar or other departments may also be recorded.

DAILY PAYROLL REPORT—Form listing all the employees who worked on a given day, the number of hours each worked, and the pay each earned.

DAILY PRICE BOARD—Blackboard listing the main items to be purchased (e.g., meats) along with the latest prices; ideally it is updated daily.

DAILY PURCHASE SHEET—Form listing the par stock for each item to be purchased, the amount on hand, and the amount that should be ordered that day to achieve the par stock level.

DAILY RECORD OF PURCHASES AND ISSUES—Multicolumn form more extensive than the basic **daily food receiving report** but used for the same purpose—to summarize the purchases and the disposition of those purchases for a given day.

DAILY REPORT OF FULL BOTTLE SALES—Record of the number and type of whole bottles of liquor sold that day to customers.

DAISY WHEEL—Computer printer wheel with characters around the rim of the plastic hub. It offers the best computer type available.

DAMSON PLUM—Purplish plums, small and dark, used to produce flavorful preserves.

DANDELION GREENS—Weed with edible leaves that are cooked like spinach, used freshly cut for salads, or tossed in a skillet.

DANDY ROLL—Cylinder of wire that produces watermarks or other embellishments on fine menu paper.

DANGEROUS ARTICLES—**Regulatory products,** hazardous items that must be so labeled prior to transport, in accordance with the regulations of the U.S. Department of Transportation (DOT). Such products include corrosives, flammables, and poisons. By regulation, they must also be packaged safely.

DANGER ZONE—Temperature range most favorable for bacteria, i.e., about 45° to 140°F.

DARIOLE—Small cylindrical vessel used for molding and baking a certain type of cake that is also called a dariole.

DARK ADAPTATION—Chemical change in the eye resulting in the increased ability to see in dim light. Its effectiveness depends on the presence of sufficient vitamin A.

DARNE—French; thick slices cut from the middle portion of large fish such as salmon.

DASHEEN—Southern U.S. potatolike vegetable.

DATA BASE—Organized grouping of computer data in a central place to facilitate its retrieval by management.

DATA COLLECTION—Process of bringing computer data from several points to one central place for processing or storage.

DATA ELEMENT—Basic unit of information in a data base. Each data base has many data classes, each of which is made up of data elements.

DATA SET—Typically a phone dial or handset for manual computer dial-up operation used for data or voice communication. Also refers to a collection of computer data.

DATE OF ACQUISITION—The day an asset was purchased, as recorded in an establishment's books. The same data must appear in asset accounts, depreciation expense accounts, and any other records for that item.

DATE STAMPING—Stamping the date on goods as they are received so that older goods may be used up first.

DAUBE—French; meat stew. Usually the word is combined with others that indicate the kind of stew.

DAUBIERE—French; a pot used to make stews or casseroles.

DEAD-MAN CONTROL—Safety device on potentially danger-ous equipment that must continuously be activated for the ma-chine to operate. If the person dies, faints, slips, or for any other reason lets go, the machine stops automatically.

DEAD STOCK—Food items that have been in the storeroom for a long time and must be used promptly or be thrown out. See **shelf life.**

DEBENTURE—Bond or certificate acknowledging indebtedness, but not backed by collateral.

DEBIT—Accounting entry that serves to increase an asset or ex-pense account, or to decrease a liability or revenue account. The opposite of **credit.**

DEBIT MEMORANDUM—Document issued by a bank or other institution explaining why one's account has been reduced, e.g., for a service charge. The opposite of **credit memorandum.**

DEBTOR—Person or organization that owes money to a **creditor.**

DECANT—To pour a spirit or wine from its original container into a serving container, often to insure that no sediment re-mains in the portion to be served.

DECANTER—Container used in serving a spirit or wine. The wine is first poured or "decanted" from its original bottle into this new container.

DECENTRALIZED SERVICE—Service method in which food prepared in a central kitchen is sent in bulk to service pantries where it is placed onto dishes and trays and dispatched. Contrast **centralized service.**

DECK OVEN—Oven that holds up to four pans stacked. It is useful in conserving floor space.

DECLASSIFIED COST—Cost of a product broken down into cost fractions, each of which is attributable to a different ele-ment, e.g., raw materials, labor, and energy.

DECLINE PHASE—Fourth phase in **bacterial growth** when

death exceeds reproduction and the number of bacteria in the colony diminishes.

DECOCTION—Liquid that results from boiling food materials, e.g., meat or vegetable stock.

DECOMPOSITION—Breakdown of food chemicals into simpler compounds, as in food digestion or spoilage.

DECORATED TYPE—Printing type for menus in which the lines of individual letters have fancy or ornate embellishment. See **special type.**

DECORATING BAG—Cone-shaped bag of cloth, plastic, or parchment fitted with a special nozzle at the apex, through which are squeezed creams or icings for decorating pastries.

DECORATING COMB—Spatula with serrated edges for making ridged surfaces on cake icings. Decorating combs are often triangular, with each edge patterned differently.

DECORATING TUBE—Special nozzle that fits onto a decorating bag or syringe, with one of several different types of openings through which decorations of icings or creams are piped.

DECORTICATION—Process of stripping away the outer rind or hull of a grain or plant.

DECREMENT—Decrease in value of an asset during a specific period. The opposite of **increment.**

DEEP-FAT FRYING—Cooking food by immersing it in boiling fat or oil.

DEEP-FRYING BASKET—Wire basket used to hold food while it is being deep fried. When it is removed from the fat, the basket allows the food to drain.

DEFALCATION—Embezzlement of cash by an employee.

DEFAULT—Failure to make payments on a debt or to fulfill any other contractual agreement.

DEFERRED LIABILITY—Debt on which payment is postponed beyond the originally agreed-upon or usual date.

DEFERRED-PAYMENT SALE—Credit sale for which an establishment allows payment to be made later than usual, with or without installments.

DEFERRED REVENUE—Income received before it has been earned, e.g., payment received for goods before they have been delivered.

DEFICIENCY—Business condition of an enterprise in which liabilities are greater than assets.

DEFICIT—Operating at a loss; expenses exceed revenues.

DEFROSTING—To thaw a freezer so that built-up ice can be removed. This increases the efficiency of the unit and its ability to cool. The frozen foods within the unit should not be allowed to thaw at the same time or they might spoil.

DEGLAZE—To make gravy out of the residue in a pan of cooked meat, by removing the excess fat, then heating the remaining drippings with stock.

DEGREASE—To remove fat or grease from a food, e.g., skimming liquid fat off a stock.

DEGREE—Unit of temperature on the **Celsius** or **Fahrenheit** scales.

DEGREES, CELSIUS—Standard abbreviation for degrees on the Celsius scale of temperature is °C.

DEGREES, FAHRENHEIT—Standard abbreviation for degrees on the Fahrenheit scale of temperature is °F.

DEGUMMING AGENTS—Any chemical (e.g., hydrochloric acid) that can remove the gummy resins from fats to purify them.

DEHUMIDIFY—Removing moisture from the air of a room or container, either mechanically or chemically. This process can in turn remove moisture from stored foods.

DEHYDRATION—Removal of 95 percent or more of the water from a material, usually a foodstuff, by exposure to heat or chemicals. See **dessicant.**

DEHYDROASCORBIC ACID—Oxidized vitamin C.

DEHYDROCANNING—Partial (50 percent) **dehydration** of fruits and vegetables prior to canning. Such partial dehydration does not harm the food's texture.

DEHYDROCHOLESTEROL—Present in the skin. Sunlight acts on it to form **vitamin D$_3$**.

DEHYDROFREEZING—Partial dehydration (50–65 percent) of fruits and vegetables prior to freezing.

DEHYDROGENASES—Enzymes that oxidize compounds by removing hydrogen from them. More recently called oxidorductases.

DEHYDROGENATION—Process of oxidizing a compound by removing its hydrogen.

DEHYDRORETINOL—Chemical name of **vitamin A$_2$**.

DELICATESSEN—Ready-to-eat food specialties, or the store that sells them.

DELIMITED AREA—Geographical area whose name is used for the spirit or wine produced within its borders.

DELIVERED PRICE—Price that includes not only the goods themselves, but also delivery to an agreed-upon point (usually a freight terminal rather than an establishment itself).

DELIVERY SLIP—Form that describes goods being shipped. It should accompany the goods during shipment and should be checked by the receiving clerk.

DEMAND—Potential number of customers who will want to purchase a particular item at a particular price. See **supply**.

DEMAND CHARGE—Rate increase made by electrical utilities in addition to the basic cost per KWH consumed. It is charged to cover the utility's extra expenses in supplying large amounts of energy during peak demand periods.

DEMERIT—Point taken off an establishment's health rating by the health authority for each violation of sanitary requirements.

DEMERIT SCORE—Total number of demerits assigned to an establishment by the health authority in a single inspection and evaluation. See **inspection report form.**

DEMIJOHN—Bottle that is fat-bellied and encased in wicker. It holds two to ten gallons.

DEMITASSE—Small coffee cup usually reserved for serving strong coffees such as espresso. Also, the after-dinner drink of strong coffee served in a small cup.

DEMITASSE SPOON—Small spoon with an oval bowl used for stirring beverages served in demitasse cups.

DEMURRAGE—Loading charges assessed by a carrier of goods when the job exceeds an agreed-upon amount of time.

DEMY SIZE—Printing paper measuring 17.5 × 22.5 inches (44.5 × 57.2 cm). See **paper sizes.**

DENATURATION, ALCOHOL—See **alcohol, denatured.**

DENATURATION, PROTEIN—Intermediate stage between full solubility and full coagulation of protein. The reduction in activity is caused by a rupture in the hydrogen bonds of the **peptide** chains. Heat or chemicals such as acids can cause this.

DENDRITIC SALT—Salt with the same chemical structure as ordinary salt (sodium chloride) with branched rather than cubed crystals. It dissolves more rapidly than ordinary salt does.

DENSITOMETER—Device used to measure the density of a liquid or gaseous material.

DEODORIZATION—Removal of the smell and part or all of the flavor of a food, such as cabbage or fish.

DEOXYRIBONUCLEIC ACID (DNA)—Found in the nucleus of all living cells; DNA is the principal constituent of chromosomes, the structures that transmit hereditary characteristics. Its double-helix chemical structure is made up of sugar, phosphates, purines, and pyrimidines.

DEPARTMENT—Section of an establishment in which similar

or related procedures are performed, e.g., the accounting department, the cooking department.

DEPARTMENT VOID—Cancellation of a sale that was already rung up on the register. This may be due to an error, perhaps in the price of an item.

DEPECTINIZATION—Use of enzymes to remove pectin from fruit pulp.

DEPOSIT, WINE—Sediment resulting as a wine matures in the bottle. Deposits are more visible in red wines than in white.

DEPRECIATED COST—Portion of the original purchase price of an asset that has been written off as depreciation expense.

DEPRECIATION—Decrease in value of an asset over time. There are two accounting methods for calculating depreciation, accelerated and straight-line. In the straight-line method, an equal amount is deducted from the value of the asset each year. In the accelerated method, the asset is depreciated more in the initial years, less in later years. Accumulated depreciation is the total to date charged off a given asset.

DEPRECIATION RATE—Percentage of the original purchase price of an asset that is written off each year as depreciation expense.

DESCRIPTIVE COPY—Menu copy that describes the item offered for sale. Colorful descriptions can add to the appeal of an item and help to sell it.

DESCRIPTIVE MENU HEADINGS—Colorful and appealing words at the head of each group of items on the menu. For example, "Seacoast Delights" attracts more attention than simply "Seafood."

DESICCANT—Any chemical that absorbs moisture and can dehumidify a space or dehydrate a substance.

DESICCATED EGGS—Dried whole eggs, whites, or yolks, used in baking.

DESICCATION—Removal of almost all water from a substance,

which can be done chemically or naturally, as with heat or air. Foods are sometimes dessicated to preserve them.

DESSERTSPOONFUL—Quarter-ounce measure.

DETERGENT—Any organic or chemical compound with cleansing properties.

DETOXICATION—Chemical alteration of a toxic substance to make it nonpoisonous. This can be accomplished in the body by various chemical processes such as oxidation.

DEVEIN—To remove the vein from shrimp by cutting only a bit into the shrimp's flesh at the top and lifting the meat to expose the vein, which is then removed.

DEVILLED—Meat, poultry, seafood, eggs, and so on, ground or chopped and mixed with seasoning.

DEXEDRINE—**Amphetamine** drug used primarily to diminish the appetite. It has many undesirable side-effects and is addictive, hence rarely prescribed.

DEXTRIN—Intermediate chemical step in the breakdown of starch to maltose sugar due to enzyme action or heat (e.g., as in toasting bread).

DEXTROSE—**Glucose.**

DEXTROSE EQUIVALENT VALUE (DE)—Indication of the extent of **hydrolysis** of starch expressed as a percentage of the dextrose present compared to remaining starch and dextrins.

DIABETES INSIPIDUS—Disease in which the person lacks sufficient antidiuretic hormone (ADH) so that he or she produces copious amounts of dilute urine and suffers excessive thirst. It is rare.

DIABETES MELLITUS—Disease in which the pancreas produces insufficient insulin, which is required to metabolize sugar in the blood. Sufferers of this disease therefore cannot handle much sugar in their diets and are often administered supplementary insulin.

DI-ACETATE, CALCIUM—Food additive that inhibits mold and bacterial growth in bread.

DI-ACETATE, SODIUM—Food additive that inhibits mold and bacterial growth in bread.

DIACETYL—Natural flavoring agent in butter that is extracted and added to margarine to improve its flavor.

DIAMOND-BACK TERRAPIN—Small turtle that lives in fresh water and offers the best turtle meat on the market for soup preparation.

DIASTASE—Amylase found in saliva and pancreatic fluid that converts starch to dextrins.

DIASTATIC ACTIVITY—Ability of flour to feed yeast during leavening by producing sugar from its own starch and **diastase.**

DICED—Uniform cut of food into cubes that are small (quarter inch), medium (half inch), or large (three-quarters to one inch).

DICOUMAROL—Substance derived from sweet clover that blocks the action of vitamin K and so retards blood clotting. It can be beneficial as an anticlotting drug, or it can kill by causing severe internal bleeding.

DIFFERENTIAL COST—Variance in cost per unit depending on the number of units of an item produced. For example, making one pizza may be costly, but if 100 are made, the cost per pizza diminishes.

DIGESTIBILITY—Degree to which food eaten can be converted into nutrients and assimilated by the body, i.e., digested. The remainder becomes waste.

DIGESTION—Process of breaking down ingested foods into components that can be absorbed into the bloodstream, e.g., carbohydrates are broken down into glucose. Digestion is performed in the alimentary canal.

DIGESTIVE JUICES—Secretions of the mouth, stomach, pancreas, and so on, that contain enzymes vital for digestion.

DIGITAL COMPUTER—Electronic machine that uses the **bi-**

nary number system, as do most business computers. Contrast **analog computer.**

DIGLYCERIDES—Fat in which each molecule has one molecule of glycerol and two of fatty acids, unlike the three in **triglycerides.**

DIHYDROCHALCONES—Group of intensely sweet compounds artificially derived from the natural **flavanones** in various fruits.

DILATATION OF FAT—Increase in volume of fat as it changes from the solid to a liquid state.

DILUTE—To decrease the concentration of a liquid by adding more fluid.

DINNER FORK—Fork used to eat entrees.

DINNER KNIFE—Table knife used to cut food.

DIPEPTIDE—Molecule composed of two amino acids linked together; a product resulting from the breakdown of protein during digestion.

DIPHENYL—Compound that inhibits mold growth on fresh fruit.

DIPPER WELL—Container filled with running water in which ice cream scoops and similar utensils are rinsed between uses.

DIPSA—Any food that causes thirst, e.g., spicy and salty foods.

DIPSESIS—Craving to drink unusual fluids, e.g., blood.

DIPSOMANIA—Irresistible urge to drink alcoholic beverages; often used as a synonym for alcoholism.

DIRECT COSTS—Costs that are directly related to a particular operation or department. For example, the expense of flour is a direct cost to breadmaking or to the bakery department. Contrast with **indirect costs.**

DIRECT DELIVERIES—Supplies taken directly to their destination, e.g., the kitchen, without being placed in storage.

DIRECT DEPARTMENT—Any department that is involved directly in providing goods and services to the public. See also **indirect department.**

DIRECT EXPENSE—**Direct cost.**

DIRECTIVE—Statement or order from a manager or other authority figure to an employee requiring the employee to comply with a particular procedure or course of action.

DIRECT MAIL ADVERTISING—Printed advertising circulars, often with discount coupons, that are mailed to known customers, to names from a mailing list, or to all the residents in a given area, in order to solicit patronage.

DIRECT MATERIAL—Cost of raw materials that directly become a part of the finished product. For example, flour and sugar become part of the cake; the pan and oven do not.

DIRECT POSTING—Placing expense, revenue, or other entries directly into the ledger without first listing them in a journal.

DIRECT PURCHASES—Perishable food items that are not put into long-term storage but are kept near the kitchen for use within a day or so after purchase.

DIRECT SELLERS—Those selling directly from manufacturers or packers. They may provide some savings to the buyer because of the elimination of marketing agents and services.

DIRECT SHIPMENT—**Drop shipment.**

DISACCHARIDE—Any sugar whose molecules are each composed of two **monosaccharides.** For example, sucrose is composed of glucose and fructose.

DISBURSEMENT—Payment by cash or check for services rendered or goods purchased.

DISC, MAGNETIC—Any type of magnetic memory device in the shape of a disk that is either hard or flexible, fixed or removable. Used to store computer data. Contrast **drum, magnetic.**

DISCOUNT—Reduction in the price of one or more items for a specific period or for certain customers. Employees, for example, may pay 20 or 40 percent less than regular customers.

DISCOUNT EARNED—Savings in the purchase price of an item because payment was made before a certain date. See **cash discount.**

DISCOUNT LOST—Account sheet that lists discounts possible at the time of purchase that were not collected because of failure to pay on time or some other factor.

DISH DISPENSER—Device holding stacks of dishes that is continually raised by a spring-loaded or counterweight mechanism to a level convenient for removal. It may have a heating unit to keep dishes warm. It is mounted on wheels so it may be conveniently moved from the dish room to the serving area.

DISHWASHER, CAROUSEL—Dishes are carried on a circular moving belt that passes through and then around the machine, to re-enter at the front. Dishes may be loaded and unloaded by one person at a single location. Dishes not unloaded will pass through the machine again.

DISHWASHER, CONVEYOR-RACK—Dishes are moved on racks through the wash and rinse compartments by a pair of motor-driven chains.

DISHWASHER, FLIGHT—Dishes are placed on a continuous rack-belt that transports them through the wash and rinse sections of the machine and exits them through the unloading end. After exiting the final rinse section, the conveyor travels for several feet in the open to allow time for drying before the dishes are removed. Glasses and silver are placed on racks to be sent through on the conveyor.

DISHWASHER, IMMERSION—A rack of dishes is immersed in a tank of hot water and detergent that are agitated by a pump. The rack is lifted out and placed in another tank for rinsing.

DISHWASHER, SINGLE TANK STATIONARY RACK (DOOR TYPE)—Dishes are placed on a rack that is inserted by hand through a door that is then closed. They are washed by jets of water and detergent from spray nozzles above and below the rack. Dishes are rinsed and sanitized in the same compartment by jets of plain hot water, after which the door is opened by hand and the rack manually removed.

DISINFECTANT—Chemical that kills active bacteria, although it may not harm the spores.

DISPENSERS, ELECTRONIC—Devices that not only measure out the right amount of liquor for one drink but also automatically print out the price on the sales check.

DISPENSERS, METERED—Devices that measure out the desired amount of liquor for one drink and count the number of drinks given out.

DISPLAY ADVERTISING—Relatively large ads, often with pictures or drawings as well as print, that appear in the main editorial portions of a periodical. Such advertising normally attracts more attention than the cheaper **classified advertising.**

DISPLAY REFRIGERATION—Refrigerated display cases that may be open, as in a supermarket, or closed with glass doors.

DISPLAY TYPE—Type larger than that used for the text that is therefore used for headings or to emphasize certain portions of the copy.

DISTRESS MERCHANDISE—Items with a large mark-down in selling price because the owner is facing an emergency such as bankruptcy or loss of storage space.

DISTRIBUTING—Taking goods that have been received, classifying them as perishables or storable dry goods, and placing them into the appropriate storage areas.

DISTRIBUTION EXPENSES—Those costs, such as advertising and transportation, that relate to selling of goods.

DIURESIS—Increased excretion of urine.

DIURETIC—Substance that tends to increase the amount of urine, thus affecting the body's water balance. Some vegetables are natural diuretics, e.g., asparagus and parsley. As drugs, diuretics are often prescribed for high blood pressure. Their use increases potassium loss, which can be supplemented by the mineral in pill form or by eating postassium-rich foods such as bananas and oranges.

DNA—Abbreviation for **deoxyribonucleic acid.**

DOCTRINE OF PUBLIC CALLINGS—Legal principle that anyone who chooses to work, for example, in the hospitality industry must abide by the regulations designed to protect the public.

DOILY—Small placemat, usually of linen or paper, placed under dishes as protection.

DOLLY—Piece of mobile equipment on which food items or supplies are placed to facilitate their movement from one place to another.

DOMAINE—French; ownership of a vineyard estate, i.e., the producer of a given wine.

DORSAL FIN—Fin that runs along the back of the fish.

DOT—Abbreviation for the U.S. Department of Transportation, which among other things requires the labeling of hazardous materials to be transported.

DOT MATRIX—Computer printing method in which characters are formed of small dots selected and printed by the printer.

DOTTING—Topping food with small pieces, as of butter, before baking or broiling.

DOUBLE-ACTING BAKING POWDER—Baking powder that is leavened once when moistened and again when baked. See **single-acting baking powder.**

DOUBLE BOILER—Double pot with a lower section that holds boiling water and an upper section that holds food that must be cooked gently.

DOUBLE CROWN SIZE—Printing paper with each sheet measuring 30 × 20 inches (76.2 × 50.8 cm). See **paper sizes.**

DOUBLE DEMY SIZE—Printing paper with each sheet measuring 35 × 22.5 inches (88.9 × 57.2 cm). See **paper sizes.**

DOUBLE GRID—Grid that opens to hold and enclose a fish during cooking, allowing it to be turned without damage.

DOUGH CUTTER—Rectangular metal blade with a wood or plastic handle, used to cut and section dough; also used to scrape bench tops.

DOUGH HOOK—Vertical-mixer accessory made of a heavy metal arm shaped like a hook. It is used to mix dense or heavy materials such as bread dough, which requires extensive kneading. Also called dough arm.

DOWNTIME—Period when a computer is not working because of malfunction.

DRAINBOARD—Board placed under a dish rack so that water dripping off the wet dishes can be directed back into the sink. The far end should rise at least one eighth of an inch per foot of length.

DRAINED WEIGHT TEST—Weight of canned food remaining when the liquid is drained off. Two different brands of the same item may have the same total weight, but one may contain more actual food.

DRAW-PLATE OVEN—Oven in which the entire floor rolls out for easy loading and unloading.

DREDGE—To lightly coat food pieces with flour prior to searing or cooking.

DREDGER—Large shaker used to sprinkle sugar over cakes or doughnuts.

DRESS—Process of cleaning, trimming, and trussing meats, fish, or poultry.

DRIPPING PAN—Rectangular pan placed under food roasting on a spit to catch the dropping juices.

DRIPPINGS—Renderings, including juice and fat, that accumulate from meats while roasting. They may be used to baste the meat or to act as a base and flavoring for sauces and gravies.

DRIVING SURFACES—Area around foodservice establishments (especially drive-in fast food restaurants) on which customers drive their cars. These surfaces should be covered with concrete, asphalt, or treated gravel to minimize dust. They should also drain well after rain and be kept clean.

DROP FLOWER TUBE—Nozzle with a star-shaped opening used for cake decorating. Each tube can produce two different flower shapes, plain or swirled.

DROP SHIPMENT—Shipment of goods direct from the producer or supplier to the customer. The middle step to the distributor is eliminated.

DROP TEST—Ascertaining if a loaded package or its contents will break or leak by dropping it from a given height. This is done to test the strength of packaging and cushioning materials.

DRUM—Container in which liquids, especially oil, are stored and transported.

DRUM, MAGNETIC—Magnetic memory device for computers that is cylindrical rather than disk-shaped. Contrast **disc, magnetic.**

DRUM SIEVE—Drum-shaped cyclinder used as a sieve, usually for powdered materials.

DRUPES—All fruits with a single large seed at the center, e.g., a peach or plum.

DRY—Lacking sweetness, as in a wine with a low sugar content. When applied to foods, *dry* signifies a lack of moisture, e.g., dehydrated meat.

DRY-BLANCH-DRY PROCESS—Drying fruit at a high temperature, blanching it, then drying it again at a lower temperature. This method is fast, economical, and preserves the color and flavor of food better than sun drying or hot-air drying can.

DRY FRYING—Frying with an anti-stick chemical (e.g., silicone) rather than natural fat.

DRY GOODS—Packaged food items that can be put into long-term storage for an indefinite period.

DRY ICE—Carbon dioxide in a solid state at −110°F. Rather than melting into a liquid as ordinary ice does, it vaporizes directly into gas as it absorbs heat.

DRY NONFAT MILK—Nonfat milk from which all moisture has been evaporated.

DRY STORAGE—Room for the storage of food that does not have to be refrigerated, e.g., in cans and cartons.

DRY WHOLE MILK—Whole milk with all moisture evaporated.

DUAL BIN—Maintenance of two supply areas. One area holds the normal supply from which items are drawn as needed; the other holds special emergency stock.

DUCKBOARD—Boardwalk or slatted platform laid on top of a wet or muddy area so that people can walk safely.

DUCK PRESS—Device in which a duck is compressed to extract the juices. It consists of a perforated cylinder to hold the duck, a screw-operated piston to compress it, and a spout through which the juices pass into a container.

DUE—Payable now. If payment is not received in the immediate future, a penalty payment is usually assessed.

DU JOUR—French; daily special.

DU JOUR MENU—French; menu "of the day." The term refers to a menu composed of special dishes offered on that day.

DULCIN—Synthetic sweetener that is eight times as sweet as cyclamate and 250 times as sweet as table sugar. The substance is not approved by the FDA for use in food.

DULCITOL—Alcohol derived from galactose.

DULSE—Edible seaweed that is reddish-purple in color.

DUMMY—Mockup of the menu made in advance of printing to show roughly how it will look when printed.

DUN—Brown mold growth in salted fish.

DUNNAGE RACK—Low-set stand or pallet on which supplies can be stacked to keep them off the floor.

DUODENUM—First portion of the small intestine, right after the stomach in the gastrointestinal tract. Many digestive juices (e.g., bile) do their work here.

DUPLEX—Printing paper with one color on the front and a different color on the back.

DUPLICATE CHECK—Carbon copy of a sales check that is issued to a customer. The two copies are made for control purposes and to save time by generating the kitchen copy and the cashier copy at the same time.

DUPLICATED AUDIENCE—Number of people who get the same advertising message two or more times, either in the same or different media. Such people cannot be counted more than once in measures of the **accumulated audience.**

DUST—To sprinkle powdered sugar or flour lightly on food.

DUSTLESS CLEANING—Using vacuum cleaners or wet mops to clean a floor, which does not force clouds of dust into the air and onto food.

DUTCH COCOA—**Dutch-process cocoa.**

DUTCH OVEN—Heavy pot with a dome-shaped, tight-fitting lid, often used for the slow cooking of meats.

DUTCH-PROCESS COCOA—Cocoa powder that has been treated with alkali to neutralize the natural acids and make it darker. The process was developed in the Netherlands as the name implies.

D-VALUE—Time in minutes that it takes a given temperature level to kill 90 percent of the microorganisms or parasites present in a sample of matter.

DYNAMIC EQUILIBRIUM—Process by which nutrients from ingested food are used to resynthesize the bodily tissues that undergo a normal breaking-down process. Since this process occurs throughout life, proper nutrition is important at all ages.

DYSCRASIA—Abnormal physical condition of the body or any part of the body caused by faulty development or metabolism.

DYSENTERY, AMEOBIC—See **ameobic dysentery.**

DYSPEPSIA—Any sort of discomfort related to eating. Also called indigestion.

E

EARTHENWARE—Unvitrified, soft, porous clay product that may or may not be glazed. It is used to make serving pieces and cookware.

EAU DE VIE—French; literally, water of life. Generally the term refers to spirits or, more specifically, to brandy.

EBERTHELLA TYPHI—Microorganism found in water, milk, and shellfish that causes typhoid fever.

ECUELLE—French; deep dish used to serve vegetables.

EDEMA—Excess retention of water by the body or part of the body that causes swelling. The various causes include prolonged protein deficiency and kidney disease.

EDIBLE PORTION (EP) WEIGHT—Net weight of meat after all the unusable portions and waste have been removed.

EFFICIENCY—Ratio of output to input, times 100 percent. For example, if 10 units of energy are used by an oven but only 5 units produced, its efficiency = $5/10 \times 100\% = 50\%$.

EFFICIENCY, ADVERTISING—Evaluation of the actual performance of advertising by comparing it to a given standard of performance.

EGG ALBUMINS—Proteins that compose about 10 percent of the egg white. Included are ovalbumin and conalbumin.

EGGBEATER—Small hand-held device used to whip eggs or other substances into a frothy mixture.

EGG COOKER—Machine that submerges eggs in hot water for cooking and automatically removes them at the end of the desired time. The water may be heated by steam, gas, or electricity.

EGG GRADES—The four grades of eggs, in order of descending quality, are AA, A, B, and C. Grade AA eggs have clean, unbroken shells and firm egg whites. Grade A eggs have clean, unbroken shells and somewhat firm egg whites. Grade B eggs have stained shells, an irregular shape, or a weak egg white. Grade C eggs have so many flaws that they may not, by federal regulation, be used in foodservice.

EGG HOLDER—Utensil used to hold eggs for boiling.

EGG NOODLES—Noodles made with eggs in addition to flour and water. They have a richer flavor than plain noodles.

EGGPLANT—Large, pear-shaped, purple-skinned vegetable.

EGG-SIZE CLASSES—Categories of egg sizes are jumbo, extra large, large, medium, and small.

EGG TIMER—Traditionally, a small hourglass in which fine sand runs through a small aperture from an upper glass bulb into a lower bulb in three minutes. More recently they are made in a variety of shapes and forms.

EGRESS—Exit; a way to go out of a place. See **means of egress.**

ELASTIN—One of the proteins in meat responsible for holding muscle fibers together. It is insoluble and not altered by cooking; the more of it present, the tougher the meat.

ELECTRONIC DATA PROCESSING (EDP)—Manipulation of business data with computerized equipment to produce usable information for management.

ELECTRONIC DETERGENT DISPENSER—Device in some

dishwashing machines that monitors the concentration of detergent in the dishwater and automatically releases more when it is needed.

ELECTRONIC HEATING—Cooking food by running a high-frequency electric current through it. The current produces heat.

ELECTRONIC REGISTER—In addition to recording the price of each item ordered and adding up a total, as a mechanical register does, an electronic register can be programmed to function as a **precheck machine.** It can also automatically update the tally sheet.

ELECTRONIC STORE AND FORWARD—Portion of the memory file reserved to store data for analysis and communication.

ELECTROPURE PROCESS—Pasteurization of milk by running low frequency electricity through it.

ELIXIR—Liquid produced by dissolving various substances in alcohol or wine with a high alcohol content; it is usually sweet.

EM—In printing, a unit of measurement equal to the **point size** of the type used.

EMACIATION—Severe loss of weight and deteriorization of bodily structures caused by disease or extremely insufficient diet.

EMBOSS—To create a raised or depressed image on paper by pressure.

EMBOSSED FINISH—Paper with nonsmooth surface that resembles leather or cloth. Useful for menu covers.

EMPLOYEE MEALS—Free or subsidized meals given to employees while on duty. The cost of these meals should be entered into a separate account since they are an employee benefit and produce little if any sales revenue.

EMPLOYEES' CAFETERIA COST RECORD—Record of the actual cost of meals provided to employees by establishments that have employee cafeterias.

EMPLOYEES' MEALS WORKSHEET—Form on which is listed, for each day, the number of meals served to employees, the cost of the food issued, and the sales income they produce.

EMPLOYEE TURNOVER COSTS—Cost incurred directly or indirectly when an employee quits or is fired, including advertising, interviewing and training.

EMPTY-FOR-A-FULL SYSTEM—**Bottle-for-bottle system.**

EMULATOR—Program that allows communication between two computers of different manufacture.

EMULSIFYING AGENTS—Substances such as albumin, gums, and soaps that aid in the formation of an **emulsion.**

EMULSIFYING SALTS—Sodium citrate, sodium phosphate, or sodium tartrate, all of which aid in the formation of an **emulsion.**

EMULSION—Unstable mixture of two fluids, e.g., oil and water, that tend to separate. They will meld temporarily if shaken or stirred, or for a longer period with the addition of **emulsifying agents.**

ENAMELWARE—Cookware made of metal with a protective enamel coating commercially baked onto the cooking surface. This makes them easier to clean.

EN BROCHETTE—French; on a skewer.

ENCYST—Process by which a parasite forms a **cyst.**

ENDEMIC HEMOPTYSIS—**Pulmonary paragonimiasis.**

ENDOCRINE GLAND—Any gland that secretes hormones directly into the bloodstream. The thyroid, for example, secretes hormones controlling **metabolism.**

END OF MONTH (EOM)—Time when inventories are normally taken.

END OF YEAR (EOY)—Time when annual financial statements are prepared.

ENDOPEPTIDASES—Enzymes such as pepsin that help metabolize protein by splitting the peptide bonds that hold the amino acids of protein together.

ENDOSPERM—Inner portion of the cereal grain. About 85 percent of the grain's mass, it contains most of the protein and carbohydrate.

ENDPRODUCT—Final output in the production of an item, e.g., the food order to be served to a customer.

END RATE—Amount actually charged an advertiser after all his discounts have been deducted from the **card rate.**

ENERGY—Capacity to sustain action. Most foods contain stored chemical energy. Eating provides each person's energy needs in the form of **calories.**

ENERGY, AVAILABLE—Amount of energy derived from food that is actually available to the body. The remainder is lost through digestion and other bodily processes.

ENGLISH SERVICE—Style of service in which a host helps to apportion food onto plates that are then distributed to other guests by the waiter. Such service is usually done only at private parties or other special events. Contrast **American service.**

ENOCIANINA—Food-coloring additive derived from red grape skins.

ENOLASE—Enzyme important in the metabolism of carbohydrates.

ENOLOGY—Study or science of wine. Also spelled oenology.

EN PENSION—French; payment plan in which meals are included with the price of lodging, i.e., the **American plan.**

ENRICHED RICE—White rice with added vitamins and iron.

ENRICHMENT—Addition of vitamins and other nutrients to food; also called **fortification.** Enrichment may also signify adding a rich ingredient to a mixture, such as butter to a sauce.

ENTAMOEBA DYSENTERIAE—One-celled organisms, commonly called **amoebas,** that cause **amoebic dysentery.**

ENTAMOEBA HISTOLYTICA—One of the protozoan parasites that can cause **amoebic dysentery.**

ENTERIC—Intestinal; pertaining to the intestines.

ENTEROGASTRONE—Hormone in the small intestine that inhibits stomach activity. It is released when food in the stomach passes into the small intestine.

ENTEROPATHOGENIC—Anything that can cause a disease in the intestines, e.g, a poison, microorganism, or parasite.

ENTEROTOXEMIA—Illness caused by toxins secreted within the intestines by pathogens.

ENTEROTOXIN—Poisons produced by various strains of **staphylococci** bacteria. These affect the mucous lining of the intestines and account for most staphylococcal food poisoning.

ENTOLETER—Machine with a rapidly spinning disc that kills insects in any food processed through it.

ENTREE—French; main course of a meal. It is usually the most expensive item of the meal.

ENTREE SALES RATIO—Index of entree popularity. It is computed by dividing the number of sales of a specific entree by the total number of all entree sales in the same period.

ENTREPRENEUR—Person who owns his own business, e.g., a restaurant.

ENVELOPE STUFFER—Advertising leaflet inserted in an envelope with a bill or other mail.

ENVIRONMENTAL END—Poptop openers on beverage cans that remain in place after opening rather than becoming separated. They are less likely to be discarded and add to environmental pollution.

ENVIRONMENTAL HAZARD—Unsafe condition that exists in the area where employees work or customers eat.

ENVIRONMENTAL INFORMATION—Information about the economic, political, and social environment in which an establishment operates. This information includes the immediate physical location as well as the state, country, and so on. Trends at any of these levels might affect the future of the establishment.

ENVIRONMENTAL PROTECTION AGENCY (EPA)—Federal agency that among other things regulates **restricted use pesticides.** It works in conjunction with state regulators to certify those allowed to use such pesticides. It also develops regulations concerning waste disposal.

ENZYME—Protein that facilitates a biological reaction in the body. They affect innumerable body processes, including those involved in digestion.

ENZYMES, AMYLOLYTIC—Enzymes that chemically break up starch.

EOSINOPHILIC MENINGOENCEPHALITIS—Inflammation of the brain and the membranes that surround it caused by the parasitic worm **Angiostrongylus cantonensis.**

EPICARP—Outer peel of citrus fruits; contains the color and oil of the fruit.

EPICURE—One knowledgeable about and appreciative of food and wine.

EPIDEMIC—Sudden increase in the incidence of a given disease among the human population in a specific area, usually due to contagion or contamination from a common source.

EPINEPHRINE—**Adrenaline.**

EPITHELIUM—Outer layer of cells in the skin.

EPIZOOTIC—Sudden increase in the incidence of a given disease in a specific area among animals rather than humans. Contrast **epidemic.**

EPSOM SALTS—Magnesium sulphate, a laxative.

EQUILIBRIUM MOISTURE CONTENT—The amount of moisture in a substance that is in equilibrium with that of the air. The substance will not gain moisture from or lose it to the surrounding air.

ERASURE-PROOF PAPER—Paper that cannot be erased. If a mistake is made, it must be crossed out. Often used to print customer checks as a protection against unauthorized changes.

EREPSIN—Group of enzymes in intestinal juices that aid in the digestion of protein.

ERGOCALCIFEROL—Vitamin D$_2$.

ERGONOMICS—Science of matching equipment design to the requirements of the people who operate it so that efficiency and productivity are increased.

ERGOSTEROL—Sterol derived from yeast that can be converted to **vitamin D$_2$.**

ERGOT—Fungus that grows on rye grains. If the infected rye is eaten (e.g., in bread), **ergotism** results.

ERGOTISM—Poisoning caused by the ingestion of **ergot.** Symptoms include headache, drowsiness, and gangrene of the fingers and toes.

ERUCIC ACID—Unsaturated fatty acid contained in many vegetable oils.

ERYSIPELOID—Skin disease caused by the bacilli **Erysipelothrix,** which are found in infected meat, fish, and poultry. They enter through cuts in the skin, particularly on the hands, of those who handle food. Symptoms include skin reddening, itching, and eruptions.

ERYSIPELOTHRIX—Bacilli that cause **Erysipeloid.**

ERYTHEMA—Reddening of the skin. Visible erythema on an employee may indicate that he or she has an infection and should not handle food until the infection is healed.

ERYTHROCYTES—Red blood cells, the oxygen-carrying cells that are dependent in part on the dietary intake of iron. See **blood cells, red.**

ERYTHROSINE BS—Red-coloring food additive used, for example, in cherries.

ESCALATION PRICE—Adjusted price resulting when certain

contractually agreed-upon events occur, e.g., if labor or shipping costs go up.

ESCALATOR CLAUSE—Stipulation in a purchasing contract that allows the purchase price to be raised under certain conditions, e.g., if labor or shipping costs go up.

ESCAPE CLAUSE—Provision in a contract stipulating that one party can nullify or modify the contract under certain agreed-upon conditions, e.g., an employees' strike.

ESCARGOT CLAMPS—Small pair of silver tongs designed to hold an escargot shell as the meat is extracted with a fork.

ESCARGOT FORK—Small table fork with two long tines used to extract the snail from its shell.

ESCARGOTIERE—French; a metal plate with small depressions for holding snails in their shells. It is used both for cooking and serving.

ESCARGOTS—French; snails. They are traditionally served in the shell with a garlic butter.

ESOPHAGUS—Tube through which food passes from the mouth to the stomach in the human body.

ESPRESSO—Italian; strong, heavy coffee made by forcing steam through a finely ground dark roast and traditionally served after a meal. Also spelled (incorrectly) **expresso.**

ESSENCE—Flavorful liquid extract obtained by stewing fish meat, poultry, game, or certain vegetables at a low temperature for a long time; used to enrich or flavor certain sauces.

ESSENTIAL OILS—Water-insoluble oils derived from plants (e.g., mint, almond) that are used as food additives to provide flavor and odor. They are so named not because they are essential in the diet but because each provides the characteristic essence of the plant from which it is derived.

ESSEX TUBE—Nozzle for a cake-decorating bag or syringe with a deep-cut opening that gives sharply defined shapes to icing decorations.

ESTATE BOTTLING—Wine production in which the owner of a vineyard handles the entire process of growing grapes, producing wine, and bottling it at the vineyard itself.

ESTER—In organic chemistry, any compound composed of an acid and an alcohol, e.g., fats and waxes. These volatile and often fragrant compounds are developed in spirits and wines when organic acids combine with the alcohols and are mainly responsible for the **bouquet.**

ESTERASES—Enzymes that chemically break down **esters.**

ESTROGEN—Female sex hormone, sometimes given to cattle to increase their growth.

ETHER—Organic compounds in wine that smell sweet and contribute to a wine's **bouquet.**

ETHYL ALCOHOL—Drinking alcohol, found in wines and spirits.

ETHYLENE—Gas that accelerates the ripening of fruit.

ETHYLENEDIAMINE TETRA-ACETIC ACID (EDTA)—Food additive that combines with metallic impurities chemically and renders them harmless. Useful in preventing a metallic taste in canned foods.

ETHYL FORMATE—Ingredient in many artificial fruit and other flavors.

ETIOLOGICAL AGENT—Any substance that can cause disease.

ETIOLOGY—Origins or causes of a disease.

EUROPEAN PLAN—Hotel payment plan that covers only the room and no meals. Contrast **American plan.**

EUTROPHIA—State of being well nourished.

EVAPORATED MILK—Milk that has had about 55 percent of its water extracted; no sugar is added, as is the case with **condensed milk.**

EVAPORATOR—Section of a refrigeration unit in which the

compressed refrigerant gas expands and removes heat from the interior air.

EVISCERATE—To remove the viscera or internal organs (heart, stomach, intestines), as is done to a meat carcass during butchering.

EWE—Mature female sheep that weighs between 60 and 100 pounds and is over 20 months old.

EXCESS PACKAGING—Supplier's use of more or heavier packaging than required to ship goods. The total weight is correct, but contents are reduced.

EXCESS TRIM—Meats delivered by a supplier that have more bone and fat than allowed in the purchase specifications.

EXCISE TAX—Tax set by the government for the privilege of selling specified kinds of items.

EXIT ACCESS—Unobstructed path to an exit connecting an establishment with a public way. See **means of egress.**

EXIT DISCHARGE—Unobstructed space between the end of an exit and a public way. See **means of egress.**

EXOTOXIN—Poisonous substance secreted by bacteria into the surrounding cells. It is characteristic of **botulism** bacteria, among others.

EXPANDED TYPE—Printing type with characters or spaces between characters that are wider than usual. The opposite of **condensed type.**

EXPANSION VALVE—Device in a refrigeration unit that is controlled by a thermostat and releases the refrigerant gas into the **evaporator** as needed.

EXPECTED LIFE—Period in which a particular asset is normally able to serve a useful function.

EXPELLER CAKE—Protein-rich remainder of various seeds (e.g., sunflower) after they have been pressed for oil.

EXPENDITURE—Cash (or other assets) paid in exchange for goods or services.

EXPENSE—Outlay of funds or a business cost chargeable to a specific time period.

EXPENSE ACCOUNT—Accounting sheet used for a specific type of expense, e.g., print advertising or radio advertising.

EXPENSE CONTROL—Any approach to keeping future costs down, e.g., holding supervisors responsible for certain costs in their departments.

EXPENSE DISTRIBUTION—Identifying in the business records an expense and the products for which it was incurred.

EXPIRATION DATE—Final day that a food product can be used safely. After this point it may be stale, rotten, or have lost much of its nutritive value. Contrast **freshness date.**

EXPRESSO—**Espresso.**

EXTENDED COST—In yield testing, the total cost of the material tested.

EXTENDED INVOICE—Cost of each item on the invoice multiplied by the quantity ordered.

EXTENDED TYPE—**Expanded type.**

EXTENSION—Unit price and the number ordered, i.e., the total cost. Used on many types of cost-control forms.

EXTENSION RING—Accessory to a vertical mixer consisting of a clamped-on metal band that adds height to the sides of the mixer bowl to prevent the ingredients from being thrown out.

EXTENSOMETER—Device that stretches dough to measure its baking quality. Good dough will have the proper elasticity, neither too weak nor too strong.

EXTERNAL ATMOSPHERE—The atmosphere of the neighborhood in which an establishment is located, as well as its own exterior building and grounds. External atmosphere plays a large role in the kind of clientele attracted. Contrast **internal atmosphere.**

EXTERNAL AUDIT—Review of accounting records done by an

outside company, presumably impartial and objective. Contrast **internal audit.**

EXTERNAL INFORMATION—Sum of **competitive information** and **environmental information.** The opposite of **internal information.**

EXTERNAL TRANSACTION—Ordinary business transaction with a person or organization that is not part of the establishment. Contrast **internal transaction.**

EXTRACT—Meat flavor commercially leached out of meat and concentrated; used to flavor soups, sauces, and so on. Also refers to flavors leached out of other foods, e.g., vanilla.

EXTRACTION RATE—Percent of the original wheat grain that remains in the flour after milling. Whole grain flour yields 100 percent; when bran and other portions are excluded, the yield is lower.

EXTRAORDINARY EXPENSE—Unusual or abnormally large expense, e.g., the cost of replacing goods lost in the storeroom during a flood.

EXTRA SEC—French; extra dry. However, it is applied to dry champagne that is actually slightly sweeter than **brut.**

EXTRA SELECT—Shucked oysters with a count of 160 to 210 per gallon.

EYELET—**Grommet.**

EYE MOVEMENT PRINCIPLE—Premise that customer's eyes move from the center of the menu page, then to the right corner, and then around the menu. The most important item therefore should be listed in the center.

F

FACSIMILE—Reproduction of a document (e.g., a handwritten note of welcome from the owner to the patrons), often added to copy that is set in type and published in the menu.

FACTOR OF PRODUCTION—Any of the factors or components (e.g., raw materials, labor) that contribute to producing an item.

FACTORY SERVICE—Overhead expenses of a factory that add to the price of the products it manufactures.

FACULTATIVE—Ability of a microorganism to survive in more than one way of life, e.g., bacteria that can survive with or without free oxygen.

FAHRENHEIT—Method of measuring heat in which 32 degrees is the freezing point of water and 212 degrees the boiling point. It is 100/180 of a **Celcius degree.**

FAHRENHEIT-CELSIUS CONVERSION—$°C = 5/9 \, (°F - 32°)$.

FAIR MARKET VALUE—Value of an item, as determined by experienced experts, based on normal bargaining in the open market.

FAIR-TRADE PRICE—Resale price of an item set by the manufacturer so retail prices do not vary from dealer to dealer.

FALSE SEAM—Defect in the manufacture of sanitary double-seamed cans in which the two seams do not interlock.

FARINA—Starch derived from all forms of wheat except durum, e.g., spring wheat; cooked as a breakfast cereal. Contrast **semolina.**

FARINACEOUS—Usually, finely ground meal or flour from potatoes or other vegetables. It literally means high in food starch.

FARMER'S MARKET—Public market at which farmers can sell their produce directly to customers. As a rule, the produce is fresher than at usual outlets, and cheaper because middlemen are eliminated.

FASCIOLOPSIS BUSKI—Intestinal parasite found in a group of plants called **caltrops.** It is destroyed by heat. Infected uncooked caltrops can cause nausea, vomiting, and abdominal pain.

FAT—An **ester** of **fatty acids** and **glycerol.** Fats are soluble in such organic solvents as benzene but not in water. See, e.g., **triglycerides.**

FAT EXTENDERS—Food additives such as glyceryl monostearate that reduce the fat level in food without changing its texture.

FAT, NEUTRAL—Substance that contains one or more **fatty acids,** i.e., **triglycerides,** and is the principal form in which energy is stored by the body. It is soluble in such organic solvents as benzene but not in water.

FAT PERCENTAGE MEASURING KIT—Compact, portable assembly of equipment used to measure the fat content of ground beef. Fat is rendered from a beef sample by heating, is measured in a calibrated tube, and the measurement is expressed in terms of percentage of fat per given weight of meat.

FAT, SATURATED—These are primarily animal fats, of which saturated **fatty acids** are a component. They are found as well in animal products, e.g., milk, butter, and cheese, and also appear in coconut, chocolate, and cocoa. Saturated fats contain large amounts of **cholesterol.** They are implicated in many diseases, especially heart and circulatory problems because of the cholesterol's tendency to build up deposits in the blood vessels and hinder blood flow. They are also implicated in certain cancers, e.g., of the colon and breast. They are sometimes called hard fats, in part because of their tendency to harden at room temperature and below. See **fat, unsaturated, fatty acids, saturated,** and **fatty acids, unsaturated.**

FAT-SOLUBLE VITAMINS—See **vitamins, fat-soluble.**

FATTY ACIDS—Organic acids chemically composed of long chains of carbon that, when combined with **glycerol,** form **fat.** Examples include **acetic acid** and **butyric acid.**

FATTY ACIDS, ESSENTIAL—Three unsaturated **fatty acids** are essential to the human body: linoleic, linolenic, and arachidonic. Linoleic and linolenic acids are derived primarily from plant oils (e.g., corn and peanut), and arachidonic from animal fats. Linoleic acid must be included in the diet because the body cannot synthesize it as it does the other two, but all three are enriched by dietary intake. See **fatty acids, unsaturated,** and **fatty acids, saturated.**

FATTY ACIDS, NONESTRIFIED—Fatty acids that are free in the blood and not chemically connected with **glycerol** into an **ester.** They provide energy to the muscles during prolonged exercise and can be converted into other fatty acids.

FATTY ACIDS, SATURATED—**Fatty acids** in which each carbon atom in the chain is attached to the maximum number of hydrogen atoms. It is believed that such fats should be limited in the diet. See **fat, saturated, fatty acids, unsaturated,** and **fat, unsaturated.**

FATTY ACIDS, UNSATURATED—Fatty acids in which each carbon atom in the chain has fewer hydrogen atoms attached than the maximum possible. They are believed to be more healthful in the diet than saturated fatty acids. See **fat, saturated, fatty acids, saturated,** and **fat, unsaturated.**

FAT, UNSATURATED—These are primarily oils, of which unsaturated **fatty acids** are a component. They appear in some animal foods, but they are primarily plant in origin. They contain little or no **cholesterol,** and are believed to be helpful in lowering blood cholesterol levels. For these and other reasons, they are thought to be beneficial in the diet. See **fat, unsaturated, fatty acids, saturated,** and **fatty acids, unsaturated.**

FEASIBILITY STUDY—Intensive and detailed analysis of the market, performed in order to plan site location, judge type and location of competition, size of operation, cost, financing, and budgeting. The study determines the likelihood of the operation's success.

FEBRILE—Feverish; frequently characteristic of people with infectious diseases.

FECULA—Any food composed almost entirely of starch.

FEEDBACK—Comparison of output to input made within a computer to correct errors in the system.

FEHLING'S TEST—Test to determine whether sugars are chemically reducing or nonreducing. See **reducing sugar.**

FEINTS—First and last portions of a distillation of spirits. These are the less desirable parts. Also called "heads and tails."

FENCE ATTACHMENT—Device attached to the carriage tray of a food slicer to hold small items, such as tomatoes, for slicing. May be used singly or in rows.

FERMENTATION—Breakdown of a compound that does not require the use of oxygen. Such chemical changes can alter the makeup of food. In alcoholic beverages, for example, yeast breaks down sugar into carbon dioxide and ethyl alcohol. In fermented milk, bacteria convert lactose sugar into lactic acid.

FERRIC AMMONIUM CITRATE—Sometimes used as a food additive for its iron content.

FERRITIN—Protein form in which iron is stored in the liver, bone marrow, and other bodily tissues.

FEUILLETTE—French; a half-bottle of wine. It may also mean a small cask of wine.

FIBER—That part of food that cannot be digested or absorbed. It is believed to be beneficial in many illnesses; recent research suggests it may help prevent certain forms of cancer. Foods high in fiber content include wholemeal cereals and flour, root vegetables, nuts and fruit. Fiber is also called roughage.

FIBRINOLYSIN—Enzyme that liquefies coagulated blood by destroying the fibrin in the clot.

FIDDLEHEAD FERN—Edible ferns picked during the fiddlehead stage, i.e., before the fronds have unfolded. Since some ferns are poisonous, novices should not attempt to gather their own for eating.

FIDELITY BOND—Insurance covering an establishment for losses caused by dishonest employees, such as theft and embezzlement.

FIFTH—Standard bottle size used for wines and distilled spirits. It is one fifth of a gallon or 25.6 ounces.

FIG—Small, round, white, purple, or red fruit of the mulberry family. Figs are very sweet and may be eaten raw, dried, or cooked.

FILE—Group or block of related records or information stored in the computer, usually accessible by file name.

FILET—Choicest cut or tenderloin of beef, pork, mutton, or veal with no bone. Also refers to boned fish.

FILL-IN LETTER—Promotional letter with the in-common portions printed but certain other portions left blank (e.g., name and address) so the letter can be personalized.

FILM YEASTS—Yeasts that form a film over pickles and pickling brines.

FILTER—Fine screen used to clarify liquids such as wines.

FILTH TEST—Means of measuring the level of contamination in human food, i.e., the presence of insects, rat hairs, and so on. A small sample of food is drawn for close examination, in which foreign materials are identified and counted.

FINANCE—To supply an establishment with money, as through loans or credit.

FINDER—Person who locates suitable buyers for a supplier or suitable suppliers for a buyer, for a fee.

FINE—To clarify wine by adding substances that combine with the floating particles and settle with them to the bottom. Also, to filter wine.

FINES HERBES—French; chopped herbs including chervil, chives, marjoram, parsley, tarragon, and thyme. See **herbs.**

FINGER BOWL—Small silver or glass bowl placed on a doily and silver underliner, filled one third with warm water and lemon juice or fragrance. It is used by a guest to clean his fingers after eating messy foods such as lobster.

FINING AGENT—Any substance that can clear a liquid of suspended matter by combining with that matter to form a precipitate.

FINISH—Amount of fat and its distribution around a cut of meat. One of the three characteristics checked in **meat grading.**

FINISHED GOODS—Produced goods that are ready for sale as opposed to finished parts that will be incorporated into the further processing of larger assemblages.

FINISHING OVEN—Small oven mounted on top of an upright broiler, used to finish cooking items that are partially cooked in the broiler by utilizing exhaust heat from the broiler. It can also be used to hold or warm foods that are ready to serve.

FIRE POINT—Temperature at which a cooking oil will burn (around 340°C or higher).

FIRM CONTRACT—Legal document that obligates a buyer and seller to meet certain terms regarding a purchase.

FIRMING AGENT—Any substance (e.g., calcium carbonate) that converts pectic acid from a liquid into a solid gel. It helps keep fruit containing pectin firm.

FIRM PRICE—Selling price fixed at the time of a sales contract and not open to further negotiation.

FIRST AID—Emergency or improvised treatment given to an accident victim before he can be brought to professional medical attention.

FIRST IN/FIRST OUT (FIFO)—Principle that goods purchased first should be used first. This helps reduce food spoilage. Compare **Last In/First Out.**

FIRST PROOF—First printing of an advertisement or menu used for proofreading to find errors before a large number are run off.

FISCAL YEAR—Any period of 12 consecutive months considered convenient for budgeting and accounting purposes (e.g., October to September).

FISH—Fish is high in protein and low in fat. There are numerous varieties. Below is a list of some of the more popular fish in the United States.

Albacore: One of the Pacific tuna, with the lightest meat. Canned, it is labeled white meat.

Anchovy: Fish of the herring family, found on both the Atlantic and Pacific Coasts. Not usually eaten whole but pickled and salted.

Blackback: Fish with a white, firm flesh; abundant in the Northeast in the fall and winter months. It is a type of flounder.

Bluefish: Fish with dark meat and oily flesh; abundant in the Northeast from May to November and on the Gulf Coast in the winter months.

Butterfish: Fish with nonoily flesh; abundant in the Northeast in summer and on the Gulf Coast in winter.

Carp: Lean, firm fish from the Great Lakes; abundant in spring.

Catfish: Southern freshwater fish with delicate white flesh.

Cod, Atlantic: One of the most abundant fish in the United States, particularly in the Northeast during the spring and summer months. It has a flaky, nonoily flesh.

Cod, Pacific: Fish with a flaky, nonoily flesh; abundant on the Pacific Coast all year long.

Croaker: Lean fish abundant in the Midatlantic states from March to October.

Cusk: Delicate, lean fish; abundant in the Northeastern states in spring and summer.

Dolphin: Also called mahimahi in Hawaii, where it is abundant. It has a firm flesh.

Eel: Fresh- or saltwater snakelike fish without scales. Conger is the most popular variety.

Flounder: Group of fish including **fluke, yellowtail,** and blackback. Flounder is available all year in the Atlantic, Gulf, and Pacific states. It has a flaky, delicate flesh.

Flounder, starry: Flounder found in the Pacific Northwest.

Flounder, yellowtail: Flounder found in the Gulf and Midatlantic States from summer to winter.

Fluke: Flounder abundant in the Northeast and Midatlantic states all year long.

Grouper: Fish with a delicate, lean flesh; abundant on Southern and Gulf Coasts from April to December.

Haddock: Fish with lean, nonoily flesh; abundant in the North Atlantic from March to November.

Hake: Fish with a lean, delicate flesh; found on the Gulf and Pacific coasts. Most abundant in August and September.

Halibut: Fish with delicate, white flesh abundant in the Northwest and Northeastern states during spring and summer.

Lake sturgeon: Firm, delicate freshwater fish; usually smoked. A major source of caviar.

Lake trout: Firm, oily freshwater fish; abundant in the Great Lakes from May to October.

Lingcod: Fish with a delicate, lean flesh; most abundant in the Pacific Northwest from October to May.

Mackerel, Atlantic: Fish with a dark, oily flesh; most abundant in the New England states in summer.

Mackerel, King: Fish with an oily flesh; most abundant in the Gulf States from November to March.

Mackerel, Spanish: Fish with lighter flesh than the other mackerels. Available all along the Atlantic Coast and parts of the Pacific Coast.

Mullet: Fish with firm, medium-oily flesh; most abundant in the Gulf and Florida from April to November.

Northern pike: Lean, flaky freshwater fish. No longer fished commercially.

Ocean perch: Also known as redfish and rockfish. Fish with flaky, white flesh; found on both coasts.

Pollack: Fish with white, nonoily flesh; found in the Northeast and Midatlantic states. Most abundant from October to December.

Pompano: Fish with firm, white flesh; abundant in Florida from March to May.

Porgy: Fish with delicate, white flesh; abundant on the Atlantic coast.

Rainbow trout: Delicate white-fleshed freshwater fish; available throughout the United States.

Redfish: Fish with firm, light flesh; abundant in the Gulf states from November to February.

Red snapper: Fish with delicate, white flesh; abundant in the Atlantic and Gulf coasts during the summer months.

Rockfish: Group of fish of over 50 varieties abundant in the Pacific Northwest. They have a firm, white flesh.

Salmon: Species of fish including chinook, coho, sockeye, pink, chum, and Atlantic salmon. Salmon have firm, fatty flesh and are one of the most prized of American fish.

Salmon, Atlantic: Salmon found in Atlantic waters; usually sold smoked.

Salmon, chinook: Salmon found in the Pacific Northwest from May to October.

Salmon, chum: Salmon found in the Pacific Northwest from August to October. It is of poor quality and is usually canned.

Salmon, coho: Salmon found in the Pacific Northwest from June to September.

Salmon, pink: Salmon found on the Pacific coast from June to November. It has a pink, oily flesh and is usually sold canned.

Salmon, sockeye: Salmon found in the Pacific Northwest; abundant in the summer months. It has a pink, oily flesh.

Sardine: Fish with dark, oily flesh, found on both coasts. Most sardines in the U.S. are canned.

Sea bass, black: Bass with white, flaky flesh; abundant in the Midatlantic states in spring.

Sea bass, white: Bass with white, flaky flesh; found on the Pacific Coast from May to September.

Sea trout: Fish with delicate, lean flesh; abundant on the Gulf Coast during spring and fall.

Shad: A fatty, bland fish found in Northeastern states and Alaska. The roe is highly prized.

Smelt: Small, oily fish. Lake smelt are abundant in the Great Lakes during March and April. Sea smelts are found in the Gulf and Midatlantic states.

Sole, gray: Fish with firm, white flesh; found in the Gulf and Atlantic states.

Sole, lemon: Fish with firm, white flesh; found in the Gulf and Atlantic states.

Sole, petrale: Fish with firm, white flesh; found in the Pacific states.

Swordfish: Fish with firm, medium-oily flesh; found in the tropical waters of the Pacific and Atlantic.

Tilefish: Fish with firm, light flesh; abundant in the Midatlantic and Northeastern states.

Tuna, albacore: Tuna with light flesh; abundant in Californian and Mexican waters.

Tuna, yellowfin: Tuna with light flesh, but not as light as albacore. It is abundant in California and waters south of California.

Whitefish: Flaky, white freshwater fish; abundant in the Great Lakes from May to August.

Whiting: Light, nonoily fish found in Northeastern and Midatlantic waters. Most abundant in the summer months.

Yellow Perch: Fish with firm, white flesh; abundant in freshwater areas from April to November.

FISH FORK—Medium-sized fork with broad, flat tines used to eat fish. May also be used for desserts.

FISH KETTLE—Utensil for cooking fish, containing a metal grid to hold fish while cooking and for removing whole fish without breaking the flesh. Also called a fish poacher.

FISH KNIFE—Medium-sized table knife with a broad, flat blade used to cut and remove bone from fish.

FISH MEAL—Inedible fish or fish parts that are dried and powdered into a high-protein meal. Used as fertilizer, animal food, or, after further processing, human food.

FISSION—Asexual method of reproduction in which a single microorganism splits into two or more equal parts.

FIXED ASSET—Permanent item of equipment or furnishings that cannot readily be converted to cash. Contrast **current assets.**

FIXED ASSET RATIO—Index of the amount of revenue generated by an establishment's fixed assets; calculated by dividing net sales by the net value of fixed assets (i.e., the value after depreciation has been subtracted).

FIXED COSTS—**Fixed expenses.**

FIXED EMPLOYEES—Employees whose presence is required regardless of the amount of business being generated, e.g., accountants or managers. Contrast **variable employees.**

FIXED EXPENSE—Cost of running an establishment that is the same amount regardless of the quantity of production. The manager's salary, for example, normally remains the same day to day regardless of the sales volume.

FIXED MARK-UP—Purchasing plan in which a supplier agrees to sell to an establishment at a price that includes his own costs plus a set percent mark-up for profit.

FIXED MENU—Menu that remains the same for an indefinite period. Such a menu is most common at an establishment where the clientele changes continually. Contrast **changing menu** and **combination menu.**

FIXED RESALE PRICE—Minimum retail price as established by contract by the manufacturer of an item. The individual retailers who sign the contract can charge more but not less.

FIXED STANDARD—Performance standard used on a long-term basis without change.

FLAGELLA—Organs of movement in some one-cell organisms. They are shaped like long, thin threads and create movement by whipping side to side.

FLAGON—Old term for wine flask.

FLAMBE—French; any meat dish or dessert presented flaming by igniting the spirits poured over it.

FLAMEPROOF—Any material that will not ignite at any temperature. Contrast **flame-resistant.**

FLAME RESISTANT—Any material that will burn only when subject to a direct flame, but will not support combustion on its own. Contrast **flameproof.**

FLAME RETARDANT—Any chemical added to packaging, furnishings, or construction materials to make them resist burning.

FLAMEWARE—Cooking utensils that have been specially hardened so that they will not crack when exposed to direct flame.

FLAN—Metal disk used to hold the flan, or baked custard tart, while cooking.

FLASH FREEZING—Food-preserving process in which temperatures are dropped very quickly and briefly, and then raised to usual freezing levels. This causes the liquids in the food to form fine rather than large crystals, thereby producing less tissue breakage and flavor loss.

FLASH PASTEURIZATION—Killing the microorganisms in milk by pasteurizing at a temperature higher than usual and for less time.

FLASH POINT—Temperature at which cooking oils will first burn (around 290°C to 330°C) but not sustain combustion. See **fire point.**

FLASK—Flat-sided bottle for convenient carrying of alcoholic beverages. Available in volumes from eight to thirty-two ounces.

FLAT BEATER—Accessory to a vertical mixer made of interconnected metal bars in a flat plane. It is normally used to mix, cream, and mash medium-consistency foods at medium speeds. Also called a paddle.

FLAT FISH—Fish, such as sole, flounder, halibut, and rock cod, that swim on the bottom of the ocean.

FLAT SOURS—Bacteria that flourish at high temperatures and

can turn canned food sour. They do not produce gas, thus leaving the ends of the can flat, and there is no external sign of their presence.

FLATTEN—To make something stale or tasteless. Also, to beat meat flat with a mallet in order to tenderize it.

FLATULENCE—Excessive gas in the stomach or intestines created during the digestion of food.

FLATWORMS—Parasitic worms such as tapeworms that are flat in appearance. Some flatworms infest human food, although proper cooking will usually kill them. See **cestodes** and **trematodes**. Contrast **roundworms**.

FLAVANONE—A type of **flavonoid**.

FLAVEDO—Spanish; **epicarp**.

FLAVIN—Food-coloring additive derived from the oak *Quercus tinctoria*.

FLAVONOIDS—Pigmenting compounds found in many different types of plants, including flowers and vegetables.

FLAVOPROTEINS—Group of proteins that serve as oxidizing enzymes during metabolism.

FLAVOR POTENTIATOR—Any substance that enhances the flavor of a food without distorting it, e.g., **monosodium glutamate** (MSG).

FLAVOR PROFILE—Identifying and analyzing the various components of a food flavor.

FLAVORS, SYNTHETIC—Organic compounds (usually **esters**) synthesized in the laboratory that approximate the flavor of natural foods.

FLIGHT LINKS—Parts of the conveyor surface on a flight-type dishwashing machine that hold items to be washed and carry them through the machine. See **dishwasher, flight type**.

FLINTY—Metallic, pungent flavor in extremely dry wines, especially those from Chablis.

FLIPPER—A **swell** of a sealed can that appears when the can is struck. Otherwise the can retains its normal shape.

FLOPPY DISC—Flexible computer memory disc encased in a square wrapper when not in use. It measures about seven inches in diameter, as compared to a "minifloppy," which is around five inches.

FLORIDEAN STARCH—Starch derived from the red algae (genus *Florideae*).

FLOUR—Fine, soft powder resulting from sifting and grinding the meal of a grain, particularly wheat. The following are among the more common types.

All-purpose: Mixture of hard and soft wheat flour; used for all cookery except fine cakes.

Bread: Made from hard wheat flour; usually available only wholesale.

Cornmeal: Meal ground from yellow or white corn; used in breads and puddings.

Cracked wheat: Coarse flour made by cutting rather than grinding the whole wheat grain.

Cake flour: Made from soft wheat, and contains 7 to 8.5 percent protein.

Family flour: Soft and hard wheats blended to make an all-purpose flour.

Graham: Made from unsifted whole wheat.

Hard wheat: Made from wheat with a strong, high-gluten quality; suitable for bread baking.

High-ratio: Very fine and powdery, this flour can be combined with up to twice as much sugar as other flours, as in cake baking.

Instant: Flour that has been processed so that it has a granular texture and dissolves easily in hot and cold liquids.

Middlings: Coarse flour made from the grain's outer coat.

Pastry or Cake: Made from soft wheat flour.

Potato: Made from potatoes. This four is a good thickening agent and is used in baking combined with other flours.

Rye: Dark flour made from rye grains. It is used to make

pumpernickel or is combined with wheat flour to make rye bread.

Self-rising: Contains salt and baking powder so that the dough rises without requiring yeast.

Semolina: Grainlike portions of wheat remaining in the bolting machine after fine flour has been sifted through. It is a hard wheat flour ideal for making pasta.

Soft wheat: Made from wheat with low gluten and a high starch content. It is suitable for use in making pastries and cakes.

Strong flour: Hard wheat or bread flour, so called because of its strong quality of gluten or protein.

Whole wheat: Dark flour that contains the whole grain including the germ, endosperm, and bran. This flour is often stoneground and unsifted. It is thought to be the most nutritious of flours.

FLOUR STRENGTH—Ability of flour proteins to hold the carbon dioxide produced during fermentation. Stronger flour holds more gas and yields a larger loaf.

FLOWER NAIL—Nail-shaped device that is held by the stem and rotated in one hand, as decorative flowers are extruded from its head with icing squeezed from a bag held in the other hand.

FLOWERY—A pleasant blossomlike fragrance characteristic of some white wines.

FLUID BED DRYER—A device that dries food particles (e.g., grain) with jets of hot air.

FLUKES—Parasitic **trematode flatworms.**

FLUORIDE—Compound that occurs in trace amounts in bone, skin, fish, and tea. It is added in small amounts to water (fluoridation) to inhibit tooth decay. Large amounts are poisonous.

FLUSH COVER—Menu cover that has been trimmed to the same dimensions as the inside pages. More often, however, the cover is larger; see **overhang cover.**

FLUSH PARAGRAPH—Any paragraph printed without an initial indentation.

FLUTE—Stemmed wine glass with a funnel-shaped bowl. Also, to decorate with grooves, as in pastry.

FLUTED TUBE—Nozzle with tightly curved openings used with a cake-decorating bag or syringe. It is used to make lilies of the valley and scalloped or ribbon icing borders.

FOAM CAKE—Cakes dependent on egg foam for lightness and texture.

FOB PRICE—Price including not only the cost of purchase but also cost of delivery to a designated point. See **free on board.**

FOIE GRAS—French; goose liver. Often used in paste form to spread as an appetizer.

FOLDING IN—Method of blending ingredients whereby a light, aereated product, such as beaten egg whites, is incorporated into the end product, such as a custard or sauce, to make it lighter and fluffier.

FOLD TESTING—One of the techniques used in **grain testing** of paper. A sample sheet is folded by hand. If the crease comes out straight and smooth, that is the direction of the grain. If the crease is irregular and rough, that is not the direction of the grain.

FOLIC ACID—A B vitamin found in liver and dark-green vegetables. It is important in the synthesis of **amino acids** and the **purines** and **pyrimidines** that appear in **nucleic acid.** Insufficient intake results in **folic acid deficiency.**

FOLIC ACID DEFICIENCY—Caused by insufficient dietary intake or bodily utilization of **folic acid.** Symptoms include anemia and disturbances of the entire gastrointestinal tract, from cracked lips and stomatitis to flatulence and diarrhea.

FOLIO—Printed page number, as in a menu.

FONDU, FONDUE—French; melted to a ready-to-pour consistency, e.g., cheese. Fondue also refers to a dish of steak cubes cooked by the customer at his table by dipping the cubes into a pot of oil heated over Sterno. Once cooked, the steak is dipped into a savory sauce and consumed.

FOOD AND BEVERAGE CONTROL OFFICE—Section or group within the accounting department that deals with costs and revenues relating to food and beverages.

FOOD AND BEVERAGE MANAGER—Person in charge of the food and beverage department. His or her prime responsibility is to ensure that the operation shows a profit.

FOOD AND DRUG ADMINISTRATION (FDA)—Government agency that among other things is responsible for inspecting food-processing operations and developing guidelines for their proper regulation by state and local agencies.

FOODBORNE ILLNESS—Disease, injury, or other harm caused by contaminants in ingested food.

FOOD CHECKER—Person assigned the task of **post-checking**, i.e., ensuring that both the check and the order include the same items.

FOOD CHOPPER, BOWL TYPE—Chopping machine that operates with the combined action of a revolving metal bowl and rapidly spinning blades. Food is put into the bowl, which revolves in the opposite direction from the spinning blades; the food is chopped as it passes through the blades. Also called a Buffalo chopper.

FOOD-CONTACT SURFACE—Surfaces of pots, pans, ladles, utensils, and countertops with which food comes into direct or indirect contact.

FOOD COST—Cost to an establishment of the food it sells to the customers.

FOOD COST, ACTUAL—**Actual food cost.**

FOOD COST PERCENTAGE—Ratio of the cost of food to the revenue it produces upon resale, multiplied by 100, i.e., food cost divided by food sales × 100%.

FOOD COST, POTENTIAL—See **potential food cost.**

FOOD FILE—Rack and slide assembly in a refrigerator or food warmer to hold several sheet pans by their rims.

FOOD FILE, MOBILE—Rack and slide device to hold several pans. It may be inserted and removed from the refrigerator as a complete unit and rolled from place to place.

FOOD GRINDER—Machine for chopping food into very small pieces. The food is pushed through a small hopper with a stomper until it is picked up by a screw, which in turn forces it through a set of turning knife blades from where it is extruded through a grid of sharp-edged holes. Grinders may be powered by a self-contained motor or operated as an accessory to a vertical mixer.

FOOD MILL—Utensil used to **purée** or rice cooked foods. Also called a purée sieve.

FOOD MIXER—Machine that mixes solids and liquids. With different attachments it can beat, mix, knead, whip, emulsify, slice, sieve, strain, chop, or grind. See **vertical mixer** and **horizontal mixer.**

FOOD MOLDER—Machine that apportions and molds soft foods into units of desired size and shape, such as patties, meatballs, or fish cakes. The food is placed in a hopper from which it is forced into molds, automatically removed from the molds, and placed automatically on a tray or other suitable receptacle.

FOOD ORDER BOOK—See **order book.**

FOOD POISONING—Toxic reaction of the body to foreign chemicals or bacteria in contaminated food. See, for example, **botulism** or **salmonella.**

FOOD PORTION CONTROL REPORT—Form on which the actual number of each item sold that day can be compared with the anticipated number. If there are large discrepancies, the information can help make future purchasing and customer estimates more accurate.

FOOD PROCESSOR—Originated in France under the trade name of Cuisinart. It is a machine that speedily performs a variety of functions, such as puréeing, emulsifying, chopping, slicing, shredding, and whipping, through the action of a set of rapidly spinning blades in the bottom of the container.

FOOD PRODUCTION SHEET—Form that shows, for a single meal, how many of each item were prepared, how many were forecast to be sold, and how many were actually sold.

FOOD RESEARCH INSTITUTE—Private, nonprofit organization that investigates the causes of foodborne illnesses and provides information useful in preventing them.

FOOD SAFETY AND QUALITY SERVICE—Agency within the U.S. Department of Agriculture responsible for inspecting and grading meat, poultry, and other food products.

FOOD STOREROOM INVENTORY—Counting the number of each food item on hand in the storeroom.

FOOD STOREROOM REQUISITION—Form used when a department within an establishment, e.g., the coffeeshop, requests food from the storeroom.

FOOD TEST—Test of net yield, quality, and price of the different brands of a given food item in order to determine which is the best buy.

FOOD WARMER, FREE-STANDING—Countertop unit with an electrically heated open well in which liquid or solid foods are kept hot for service.

FOOD-WASTE DISPOSAL—Machine that grinds up food waste, mixes it with water, and flushes it into the sewage system. There are many different designs. The two main ones are the horizontal downswing hammer mill type and the vertical type with fixed-tooth impeller, swinging hammer, and rotor shredder. All require adequate sewage facilities and water supply, and care must be taken to avoid amounts and materials that the machine cannot handle. Some have devices to prevent the entrance of objects such as flatware.

FOOD-WASTE GRINDER—Garbage-disposal unit connected

with the plumbing system to facilitate the removal of organic waste.

FOOLSCAP—Printing paper each sheet of which measures 13.5 × 17 inches (34.3 × 43.2 cm). See **paper sizes.**

FOOT-CANDLE—Measure of the illumination provided by a light source in a given area; equivalent to the illumination provided by one candle from a distance of one foot. The minimum standard for safety is 20 foot-candles on work surfaces and 10 elsewhere.

FORCED ISSUES—Those items the storekeeper tells the chef are **dead stock** and must be used soon.

FORCED-SALE VALUE—Price for items when the owner must sell as soon as possible, as in liquidation proceedings.

FORECAST—Prediction of the amount of future sales volume and/or profit based on current trends.

FORECASTING—Projecting sales into the future for a given period.

FOREGROUND PROCESSING—Computer processing that takes priority over **background processing.**

FORK, BROILER—Sturdy fork with a long handle and two sharp prongs, used to lift and turn meats as they are broiled.

FORK, CARVER—Two-tined fork with a wooden handle used to hold roasts while carving them.

FORK, COOKING—Sharp-pronged fork used in cooking to hold, turn, and handle food. There are many different sizes and designs.

FORK, COOK'S—Multipurpose fork with a long wooden handle and two sharp tines.

FORMAL BUYING—Competitive buying in which several different vendors are invited to submit bids in writing. Contrast **informal buying.**

FORMAT—Description of how the menu should look, stating the size, type style, kind of paper, and so on.

FORTIFICATION—Addition of nutrients to food to supplement those it already contains. See **enrichment**.

FORTIFIED WINES—Wines to which brandy has been added to increase the natural alcoholic strength.

FORTRAN—Acronym for Formula Translating System, an early computer language with application to scientific and technical matters.

FOUNTAIN—In pastry making, the well of flour into which wet ingredients are stirred.

FOUR SPICES—Common mixture of spices that includes white pepper, cloves, ginger, and nutmeg.

FOWL—Birds, usually referring to edible species such as chicken, ducks, and turkeys.

FOXINESS—Strong grapey characteristic of wine, especially those produced in the Eastern United States from American grapes.

FRANCAISE, A LA—French; food prepared in the French style of that item.

FRANCHISE—The right or license to sell a company's goods or services in a particular territory, usually exclusively but at least with very limited competition.

FREE FATTY ACID (FFA)—Any fatty acid that is not linked to a glycerol molecule in a fat or oil. Such fat breakdown indicates deterioration in a food.

FREE ON BOARD (FOB)—Clause in sales contract that stipulates that the seller will deliver the purchased goods to a freight terminal of a given city at no extra charge. Beyond that point the buyer must pay for transportation. See **FOB price**.

FREE VENT—The placement of food over steam to allow it to cook.

FREEZE CONCENTRATION—Concentrating a juice or other liquid by freezing out part of the water.

FREEZE DRY—Process by which the product is frozen, a vacuum is created, and the moisture in the product evaporates without turning to water.

FREEZER BURN—An alteration of a food's texture, color, or flavor caused by loss of water vapor when stored in a freezer. It is caused by improper wrapping.

FREEZER, REACH-IN—Cabinet for holding frozen food at 0°C or colder, with a door that swings open or a drawer that may be pulled out.

FREEZER, WALK-IN—Compartment for holding foods at 0°C, or colder that is large enough for a person to walk into.

FREEZING POINT OF WATER—At standard atmospheric pressure, this is 0°C, or 32°F.

FREIGHT IN—Transportation costs for incoming goods paid by the buyer.

FREIGHT OUT—Transportation costs for outgoing goods paid by the seller.

FRENCH—To make meat less stringy by cutting the fibers diagonally. Also, to cut green beans lengthwise prior to cooking.

FRENCH FOLD—Advertisement or menu composed of one large sheet printed on one side only and then folded to make four smaller pages.

THE FRENCH INSTITUT NATIONAL DES APPELATIONS D'ORIGINE DES VINS EAUX-DE-VIE (INAO)—Organization that certifies the source and quality of wine.

FRENCH KNIFE—Multipurpose knife, usually eight to twelve inches long, with a blade that is widest near the handle and tapers gradually to a pointed tip. It is useful for slicing, chopping, and dicing.

FRENCH SERVICE—Elaborate service in which the kitchen does only part of the work. The final preparation and apportioning is done at the table.

FRENCH WHIP—Instrument with medium-gauge wire loops for beating and mixing medium to thick sauces.

FREON—Trade name for any of several nonflammable fluorocarbon gasses used as a refrigerant in most foodservice refrigerators and freezers.

FRESHNESS DATE—Last date that a food product will still be in peak condition. After this point it will continually lose quality, although it can safely be eaten for several days beyond this date. See **expiration date.**

FRINGE BENEFITS—Labor costs other than salary paid for by the establishment that provide a service; such as pensions and various types of insurance.

FRITTERS—Batter-fried, sliced, or chopped foods.

FRIZZANTE—Italian; crackling or semisparkling, used in reference to wine.

FRONT OF THE HOUSE—Customer's area in a foodservice establishment, i.e., the dining room. Contrast **back of the house.**

FROSTED FOODS—Foods frozen by **flash freezing.**

FROSTING—Final decorative layer or coating, such as buttercream, caramel, chocolate, coconut, fudge, and marshmallow applied to cakes or other pastries.

FROZEN STORAGE—Insulated and deeply chilled storeroom for foods that must be kept below the freezing point (32°F) until ready for use. Contrast **refrigerated storage.**

FRUCTOSAN—Any compound whose molecules are formed by combining units of **fructose.**

FRUCTOSE—Fruit sugar. See **sugar.**

FRUIT AND VEGETABLE TEST—Comparison of the different brands of a given fruit or vegetable to see which gives the greatest amount of acceptable quality produce for the money.

FRYING—Method of cooking in fat, such as **sautéeing** and **deep-fat frying.**

FRYING PAN—Shallow pan with a single long handle used to fry foods.

FRY KETTLE—A tank used for deep frying that heats the fat and holds it at a constant temperature, usually 300°F to 400°F. Models may be countertop or freestanding, with capacities from 15 to 50 pounds.

FUEL-AIR RATIO—Amount of air relative to the burning fuel in gas-burning stoves and gas-, coal-, and oil-burning furnaces. Fuel needs oxygen in order to burn.

FULL CONVENIENCE KITCHEN—Kitchen with minimal equipment set up mainly to handle already processed, composed, and cooked food items. Contrast **full production kitchen.**

FULL PRODUCTION KITCHEN—Kitchen equipped so that almost all menu items can be prepared from scratch. Contrast **semiconvenience kitchen, full convenience kitchen,** and **short order kitchen.**

FUMET—French; a strong bouquet in a wine.

FUNCTION SHEET—List of specific details (type and number of entrees, wines to be served, and so on) regarding banquets to insure that they run smoothly.

FUND—An asset, normally cash, set aside from all other assets for a specific purpose, e.g., a petty-cash fund.

FUNDED RESERVE—Money accumulated in a special account to take care of some future need, e.g., a reserve for bonuses or new equipment.

FUNGIBLE—Items that are of the same type, equivalent, or interchangeable with one another, e.g., a tray of chocolate chip cookies.

FUNGICIDE—Any chemical that kills fungi such as mildew and mold.

FUNGUS—Flowerless plant such as the mushroom, yeasts, and molds. Some fungi benefit foodservice, such as the molds that form on certain cheeses, but other fungi cause disease or spoil food, such as molds that ruin bread or wine. For such reasons, careful hygiene in handling and storing all food products is important.

FUSEL OIL—Byproduct of alcohol fermentation composed of several organic acids and alcohols. It contributes flavor to alcoholic beverages.

FUSTIC—Yellow food-coloring additive derived from certain trees.

FUTURES-AND-CONTRACT PURCHASING—Type of formal buying in which contracts are established in the present for goods to be delivered in the future. Since the price is set in the present, the establishment can predict related costs for the duration of the contract.

G

GAIN—Income, profit, or any other kind of financial benefit.

GALACTOSE—Simple sugar similar to **glucose** found in molecules of milk sugar (lactose).

GALACTOSEMIA—Inborn inability to metabolize **galactose** completely. An entirely galactose-free diet must be followed or the partially metabolized byproducts will cause mental and physical retardation.

GALLATES—Group of antioxidant compounds derived from gallic acid, which comes from various plants.

GALL BLADDER—Organ that stores liver bile until it is needed in digestion.

GALLSTONE—Stone formed from **cholesterol** and various calcium compounds in the gall bladder. A low-fat diet aids in prevention and treatment.

GALVANIZED SURFACE—Surface coated with zinc. Galvanized containers should not be used for acid foods such as sauerkraut because the acid may dissolve the zinc and cause poisoning.

GAME—Wild animals and birds that are hunted for sport. American game can be divided into four categories: water fowl, upland game, small game, and big game. The following are the most popular types.

Pheasant: Game bird of the *Phasianus Colchicus* species; the most highly prized of game birds. Pheasant is often hung for four to twelve days so that the bird develops its characteristic flavor. They should be well larded as they have a tendency to dry out.

Pigeon: Game bird of the *Columidae* family. Pigeons have a robust, gamey flavor. Their flesh has a tendency to dry out quickly.

Quail: Migratory bird related to the partridge family. Quail weigh between two and six ounces and have light colored flesh. Popular species include the California quail, the mountain quail, and the crested quail.

Rabbit: Rodent that is best eaten when young. Rabbit has white, closely grained, easily digested flesh that is high in protein and low in fat.

Squab: Pigeons that are four weeks old or less and weigh from eight to fourteen ounces. They have tender, dark, and delicate flesh.

Venison: The flesh of any deer including elk, moose, or reindeer. Venison has dry, lean flesh. Older venison should be marinated and larded to prevent it from drying out.

Wild duck: There are numerous types of wild duck, including black mallard, canvasback, bufferhead, and baldpate. Wild duck often has a fishy taste that does not appeal to everyone. Marinating the bird helps alleviate this somewhat.

GARAGE POSTER—Advertising poster placed on the wall of business garages or a parking lot.

GARDE-MANGER—French; place where food is stored and basic preparatory work is done before the food's removal to the kitchen to be cooked. It is also used to designate the person in charge of this work.

GARNISH—Tasty, decorative addition that enhances the visual appeal as well as the flavor of the food to which it is added.

GAS PACKING—Putting foodstuff into containers that are gas tight and replacing the oxygen with a gas such as nitrogen that does not sustain aerobic bacterial life. The procedure also prevents direct oxidation of the food.

GAS STORAGE—Preservation of fruits and vegetables by storage in a chamber filled with a combination of gases (e.g., nitrogen, carbon dioxide, and oxygen). The exact combination depends on the item to be stored.

GASTRIC—Anything pertaining to the stomach. For example, digestion is a gastric process.

GASTRIC JUICES—Enzymes such as pepsin that are secreted in the stomach and aid digestion.

GASTRIC LAVAGE—Flushing poison out of the stomach by introducing large amounts of water and pumping it out.

GASTRIN—Hormone secreted in the stomach in response to the presence of food. Gastrin in turn stimulates the production of gastric juice.

GASTRITIS—Stomach inflammation caused by **pathogens.**

GASTROENTERITIS—Inflammation of the stomach and intestines usually caused by viruses, bacteria, or food-poisoning toxins.

GASTROINTESTINAL TRACT—Entire digestive tract, from the mouth to the end of the large intestine.

GASTRONOME—A lover of good food. See **gourmet.**

GAUGE GLASS BRUSH—Narrow cylindrical brush with a long thin handle used to clean the glass gauge tube of a coffee urn.

GAUGE PLATE—Adjustable surface on a slicer or meat saw

against which the item to be cut is placed. The position of the gauge plate determines the thickness of the slices.

GELATIN—Protein derived by boiling beef bones, cartilage, hooves, tendons, and similar animal tissues. It is used to make jellylike dishes and combines well with other foods since it adds no flavor or color of its own. Gelatin may be made in the kitchen of a foodservice establishment or bought commercially in a powdered or crystal form.

GENE—Determinant of inherited characteristics within cells. Composed principally of sugar, phosphate, and other organic compounds. See **chromosome.**

GENERAL ACCOUNTING—All accounting other than **cost accounting.**

GENERAL OVERHEAD—Another term for the sum of administrative expenses and selling costs.

GENERAL-USE PESTICIDES—Pesticides that can be used safely by anyone who reads and follows the instructions. Contrast **restricted-use pesticides.**

GENERIC EXPENSES—Costs relating to an entire class of items, e.g., baked goods, rather than only to particular items within the class, e.g., doughnuts.

GENERIC WINE—General wine categories, such as chablis or burgundy. Contrast **varietal wine.**

GERBER TEST—Chemical test to measure the fat content in milk.

GERMAN COCKROACH—Smallest of the three principal varieties that infest foodservice establishments. It is about a half-inch long and of a light-brown color. See **cockroaches.**

GERM, CEREAL—Inner portion of cereal grains that acts as a seed. Germs contain chromosomes for the next-generation plant.

GERM, DISEASE—Any one of the bacteria and viruses that cause disease.

GERMICIDE—Disinfectant.

GERMINATION—Initial growth of any living thing, e.g., a sprout.

GERMPROOF—Substance that is sufficiently dense and solid to prevent microorganisms from passing through it, e.g., seals on food containers.

GHEE—Butter derived by evaporating water from milk; the butterfat is clarified but not churned. Used especially in Indian cooking.

GHERKINS—Tiny cucumbers that make excellent fancy pickles.

GIBBERLIN—Plant-growth regulator, derived from fungi, used to speed the germination of barley for brewing.

GIBLETS—Poultry heart, gizzard, liver, and trimmings.

GINGKO NUT—Small aromatic nut often used in Chinese cookery.

GIZZARD—Muscular second stomach found in turkey and other fowl. Cleansed of partially digested food, it can be used in a variety of dishes, e.g., it is one component of giblets.

GLASSINE—Smooth, thick paper resistant to grease and the passage of air and moisture. Used widely for wrapping and packaging foods.

GLASS WASHER, BRUSH TYPE—Small machine for washing glasses individually. Glasses are submerged upside down by hand in a tank containing a revolving brush, where they are scrubbed inside and out by the combined action of brushes and forced circulation of water.

GLIADIN—Alcohol-soluble protein found in wheat and rye.

GLOBINS—Group of pure proteins that often enter into chemical reactions with nonprotein compounds. For example, iron combines with globin to form hemoglobin.

GLOSS AGENT—Any chemical additive that makes a paper's finish reflect more light and gives it a smooth, shiny appearance.

GLOSSITIS—Enlarged and inflamed tongue caused by many factors, including strong foods and vitamin deficiency.

GLUCAGON—Pancreatic hormone that increases the level of blood sugar.

GLUCARIC ACID—An acid derived from glucose.

GLUCOASCORBIC ACID—An organic acid that destroys **vitamin C** (ascorbic acid).

GLUCOMETER—Device for measuring the amount of sugar in syrups or other liquids.

GLUCONO-DELTA-LACTONE—Compound used in chemical leavening to produce carbon dioxide in reaction with bicarbonate.

GLUCOSAN—Any substance such as starch whose molecules are made up of multiples of glucose.

GLUCOSE—The most elementary chemical form of sugar. Glucose in the bloodstream is the primary bodily source of energy, hence it is also called blood sugar. In food products it is often called dextrose.

GLUCOSE SYRUP—Syrup containing **glucose** and other sugars derived from a partial **hydrolysis** of corn or potato starch. If derived from corn, it is called corn syrup.

GLUCOSE TOLERANCE TEST—Test for diabetes and hypoglycemia, or low blood sugar. Blood sugar levels are measured in a fasting subject before and at fixed intervals after a measured amount of glucose is ingested. Diabetics show higher levels of blood sugar and take longer to recover to normal; hypoglycemics show lower levels.

GLUCOSIDES—Any compound composed of glucose and another organic substance, e.g., **flavonoid.**

GLUCURONIC ACID—An acid produced by glucose oxidation that combines with various toxic substances and then is excreted with them in the urine. In addition to helping the body get rid of toxins, it is found in certain **polysaccharides.**

GLUTAMIC ACID—One of the nonessential amino acids.

GLUTELINS—Proteins soluble in weak acid or alkaline solutions but not in neutral ones or pure water.

GLUTEN—Protein substance in wheat flour that gives cohesiveness to dough and structure to baked products.

GLYCERIDES—Components of fat. Each glyceride is an **ester** of **fatty acids** and **glycerol.**

GLYCEROL—Alcohol that combines with **fatty acids** to form fat. In pure liquid form, glycerol is used as a solvent for flavoring additives.

GLYCEROSE—Simple sugar with only three carbon atoms per molecule.

GLYCERYL LACTOSTEARATE—Emulsifying agent used in shortening.

GLYCERYL MONOSTEARATE (GMS)—Nongreasy fat used to subdue fat spattering during frying, to form emulsions and to coat foods to seal in moisture and softness, as in baked goods.

GLYCINE—One of the nonessential amino acids. It can be used as a sweetening additive.

GLYCININ—One of the proteins in soybeans.

GLYCOGEN—Chemical form in which glucose is stored in the body, mainly in the liver and muscles. Each molecule is composed of glucose molecules.

GLYCOLIPID—Any fat (lipid) that contains carbohydrates.

GLYCOPROTEIN—Any compound composed of both carbohydrate and protein, e.g., cartilage.

GLYCOSIDE—Any compound whose molecules are composed of a sugar molecule and a nonsugar molecule.

GLYCOSURIA—The presence of glucose in the urine in abnormally large amounts. It is a symptom of some diseases, including kidney disease and diabetes.

GLYCYRRHIZIN—Sweetener derived from the licorice plant.

GOBLET—Wide-mouthed drinking vessel that was once made of silver or silver plate but now usually made of glass.

GOITER—Swelling of the thyroid gland in the neck caused by iodine deficiency.

GOITROGENS—Substances found in soybeans and vegetables such as turnips and cabbage. They inhibit the secretion of thyroid hormones and in excess can cause goiter.

GONG BRUSH—Stiff-bristled brush with a short wooden handle used for scrubbing pots and pans. Also called a pot and pan brush.

GOOD GRADE—Third highest of eight grades of meat. See **meat grading.**

GOODS—Commodities, items of value, and merchandise.

GOODS RECEIVED FORM—Form on which the receiving clerk lists and describes the goods received that day.

GOODS RECEIVED WITHOUT INVOICE FORM—Form used by the receiving clerk when supplies are not accompanied by an invoice. Items received are listed and described, and a copy of the form is sent to the accounting department.

GOODWILL—Good reputation developed by an establishment over time that increases its sales revenues and can be expected to continue to do so. It is a major advantage over a new concern in the same region.

GOOSEBERRY—Berry related to the red currant. Ripe berries range in color from red to green and some species are hairy. They may be eaten fresh or cooked. Gooseberries are not very popular in the United States.

GOSSYPOL—Poisonous compound in cottonseed that must be removed to make the seeds edible; the seeds are ground into a flour used as a food additive or are pressed into cottonseed oil. Though not proven toxic to man, gossypol has negative effects on animals, e.g., chickens fed it produce eggs with discolored yolks.

GOURMAND—Someone who eats too much and indiscriminately. Contrast **gourmet.**

GOURMET—Someone very knowledgeable about fine food and drink.

GRADE—Indication of the quality of meat or some other food product, used to differentiate quality levels in market products.

GRADE PLACARD—Sign issued by the health authority to be displayed publicly within a foodservice establishment. It shows the grade of the establishment at the last health inspection. See **grading of establishments.**

GRADE STAMP—Stamp on delivered meats or other products that indicates the grade of the product. The receiving clerk should compare the product to the grade claimed on the invoice.

GRADING OF ESTABLISHMENTS—Grades on safety and sanitation assigned by the health authority on the basis of the **demerit score** as entered on the **inspection report form.** Grade A corresponds to 10 or fewer demerits, Grade B to 11–20 demerits, and Grade C to 21–40 demerits. More than 40 results in an immediate suspension of the permit.

GRAIN—Direction in which the majority of paper fibers lie in a sheet of paper. See **grain testing** and **with the grain.** Grain also signifies the seeds of cereal grasses, such as wheat and oats.

GRAIN SPIRITS—Alcoholic beverages distilled from grains such as rye and barley.

GRAIN TESTING—Checking a sample of paper prior to printing to determine the direction of its **grain.** See **tear testing** and **fold testing.**

GRANDE MARMITE—French; large round pot with two loop handles; it corresponds to the American stockpot.

GRANULATE—To form a substance into grains, e.g., sugar.

GRAPE—One of the most versatile berries known to mankind. Grapes come in a variety of colors, but all grow in clusters on vines. They can be eaten fresh or cooked, converted into juice and an endless variety of wines. Dried grapes become raisins.

GRAPEFRUIT—Citrus fruit grown in large clusters, with or without seeds, with pink or white flesh (the peel is yellow). It may be served in halves to start any meal, or sectioned for fruit cups, salads, or desserts.

GRAPEFRUIT KNIFE—Small knife with a curved blade used to cut out the pulp of grapefruit sections.

GRAPE SUGAR—**Glucose** derived from grapes.

GRAPHICS—Displays of pictorial symbols or graphs, rather than words alone.

GRATE—To scrape a food like cheese against a rough surface, e.g., a **grater,** thus producing a pile of large shreds or particles.

GRATER—Utensil with a rough surface pierced with holes, used to shred or grate foods such as cheese or vegetables.

GRATING—Fine shredding of vegetables, fruit rinds, cheese, spices, and so on.

GRAVURE—Printing process in which the image or letters form a depressed surface in the printing plate. Ink fills up the recesses, is scraped off the flat surfaces, and transferred from the recesses to the paper. Contrast **letterpress printing.**

GRAVY—Opaque sauce, thickened with flour or cornstarch, made with meat juices and served over meat, bread, rice, or potatoes.

GREASE SALES—Income from the sale of cooking byproducts such as grease, bones, or oil (e.g., to soap companies).

GREEN S—A food-coloring additive.

GREEN TEA—A nonfermented tea. Contrast **black tea.**

GREEN WINE—Light, very young wine.

GRENADINE—Pomegranate syrup used in mixed drinks for its red color and sweet flavor.

GRIDDLE—Unit consisting of a metal plate, heated by gas or

electricity, on which food is cooked by direct contact with the surface. The food is usually cooked first on one side and then turned over to cook on the other side. However, some models have devices to cook both sides at once, e.g., covers with infrared elements, a heated metal cover, or a tight-fitting lid that traps steam over the item.

GRIDDLE BROILING—Cooking on a hot, dry surface and removing liquid fat from the food item as it accumulates.

GRIDIRON GRILL—Utensil composed of several parallel iron bars attached to a frame. It is used to grill foods like steaks or fish, often over a charcoal fire.

GRILLARDIN—French; the chef who grills foods.

GRILLING—Cooking on a flat heated surface or griddle at moderate temperatures, i.e., 325°–400°F. The meat juices tend to evaporate quickly on the surface of the meat, thus "sealing in" most of the nutrients with the meat.

GRIND—To rub a food such as pepper between two hard or rough surfaces, thus converting it into a powder. Also, to process meat into small pieces, such as ground beef.

GRITS—Ground hominy. Eaten as a breakfast food in the South. It is boiled like cereal and often served over or with eggs.

GROATS—Endosperm of oats.

GROMMET—Metallic circle with a hole in the center. When manufactured into a paper tag (e.g., a meat tag), string or wire is fed through the hole to connect the tag to the item.

GROSS COST OF MERCHANDISE SOLD—Purchase price of goods (including insurance and freight) that are in turn sold at the retail level.

GROSS FOOD COST—Cost of all food purchased by an establishment, including food not sold to customers for a profit, i.e., that which is wasted or sold to employees at cost. Contrast **net food cost.**

GROSS FOOD SALES—Total income from all sales of food to customers.

GROSSIER—French; coarse or harsh wine.

GROSS INCOME—Total income before expenses are deducted.

GROSS LOSS—Amount by which the total cost of goods sold exceeds the revenue produced when the goods are sold.

GROSS PROFIT—Total revenues on food sold minus the total cost of that food to an establishment.

GROSS PROFIT PER ITEM—Difference between the food cost to an establishment and the selling price to the customer for a single menu item.

GROSS SALES—Total dollar value of all sales for a given period.

GROSS WEIGHT—Total weight of a product, including the container and its contents.

GUARANTEE—Purchaser who receives a **guaranty** for the item bought.

GUARANTEED POSITION—In print advertising, the location in the publication guaranteed by the publisher. See **position request.**

GUARANTY—Company's promise to make restitution to unsatisfied customers with legitimate complaints. Also spelled guarantee.

GUAVA—Tropical American pear-shaped edible fruit typically eaten raw or used in the preparation of jelly and jam.

GUERIDON—In French service, a side table, usually on wheels, at which the waiter prepares food at tableside.

GUM ACACIA—Sap from the stems of the *Acacia senegal* and other Acacia plants. It is used as a stabilizer and thickener in the production of gumdrops and other jellies.

GUM ARABIC—**Gum acacia.**

GUMS—Thick viscous substances derived from a variety of

plants. They are not digestible but can be used in foods as thickeners and stabilizers.

GUSTATION—Overall sense of taste, composed of the four basic taste qualities–sweet, sour, salty, and bitter.

H

HACKBERRY—North American fruit, resembling cherries, that grows on *Ulmaceae* trees. It is purple and very sweet.

HAFF DISEASE—Paralysis caused by the consumption of antithiamine, which prevents the body's utilization of **thiamine.** The principal source is incompletely cooked freshwater fish.

HAIRLINE CRACK—A fine, barely visible crack in a glass bottle caused by a sharp blow or heat stress.

HAIR RESTRAINTS—Hair bands, caps, or nets that keep hair close to the head, prevent the hair's movement, and discourage head scratching. They reduce the transmission of contaminants from hair to food.

HAIR TUBE—Nozzle for a cake-decorating bag or syringe with multiple tiny openings for making clusters of icing strings that look like hair or grass.

HALF AND HALF—Commercial mixture of half 18 percent cream and half 3.5 percent milk.

HALLUCINOGEN—Any substance that produces hallucinations, i.e., makes a person perceive things that are not there. Certain foods, such as some poisonous mushrooms, contain hallucinogens.

HALOPHILIC BACTERIA—Bacteria that grow in high salt concentrations that inhibit the growth of most bacteria.

HAM HOLDER—Round metal rack that will hold one ham in an upright position for cooking or carving.

HAMPER—Container for carrying fruits and vegetables during shipment.

HAM SLICER—Slicing knife with a long narrow blade and a square tip.

HAND PARER—Small tool with a sharp-edged slot in the blade, used to cut the peel or thin strips from the surface of fruits and vegetables. Some models have a swivel-action blade.

HAND TRUCKS—Carts set on wheels, often with two or more decks, used to move supplies within an establishment.

HANGING—Suspending meat in the cool dry air of a special room, thus allowing it to age. This improves its flavor and increases tenderness.

HARD BALL—Sugar and water mixture cooked at 254°F until it forms a hard ball when a spoonful is dropped into chilled water.

HARD COPY—Printed output from a computer, as opposed to temporary output on the screen.

HARD CRACK—Sugar and water mixture boiled at 290°F until it becomes brittle when a spoonful is dropped into chilled water.

HARD LIQUOR—Beverages that contain at least 40 percent alcohol (80 proof).

HARDWARE—Physical machinery of a computer system, including disc drives, storage units, keyboards, and video display terminals.

HARD WATER—**Water hardness.**

HAUT—French; literally means "high." Used in reference to wines, but usually refers to geographic area rather than to quality.

HAUT CUISINE—Traditionally elaborate French cooking; usually served in elegant (and expensive) establishments.

HAYBOX COOKING—Placing hot food in a well-insulated container so that it can continue cooking by its own heat without the use of any further fuel.

HAZE—Cloudiness that appears in beer caused by small amounts of gum or other residues from the plants used in brewing.

HEAD MARGIN—Unused space on a page that lies above the first line of print.

HEAD-ON LOCATION—Billboard or other outdoor advertising display so positioned that oncoming traffic can see it directly.

HEADS—Alcoholic spirits developed during early distillation. See **feints.**

HEADSPACE—Empty space in a sealed can, bottle, or other container that is above the level of the contents.

HEALTH OFFICER—Medical doctor who administers public health programs. The doctor's responsibilities include identifying health hazards, enforcing regulations to remove them, and educating those responsible on how to avoid them.

HEART OF THE HOUSE—Employee's domain of an operation, revolving largely around the purchasing of food, its storage, and preparation. Also called **back of the house;** contrast **front of the house.**

HEART OF PALM—Vegetable taken from the tender central part of a palm stalk.

HEAT DEFLECTION TEMPERATURE—Temperature at which plastic will become soft enough to bend if any pressure, such as the contents of a container, is placed on it.

HEAT ENERGY—Energy that tends to elevate the temperature of a substance or space. See **sensible heat, latent heat,** and **usable heat.**

HEAT LAMP—Device widely used in kitchens and serving areas that keeps food warm by infrared radiation. The most common type consists of a 250-watt infrared bulb installed in a reflective shade.

HEAT OF COMBUSTION—Heat in calories produced by total combustion of a known amount of a given food substance.

HEAT TRANSMISSION—Movement of heat energy through open air (as from a stove) or through liquid and solid materials (as through the walls of refrigerated storerooms). Insulation inhibits this process. See **conduction, convection,** and **radiation.**

HEAVY DUTY BROILER—**Upright broiler.**

HEAVY WHIPPING CREAM—Cream of 30 to 40 percent milkfat.

HECTOLITER—Liquid measurement equaling 100 liters or 26.418 gallons.

HEDONIC SCALE—Rating scale, usually of ⅃ine points, on which a customer ranks his or her like or dislike of a particular food.

HEIFER—Cow 17 to 24 months old that has never had a calf.

HELMINTH—Any of the parasitic worms, including **cestodes, nematodes,** and **trematodes.**

HEMAGGLUTININS—Poisonous substances found in legumes such as soybeans and sweet peas. They are destroyed by cooking. These substances tend to increase the clotting of the blood.

HEME—Reddish iron-containing compound that combines with the protein globin to form **hemoglobin.**

HEMOCHROMATOSIS—Hereditary disease in which too much iron is absorbed by the body. The excess iron gets deposited in tissues and organs such as the liver and heart, interfering with their functions. It can also turn the skin bronze colored.

HEMOGLOBIN—Source of the color in red blood cells. It is the medium by which oxygen is transported within the body.

HEMOLYSINS—Various substances produced by microorganisms that are responsible for the process of **hemolysis.**

HEMOLYSIS—Substance capable of destroying red blood cells. Various pathogens such as **streptococcus pyogenes** can do this.

HEMORRHAGE—Large or uncontrolled flow of blood. It can be caused internally by a variety of poisons and parasites.

HEMOSIDERIN—One of the forms in which iron is stored within the body.

HEN—Female of domestic poultry, e.g., chicken or turkeys. Also called fowl.

HEPATIC—Anything pertaining to the liver, e.g., an infection or other disease.

HEPATITIS—Inflammation of the liver. The type called infectious hepatitis can be caused by drinking or eating food (e.g., oysters) infected with the responsible **virus** or **ameba.**

HEPTYL PARABEN—Preservative used in beer.

HERB BOUQUET—Seasoning made up of mixed herbs.

HERBS—General term for aromatic plants with no woody stems above ground. Herbs are used to season dishes and are best used fresh. The following are the most popular herbs used today.
Angelica: Plant of the parsley family, cultivated in France. The leaves are used to flavor salads and the green stalks are often candied.
Anise: Dried seed of a plant from the celery family. Anise is produced in Spain, the Netherlands, and Mexico. It is used in liqueurs and sweets.
Basil: Mint family herb grown in Europe and the U.S. It is used in tomato, egg, and game dishes.
Bay leaf: Dried leaves of the laurel tree, grown in Turkey and Portugal. It is used in bouquet garni, stocks, and stews.
Borage: Hairy leaves of a southern European plant, used fresh in salads or dried as an herb.
Burnet: Used to season salads.
Camomile: Dried flowers of this herb are steeped and the brew given as a tonic tea.
Caraway Seed: Dried pungent seeds from an herb of the carrot family, grown in Holland and Poland. It is used in rye breads, liqueurs, sauerkraut, and potato dishes.
Cassia: Tropical herb with pods that taste like cinnamon.

Chervil: Herb of the carrot family with a flavor similar to
parsley. It is used in salads, omelettes, soups, and stews.

Chicory: Plant also known as endive or succory. The mature
roots are roasted, ground, and used with coffee.

Chives: Small, mild variety of onion used for soups, salads,
and in potato dishes.

Comfrey: Rough, boraginaceous plants used in salads or
cooked.

Cress: Another name for watercress, a salad plant with pep-
pery-flavored leaves.

Cumin: Ground seeds of this plant are used as a spicy seasoning in many Mexican foods, curries, and the like. Also
spelled cummin.

Dill: Herb of the carrot family with aromatic leaves, seeds,
and stems used in pickling, soups, and egg and fish
dishes.

Fennel: Seed from a plant of the carrot family with a flavor
similar to anise. It is used with fish, baked goods, and
bean dishes.

File: Powder made from dried sassafras leaves. It is used to
thicken gumbos in Creole cookery.

Garlic: Strong-flavored bulb of the onion family. Each bulb is
made of smaller sections called cloves. It is used to flavor
soups, meats, stews, and salads.

Horehound: A weed of the mint family used as an herb because of its bitter flavor. It is sometimes used as an ingredient in cough remedies.

Horseradish: Species of scurvy grass with white-fleshed, pungent roots. It is used grated and used in sauces, as a food
seasoning, and as a relish. The flavor is sharp and piquant.

Marjoram: Aromatic herb of the mint family. It is used to
season veal, cheese, egg, poultry, and fish.

Mint: Small aromatic plants, including spearmint, peppermint, and pennyroyal. It has a cool, fresh flavor and is
used to season lamb dishes, salads, and cool drinks.

Oregano: Herb of the mint family; also known as wild marjoram. It is used in Italian and South American cookery.

Parsley: Hardy biennial plant with leaves that are used as a garnish or in flavoring soups, stews, potatoes, and stuffings.

Râpé: Mustard-family herb, the seeds of which yield an oil useful in cooking.

Rosemary: Aromatic shrub of the mint family. The leaves are used to flavor tomato, egg, fish, meat, and vegetable dishes.

Rue: Strong-scented herb whose leaves are used for seasoning.

Saffron: Dried stigmas of a species of purple crocus. Saffron is bright orange-yellow with a slightly bitter taste. It is used as a coloring agent in Mediterranean cookery.

Sage: Strongly-flavored herb of a shrub belonging to the mint family. The leaves are gray-green with a strong, musty flavor. It is used in pork and poultry dishes.

Salad burnet: Perennial herb with a cucumber flavor. It is used as a salad green.

Savory: Aromatic herb of two types, summer and winter. Savory has a flavor similar to thyme and is used to flavor fish and egg dishes.

Shallots: Herb of the lily family with a flavor similar to garlic and onion. Shallots are used to flavor meat, poultry, and sausage.

Sorrel: Herb of the dock family with an acidic flavor. It is used in soups, and in spinach and egg dishes.

Tarragon: Herb from a plant related to the wormwood family. It is used to flavor stews, sauces, fish, eggs, and chicken dishes.

Thyme: Garden herb with strong flavor; used to season poultry, meat, stuffings, and in bouquet garni.

HERMETIC SEAL—Seal on a bottle or other container that is able to prevent air and fluids from seeping out or in.

HESPERIDIN—Nutrient from the **pith** of citrus fruits, especially oranges, that aids in developing blood-vessel strength.

HEURISTIC—Attacking a computer problem by the trial-and-error method.

HEXAMIC ACID—An artificial sweetener.

HEXAMETHYLENE TETRAMINE (HMT)—A food preservative.

HEXOSANS—Any **polysaccharide** composed of **hexose** sugars.

HEXOSE—Any sugar with molecules that have six carbon atoms each, e.g., glucose.

HEXURONIC ACID—Acid resulting from oxidation of a **hexose** sugar.

HICKEYS—Stray dots and other marks that detract from the appearance of copy printed through offset-lithography.

HIGHBALL GLASS—Plain cylindrical bar glass holding five to ten ounces.

HIGH DENSITY LIPOPROTEIN (HDL)—**Cholesterol** with only 50 percent lipid and 50 percent protein. It contains more protein than does **low density lipoprotein** or LDL. Also called alpha cholesterol. HDL is safer than LDL and helps rid the body of excess cholesterol.

HIGH GLOSS INK—**Printing ink** with extra varnish to give it a very glossy appearance.

HIGH-LEVEL LANGUAGE—Computer programming languages that are closer to English than **machine-language** ones. Examples include BASIC, COBOL, and RPG.

HIGHLIGHT—Lightest part of a printed photograph. Also, to emphasize part of a menu or advertisement with special type or graphics.

HIGH QUALITY PROTEIN—Protein that contains more of the essential amino acids. If it contains them all, it is called complete protein.

HIGH-RATIO SHORTENING—Shortening with a higher proportion of **monoglycerides** and **diglycerides** than **triglycerides**. It can interact with more sugar during baking than other kinds, yielding a sweeter product.

HIGH TEMPERATURE SHORT TIME PASTEURIZATION—See **flash pasteurization**.

HIGH WINES—Middle part of a distillation, as distinguished from the **feints.**

HINDSADDLE, MEAT—The back part of a full veal or lamb carcass that has been cut in half through the twelfth and thirteenth ribs.

HISTAMINE—Derivative of **histidine.** It constricts the lung's bronchioles, lowers blood pressure, and stimulates gastric acid secretion.

HISTIDINE—Amino acid that is nonessential to adults but that may be essential for growing children; the source of **histamine.**

HISTONES—Proteins that are not soluble in diluted ammonia but are soluble in plain water.

HISTORICAL BASIS—Cost-accounting technique in which actual costs such as overhead are not determined until the end of a given period.

HOCHGEWACHS—German; superior wine growth or vineyard.

HOGSHEAD—Barrel with a capacity of 60–72 gallons used for wines and spirits.

HOME-STYLE SERVICE—Method of service in which at least some food is served in large dishes and guests help themselves. Also called family-style service.

HOMINY—Inner corn kernels that have been bleached. They are eaten whole or ground into **grits.**

HOMOGENIZATION—Reduction of the size of fat globules in milk through high-speed blending so that the cream does not rise but rather remains in a stable emulsion with the milk.

HOMOGENOUS COSTS—Group of costs related to the same set of functions, items, or departments, e.g., utility expenses.

HONEY—Sweet liquid made from flower nectar by working bees. It is condensed through evaporation in the hive and used as a sweetener in food production. The flavor varies according to the type of blossom from which the nectar is taken.

HONEYCOMB TRIPE—The best part of **tripe**. It is served boiled.

HONEYDEW MELON—Fruit of the muskmelon family. It has a yellowish rind and sweet greenish flesh.

HOOD—Canopy installed over cooking equipment to collect and exhaust heat, grease, smoke, and steam from the kitchen. It is used in conjunction with fans, filters, and sometimes with fire-extinguishing and pollution-control devices.

HOPS—Blossoms used in brewing because they retard bacterial growth and provide a slightly bitter taste.

HORDEIN—A protein found in barley.

HORIZONTAL MIXER—Large food mixer used in high-volume bakeries and kitchens. It consists of a horizontal cylinder in which a rotating shaft is driven by a heavy-duty motor.

HORMONES—Chemical messengers secreted by the endocrine glands that travel through the bloodstream and produce effects on distant parts of the body.

HORN—Small utensil used to scrape up remains from mortars and mixing bowls. Traditionally made of horn.

HORS D'OEUVRES—French; bite-size morsels often picked up by the fingers and eaten as appetizers.

HORSEPOWER—Unit of energy equivalent to 34,000 **BTU's**.

HORSERADISH—Root of a mustard-family plant that is ground and used as a relish or seasoning in a number of different condiments and sauces. It is sharp and piquant.

HORTVET FREEZING TEST—A check of any change of the freezing point of milk to estimate how much excess water it contains.

HOST BAR—Bar at a private party at which the host has arranged to pay for all the drinks consumed by his guests. Contrast **cash bar.**

HOST COMPUTER—Computer that initiates and controls communication with one or more other computers and is typically larger than the others.

HOST, HOSTESS—Man or woman who receives customers into the dining room, leads them to a table, and issues them menus.

HOST, PARASITIC—Plant or animal in which a parasite lives.

HOTEL BROILER—See **upright broiler.**

HOTEL PAN—See **counter pan.**

HOT-FOOD SERVER—Electrically heated cabinet with one or more drawers that is used to keep items such as rolls warm for service. It may have controls to regulate moistness or crispness. The cabinet may be mounted on a countertop or may sit on the floor. Also called a roll warmer.

HOT TOP—Cast-iron or steel plate used as a cooking surface on some electric and gas ranges. Some are thermostatically controlled. They may also be used as griddles. Also called boiling plate, closed top, uniform heat top, or hot plate.

HOT-WATER DISPENSER—Machine that apportions hot water for mixing hot instant beverages. Connected to a water supply, it heats water electrically to the desired temperature.

HOT-WATER JACKET—Accessory to a vertical mixer that fits around the base of the mixing bowl and is used to keep the contents of the bowl warm during mixing. As an ice jacket, it is used to cool instead.

HOUSEFLY—Ordinary fly that is exceedingly dangerous in food-service establishments. It carries pathogens of a large number of human diseases, e.g., dysentery, staphylococcal infections, streptococcal infections, and typhoid.

HOUSEKEEPING, COMPUTER—Performing functions important to the operation of a computer system but not necessary to solve a given problem.

HUCKLEBERRY—Type of blueberry that is small and blue-black in color.

HULL—Outer covering of cereal grains. It is rich in fiber. Also called **husk.**

HUMECTANT—Any substance such as sorbitol or glycerol that absorbs moisture and can be used to regulate the moisture level in a food, such as marshmallows.

HUMIDITY—Amount of water vapor in the air of a given space. See **absolute humidity** and **relative humidity.**

HUMULONE—Group of resins in hops that accounts for their bitter flavor.

HUSK—Woody outer covering of cereal grains. It is high in fiber but low in nutritive content. Also called **hull.**

HUTCH—Piece of furniture, usually in the dining room, with shelves and drawers in which silverware, plates, napkins, and the like may be kept.

HYBRID RESERVE—Cash reserve set up to handle two or more different functions or needs, e.g., repairs and excess energy costs.

HYDRALAZINE—Drug used to fight hypertension that may diminish the body's supply of vitamin B_6 among its possible side effects.

HYDROCHLORIC ACID—One of the gastric juices that help digest food. Too much can cause stomach overacidity or contribute to ulcer formation.

HYDROCOOLING—Chilling vegetables by washing them in ice water or by evaporating the water on them in a vacuum chamber.

HYDROGENATE—To add hydrogen to vegetable oils to make them more saturated and firm, i.e., solid, as in the production of margarine.

HYDROGEN PEROXIDE—Common antiseptic agent. It can be used as a milk preservative, but since it also destroys many of the nutrients, it is not often used for that purpose.

HYDROGEN SWELL—A **swell** caused by hydrogen gas formed

within a sealed can when food acids, e.g., citric acid, react with the metal of the can. Such food is safe to eat.

HYDROLYZE—To split up a large molecule into two smaller ones with the addition of water. The H_2O molecule also splits, with H going to one and OH to the other of the new molecules. This occurs, for example, when proteins are split into their component amino acids.

HYDROMETER—Instrument for measuring the density of liquids. A variety of special-purpose hydrometers are made for evaluating specific liquids, e.g., wine, vinegar, syrups. It consists of a glass tube with a graduated stem that is placed in the liquid to be tested. The density is shown by the level at which the stem floats.

HYDROSTATIC TEST—Test of the pressure inside a fire extinguisher. Reduced pressure may cause the extinguisher to malfunction.

HYDROXYBENZOIC ACID ESTERS—Compounds used as food preservatives.

HYDROXYPROLINE—One of the nonessential amino acids.

HYGIENE—All conditions and practices, such as sanitation, that are conducive to good health.

HYGROMETER—Device that measures the amount of humidity in a given space.

HYGROSCOPIC—The ability of any substance, such as calcium chloride, to absorb water readily, thus making it useful as a drying agent.

HYPERCALCEMIA—Toxic condition involving excessive calcium levels in the blood. Symptoms include constipation, vomiting, and weakness. Death may result.

HYPERCHLORHYDRIA—Excessive secretion of hydrochloric acid in the stomach.

HYPERPHAGIA—Physical condition creating abnormal feelings

of constant hunger, even when the body does not need food. Usually the afflicted individual overeats and may become obese.

HYPERTENSION—High blood pressure. A common cause is an excess of sodium through the salt in the diet and the increased water retention it creates.

HYPERTHYROIDISM—Excessive secretion of thyroid hormones, resulting in an abnormally high rate of metabolism.

HYPERVITAMINOSIS—Toxic state caused by the body's retention of an excess of certain vitamins, e.g., A, D, and nicotinic acid, usually by ingesting them. Excesses of certain other vitamins (e.g., C) are excreted by the body and are thus less dangerous.

HYPHAE—Tube-shaped cells that make up the mass of a fungus.

HYPOGLYCEMIA—Condition of low blood sugar, or glucose, in the body. The opposite of **diabetes.**

HYPOKALEMIA—Acute shortage of potassium in the body. Its symptoms include muscular weakness and a mental disorientation resembling senility. It is a not uncommon effect of **diuretics.** The condition can usually be cured by adding potassium-rich foods, such as bananas, or a potassium supplement to the diet.

HYPOPROTEINAEMIA—Abnormally low level of protein in the body.

HYPOSITE—Any food low in calories.

HYPOTHALAMUS—Part of the brain that controls many important bodily functions, including hunger and thirst.

HYPOTHYROIDISM—Undersecretion of thyroid hormones, resulting in a sluggish rate of metabolism. If this occurs doing the early years of growth, it results in mental and physical retardation.

I

ICED-TEA GLASS—Tall cylindrical drinking glass that holds about 12 ounces. Interchangeable with a Tom Collins glass.

ICED-TEA SPOON—Long-handled spoon with a small bowl used to stir drinks served in tall glasses or to eat desserts such as parfaits.

ICE JACKET—See **hot-water jacket.**

ICHTHYISM—Any poisoning caused by the ingestion of fish.

ICING—Sugary concoction used as the outer coating over cakes, cupcakes, and the like.

IDEAL STANDARD—Description of costs if an establishment were to be run in a completely efficient way.

IDLE-TIME EXPENSES—Costs incurred when employees or equipment are not working productively because of lack of business. Costs remain high while revenues slip down.

ILEUM—Last segment of the small intestine, beginning where it joins the large intestine.

ILLEGAL SUBSTITUTIONS—Serving of a product of lesser quality or value than that stated in the menu. It is illegal unless the customer was properly informed when ordering.

IMAGE—The combination of the elements that make up a restaurant—including food, service, menu, location, price, market attractiveness, the personality and philosophy of management— and how this combination is viewed by those outside the establishment, i.e., potential and actual customers.

IMMUNITY, ACTIVE—Resistance to disease-causing organisms or substances that the human body develops after exposure. See **immunity, passive.**

IMMUNITY, PASSIVE—Resistance to disease-causing organisms or substances that is not developed by the human body itself but rather is formed elsewhere and transferred to the body, as by injection with a vaccine. See **immunity, active.**

IMPACT STRENGTH—Measure of the ability of a packaging material to withstand breakage when dropped or hit.

IMPERIALE—French; a large wine bottle with a volume of six liters.

IMPERIAL SIZE—Printing paper sheets that measure 22 x 30 inches (55.9 x 76.2 cm). See **paper sizes.**

IMPLIED CONTRACT—An agreement between parties that is not set down in writing but is followed as though it had been. The presence of an agreement can be legally inferred.

IMPOSITION—Placement of individual pages on a large sheet so that, after printing and folding, they will be in the right order.

IMPREST FUND—Petty-cash fund from which money in small amounts can be withdrawn for various minor purchases, e.g., postage, and that is periodically replenished to its maximum amount when receipts for the missing amounts are produced.

IN-AD COUPON—Coupon for a discount offered by a product's manufacturer that is printed along with a local merchandiser's ad.

INANITION—Exhaustion caused by extreme malnutrition.

INCINERATOR—Furnace in which combustible rubbish can be burned.

INCOME—Money or other assets received by an establishment in return for sales of goods or services.

INCOME ACCOUNT—Account sheet on which are recorded all items regarding a particular type of revenue, e.g., liquor sales by the bottle or cigarette sales.

INCOME STATEMENT—Financial statement for a given period that itemizes revenues, expenses, and the resulting profit or loss.

INCOMPLETE COMBUSTION—Incomplete burning of any

fuel, such as natural gas. This wastes fuel and can lead to carbon buildup (soot) on the burners, which in turn wastes more fuel.

INCOMPLETE TRANSACTION—Business deal that has been initiated but will be culminated later. For example, goods may be purchased on credit and paid for later.

INCREMENT—Increase in value of an asset during a specific period. Contrast **decrement.**

INCREMENTAL COSTS—Additional costs required for an establishment to increase output.

INCUBATION PERIOD—Period following the invasion of microorganisms into a host before disease symptoms appear. The microbes multiply rapidly during this time and may be contagious.

INCUR—To acquire responsibility for something, e.g., a cost or debt.

INDEBTEDNESS—State of having a debt or any other sort of liability.

INDEX, COMPUTER— Computer-stored table or list of the **addresses** of records in a data base or file.

INDEX PAPER—Inexpensive paper noted for its stiffness. See **paper types.**

INDIGO CARMINE—Blue food-coloring additive derived from the indigo fern.

INDIRECT COSTS—Any cost that is not direct, i.e., not clearly identified with a specific department or operation. Such overhead-type costs should be apportioned among all relevant departments.

INDIRECT DEPARTMENT—Any department that serves the **direct departments,** e.g., the storeroom, personnel office, and the like.

INDIRECT LABOR—Employee expenses that are not directly related to producing goods or services for sale but are important for maintenance of an establishment, e.g., repairmen and janitors.

INDIRECT MATERIAL—Supplies that do not become a part of produced goods but are used up in the process of running an establishment, e.g., energy.

INDUCTION PERIOD—Time during which fats remain fresh due to the action of the **antioxidants** they contain. After this period, fats go rancid quickly.

INFECTION, FOODBORNE—Illness caused by the ingestion of a food containing the infection-causing organism. See also **intoxication, foodborne.**

INFESTATION—Invasion of parasites or other pests in food or a place, e.g., the kitchen.

INFORMAL BUYING—Handling purchasing negotiations orally, either in person or over the phone. Contrast **formal buying.**

INFORMATION SYSTEM—System for the orderly flow of reports and other needed information to managers so they can make timely and accurate decisions.

INFORMING GRAPE—Main grape that gives a wine its distinguishing character.

INFRARED ENERGY—Electromagnetic energy with wavelengths just below those of visible red light. The **radiant energy** they supply can be used for cooking, e.g., in quartz broilers.

INFRARED OVEN—**Quartz oven.**

INFUSION—Flavored liquid that results from steeping. For example, tea is an infusion that results from steeping tea leaves in hot water.

INGREDIENT ROOM—Area for measuring, cleaning, mixing, forming, and otherwise preparing foods before they are sent to the chef for actual cooking.

INHIBITION, COMPETITIVE—The competition of one substance for the enzymes required by another substance, thus interfering with the latter's reactions. Sulfa drugs inhibit bacterial growth in this way.

INLINE-SHADOW TYPE—Printing type in which each character has both an inline and a shadow, for double emphasis. See **special type.**

INLINE TYPE—Printing type in which the body of each letter is in outline. See **special type.**

INOSITOL—Compound similar to hexose sugar that is present in certain foods such as bran. It is synthesized by the human body and is not known to be essential.

IN-PROCESS INVENTORY—Food items immediately on hand during the cooking and preparation of menu items.

INPUT—Movement of data into the main computer memory for storage or processing.

INPUT-OUTPUT (I/O)—Overall term for computer operations.

INSERT—Advertising leaflet printed separately and inserted in a newspaper or periodical.

INSET—Stainless steel vessel, made in various shapes and sizes, designed to hold foods in a steam table or food warmer.

INSIDE HANDLES—Handles on the inside of doors to lockable storerooms. They are needed so that a person can get out if accidentally shut in.

INSIDE SALES TOTAL—Total dollar value of all sales of food and beverage items purchased in a given period that are meant to be consumed on the premises. Contrast **carryout sales total.**

INSOLVENCY—Financial inability of a company to pay its debts.

INSPECTED AND PASSED STAMP—U.S. Department of Agriculture's approval, indicating that the food product is fit for human consumption.

INSPECTION REPORT FORM—Form on which a health authority lists the violations discovered and states the **demerit score.** See also **grading of establishments.**

INSTALLMENT SALE—Selling property or goods in return for a series of partial payments rather than one lump sum.

INSTITUTIONAL ADVERTISING—Advertising usually paid for by a group or organization of businesses and directed toward increasing consumption of a general type of product (e.g., milk) rather than a specific brand. The purpose is to increase sales for all producers, suppliers, and retailers.

INSTRUCTION, COMPUTER—Coded program step commanding the computer to do a particular operation in a program.

INSULATION—Materials such as fiberglass that resist the transmission of heat energy.

INSULIN—Protein hormone produced by the pancreas that controls the metabolism of carbohydrates, i.e., sugars. The diabetic usually does not produce enough insulin and must therefore have it supplemented either by pills or injection.

INSURABLE VALUE—The cost, as insured, to replace destroyed or stolen items minus a percent of the total for depreciation based on age.

INTANGIBLE ASSET—An asset that is not physical, such as property or cash, but that still has value, such as a franchise, a special recipe, or a trademark.

INTELLIGENT TERMINAL—Computer terminal with extensive logical, arithmetic, and data storage capability.

INTERACTIVE SYSTEM—Computer system capable of both conversational mode and real-time processing.

INTERBAR TRANSFERS—Transfer of beverages from one bar to another within the same establishment.

INTERFACE CIRCUIT—Circuit that allows two or more computer systems to be connected to each other.

INTERFUND TRANSFER—Transfer of money from one fund to another.

INTERIM FINANCIAL REPORT—Report on an establishment's financial condition made at some time other than the end of the fiscal year, i.e., a report on developments so far in the current year.

INTERKITCHEN TRANSFER—Form that can be used to requisition items from one kitchen to another at establishments with more than one kitchen.

INTERMEDIATE HOST—Any animal in which some parasitic worms complete their development prior to infesting humans or any other primary host. For example, lung and liver flukes complete this stage in snails before they are able to infect a human.

INTERNAL ATMOSPHERE—Overall atmosphere or feeling tone of the area where customers eat. This atmosphere can help build a positive mood and encourage customers to return. Contrast **external atmosphere.**

INTERNAL AUDIT—Audit done by the accounting section of an establishment itself. Contrast **external auditing.**

INTERNAL INFORMATION—Information on costs and revenues within the establishment gathered by the manager. Contrast **external information.**

INTERNATIONAL UNITS (IU)—Internationally agreed-upon standards of measurement for drugs and nutrients such as vitamins.

INTERPRETER, COMPUTER—Computer-language translator that translates a group of source statements for immediate execution rather than waiting as a compiler does.

INTESTINAL JUICES—Digestive enzymes such as amylase and lipase that are secreted by glands in the small intestine.

INTESTINE, LARGE—Final segment of the digestive tract. Waste is collected here, and normally some of its water is absorbed before elimination.

INTESTINE, SMALL—Segment of the digestive tract between the stomach and the large intestine. Digestion is completed here and the nutrients are absorbed into the bloodstream.

INTOXICATION, FOODBORNE—Poisoning caused by the ingestion of a substance that is toxic, e.g., excessive alcohol, bacteria, or mercury in contaminated fish. See also **infection, foodborne.**

INULIN—**Polysaccharide** in which each molecule is composed of molecules of fructose.

INVENTORY—Physical count of the total number of each item present in an establishment's storerooms. Once the total and the price for each are known, the dollar value of everything can easily be computed.

INVENTORY BOOK—Inventory record that can be used instead of inventory sheets. The main difference is that the items are listed once, and the quantities and values are listed at periodic intervals.

INVENTORY, BOOK—See **book inventory.**

INVENTORY CERTIFICATE—Written statement that describes an establishment's inventory. It is given by management to auditors during the audit process.

INVENTORY CONSUMPTION RECORD—Form listing all the types of liquors sold by an establishment along with the previous inventory and additions during the period. When one subtracts the current inventory, the result is the amount used during the period.

INVENTORY, CONTINUOUS—See **continuous inventory.**

INVENTORY CONTROL—Control of merchandise on hand with records and other accounting means, as well as the physical security of the goods themselves.

INVENTORY CONTROL CLERK—Employee with keys to the storeroom who ensures that all receipts and issues are for legitimate purposes and are properly recorded.

INVENTORY OVER—Actual inventory exceeds the **book inventory.** This is caused by a mistake in the records. Contrast **inventory short.**

INVENTORY PROFIT—Increase in the value of goods in the storeroom created by rising prices in the open market.

INVENTORY, RETAIL METHOD—See **retail method of inventory.**

INVENTORY SHEETS—Columnar sheets on which inventories are recorded. There are columns on each page for lists of items, quantity, cost of each, and the total value. Compare **inventory book.**

INVENTORY SHORT—**Book inventory** exceeds the actual inventory. Contrast **inventory over.**

INVENTORY TEST-CHECKS—Irregularly timed check on certain stored items to compare the number actually on hand to that supposedly on hand according to the **bin cards.**

INVENTORY TEST SHEET—Form used to reconcile differences between the amounts of goods available according to the books and the actual amounts on hand according to inventory.

INVENTORY TURNOVER—Estimated number of times each month that the total volume of goods in the supply room is used up. It is calculated by dividing food cost for the month by the average inventory.

INVENTORY VARIATION—Difference between the inventory at the beginning of an accounting period and that at its end.

INVERTASE—Enzyme that splits the **disaccharide** sucrose (table sugar) into its component **monosaccharides** glucose and fructose.

INVERT SUGAR—**Fructose** and **glucose** mix derived from hydrolyzing **sucrose.** See **invertase.**

INVESTMENT—To buy property or other assets that are likely to produce income in the future, either directly or indirectly.

INVOICE—Form that lists and describes goods ordered and their cost. It should accompany their shipment.

INVOICE COST—Final net price for a purchase after deducting discounts, as stated on an invoice.

INVOICE RECEIVING—Receiving technique in which actual goods received are compared with what the accompanying invoice says should be in the shipment.

INVOICE REGISTER—Business record in which invoices are listed in the order they are received from suppliers.

INVOICE STAMP—Rubber stamp used to print on invoices a short form that can be filled in by the receiving clerk and others as needed. The form can include lines for the date received, the quantity received, the price, and the date paid.

INVOICE, SUBSTITUTION—See **substitution invoice.**

IODINE—An element essential for proper thyroid function. Since many areas lack natural sources (which include seafood), iodine is frequently added to table salt during processing. Deficiency results in goiter.

IODINE VALUE—Chemical indication of the degree of fat's unsaturation. The higher the number the greater the unsaturation. See **fat, unsaturated.**

IODIZED SALT—Salt with iodine compounds added to prevent deficiency and the development of goiter.

IODOPHOR—Any iodine-containing compound that can kill bacteria.

ION-EXCHANGE RESINS—Resins that collect ions (as from hard water) and later release them under the proper chemical conditions. Used to soften hard water.

IONIZATION—The splitting of molecules into positively charged and negatively charged ions.

IRISH MOSS—Red seaweed from which **carrageenan** is derived.

IRON—A mineral essential to health. It plays a major role in the transfer of oxygen in the body, among other important functions. Too little can cause **anemia,** too much can cause **hemochromatosis.** Found in various foods such as liver and cereals.

IRON, REDUCED—Iron food additive produced by the reduction of iron oxide.

IRRADIATION—Sterilizing food products with nuclear radiation to improve their shelf life. The food does not become radioactive, although some chemical changes that may affect the flavor do take place.

IRREGULARITY—Any deliberate or accidental error in the business records.

ISINGLASS—Fish membrane used to clarify liquids such as beer.

ISLAND POSITION—Location for print advertisements at the center of a page and surrounded by editorial content. Such a position attracts more attention than most others.

ISLETS OF LANGERHANS—Parts of the pancreas that produce insulin.

ISOENZYME—Any combination of different enzymes with a similar function.

ISOLEUCINE—One of the essential amino acids. Rich sources include soybeans, other legumes, nuts, chicken, meats, and fish.

ISOLIMONIN—Substance responsible for the bitter taste of the navel orange peel. Contrast **limonin.**

ISOMERS—Molecules all with the same number and type of atoms but with them differently arranged. This sometimes imparts different chemical properties.

ISORIBOFLAVIN—A compound that interferes with the function of riboflavin (vitamin B_2).

ISSUING—Supplying food from the storerooms to the cooks and other production personnel, usually by requisition.

ISSUING PROCEDURES—Established procedures for issuing goods from the storeroom, i.e., when properly requested and accounted for.

ITALIC TYPE—Variation of a typeface in which the letters are slanted to the right. Used in printing to add emphasis and to set foreign terms.

ITEM POSITION—Location of an item on a list of several menu entries. The first, second, and last items commonly get the most attention, so high-profit items should be listed in these spots.

J

JAGGER—Device with a sharp wheel used to cut pastry.

JAM—Fruit that is mashed and cooked with sugar syrup to a thick spreadable consistency.

JAMBONNIERE—French; a braising pan for ham, specially shaped to hold and fit one whole ham.

JAPANESE ROULETTE—"Game" sometimes played in Japan of eating puffer fish, which is safe only if it is prepared correctly— otherwise it is deadly poisonous.

JARDINIERE—French; food preparation involving assorted herbs and diced vegetables.

JARRA—Spanish; metal or wooden jar used in sherry production, about 12 liters in volume.

JASMINE—Blossoms from several plants of the olive family; used to flavor various Oriental dishes and tea.

JEJUNUM—Middle segment of the small intestine.

JELLY—A gelatinous substance based on meat stock, or the combination of fruit juice, sugar, and pectin.

JERKED BEEF—Air-dried beef available in long thin strips. Also called jerky.

JEROBOAM—Oversize wine bottle that holds 104 ounces or four regular bottles. Also known as a double magnum.

JERUSALEM ARTICHOKE—Sunflower-family plant with a sweet edible root that may be eaten raw or cooked like a potato.

JERUSALEM MELON—Juicy melon from the Mediterranean region.

JICAMA—Tuber from South America that resembles in both appearance and flavor the Chinese **water chestnut.**

JIGGER—Standard measurement for cocktails equal to 1.5 ounces.

JOB ANALYSIS—Examination of the workload of an establishment for the purpose of deciding which positions or jobs should do which tasks.

JOB CONTROL LANGUAGE (JCL)—Language used to describe the job to be done by the computer and the steps needed to accomplish it.

JOB DESCRIPTION—Statement of the task an employee must perform in a given job.

JOB NUMBER CONTROL LIST—List of all the jobs that must be filled to staff an establishment adequately, along with the schedule for each. The jobs are numbered so that, when hiring, each particular slot can be filled with an appropriate person.

JOB ORDER—Order for a specific number of particular products. A cost sheet can be maintained for each job, on which are listed all the costs relating to it.

JOB SPECIFICATION—Statement of the qualifications necessary for a person to handle a particular job, including education and experience.

JOINT COST—Cost of equipment used to produce two or more different items. In calculating the costs per item, a proportion of the joint cost must be allocated to each.

JOINT PRODUCT—Two or more related items derived from the

same material. For example, both cookies and cake are derived from flour.

JOURNAL—Book in which business transactions, including sales and purchases, can be recorded as they occur.

JOURNAL SHEETS—Lined sheets on which all business transactions are recorded as they occur, usually in chronological order. This contrasts with account sheets, where transactions for each account are listed separately.

JOWL—Face meat of the hog.

JUICE EXTRACTOR, TYPE D—Accessory to a vertical mixer or a self-contained machine that grinds whole fruit, discharging the juice and desired portion of the pulp through a removable screen. Some hospitals also use it to extract juices from beef and liver for special diets.

JULIENNE—French; vegetables cut in thin strips.

JUNIPER BERRIES—Berries of a tree of the cedar family. The essence is used to flavor and season foods such as soups and stews, and in making gin.

JUSTIFY—To arrange the type and spacing so that lines of the text all come out the same width, except at the end of the paragraphs.

K

K—Abbreviation for kilo, or one thousand (1,000), as when defining computer storage capacity in number of bytes.

KABINETT WEIN—German; wine of high quality.

KALE—Cabbagelike vegetable consisting of loose, curly leaves. It can be boiled and served like spinach or added to soup.

KARAYA GUM—Derived from the *Sterculia* tree in India; used in food as a stabilizing agent.

KCAL-BTU CONVERSION—One Kcal equals 3,968 **BTUs.**

KEG—Barrel for beer or wine that contains no more than 10 gallons.

KELLER—German; cellar.

KERATIN—Indigestible protein in such animal products as fingernails, feathers, hair, and hoofs. It is used as fertilizer.

KETONE BODIES—Endproducts of the metabolism of **fatty acids** in the human body. Since they are oxidized slowly, overproduction can occur fairly easily and may lead to **ketosis.**

KETONEMIA—Presence of **ketone bodies** in the bloodstream.

KETONIC RANCIDITY—Rancidity of fats (as in butter) caused by certain molds that metabolize **fatty acids** into **ketone bodies.**

KETOSIS—Excessive levels of **ketones** in body tissues. Acidosis of the blood is one symptom of the condition. Excess production occurs, for example, when a person ingests too little carbohydrate in an effort to lose weight, thus burning up his fat stores at an accelerated rate.

KEYBOARD—Computer panel where the numeric keyboard standard keys and feature keyswitches are located.

KEY INDICATORS—Statistics, such as food-cost percentage, that reveal basic revenue and expense trends.

KEYLOCK—Lock on the keyboard of a computer that controls the cashier, manager, or training mode operation.

KEY LOGBOOK—Book that must be signed each time a person uses the keys to the storeroom. The time the keys were withdrawn and returned can also be cited.

KICKBACK—An illegal practice in which a supplier gives money or goods to the purchasing agent personally in return for his promise to buy those products exclusively.

KIDNEYS—An organ meat. The kidneys are the glands that purify the blood and produce urine. Although rich in nutrients, they are not very popular as food in the United States. Before cooking, they should be examined for the presence of kidney stones.

KILOCALORIE (KCAL)—Standard unit of energy in food. It is also called Calorie, spelled with a capital C. Confusingly, both as kilocalorie and as Calorie, each unit is equivalent to one thousand calories, the word spelled here with a lowercase c.

KILOGRAM—Measurement of mass or weight equal to 1,000 grams, or about 2.2 pounds.

KILOWATT-HOUR (KWH)—Unit of measurement of electricity consumption. One KWH equals the energy expended by one kilowatt in one hour.

KIPPER—Process by which herring or other fish is cleaned or preserved by drying, salting, or smoking.

KISSING CRUST—Crust of a bread loaf that expands over the pan's edge during baking. If multiple pans are lined up, it touches the crust of adjacent loaves.

KITCHEN CONTROL—Scheduling of employees and kitchen equipment so that the right amount of food will be ready at the right time.

KJELDAHL DETERMINATION—Procedure for determining the amount of nitrogen (usually as protein) in a food.

KNEADING—Process of mixing and working dough to improve texture and redistribute yeast cells, among other things; it is also a way to add more flour.

KNIFE REST—Small utensil on which a soiled knife can be placed so as not to stain the tablecloth.

KNIFE SHARPENER—Machine that grinds the cutting surface of knives or other sharp tools to a keen edge, usually by means of a spinning wheel of some abrasive material. The machine may be a self-contained unit or an attachment to some other machine such as a vertical mixer.

KNOCKED DOWN (KD)—Used to describe machines or equipment shipped by the seller in pieces or segments that must be assembled by the purchaser.

KNUCKLE—Ankle joint with its associated meat.

KOHLRABI—Cabbage-family vegetable with a bulbous end. It looks like a turnip and can be used in the same way.

KOJI—Enzyme derived from molds that **hydrolyzes** protein.

KOSHER—Preparation and service of food in accordance with Jewish dietary laws.

KREIS TEST—Test for the presence of rancidity in fats.

KRONA PEPPER—Red pepper much milder than cayenne. It is used as a seasoning.

KUMQUAT—Small citrus fruit with sweet-tasting skin and very acidic, tart pulp.

KWASHIORKOR—A particular type of malnutrition caused by an extreme lack of protein but sufficient carbohydrates in the diet. It is most common in children of one to three. The most visible symptom is a characteristic swollen belly. Contrast **marasmus.**

KWH-BTU CONVERSION—One **KWH** of electricity equals 3,412 **BTUs** of energy.

L

LABELER—Device that affixes labels to packages. Stamped appropriately, it can be used, for example, to date packages on receipt.

LABEL, GUMMED—Piece of paper with adhesive on one side, which must be moistened before sticking it onto a package. Various information is written or printed on the other side.

LABEL, PRESSURE-SENSITIVE—Label with an adhesive side that does not have to be moistened before application (as does a gummed label.) Since the adhesive is already sticky, it must merely be pressed against a package or other surface.

LABOR COST—Total cost of all employees who comprise the work force in an operation.

LABOR COST ANALYSIS—Determination of appropriateness of labor costs in an operation and, if they are excessive, where the problems lie.

LABOR COSTING—Calculation of the labor cost for each menu item by multiplying total preparation time by hourly wages and dividing by the number of servings prepared.

LABOR COST PERCENTAGE—Percentage calculated by dividing the cost of labor by the total amount of sales, then multiplying by 100 percent.

LACTALBUMIN—One of the main proteins in milk; part of the whey.

LACTASE—Enzyme that aids in the metabolism of lactose by dividing each molecule into **glucose** and **galactose.**

LACTIC ACID—Acid formed from **lactose** as milk turns sour. Also, in the human body during vigorous exercise, glucose metabolism results in the buildup of lactic acid in the muscles, which makes them sore.

LACTIC ACID BACTERIA—Bacilli that ferment milk sugar (lactose) into **lactic acid,** thus making the milk sour.

LACTIC FERMENTS—Interaction of **lactic acid** in milk (see **lactic acid bacteria**) with the gluten protein in flour dough in a kind of fermentation that helps to raise the bread loaf.

LACTOCHROME—Substance responsible for the color of milk.

LACTOMETER—Specialized **hydrometer** that measures milk density to determine the butterfat content.

LACTOSE—Disaccharide in milk composed of glucose and galactose; commonly called milk sugar.

LACTOSTEARIN—Glyceryl lactostearate, an emulsifying agent.

LADING—Goods that are packed into containers and shipped. See **bill of lading.**

LADLE—Utensil with a round bowl of any of several standardized sizes attached to a long upright handle with a hook on the end. It is used to measure and serve portions of soup or sauces.

LAG PHASE—First phase in **bacterial growth,** characterized by a delay in colony growth as the bacteria adjust to a new host environment.

LAGER—Beer that is stored to allow sedimentation and to improve the flavor. Most American beers are aged this way.

LAGER BEER—Light-colored, smooth, highly carbonated beer. Most American beers are of this kind.

LAIRAGE—Site where meat-producing animals are kept prior to slaughter.

LAMB—Lamb is a sheep less than twelve months old. The three types of lamb are baby lamb, which is milk-fed and less than six weeks old; spring lamb, which is milk-fed and up to four months old; and grass-fed, which is four months to one year old. Mutton is a sheep over twelve months old; it has a strong flavor. Quality lamb is well fed, finely grained, and has a pinkish color. Lamb variety meats include the brains, heart, kidneys, liver, sweetbreads, and tongue. USDA grades for lamb in descending order of quality are: prime, choice, good, utility, and cull. The basic cuts are as follows:

Baron: Cut that includes the saddle and two legs.

Breast: Portion of the foresaddle below the rib. It includes the spareribs.

Crown roast: Entire lamb loin, usually served filled with mashed potatoes.

Lamb hotel rack: Portion separating the plates from the rack by a straight cut across the ribs no more than four inches from the ribeye muscle.

Lamb legs, double: Portion of the hindsaddle remaining after the loin is removed. It is a tender but uneconomical cut because of the ratio of bone to meat.

Lamb loin, double: Anterior portion of the carcass remaining after the removal of the foresaddle.

Lamb shoulder, square cut: Portion of the foresaddle prepared by two straight cuts passing through the first rib to the fourth rib perpendicular to the chuck. This is an economical cut, with meat that is less tender than the legs or loin.

LANGOUSTINE—French; tiny lobster or prawn.

LANGUAGE, COMPUTER—All symbols, including characters, letters, and numbers, used in programming a computer, as well as the rules by which these symbols may be used.

LAPPING—A way cashiers may steal from an establishment by trying to cheat a customer with an intentional mistake and, when caught, "correcting" the mistake with money taken from another customer.

LARD—Rendered pig fat.

LARDING—Cooking lean meat with added fat so that it does not become too dry. Strips of fat are connected to the lean meat's surface with a **larding needle** prior to cooking. Also see **lardon.**

LARDING NEEDLE—Long needle with a grip at the eye end, used to hold a piece of bacon or other fat strip as it is threaded into the surface of a cut of meat during **larding.**

LARDON—Fat inserted into the surface of meat or fish during the **larding** process.

LARD SUBSTITUTE—Shortening made from vegetable oil rather than lard.

LARGE-SCALE INTEGRATION—Practice of placing hundreds of separate computer circuits on a single large component.

LARVA—Wormlike stage in the metamorphosis of certain animals and insects, e.g., the maggot of the housefly.

LASSITUDE—Pronounced fatigue and weakness that can be caused by anemia, malnutrition, or disease.

LAST IN/FIRST OUT (LIFO)—The money value of inventory in which it is assumed that the goods recently acquired (at higher prices) are used first. This is an accounting technique only and does not affect which goods are actually used. Compare **first in, first out (FIFO)**.

LAST PRICE—Latest price quoted by a supplier for goods offered for sale.

LATENT HEAT—Water vapor or humidity in the air that increases the feeling of warmth. Contrast **sensible heat.**

LATHYRISM—Disease that results when over 50 percent of the diet consists of chick peas. Symptoms can include spinal cord degeneration.

LAVER—One of the group of edible seaweeds.

LAXATIVE—Any substance that accelerates the passage of waste through the large intestine either by absorbing water, thus increasing the volume of waste, or by irritating the intestine.

LAYER CAKE PAN—Round metal pan with a straight wall of medium height that comes in a variety of diameters, used to shape and bake round cake layers.

LAYOUT—Tentative sketch indicating approximately how a menu or ad will look after printing.

LEAD—Toxic metal that is excreted slowly and thus tends to build up in the body if repeatedly ingested. Sources include contaminated food, industrial exposure, and the ingestion of lead-based paint or insecticides.

LEAD, ELECTRICAL—Connection over which electrical signals are sent, as in computers.

LEADERS—Rows of dots or dashes to connect related parts of the text, e.g., to connect each menu item to its corresponding price.

LEAD GLASS—The glass most used commercially. It is shaped by blowing molten glass into a mold and contains lead oxide.

LEADING—Space between adjacent lines of print in a menu or ad, usually measured in **points.** Too little makes a paragraph dense and difficult to read; too much looks awkward.

LEAD POISONING—Toxic condition of the body caused by the presence of excess lead. Symptoms include kidney and liver damage, inflammation of nervous tissue, severe colic, and muscular weakness. Effective medical treatment is available, but the disease may be fatal.

LEAD TIME—Time required for goods actually to arrive after an order has been placed. Lead time should be considered in deciding when to place an order.

LEAF TUBE—Nozzle for a cake-decorating bag or syringe with a V-shaped opening; used to make leaf-shaped icing decorations.

LEAKER—Can that has developed a crack or hole so that its contents can ooze out.

LEAKER SPOILAGE—Spoilage of sterilized food that occurs because bacteria have leaked through pores or cracks in the packaging.

LEASING—Renting rather than buying pieces of equipment. It can be an attractive option for establishments that lack the capital or borrowing power to buy all they need or for those who want higher tax deductions (the entire expense is deductible).

LEAVE BEHIND—Sales brochure or leaflet left by salesmen with potential customers at the end of a sales call.

LEAVENING—Fermenting bread dough with yeast; making it rise before baking.

LECITHIN—A fat that contains phosphoric acid and choline, found in such foods as soybeans and corn. It is an important part of cell walls in the human body and is involved in the liver's metabolism of fat. It is also used as an emulsifier, as in chocolate.

LEDGER—Book in which each account is kept on a separate page. All transactions regarding that account can be kept together in chronological order.

LEEK—Vegetable related to the onion but milder in flavor, often used as a seasoning.

LEES—Sediment that settles out of wine in the cask.

LEFTOVERS—Food not sold on the day it is prepared. More accurate forecasting can usually reduce this problem.

LEGER—French; light wine without much body.

LEGUMES—Beans, lentils, peas, and other seeds of leguminous plants. These vegetables contain high-quality proteins that include all eight essential amino acids. See **beans and legumes.**

LEGUMIN—Protein characteristic of legumes such as beans.

LETHAL DOSE 50% (LD50)—Amount of pesticide or toxin required to kill 50 percent of a given amount of insects or other animals.

LETTERPRESS PRINTING—Printing process in which the letters form a raised surface on which ink is spread and against which the paper is pressed. Contrast **offset lithography** and **gravure printing.**

LETTERSPACING—Amount of space between each letter in a word or between numbers; usually measured in **points.** More space makes words cover a larger area and also may make them more legible.

LEUCINE—One of the essential amino acids. Rich sources include cereals, legumes, nuts, meat, fish, and milk.

LEUCOCYTES—White blood cells; the blood cells that help the body resist infection.

LEUCOPOENIA—Decrease in the number of **leucocytes,** often caused by malnutrition, that weakens the body's resistance to disease.

LEUCOSIN—One of the main proteins in wheat.

LEVITIN—Protein in egg yolk that contains sulfur.

LIABILITY—An amount of money owed.

LIAISONS—Any number of ingredients, including eggs, butter and cream, butter and flour, starch and liquid, added to a soup or sauce just prior to service to enhance richness or consistency.

LID REMOVER—Special tool designed to remove the covers from plastic tubs and pails easily.

LIGHTEN—To add eggs, milk, or some other fluid to a mixture to make it softer, as in cake baking.

LIGHT WHIPPING CREAM—Cream with 30 to 35 percent milkfat.

LIGNIN—Aromatic substance in the cell walls of plants.

LIME GLASS—The most brittle glass used in foodservice. It is shaped by pressing in a mold, and is inexpensive.

LIME—Citrus fruit similar to lemon, but smaller and with a green peel, used to flavor cocktails or desserts. Because it contains more citric acid than lemon, it is more sour.

LIMITED LIABILITY—Legal responsibility to pay that is limited by law or by contract.

LIMITED MENU—Menu that offers only about six to twelve entrees in order to save on labor costs and food waste. Usually only the most popular items are included.

LIMONIN—Substance responsible for the bitter taste of the Valencia orange peel. Contrast **isolimonin.**

LINE—In baking, to mold a layer of dough along the inside of a pan. Also, to place foil, some other nonfood layer, or a thin layer of some food, along the inside of a pan.

LINE FEED (LF)—Automatic advancement of the computer printer to the next line of the printout. It is activated when the LF key is pressed.

LINE OF CREDIT—Advance agreement by a bank to lend a customer as much money as he needs up to an established limit. Also called credit line.

LINE PRINTER—Computer device that prints out an entire line at once rather than one character at a time. Speed is increased but quality is reduced.

LINE SPACING—**Leading.**

LINES PER MINUTE (LPM)—A measurement that indicates how fast a computer printer is.

LINGONBERRY—Small berry that resembles a cranberry.

LINOLEIC ACID—One of the essential **fatty acids.** It is not synthesized by the human body and must be included in the diet. Rich food sources include soy bean and corn oil.

LINOLENIC ACID—One of the essential **fatty acids.** It is synthesized by the human body but is enriched by diet. Rich food sources include soy bean and corn oil.

LIOTHYRONINE—Strongest of all the thyroid-gland hormones. It increases the metabolism rate; because of this it is sometimes used in supplement form in weight-loss programs.

LIPASE—Intestinal and pancreatic enzyme that breaks down **lipids** into their component **glycerol** and **fatty acids.** Lipase may also be produced by certain bacteria.

LIPIDS—All fats and related compounds (e.g., wax) that contain **fatty acids.** Lipids are found in all living cells.

LIPOCHROMES—Pigmenting compounds from plants. They are soluble in **lipids.**

LIPOLYSIS—Hydrolysis of **lipids** into **glycerol** and **fatty acids.**

LIPOLYTIC RANCIDITY—Rancidity in uncooked fat caused by **lipase** produced by bacteria. Cooking inactivates lipase and prevents this form of deterioration.

LIPOPROTEIN—Any compound composed of both a **lipid** and a protein.

LIQUEUR—See **liquors and liqueurs.**

LIQUEUR DE TIRASE—French; sugar solution added to champagne during bottling to produce a second fermentation in the bottle.

LIQUEUR D'EXPEDITION—French; sugar solution added to champagne during disgorging to ensure the correct degree of sweetness.

LIQUEUR GLASS—Bar glass with a short stem and narrow tulip-shaped bowl that holds three ounces. There may be a line at the one-ounce level for drink measurement.

LIQUIDATION—Conversion of inventory into cash through sales.

LIQUIDATION VALUE—Price of assets to be sold during liquidation proceedings.

LIQUORS AND LIQUEURS—The term *liquor* refers to a distilled beverage with a high alcoholic content. The term *liqueurs,* on the other hand, applies to composite alcoholic drinks made from a mixture of spirits and syrups.
Abricotine: Sweet, apricot-flavored after-dinner liqueur with a brandy base.
Absinthe: Green alcoholic liqueur distilled from wormwood and flavored with anise. Because it is toxic and causes brain damage, is outlawed in France and the United States.
Advocaat: Dutch egg and brandy liqueur.
Amaretto: Almond-flavored after-dinner drink made in Italy.
Amer Picon: Heavy, orange-flavored sherry originating in Spain.
Amontillado: Pale, dry, nutty-flavored sherry from Spain.
Anisette: Sweet aniseed-flavored liqueur from France.

Applejack: American apple brandy distilled from hard cider.

Aquavit: Colorless distilled alcohol from Denmark, Sweden, and Norway with caraway flavoring.

Armagnac: Brandy from Southwest France.

Arrack: Highly alcoholic Asian drink; also called "The original spirit."

B and B: Bénédictine and brandy liqueur.

Bailey's Irish Cream: Chocolate-flavored whiskey and cream liqueur from Ireland.

Bénédictine: Sweet, spicy liqueur produced by Benedictine monks in Normandy, since 1510.

Blended whiskey: Combination of several whiskeys of at least 80 proof and possibly other spirits as well.

Bourbon: Whiskey distilled from at least 51 percent corn. The best bourbons are aged at least two years in charred, white oak barrels. Bourbon has a sweet, robust flavor.

Brandy: Fermented fruit distillation, oak aged, usually bottled at 80 proof. The best brandies include **cognac, armagnac, and calvados.**

Cacao, crème de: Chocolate liqueur that is either brown or colorless.

Calvados: Dry brandy made of apple distillates in the Normandy area of France.

Campari: Reddish, very dry apéritif from Italy.

Canadian whiskey: Whiskey with a higher proportion of rye and a lighter body than American whiskeys; produced only in Canada.

Cassis, crème de: Black currant liqueur from the Dijon area of France.

Chartreuse: Greenish yellow herbal liqueur produced by the monastery of Chartreuse near Grenoble, France.

Cheri-Suisse: Swiss liqueur with a chocolate-cherry flavor.

Cognac: Brandy made in the Cognac region of France. Cognacs are distilled twice in pot stills and aged in oak for at least two years.

Cointreau: Brand of colorless curaçao, made from the peel of small green oranges from Curaçao.

Creme de Cassis: Red currant-flavored liquor.

Curaçao: Orange liqueur made from the peel of small green oranges from Curaçao.

Cynar: Italian apéritif made from artichokes.

Drambuie: Liqueur made from malt whiskey and honey.

Dubonnet: French vermouth apéritif with a sweet but slightly bitter taste.

Fernet: Bitter, herbal liqueur from Turin, Italy.

Galliano: Sweet, herbal liqueur with a slight vanilla flavor from Italy.

Gin: White liquor that has been redistilled with the flavor of Juniper berries. It has a pure, clean taste.

Grand Marnier: Cognac-based orange liqueur made from the same type of oranges as curaçao.

Irish mist: Irish liqueur made from Irish whiskey and honey.

Irish whiskey: Whiskey made from unmalted barley, wheat, rye, and oats. The Irish use a traditional three-distillation process to create this light, clean, barley-flavored liquor.

Jack Daniel's: Tennessee bourbon sour-mash whiskey made by filtration through sugar-maple charcoal. The Jack Daniel's distillery is the oldest in the United States.

Jamaica rum: Butter-flavored rum made by a double distillation process and aged in oak barrels.

Kirsh: Cherry brandy made in the area where France, Switzerland, and Germany meet.

Lillet: Bitter white apéritif produced in France.

Madeira: Fortified wine from the island of the same name. Madeira has a rich, caramel flavor.

Maraschino: Cherry liqueur made in Italy.

Marsala: Fortified, dark, sweet wine made in the Sicilian port of Marsala.

Menthe, crème de: Sweet, green or white mint liqueur.

Noyau, crème de: Almond-flavored liqueur made from the kernels of peaches and apricots.

Ouzo: Absinthe-type apéritif from Greece. It turns white when water is added.

Pastis: Licorice-flavored french apéritif similar to Pernod.

Peppermint schnapps: White, peppermint-flavored liqueur popular in the U.S.

Pernod: Licorice-flavored liqueur originally made as a substitute for absinthe.

Poire-Williams: Brandy liqueur made from Bartlett pears.

Port: Fortified wine originally made in Portugal. There are many types of port including white, red, ruby, or tawny. Most ports are blended and aged in wood.

Rum: Liquor created either by the distillation of the fermented juice of sugar cane or by extracting the sugar acid and making the rum from the molasses. Many countries in the Caribbean produce their own traditional rums. Rums may be light or dark.

Sambucca: Sweet anise-flavored liqueur.

Schnapps: White, grainy-tasting, hard liquor drunk in Northern Europe.

Scotch: Whiskey from Scotland. Whiskeys are usually blended, with at least 60 percent consisting of grain whiskeys and 40 percent consisting of a variety of malts from different parts of the country. Single-malt scotch whiskey is unblended and made entirely of malt whiskey.

Slivovitz: Plum brandy made in various countries of Central Europe and the Balkans.

Sloe gin: Liquor made with macerated sloe berries and gin and matured in wood.

Sour mash: Process in the production of bourbon in which residue from a previous fermentation is added to the new mash to reinforce the flavor and bouquet.

Southern Comfort: Whiskey flavored with peaches, oranges, and herbs.

Straight whisky, whiskey: Whiskey that has not been blended.

Tequila: Mexican spirit made from the sap of the mezcal, a type of aloe plant.

Tia Maria: Jamaican coffee liqueur with a rum base.

Triple sec: Refined form of Curaçao.

Vandermint: Mint chocolate liqueur made in the Netherlands.

Vermouth: Aromatized wine of over 150 varieties. Each vermouth is made in a slightly different way, though all are macerated for periods of between six months to a year or more. Some of the flavorings used to aromatize vermouths include bitters, camomile, gentian, vanilla, and citrus peels.

Vodka: Neutral spirit distilled from a wide variety of raw materials including grain, potatoes, sugar, beets, and molasses.

Whiskey, whisky: Spirit distilled from grain, including a proportion of barley malt. The spelling of the term in the United States and Ireland includes the *e*, while in Scotland and Canada it does not.

LIQUOR PRICE LIST—Form used only by the control office that lists all the types of liquor sold, the cost and sales price for each. The latter is calculated from the percentage mark-up.

LIQUOR RECEIVING AND ISSUES REPORT—Section in the **daily liquor receiving and issues report** regarding totals to date.

LIQUOR STOREROOM INVENTORY—Physical count of all the bottles of each brand in the liquor storeroom.

LIST PRICE—Price of an item as printed in a catalogue or other listing. The actual selling price is usually discounted.

LIVETIN—One of the proteins in egg yolk.

LOAD-FACTOR PRICING—Charging a lower price when demand is low to attract more customers, but a higher price for the same items when demand is high. Hotels, for example, often charge less off-season.

LOADING—Adding a premium to the price in installment sales to cover the added expenses involved in such sales.

LOAF PAN—Oblong pan with deep sides, used to shape and bake breads and meat loaves.

LOBSTER FORK—Small three-tined table fork with one long central tine for extracting lobster meat from the shell.

LOBSTER PICK—Table utensil with a long central tine for picking the meat from lobsters or crabs.

LOCAL RATE—Rate for advertising charged to local merchandisers. It is usually lower than that charged national manufacturers.

LOGANBERRY—Berry resulting from crossing red raspberry and blackberry plants.

LOGO—Distinctive symbol that identifies a particular restaurant and may express its theme, e.g., a coat of arms or a photograph of some part of the interior.

LOG-ON—Signing on of a cashier, clerk, or manager on an electronic cash register.

LOG PHASE—The second phase in **bacterial growth,** characterized by rapid reproduction and a huge increase in the size of the colony.

LONG-GRAIN RICE—Rice grains over six millimeters in length. It stays light and fluffy when cooked and is the best kind to accompany stews and other meat dishes. Contrast **short-grain rice.**

LONG-TERM CONTRACT—Agreement to purchase goods that will not be fulfilled until a future fiscal year.

LOOSE PACKING—Partially filling produce containers in order to leave room for shifting during transport. Such packing can easily cause bruising of fresh items. Contrast **bulge packing.**

LOQUAT—Small, yellow, plumlike fruit, similar to a kumquat.

LOSS—Amount by which the costs to an establishment of making an item exceeds its selling price.

LOST-TIME ACCIDENT—Accident that causes the injured person to stay away from the job to recover.

LOST USEFULNESS—Depreciation of an asset.

LOT—Any group of items, whether similar or not, that are purchased together in a single transaction.

LOW DENSITY LIPOPROTEIN (LDL)—Cholesterol with 89 percent lipid and 11 percent protein. It contains less protein than **high density lipoprotein** or HDL. LDL is considered more dangerous than HDL. Excess LDL is linked with the development of coronary heart disease.

LOW-TEMPERATURE STORAGE—Frozen-food storage at temperatures of 0°F (−12°C) or less.

LOW WINES—Spirits produced by the first distillation in a series of distillations of Scotch whiskey.

LUG—Shallow wooden box used to pack fruits and vegetables for shipment; contents weigh 30 to 32 pounds.

LUMP-SUM PURCHASE—Purchase of a set of different assets for a total price that is not broken down to the amount due each separate item, e.g., a complete set of office equipment.

LUNG FLUKE DISEASE—**Pulmonary paragonimiasis.**

LUTING—Sealing joints or surfaces with a claylike cement.

LYCOPENE—Red derivative of **carotene** responsible for the color of tomatoes. The synthetic form is used as a food-coloring additive.

LYMPH—Body fluid that conveys water, nutrients, oxygen, and so on, from the bloodstream to the tissues and carries tissue waste products through the "filters" of the lymph modes before returning eventually to the bloodstream.

LYMPHATIC SYSTEM—Network of vessels through which **lymph** flows.

LYMPHOCYTIC CHORIOMENINGITIS—Mild viral infection that can be spread by rodents or infected pork.

LYSINE—One of the essential amino acids. Rich sources include legumes, meat, fish, and cheese.

M

MACASSAR GUM—**Agar-agar,** a gel formed from seaweed.

MACERATE—To soften a food or other material by soaking it in a fluid such as water or milk.

MACHINE CLEANING—Washing dishes and other utensils with mechanical devices such as dishwashers. Contrast **manual cleaning.**

MACHINE LANGUAGE—Precise computer language that requires a **compiler** or **interpreter** to translate higher-level programs into machine language.

MACHINE SERVICE CAPACITY—Potential ability of a machine, whether purchased or rented, to provide service to an establishment.

MACHINE SYSTEM FOR RECORDING SALES—System used in many fast-food establishments in which the server places the customer's order directly onto a machine, which automatically records the price and computes the total. This contrasts with the manual system at more traditional establishments.

MACHUPO VIRUS—Rodent-transmitted virus that causes Bolivian hemorrhagic fever in humans.

MACROCYTE—Abnormally large red blood cell; a characteristic of pernicious anemia, which is caused by the inability to absorb vitamin B_{12}.

MADERISE—French; a darkened white wine with a woody character caused by exposure to heat and air.

MAGMA—Combination of sugar crystals and sugar syrup.

MAGNESIUM—Metallic element essential for the proper functioning of muscles, nerves, and certain enzymes. It is found in chlorophyll and is therefore present in green plants.

MAGNESIUM DEFICIENCY—A dietary lack or inordinate loss of magnesium, as may be caused by alcoholism or prolonged diarrhea. The chief symptoms are neuromuscular, with uncontrollable muscular contractions and cramps; heart rhythm may be affected.

MAGNETRON—Part of a microwave oven that converts ordinary electrical current into the high-frequency radio waves used to cook food.

MAGNUM—Wine bottle of 52 ounces, twice the normal size.

MAIGRE—French; thin or weak, used in reference to wine.

MAILLARD REACTION—Reaction that occurs when the protein in a stored food chemically interacts with the sugar, resulting in a brown color and a loss of nutrients.

MAIN DISH SALAD—Salad served as the main entree.

MAINFRAME—Computer's central processing element, where the arithmetic units, main memory, and registers are found.

MAIN MEMORY—Storage device in computers that acts faster but holds less data than the auxiliary storage.

MAINTENANCE EXPENSE—Costs of cleaning, adjusting, and repairing equipment to keep it in good operating order.

MAITRE D'—Short form of **maître d'hotel.**

MAITRE D'HOTEL—French; literally, the master of the house. In foodservice, it is the person in charge of the dining room.

MAIZE—British term for corn.

MAKEREADY TIME—Cost of labor and energy used to ready equipment (e.g., a pizza oven) for a period of service (e.g., the daily cooking).

MAKEUP, DOUGH—The shaping of bread or pastry dough into the form desired.

MAKEUP MENU—List of the various side dishes that will accompany an entrée for a banquet.

MAKEUP, PRINTING—Breaking up the typeset lines and illustrations into separate pages of the right length for the menu.

MALFEASANCE—Wrongdoing, as when an employee pilfers from the storeroom.

MALIC ACID—Acid found in many fruits such as apples and plums.

MALNUTRITION—Condition caused by an imbalance between what a person eats and the nutrients he needs to stay healthy. It can occur because of disease or an improper diet.

MALT—Grain, typically barley, that has germinated slightly to form the enzyme diatase, which causes the starch in grains to be converted into sugars during fermentation.

MALTASE—Enzyme that splits each molecule of maltose into two glucose molecules.

MALT EXTRACT—Mixture of **maltose** and other products that result from the breakdown of barley or wheat starch.

MALTOL—Bittersweet food additive used in the production of chocolate and other sweets.

MALTOSE—Malt sugar. A disaccharide in which each molecule is composed of two glucose molecules.

MANAGEMENT INFORMATION SYSTEM—Computer-assisted process of supplying management with appropriate information to help in decision making.

MANAGEMENT PROFICIENCY RATIO—Index of management's effectiveness calculated by dividing net profit after taxes by total assets.

MANCHETTE—Paper frill used to decorate the projecting bones of roasts or chops.

MAN DAYS—Total number of hours spent on a project by a group of workers, divided by the number of hours worked each day.

MANGANESE—Metallic element essential for the functioning of certain enzymes and the synthesis of protein, among other things. Best sources are whole grains, peas, and some leafy vegetables.

MANGO—Tropical pear-shaped fruit with an orange or yellow-red rind.

MAN HOURS—Total number of hours taken times the number of employees involved to complete a given task.

MANNITOL—Alcohol derived from mannose sugar.

MANUAL CLEANING—Washing dishes and other utensils by hand. Contrast **machine cleaning.**

MANUAL SYSTEM FOR RECORDING SALES—Sales checks and duplicates are written out by hand, usually by the server. This contrasts with the machine system.

MAPLE SYRUP—Syrup derived from sap collected from particular species of maple trees, especially black maple, rock maple, and sugar maple. The sap is very thin and is boiled down to produce a thick, sweet syrup.

MARASMUS—Progressive wasting away of the body in infants suffering from severe malnutrition caused by a lack of protein and total calories. Contrast **kwashiorkor.**

MARBLING—Thin streaks of fat running through meat. Marbling increases tenderness.

MARGARINE—Butter substitute made by mixing skim milk and refined vegetable oil (e.g., corn oil) and churning it.

MARGINAL INCOME—Amount of sales revenue minus the direct costs involved in producing the items sold.

MARGIN OF SAFETY—Amount by which sales revenue exceeds the breakeven point.

MARINADE—Acidic solution of vinegars and spices used to make meats more tender, moist, and flavorful.

MARINATE—Process of soaking food in a **marinade** to tenderize and flavor it.

MARK-DOWN—Reduction in the original selling price, as for day-old baked goods.

MARKET—Region in which an establishment's products and those of its competitors are sold.

MARKET COST INDEX—Form on which costs for standard items can easily be updated; useful in adjusting the potential cost percentage quickly.

MARKETING COST—Cost of attracting customers, then selling and delivering their goods.

MARKETING REPORTS—See **agricultural marketing reports.**

MARKET MIX—Variety of services (types of menu items, cocktails, dancing) and facilities (parking, decor, banquet rooms) an establishment decides to offer.

MARKET QUOTATION SHEET—Sheet on which items needed by an establishment are listed, along with the prices quoted from several leading suppliers. The sheet allows price comparison.

MARKET VALUE—Price agreed upon by informed sellers and buyers as fair for a given item.

MARK-ON—**mark-up.**

MARK-UP—Difference between the purchase cost and the selling price, i.e., the gross profit when the item is sold.

MARK-UP CANCELLATION—Reduction of part or all of the **mark-up** on unsold merchandise.

MARMALADE—Flesh, pulp, and shredded rind of fruits such as oranges, limes, and peaches, made into preserves by boiling with sugar.

MARMITE—In classic French cookery, a deep pot of any size made of metal or earthenware. A type of double-boiler is also called a marmite.

MARMITE A RAGOUT—French; literally, a stew pot or pan. In classic French cookery, it is a round pot with two loop handles resembling the modern sauce pot.

MARROW—Edible fatty tissue found inside bones.

MARROW SCOOP—Narrow spoon with a long handle used to remove the edible marrow from large bones.

MASH—Pulpy mixture of malt, various grains, and water. See **mashing, sour mash,** and **sweet mash.**

MASHING—In whiskey and beer production, mixing malt and ground meal with water to allow the starches to convert into sugars through the action of the **diastase** enzyme in the malt. Also refers to crushing foods such as potatoes into a soft pulp.

MASKING—Covering food completely, as with a sauce or frosting.

MASTER CONTAINER—large container that holds all the individual packages of goods going to the same destination.

MASTER RECORD SHEET—Form that lists all the bottles of liquor issued from the storeroom, the dates issued, and the label numbers. See **bottle labels.**

MASTER OF WINE (MW)—Title awarded in England to professional members in the wine trade after extensive study and an examination.

MATE—A tea from South America made from the leaves of a bush of the holly family. It is brewed like a **green tea,** which it closely resembles.

MATERIAL CONTROL—Provision of the right amount of raw materials at the right time for production, at the lowest cost possible for a given level of quality.

MAXIMUM QUANTITY LIMIT—Largest amount of a given item that an establishment needs and has room to store. The purchasing department should order enough so that goods on hand and new deliveries do not exceed this limit.

MAYSIN—One of the proteins in corn (maize).

MEAL MOTHS—Moths with larvae that eat dried flour, corn, vegetables, and other stored foods. The larvae spin webs around their feeding sites, making them easy to detect.

MEANS OF EGRESS—Passageway, stairs, or other space connecting the exit access, the exit itself, and the exit discharge.

MEASURING CUP—Cylindrical container with a particular capacity; clearly marked at precise levels to permit accurate measurement of ingredients.

MEASURING SPOONS—Spoons of standardized size, usually linked together in a set of five, for measuring ingredients in tablespoon, teaspoon, and half, quarter, and eighth teaspoon quantities.

MEAT AGING—See **aging of meat.**

MEAT CLEAVER—Cross between a large knife and a small ax. It is heavy enough to chop through bones and is used to cut meat and poultry.

MEAT EXTRACT—Substances responsible for the flavor of meat. Since they are water soluble, they may be leached out with boiling water. However, see **extract.**

MEAT FACTOR—Indication of the amount of real meat, not counting fat, in sausage and other meat products.

MEAT GRADING—Federal evaluation of meat on the basis of quality, conformation, and finish. Quality is judged on the basis of fat marbling, color, and absence of defects. In order of descending quality, the grades for beef are prime, choice, good, standard, commercial, utility, cutter, and canner. See also **pork grading** and **poultry grading.**

MEAT PACKER—Company that slaughters animals, cleans, and sells the meat.

MEAT PRESS—Heavy piece of metal with a top-mounted heatproof handle that is placed on food as it cooks on a griddle and holds it in firm contact with the surface, thus preventing curling.

MEAT PROCESSOR—Company that buys raw meat and develops it into products such as sausage or smoked ham for resale.

MEAT-PURCHASE REQUIREMENT—Calculated by dividing the expected number of customers by the **portion divider.**

MEAT SAW—Power-driven band saw used primarily for cutting steaks or chops from primal cuts of meat. It is also useful for cutting blocks of frozen food. It consists of a floor- or table-mounted base containing a two or three horsepower motor, a cutting table with movable carriage, and a continuous steel-belt saw blade that rides on two large cast-iron pulleys, one above the cutting table and one beneath. The tension of the saw blade is carefully controlled by means of a special adjuster.

MEAT SAW, HAND—Hacksaw used to cut through heavy bones and cartilage.

MEAT TAG—Tag attached to meat to simplify **control** of that item.

MEAT-TAG BOOK—Business record in which all the information from the separate meat tags is combined in one place. The information includes the meat-tag number, date of receipt, the weight, and cost per pound.

MEAT TENDERIZER, CHEMICAL OR NATURAL—See **papain** and **tenderize.**

MEAT TENDERIZER, MECHANICAL—Machine that tenderizes small cuts of meat by cutting the tough fibers and then compressing a set quantity together to form small steaks. It can also incorporate items such as onion, garlic, or cheese into meat and may be used to chop or shred lettuce, cabbage, potatoes, and the like. The machine consists of two intermeshing rows of disc knives set in a metal housing and covered with a safety guard with a slot through which the food is fed into the machine.

MEAT YIELD—Amount of usable meat yielded in a particular purchase once the excessive fat and bone have been trimmed away.

MECHANICAL OVEN—Gas or electric oven in which food is cooked on trays that move through the heated cavity on a belt or a wheel. Several round trips may be needed before it is ready to be unloaded. Mechanical ovens have a large capacity and are energy and labor efficient.

MEDALLION—Small meat fillets of various shapes.

MEDIA, COMPUTER—Physical means by which records are stored, e.g., discs or cards.

MEDIA SURVEY—Study of the effects of advertising through one or more media on sales and the cost per person reached.

MEDIUM—Any substance that is the means of transmission or growth of a microorganism or parasite, e.g., improperly cooked pork is the preferred medium for the **trichinosis** parasite.

MEDIUM SIZE—Printing paper, each sheet of which measures 18 × 23 inches (45.7 × 58.4 cm). See **paper sizes.**

MEGABYTES (MB)—One million computer **bytes.**

MELAMINE—Material commonly used for tableware, made from plastic, paper pulp, and color pigments. It is durable, machine washable, and has a good appearance.

MELEZITOSE—Trisaccharide sugar in which each molecule consists of two glucose molecules and one fructose molecule.

MELIBIOSE—Disaccharide sugar in which each molecule consists of one glucose and one galactose molecule.

MELON—Any of several types of large rounded fruits that grow on vines. Varieties include cantaloupe, honeydew, and watermelon.

MELON BALLS—Decorative round balls of melon flesh. They are about the size and shape of large marbles and are usually served as appetizers or desserts.

MELTING—Turning solid foods into liquid through heating.

MELTING POINT—Temperature at which a particular solid begins to melt and change into a liquid.

MEMORANDUM INVOICE—Temporary invoice filled out by the receiver of goods if the shipper neglects to send the regular invoice.

MEMORY, COMPUTER—Storage elements, including magnetic core or disc memories and semiconductor memories, used to store information for future retrieval and use.

MENU—List of foods available at a specific meal.

MENU BORDER—Plain or embellished lines used to distinguish special portions of the menu and set them apart from the rest.

MENU BOX—Section of the menu enclosed by lines to form a rectangular box. Boxes emphasize that section and draw attention to it.

MENU, COMPUTER—Video display of the various computer functions from which to choose.

MENU CONTRAST—Difference in darkness between menu print and the background paper. For example, dark print on light paper is easily readable; light print on light paper is not.

MENU COPY—Printed words used to name and describe items on a menu. Good menu copy helps sell.

MENU ITEM COST—Calculation of the cost to an establishment of a single portion offered for sale. The costs of the different recipe ingredients are totaled and the sum is divided by the number of portions made by that recipe.

MENU ITEM SELLING PRICE—Price at which an item is offered for sale. Calculated from the known item cost and the desired mark-up percentage.

MENU ITEM TALLY SHEET—Sheet on which all available menu items are listed, and their sales marked off as they occur. At the end of a given period, the marks for each item are totaled separately.

MENU MARGINS—Space to the left and right of the printed column in a menu. For best results, about half the width of the page should be taken up by print, the remainder left for margins.

MENU PLANNING—Determining which items should be put on sale by an establishment, based on an analysis of customer preferences in the market served, availability of raw materials, preparation skills of the cooks, and profitability.

MENU PRECOST AND ABSTRACT—Form used for **precosting** with columns for forecasts of customer choices, costs, and revenues, as well as the actual results for each.

MENU PRICING—Calculating what the selling price of each menu item should be, usually by multiplying the food cost for that item by an arbitrary fixed factor (e.g., 2.5 or 3), or by dividing the **prime cost** by a fixed percent.

MENU SEQUENCE—Order in which foods are listed on the menu. Items should be grouped according to types, such as appetizers and entrées.

MENU SPACING—Space between lines of **copy** in a menu. There should be enough space to make the writing clear. Also called **leading.**

MERCHANDISE—Items purchased by an establishment wholesale and sold retail to customers. Distinguished from items produced by an establishment from raw materials.

MERCHANDISE COST—Actual price paid by an establishment for items purchased for resale.

MERCHANDISE INVENTORY—Inventory of **merchandise** items.

MERCHANDISE RETURN—Items sent back to the supplier because they are defective or are not the items ordered. Unused portions can also be sent back for credit or actual sales income, e.g., meat bones and fat for rendering.

MERCHANTABLE LIFE—**Shelf life.**

MERCURY—Toxic metallic element found in some polluted water. It can become concentrated in certain fish (e.g., swordfish) and poison humans who eat them.

MESH—Crisscross pattern of screens, wire or plastic, that allows air flow but prevents the entry of insects. A good size is 16-mesh.

MESOCARP—White inner peel of oranges and other citrus fruits; also called albedo.

MESOPHILES—Bacteria that thrive in moderate temperatures, as contrasted with **psychrophyles** and **thermophyles.** Mesophiles account for most harmful bacteria.

MESSAGE, COMPUTER—Symbols or words intended to convey information.

METABOLIC RATE—Rate at which a living body burns up energy.

METABOLIC WATER—Water (H_2O) formed within the body from the hydrogen and oxygen atoms that connect during the oxidation of nutrients.

METABOLISM—Total set of bodily processes by which food and oxygen are converted into energy.

METABOLISM TEST—Laboratory examination used to determine the rate at which the human body "burns" food and converts it into energy.

METAL CURLS—Fine metal shavings that result when cans are opened with worn or defective can openers. These sharp pieces readily fall into the food, where they pose a hazard.

METALLIC—Term used to describe a sharp and pungent taste found in some extremely dry wines.

METALLIC INK—Ink that contains a powdered metal such as bronze, copper, or aluminum. When dried, it has a lustrous silver or gold appearance.

METALLOPROTEIN—Any compound in which a protein molecule is linked with metal atoms. For example, hemoglobin is composed of a globin protein and iron.

METAMORPHOSIS—Changes in shape and structure that many animals go through as part of their ordinary growth cycle, e.g., a housefly goes through a wormlike larvae stage (maggot) before it reaches maturity.

METHIONINE—An essential amino acid that contains sulfur. Rich sources include soybeans, nuts, meat, eggs, and fish.

METHUSELAH—Champagne bottle with a volume of 179 to 208 ounces, or seven to eight regular bottles.

METHYL ALCOHOL—Household alcohol that is poisonous when ingested. It is used to denature **ethyl alcohol** for nonbeverage use.

METHYLATED SPIRITS—Ethyl (drinking) alcohol that has been denatured by the addition of **methyl alcohol** and various color and odor agents.

METHYLENE BLUE—Blue dye that turns colorless when placed in a substance with no oxygen. It is used to test for bacteria in milk, since it will remain blue in the presence of the oxygen bacteria need to live.

METMYOGLOBIN—Compound responsible for the reddish or yellowish-brown color of meat when it has been oxidized, as during exposure to light.

MICROAEROPHILES—Bacteria that can grow in extremely small amounts of oxygen, as in sealed cans.

MICROBE—**Microorganism.**

MICROBIAL ATTACK—Invasion of a substance by rapidly growing pathogenic microbes.

MICROCLIMATE—Climate of any enclosed space, i.e., the humidity and temperature, inside a storeroom or even a package.

MICRON—Microscopic measurement of length applied to microbes and the like; a millionth of a meter.

MICROORGANISMS—Bacteria, molds, viruses, protozoa, and other microscopic forms of life.

MICROPROCESSOR—Small computer with the processing circuitry on a single chip.

MICROWAVE ENERGY—High-frequency electromagnetic energy; i.e., very short waves of energy that, when broadcast at food, make its molecules vibrate, creating friction and heat within the food that then cooks the food from the inside out.

MICROWAVE OVEN—Oven in which food is cooked by exposure to high-frequency electromagnetic radiation. Such **microwave energy** can cook small amounts of food in a very short time. Browning does not usually occur, but some models have special devices to achieve this.

MIGRATION—Movement of chemicals or microbes from one item to another with which it is in contact.

MILDEW, VINEYARD—Fungal disease that attacks vines in damp or rainy seasons.

MILK-ALKALI SYNDROME—Syndrome caused by ingesting too much milk (over one quart per day) while also ingesting alkalies (e.g., sodium bicarbonate to treat ulcers). Symptoms include appetite loss, nausea, vomiting, and weakness.

MILK CHOCOLATE—Blend of chocolate liquid, extra cocoa butter, milk or cream, and sweetening and flavorings. Often used for candy, whereas bitter chocolate is used for baking.

MILK, CONDENSED—Milk concentrated to about one third of its original volume by evaporation of its water content.

MILK DISPENSER—Self-contained refrigerated unit that holds bulk milk in 2.5- to 5-gallon containers at 35–37°F and dispenses individual portions through a faucet device.

MILK, EVAPORATED—Milk concentrated to about half its original volume by evaporation of its water content.

MILK, HOMOGENIZED—Milk in which the fat has been thoroughly blended so it will not separate out.

MILK, IRRADIATED—Milk that has been exposed to ultraviolet light to increase its vitamin D content.

MILK, PASTEURIZED—Milk that has been heated to kill any pathogens it may contain; nonharmful bacteria are not killed in the process. Contrast **milk, sterilized.**

MILK, ROPY—Milk that has sticky, threadlike patches in it; they are caused by bacteria.

MILK SICKNESS—Sickness that occurs after drinking milk from cows that have eaten snakeroot. Symptoms include appetite loss, abdominal pains, vomiting, and weakness.

MILK, STERILIZED—Milk that has been heated beyond the extent required for pasteurization, until all the bacteria and spores in it have been killed. The milk is itself changed in the process, since all the albumin precipitates out.

MILK, TUBERCULIN TESTED—Milk from cows that have been checked and certified to be free of tuberculosis. Often written as milk TT.

MILL—To grind cereal grains into flour.

MILLET—Cereal grains that are small and rich in fiber. Often they are used for food in poorer areas of the world, especially in Africa and Asia.

MILLING—Grinding wheat grains into flour.

MILLON'S TEST—Test to determine the presence of proteins in a substance.

MINCING—Chopping as fine as possible.

MINERAL OIL—Ingredient in many laxative preparations that interferes with the absorption of nutrients such as vitamins A and D in the intestines.

MINERAL SALTS—Salts containing inorganic minerals such as calcium, chlorine, phosphorus, and sodium.

MINICOMPUTER—Small and relatively inexpensive computer that performs business data processing tasks.

MINIMAX STOCK LIST—Record of the minimum and the maximum amount of each item that should be in stock.

MINIMUM LETHAL DOSE (MLD)—Minimum amount of a toxin required to produce death, although lesser amounts may cause serious disease or injury.

MINIMUM QUANTITY LEVEL—Amount of a given item on hand that should be able to sustain an establishment's needs until newly ordered quantities arrive. When this level is reached, it is time to order more.

MINIMUM STAFFING—Keeping labor costs down by scheduling the fewest number of people needed.

MIPS—Acronym for millions of instructions per second, the measure of a computer's speed.

MISBRANDED—False or misleading information on containers of food.

MISCHARGING—Putting a customer's order on both his check and another customer's check, in hopes of pocketing one of the two collections.

MISE D'ORIGINE—French; wine bottled by the shipper.

MISE-EN-PLACE—French; a large wooden board used to carve foods for large functions.

MIS EN BOUTEILLE AU CHATEAU—French; wine bottled at the Bordeaux château where the grapes were grown.

MIS EN BOUTEILLE AU DOMAINE—French; Burgundy wine that is estate bottled.

MIS EN BOUTEILLE A LA PROPRIETE—French; wine bottled by the shipper.

MISSING SALES CHECKS—When sales for a given period are tallied, some of the numbered sales checks issued may not have been turned in. If a **check number issue control form** has been used, the person responsible can be identified. Servers should be instructed to prevent missing checks, which may happen because the customer kept one, the server destroyed the wrong one, or any other of a number of reasons.

MISTELLE—French; apagado—a grape **must** fortified to an alcoholic content of about 15 percent to halt its fermentation. The mistelle thus retains much of its original sweetness and can be used to sweeten other wines.

MITE—Any small insect that will infest and multiply rapidly in stored flour, meal, and other foods.

MITOSIS—Cell division, in which one cell becomes two; it is the way new body cells are produced for growth, healing, and the replacement of old cells. The body needs continual supplies of nutrients to support mitosis by providing the substances needed for new cells.

MITRED CORNERS—Two lines that meet at a right angle. Used in menu printing to designate the limits of a section.

MIXED GRILL—Combination of several grilled items such as sausage, grilled tomatoes, and mushrooms.

MIXED INVENTORY—Group of the same type of goods that were purchased in different lots mixed together in the storeroom and used in random order. Contrast **last in, first out.**

MIXER-GRINDER—Machine that simultaneously grinds and mixes meats with other ingredients.

MIXING VALVE—See **water mixing valve.**

MOBILE—Advertising material hung by dark, almost invisible thread.

MOCHA—Chocolate and coffee flavoring.

MODE, COMPUTER—Recognized method of operation, e.g., **binary mode, alphanumeric** mode.

MODEL, MATHEMATICAL—Concept, object, or process stated in mathematical terms.

MODEM—Acronym for modular-demodulator. A circuit or device that allows two computers to communicate with each other over telephone lines. Modulation occurs as signals from the computer are encoded for the telephone system. Demodulation occurs as telephone signals are interpreted by the computer at the other end.

MODIFIED AMERICAN PLAN (MAP)—Room rate structure that includes the cost of some meals, typically breakfast and dinner, consumed by a guest during his stay. See **American plan.** Also, contrast **European plan.**

MODIFIED DIET—Diet deliberately altered from the one normally consumed, usually for health reasons.

MOISTURE- AND VAPOR-PROOF PAPER—Paper used to wrap seafood for storage.

MOISTURE CONTENT—Percentage of the total weight of any material, such as food, that is water.

MOISTUREPROOF—Any container material or seal that is unaffected by moisture and will resist its migration.

MOISTURE-SET INK—**Printing ink** with pigments that precipitate out of a solution into paper when exposed to water vapor. Since these inks are virtually odorless, they are used extensively in food packaging.

MOLD—Fungi composed of **hyphae** and that grow in furry-looking colonies. Mold infests and deteriorates food.

MOLDPROOF—Any material that does not sustain the growth of mold.

MOLECULE—Group of atoms held together in a particular structure. Each molecule represents the smallest unit of a given substance, e.g., sodium chloride.

MOLISCH REACTION—Test for the presence of carbohydrates in a substance.

MOLLUSK—Shellfish with soft bodies that are partially or wholly enclosed in hard shells of mineral composition; including clams, oysters, and scallops.

MOLYBDENUM—Metallic element essential in small amounts for normal functioning because it interacts with the enzyme xanthine oxidase, which helps control metabolism. Too much molybdenum, however, is poisonous.

MONOCALCIUM PHOSPHATE—Acid portion of baking powder that releases carbon dioxide by reacting with bicarbonate.

MONOGLYCERIDE—Any fat in which each molecule of **glyc-**

erol is attached to only one molecule of **fatty acid** rather than the usual three.

MONOPHAGIA—Eating abnormality in which the person wants only one type of food and shuns others.

MONOSACCHARIDES—The simplest sugars; composed of only single molecules (e.g., glucose) rather than aggregates of two or three molecules. Contrast **disaccharides.**

MONOSODIUM GLUTAMATE (MSG)—Chemical derived from combining sodium and glutamic acid, the latter being one of the nonessential amino acids. It is used to enhance the flavor of meats and vegetables.

MORTAR—Bowl made of marble, stone, metal, or wood, in which forcemeats or other mixtures are mashed, pounded, or ground with a pestle.

MOST ECONOMICAL PURCHASE—The best buy, which is not always the cheapest one for many reasons. In addition to concerns of quality and freshness, some products (e.g., meat) have a better net yield from one supplier than from others and thus are the most economical purchase.

MOST RECENT PRICE—Use of latest price on financial records for items recently purchased, even if older items of that type already on hand had different prices. This method is simpler but not as accurate as listing each group received at its different price.

MOTHER OF VINEGAR—Film of *Acetobacter* bacteria that grows on the surface of a solution as it converts the alcohol into **acetic acid,** hence vinegar.

MOTTLE—Menu printing that is uneven or splotchy in appearance rather than solid and uniform.

MOUNTAIN LAUREL—Honey derived from the nectar of this plant is poisonous to humans.

MOVING-TRAY OVEN—Oven in which food is cooked on trays attached to chains that move from front to rear horizontally.

The trays may be unloaded at the rear of the oven or, in some models, they return to the front on a different level.

MUCOR—Group of white molds that grow on food.

MUCOSA—Moist inner lining of the gastrointestinal tract and other organs. In the small intestine, for example, digested nutrients are absorbed into the bloodstream through the mucosa.

MUFFIN PAN—Metal pan with a series of small cups into which batter is placed for making muffins, popovers, and the like.

MULBERRY—Variously colored berries of different mulberry trees. They are more often eaten cooked than raw because of the weak flavor. Their scientific names: *Morus nigra* (black mulberry), *Morus rubra* (red mulberry), and *Morus alba* (white mulberry).

MULTIDEPARTMENT ESTABLISHMENTS—Establishments with more than one foodservice operation (e.g., a restaurant and a coffee shop).

MULTIPLE-DOSE POISONS—**Rodenticides** that must be ingested by rodents several times to kill. This is a safety feature in case a person or pet accidentally eats some. Examples are fumarin, PIVAL, PMP, and warfarin. Contrast **single-dose poisons.**

MULTIPLE-PRODUCT PRICING—Calculating the price of each of several different items produced by an establishment by considering the direct costs such as raw materials or energy and the proportion of total overhead assigned to each item.

MULTIPLIER METHOD—A handy rule of thumb to calculate selling prices to be placed on a menu. See **menu pricing.**

MULTIPROCESSING—Using two or more computers to divide jobs or operations to speed up their completion.

MULTIPROGRAMMING—Several computer programs handled at one time by combining their execution, as is done in most management-information systems.

MUSCARINE—One of the ptomaine food poisons. See **pto-maine.**

MUSHROOM—An edible fungus. There are over 38,000 kinds of mushrooms in the world, of which about three fourths are edible. Below is a listing of the most popular varieties.

Barigoule: Brownish French mushroom with a rubbery texture.

Beefsteak: This mushroom grows in North America, Europe, and the British Isles. It is large, fibrous, with a meaty taste.

Bolete: A group of edible mushrooms including cepe and porcino. They are native to Northern Europe and the Pacific Northwest, and have a nutty flavor.

Chanterelle: Trumpet-shaped mushroom grown in Europe. It has a fruity taste.

Cloud ear: Popular Chinese mushroom. It is brown with a rubbery consistency.

Elm tree pleurotus: Creamy-colored mushroom native to North America and the British Isles.

Enoki: Long, thin, white Japanese mushroom.

Field mushroom: Common mushroom that grows in fields. It is similar to the cultivated mushrooms found in stores, but has a stronger flavor.

Horse mushroom: Similar to the field mushroom. It has a double collar near the cap and smells of anise.

Matsutake: Popular Japanese mushroom. Related to the pine mushroom, which grows in the Pacific Northwest.

Morel: One of the best-tasting mushrooms, native to North America and Europe. It has a spongy head and can grow to be a foot tall.

Oyster mushroom: One of the most widely cultivated mushrooms, so called because of its fishy aroma.

Polypore: A group of edible mushrooms indigenous to Europe and North America. They grow to be quite large.

Puffball: Large, white spherically shaped mushroom with a subtle taste. It is native to the British Isles and North America.

Saffron milk cap: Subtle-tasting white mushroom that grows in North America and the British Isles. It releases an orange liquid when bruised or cut.

Shitake: Popular oriental mushroom cultivated in North America. It has a brown cap and a meaty flavor.

Straw mushroom: Popular oriental mushroom cultivated in North America.

Truffle: Much revered, pepper-tasting edible fungus that grows underground. It is closer to a tuber than a mushroom. Finding truffles is difficult and specially trained dogs or pigs are often used. The best truffles are found in the Perigord region of France and in the Alba region of Northern Italy.

Wood agaric: Also known as the "red-staining mushroom" because it "bleeds" when bruised or cut. It has a white flesh and resembles the field mushroom.

MUSLIN BAG—Bag made of cotton that can be used to hold various ingredients during food preparation.

MUST—Juice that has been pressed from grapes for making wine.

MUSTARD GREENS—Leaves of the plants that produce seeds for mustard. The greens may be used fresh in salads or cooked as a vegetable.

MUSTIMETER—Device that measures the amount of sugar in a liquid, e.g., in **must.** Also known as a saccharometer.

MUTE—French; **mistelle.**

MUTTON—Meat from sheep over a year old.

MYCOTOXICOSIS—Disease resulting from ingesting food containing **mycotoxins.** Also called mycosis.

MYCOTOXIN—Poison produced by molds or other fungi. If ingested, it causes **mycotoxicosis.**

MYOGEN—One of the albumin proteins in meat, accounting for about one fifth of total muscle protein.

MYOGLOBIN—Red iron-containing protein in meat that turns brown when heated, thus accounting for the color change in meat during cooking.

MYOSIN—Fibrous globulin that accounts for about 4 percent of muscle protein.

MYRISTIC ACID—One of the **fatty acids** in butter, lard, and other fats.

N

NAPERY—Tablecloths, doilies, and napkins, of linen, cotton, or synthetic materials; traditionally called table linen.

NARINGIN—Bitter-tasting **glucoside** in grapefruit.

NASTURTIUM—Bright flower of which both the leaves and blossoms are edible. They may be used fresh, as in salads, or cooked. The scientific name is *Tropaeolum majus*. Also known as Indian cress.

NATIONAL ADVERTISING REVIEW BOARD (NARB)—Organization that screens advertisements for accuracy, honesty, and the like.

NATIONAL MARINE FISHERIES SERVICE—Agency within the Department of Commerce that inspects and grades fish products other than shellfish on a voluntary basis, i.e., when asked by the producers. See also **National Shellfish Safety Program.**

NATIONAL SANITATION FOUNDATION—National organization that sets standards for the design of foodservice equipment and maintains a testing laboratory to check equipment (e.g., refrigerators).

NATIONAL SHELLFISH SAFETY PROGRAM—Cooperative program in which the FDA and state governments determine the regions from which safe shellfish can be harvested. Shellfish from other areas cannot be legally sold. See also the **National Marine Fisheries Service.**

NATURAL FLAVORING—Flavoring derived from plant or animal products rather than from synthesized chemicals.

NATURAL FOODS—Foods that contain no artificial additives for color, flavor, or preservation.

NATURE—French; **brut.**

NEBUCHADNEZZAR—Champagne bottle of unusually large size, with a volume of 520 ounces or 20 regular bottles.

NECROSIS—Death of some or all of the cells in an organ or a tissue, which does not immediatcly cause the death of the whole organism. Characteristic of parasitic infestations.

NECTARINE—Juicy fruit, a hybrid of a peach and a plum.

NEEDLE, LARDING—See **larding needle.**

NEEDLE, TRUSSING—See **trussing needle.**

NEGLIGENCE, COSTS OF—Expenses attributable to errors, mistakes, recklessness, or fraud.

NEGOTIATED PURCHASING—Type of formal buying in which the initial contacts and price estimates are established by phone to save time, and then decisions are later confirmed in writing.

NEGOTIATION—Discussion of price between buyer and potential seller in order to reach an agreed-upon selling price for an item or items.

NEMATODE—Roundworm parasite, e.g., *Trichinella spiralis.*

NEOMYCIN—Antibiotic sometimes used in food processing and also prescribed for humans for various infections. Excessive amounts can lead to abnormalities in the absorption of fats and sugars in the intestine.

NET FOOD COST—Cost of food purchased by an establishment and sold to customers in an attempt to earn a profit. Contrast **gross food cost.**

NET FOOD COST TO DATE—Sum of the **net food costs** for all the days that have transpired since the beginning of a new period.

NET FOOD SALES—Amount of gross food sales minus all sales allowances.

NET INCOME—Total revenues minus all applicable operating costs.

NET LOSS—Amount by which expenses exceed revenues.

NET PAID CIRCULATION—Number of copies sold of a given issue of a periodical; of interest to potential advertisers in deciding which medium to use.

NET PROFIT—Portion of revenues left to an establishment after all costs have been deducted.

NET PURCHASES—Costs of items bought, including transportation or other charges but excluding discounts.

NET SALES—Amount of sales revenue that goes to an establishment, i.e., excluding tax, discounts, and returns.

NETWORK, COMPUTER—Interconnection of computer points through communication channels.

NEURINE—One of the **ptomaine** poisons, from decomposed protein.

NEUROTRANSMITTERS—Chemicals (e.g., acetylcholine, serotonin) released from nerve endings that allow for the transmission of signals between neurons in the nervous system. Each is produced within the body using certain key nutrients (e.g., choline).

NEUTRAL pH—A **pH** of 7, which is neither acidic nor basic (alkaline).

NEUTRAL SPIRITS—Alcoholic spirits distilled out at a **proof** greater than 190, i.e., almost pure alcohol with virtually no other odor and flavor element.

NEWS RELEASE—Newsworthy material submitted by organizations or establishments to publications or radio and TV. This sometimes amounts to free publicity.

NIACIN—B vitamin important for the metabolism of carbohydrates. Insufficient amounts cause **pellagra.** Natural sources include liver, meat, and cereal germ. Also called **nicotinic acid.**

NICOTINIC ACID—**Niacin.**

NINHYDRIN TEST—Test for the presence of amino acids in a substance.

NIP—Miniature bottle of an alcoholic beverage.

NISIN—Antibiotic sometimes used as a food preservative, e.g., in canned goods.

NITRATE—Compound (e.g., potassium nitrate) found in many foods naturally. Nitrates are sometimes added, e.g., in curing meat. They are converted to **nitrites** by the body, which are potentially dangerous.

NITRITE—Chemical derived from the reduction of **nitrate.** In cured meat, nitrite interacts with **myoglobin** to form **nitroso-myoglobin,** which is responsible for the reddish color of the meat. An excess of nitrites can be toxic; in addition, nitrites can be converted, during cooking, into nitrosamines, which are carcinogenic.

NITROGEN TRICHLORIDE—Compound used to bleach flour.

NITROSOMYOGLOBIN—Compound in cured meat responsible for its red color; derived from **nitrites** and **myoglobin.**

NO-HOST BAR—Bar at a private party where each guest must pay cash for the drinks he orders. Also called **cash bar.**

NOISE, COMPUTER—Extra signals or other disturbances that can interfere with the proper functioning of the computer.

NONABSORBENT CONTAINERS—Trash cans, linen hampers, and the like with inner linings that will not absorb moisture from the items deposited inside. Such containers aid in preventing the spread of microorganisms.

NONABSORBENT FLOORING MATERIALS—Materials that

do not absorb liquids and are thus less conducive to the growth of microorganisms on the floor. Such flooring materials include ceramic tile, linoleum, and terrazzo.

NONCONTROLLABLE COSTS—Expenses that cannot be anticipated (as for repairs) and that are thus beyond the control of management.

NONFEASANCE—Failure of an employee to do an essential part of his job, e.g., when the storekeeper neglects to lock the storeroom after use. See **malfeasance.**

NONOPERATING REVENUE—Income not derived from an establishment's regular or main activities, e.g., interest income on money held in the bank. Contrast **operating revenue.**

NONPOTABLE—Water that is not fit to drink. Contrast **potable.**

NONPRICE COMPETITION—Competition between rival suppliers based on quality or service, not price; each charges the same amount.

NONPRODUCTIVE ITEMS—Items such as catsup, cream, and sugar that are served to each customer but not charged for separately.

NONPRODUCTIVE ITEMS CONTROL FORM—Form that lists nonproductive items, the total quantity of each issued per day, and the number of **covers** each day. The normal amount issued per 100 customers can be calculated.

NONRESILIENT FLOORING MATERIALS—Materials such as concrete and marble that can be used to cover floors but that lack **resiliency.**

NONSKID MATS—Mats that can be laid on damp or otherwise slick surfaces that will not slip, thus making walking safer.

NONWATER-CARRIED SEWAGE—Human waste not carried away through the plumbing system, as occurs in portable toilets. Such facilities pose sanitation problems and should be kept separate from foodservice establishments.

NORDIHYDROGUAIARETIC ACID (NDGA)—Antioxidant

compound derived from the creosote bush useful in preserving fat.

NORITE—Activated carbon used to remove coloring compounds from solutions.

NORMAL VALUE—Selling price shaped by economic forces over a long period; this may or may not be the same as the **market value.**

NOTATIN—Enzyme that oxidizes glucose.

NOTE PAYABLE—Statement that an establishment owes a certain amount of money to a certain creditor.

NOTICE OF ERROR CORRECTION—Form used by the receiving clerk to inform a supplier of an error made in an invoice or in the delivery itself.

NUCLEIC ACID—RNA or DNA, present in all living cells. RNA controls protein synthesis and DNA controls heredity, two absolutely essential functions. Nucleic acids are synthesized in the body from sugar, phosphates, purines, and pyrimidines.

NUCLEOPROTEINS—Combinations of **nucleic acids** and proteins found in the nuclei of all living cells.

NUCLEUS—Control center of all living cells; contains DNA and RNA.

NUTMEAT—Edible kernel of nuts.

NUTMEG GRATER—Small **grater** used to grind whole nutmeg. It is usually kept with the nutmeg so that it can be ground as needed; the spice soon loses its fragrance after grinding.

NUTRIENT—Any substance essential for the energy, reproduction, growth, or normal functioning of living organisms. Nutrients include carbohydrates, minerals, proteins, and vitamins.

NUTRITION—Study of food in relation to dietary needs and normal bodily functions.

NUTS—Many foods designated nuts are not nuts at all but **legumes.** Nuts are a fruit with a hard shell containing an edible kernel. Below is a list of the most popular types.

Almond: The fruit of the tree *Prunus amygdalus*. There are
   two types: sweet and bitter. The bitter almond is mostly
   used in pharmaceuticals. Almonds are grown in Mediterranean countries and in California.
Betel nut: The seed of the betel palm. It is used in Asian
   countries as a dentifrice and to aid digestion.
Brazil nut: The fruit of the *Bertholletia excelsa*. The nuts grow
   in a large coconut, which holds several dozen of the nuts.
   They are grown mostly in Brazil.
Butternut: The fruit of the *Juglans cinerea* tree, a member of
   the walnut family. It has a rich flavor and is grown in
   North America.
Cashew: The fruit of the *Anacardium occidentale* tree. The
   nut is kidney-shaped with a sweet taste. It is grown mostly
   in India.
Chestnut: The fruit of the tree genus *Castanea*. The nut is
   sweet and rich and is grown in Southern Europe and
   North America.
Coconut: The fruit of the palm *Cocos nucifera*. The fruit contains a rich meat and milky liquid.
Hazelnut: Also known as the filbert, this is the fruit of the
   hazel tree. The nut is very rich and is about 65 percent
   oil. Major producers include Spain, Italy, and Turkey.
Hickory nut: Actually a group of nuts, the most popular of
   which is the pecan. Hickory nuts are the fruit of a number of North American trees of the walnut family.
Litchi: The fruit of the *Litchi chinensis* tree, native to China
   but now cultivated in many warm climates. The nut has a
   soft shell and a soft, red flesh. Also spelled lichee.
Macadamia: Originally from Australia; this fruit of the macadamia tree is now widely grown in Hawaii. It has white
   flesh and a rich, sweet flavor.
Peanut: This nut is really a bean from the *Arachis hypogaea*
   plant. Major producers include North America, South
   America, Africa, and Asia.
Pecan: The fruit of the pecan tree, which is native to North
   America. It has a tart, rich flavor.
Pistachio: The fruit of the *Pistacio vera* tree. The nut is green,

with a delicate flavor. It is grown mostly in Mediterranean countries.

Walnuts: The fruit of the *Juglans regia* tree. The nut has a very hard shell, which grows in two halves. The nut is rich and creamy.

NYCTALOPIA—So-called night blindness, a deficiency of vision in dim light caused by a lack of sufficient vitamin A.

O

OAT—Grain used extensively in cereal products.

OATEN—Comprised of oatmeal or oats.

OBESITY—Condition of being severely overweight.

OBJECTIVE VALUE—Value of an item as appraised by independent experts, regardless of selling price established on the basis of cost and mark-up.

OBJECT PROGRAM—Computer program that is ready for execution.

OBLIGATION—**Liability.**

OBLONG—A menu printed along the edge of the width, rather than the length, of its pages. The menu is held and read sideways rather than upright.

OCCUPANCY EXPENSES—Cost of maintaining and using the buildings in which an establishment is housed, including energy for heating and lighting.

OCCUPATIONAL SAFETY AND HEALTH ACT (OSHA)— Federal law that established an agency to inspect American businesses, including foodservice establishments, to assure healthful and safe working conditions for employees. See **Occupational Safety and Health Administration.**

OCCUPATIONAL SAFETY AND HEALTH ADMINISTRATION—Agency set up by the **Occupational Safety and Health Act** that inspects American businesses for violations of health and safety standards, issues citations, and assesses penalties.

OCTAVE—One-eighth of a cask of sherry, 16.5 gallons.

OENIN—Food-coloring additive derived from skins of the purple grape.

OENOLOGY—See **enology.**

OFFAL, MEAT—Entrails and other internal organs cut away from the carcass after slaughtering, leaving the skeletal muscle.

OFFAL, WHEAT—Bran and germ separated from wheat when white flour is milled.

OFFSET LITHOGRAPHY—Printing process in which ink is spread over the image area on a flat photographic plate, transferred to a rubber surface (called a blanket), then applied to paper. Contrast **letterpress printing** and **gravure printing.**

OIDIUM—Powdery mildew or fungus that can infest grapevines.

OIL—Fat of animal, vegetable, or mineral origin that is liquid at room temperature. Oil does not mix with water but may be emulsified. The use of a variety of oils in cooking has been on the increase in recent years. The following are some of the more popular types.
Almond oil: Delicate oil with rich almond flavor. This oil spoils very easily.
Babassu oil: Derived from Brazilian pine nuts.
Corn oil: Bland-tasting, light oil extracted from corn or maize. Corn oil is often used for deep-fat frying.
Grapeseed oil: Light, pale oil with a slightly nutty flavor.
Hazelnut oil: Rich, nutty oil extracted from hazelnuts. This oil goes rancid very quickly. It is particularly good for use in salad dressing.
Neroli oil: Oil derived from orange blossoms; it is responsible

for their characteristic odor. The oil is used in candy and liqueur production.

Olive oil: Full-bodied, aromatic oil. The best olive oils are from the first pressing when no heat or water is used to extract the oil.

Peanut oil: Oil extracted from peanuts. Peanut oil has a heavy quality and a slightly nutty taste but is largely unassertive. It is often used in Asian cooking.

Safflower oil: Light oil extracted from safflower seeds. It has little flavor and is high in polyunsaturates.

Sesame oil: There are two types of sesame oil, light and dark Chinese. Light sesame oil is pressed from untoasted seeds and has a mild flavor while dark sesame oil is pressed from toasted seeds and has a very nutty flavor.

Soybean oil: Oil extracted from soybeans. It is a strongly flavored oil that is high in polyunsaturates.

Sunflower oil: Pale, bland-tasting oil pressed from sunflower.

Walnut oil: Oil extracted from walnuts. It has a smooth mild walnut flavor but spoils very easily.

OIL-BASED SPRAYS—Insecticide sprays in which oil is the solvent for the toxic compounds. These are preferred where water could stain or shrink materials or create a short circuit in the electrical system. See also **water-based sprays.**

OIL DROPPER—Accessory to a vertical mixer that meters salad oil into the mixing bowl at the proper rate of flow for making mayonnaise or other emulsions.

OILS, COOKING—Oils derived by pressing corn, cottonseed, nuts, olives, and so on. Used in cooking (e.g., frying), as a base for salad dressings, or to produce solid shortening and margarine.

OILS, FIXED—Edible **triglyceride** oils in a substance, as opposed to the essential oils that provide only odor and taste.

OILS, SALAD—See **oils, cooking.**

OKRA—Slender green pods from a tall Southern plant. Used mainly in soups and gumbo because of its flavor and its thickening properties.

OLD-FASHIONED GLASS—Short, squat bar glass, wider at the top than the bottom, that holds four to ten ounces.

OLEANDOMYCIN—Antibiotic added to chickfeed in order to increase growth. It is also prescribed for certain infections in humans.

OLEIC ACID—Most abundant of all the unsaturated fatty acids; found in butter and almost all other fats. See **fatty acids, unsaturated.**

OLEO OIL—Liquid portion of processed animal fat that can be used in margarine.

OLFACTION—Sense of smell, which provides most of the experience of the sense of taste; taste buds alone are weak and can barely discern fundamental flavors.

OLIGODYNAMIC—Metals (e.g., silver) in dilute solution that will kill bacteria.

OLIVE—Fruit of the olive tree, used either green or ripe. They can be eaten whole, pitted, or stuffed.

OMELETTE PAN—Heavy, shallow skillet with a long handle. It is ideal for making omelettes and should be used only for that purpose. These pans are normally not washed after use but rather cleaned by rubbing with salt.

OMOPHAGIA—Abnormal desire to eat foods raw.

ON-ACCOUNT PURCHASE—Purchase based on credit rather than immediate payment.

ON-ACCOUNT SALE—Sale based on credit rather than immediate payment.

ON CONSIGNMENT—See **consignment.**

ONE-STOP BUYING—Purchasing a variety of different goods from the same supplier rather than from several, each of whom specializes in a different type of item.

ONE-TIME RATE—Rate charged for the single appearance of one ad; relatively expensive because there are no quantity discounts.

ON HAND—Goods that are already on the premises, immediately available for use.

ON-HAND INVENTORY—Physical count of the number of each item actually on the premises.

ONION—Edible stalks or bulbous roots of a lily-family plant. Used raw in salads and sandwiches; cooked to provide seasoning to many foods and dishes.

ONION SLICER—Machine especially designed to slice onion rings.

ON-LINE SYSTEM—Central computer-controlled operation of terminals, files, and other auxiliary devices.

ON-PAGE COUPON—Discount coupon included in an advertisement.

OOLONG TEA—A type of tea that is partially fermented.

OOTHECA—Capsule in which cockroach eggs are deposited (25–30 each). Cardboard cartons, burlap sacks, and other packaging materials should be checked for their presence upon receipt of goods, before storage.

OPACITY—Quality of menu paper that prevents the reader from seeing through the sheet to the print on the opposite side or to the next page. Generally, thin paper has less opacity. Contrast **show-through.**

OPAQUE INK—Ink through which a viewer cannot see, i.e., nontransparent. The opposite of transparent ink.

OPEN BAR—Bar at a function where the price of the ticket entitles the guest to all the beverages he wishes at no extra charge.

OPENING INVENTORY—Amount of goods on hand at the beginning of a given period.

OPEN MARKET PURCHASING—Procedure in which the purchasing agent selects several suppliers of a given item, compares their prices, and buys from the one with the best deal. Contrast **sealed bid purchasing, cost-plus purchasing,** and **co-op purchasing.**

OPEN STOCK—Food or beverage items stored in the kitchen or other production areas for use in the near future.

OPEN STOCK INVENTORY—Inventory taken on open stock, i.e., food items in the kitchen or other areas where they have been partially used or are about to be used. The total value should be added to that of the **food storeroom inventory.**

OPERATING MARGIN OF PROFIT RATIO—**Operating ratio.**

OPERATING RATIO—Ratio of net profit before taxes to net sales. Higher numbers indicate greater profitability.

OPERATING REVENUE—Income from an establishment's principal activities, i.e., selling food and drink, as opposed to **nonoperating revenue.**

OPERATING SYSTEM—Part of the computer's programming that controls and schedules other functions such as assigning file specifications, input/output control, and task scheduling.

OPPORTUNITY COSTS—Dollar figure equivalent to the potential profits given up by deciding not to take advantage of an opportunity.

OPTICAL CHARACTER RECOGNITION (OCR)—Input device that converts text printed in a special type style to computer-readable binary information.

OPTICAL READER TERMINAL—Computer terminal with a special input device that bypasses the manual input process by using light to scan existing forms of information. See **optical character recognition.**

ORANGE B—Food-coloring additive used in hot dogs. Tests with animals show that it is a carcinogen.

ORANGE BITTERS—Combination of orange flavoring and bitter herbs, used to flavor cocktails.

ORDER BOOK—Book that represents the master list of all orders placed by an establishment. For each entry, the date, supplier's name, name of the item, amount ordered, and quoted price should be listed. When the goods are received later, the date should be listed as a way of closing out the order.

ORDER CLERK—Employee in the kitchen who receives room service orders over the phone.

ORDER FORMS—Sheets in the order book that list food orders.

ORDER HOLDER—Clipping device that holds servers' orders or duplicates while the order is being prepared.

ORGANIC CHEMICALS—Chemicals found in living tissues. As a general rule, most molecules that contain carbon are organic.

ORGANIC FOODS—Foods grown with only natural fertilizers, e.g., compost or manure, and not treated with synthetic chemical pesticides.

ORGANISM—A single living plant or animal.

ORGAN MEATS—**Variety meats.**

ORGANOLEPTIC EXAMINATION—Judging beer, wine, and spirit quality with the sensory organs of sight, taste, and smell.

ORGANOPHOSPHOROUS—Chemical used in many pesticides, especially those for houseflies.

ORGEAT—Syrup made by adding almond or orange flavoring to barley water. It is used in cocktails.

ORIENTAL COCKROACH—One of the three principal varieties that infest foodservice establishments. It is about an inch long with a dark brown, shiny color. See **cockroaches.**

ORNAMENTAL RULE—Embellished line on a menu, as with curly or wavy ornamentation. See **rules.**

ORNITHOSIS—Viral disease found in poultry (e.g., turkeys) and wild birds (e.g., pigeons). Transmitted to humans, it causes symptoms resembling pneumonia.

ORTHOPHENYL PHENOL—Chemical used to inhibit mold growth on fruit after harvesting.

OSMOTIC PRESSURE—The ability of a solution to attract water molecules across a membrane.

OSMOPHILIC YEASTS—Yeasts that can grow under the high **osmotic pressure** conditions found in foods with high concentrations of salts and sugars.

OSSEIN—Substances in bone that convert to gelatin in boiling water.

OSTEOMALACIA—Bone disorder caused by inadequate vitamin D; bones become soft because of the loss of calcium.

OUTBREAK—Sudden rise in the incidence of a disease, especially when two or more people in the same group develop the same foodborne illness from eating the same contaminated food.

OUTGO—Expenditure or payment.

OUTLAY—Making a payment (or agreeing to make one) in return for goods or services.

OUTLINE TYPE—Menu printing type in which the main body of each letter is surrounded by a line for emphasis. See **special type.**

OVALBUMIN—Main albumin protein in egg white.

OVEN—Basically a heated, insulated box used for cooking. It may be classified as a roast, bake, or general-purpose oven depending on its shape and size. It may contain a single cooking compartment, or they may be stacked two, three, or four high. Some bake ovens have a steam-injection unit to produce crispy crusts. See **convection oven.**

OVERBUYING—Buying more food than is currently needed by an establishment, usually to take advantage of a quantity discount. Storage costs, deterioration over time, and other storing problems might erase the cost benefit.

OVERCURRENT DEVICE—Fuse or circuit breaker that protects a circuit from an excess of electricity, which can cause a fire.

OVEREXTRACTED—Coffee that has been in contact with coffee grinds for too long, resulting in too strong a flavor. Contrast **underextracted.**

OVERHANG COVER—Menu cover that is longer and wider than the pages within. Contrast **flush cover.**

OVERHEAD—Costs that affect the establishment as a whole (e.g., heating, insurance) and cannot be assigned to any single department.

OVER INVENTORY—See **inventory over.**

OVERLOADING OF REFRIGERATION UNIT—See **refrigerated storeroom overloading.**

OVERORDERING—**Overbuying.**

OVERPRINTING—Printing a second time on an area of the menu that has already been printed on once, to add colors or stamping, such as emblems or seals.

OVERPRODUCTION— Preparation of more food than can be sold that day. The excess can in some cases be stored overnight and sold later; in other cases it becomes waste.

OVERPROOF—Spirits with over 100 proof, i.e., over 50 percent alcohol.

OVERSTAFFING—Keeping more employees on the payroll than are actually needed to get the job done. Overstaffing obviously hurts the profitability of the operation.

OVERTIME COSTS—Costs incurred when employees work past their scheduled time. Overtime should generally be avoided whenever possible, since the rate of pay is usually 50 percent higher than straight time.

OVERTIME REPORT—Control form used by a supervisor to explain how much overtime he or she authorized, why it was done, and the period in which it occurred.

OXALIC ACID—Substance found in small amounts in chocolate, spinach, and rhubarb. Large amounts are poisonous.

OXIDASES—Enzymes that oxidize other chemicals by removing hydrogen from them and using it to make water.

OXIDATION—State that occurs when a molecule gains oxygen or loses hydrogen. The opposite of **reduction.** Such chemical reactions may lead to food deterioration.

OXYMYOGLOBIN—Combination of oxygen and myoglobin (muscle protein) that is responsible for the bright-red color of meat exposed to air. Meat not so exposed is a darker red.

OXYNTIC CELLS—The stomach glands that produce hydrochloric acid for digestion.

OYSTER KNIFE—Knife with a thin, strong, sharp, pointed blade, used to pry open oyster shells.

OZONE—Gas in which each molecule is composed of three oxygen atoms. A powerful antiseptic, it is often used to preserve food.

P

PACKAGE, COMPUTER—Generalized programs and procedures for the performance of data-processing operations to insure that they are applicable across company lines, as compared to programs designed for a particular job.

PACKAGE INSERT—Any promotional material or instructions included in a package of goods by the producer or distributor.

PACK DATE—Date when a food product was processed and packaged. This date should be indicated on the package in some way.

PACKING SLIP—Document that accompanies goods when they are shipped that describes the nature and number of those goods.

PADDLE—**Flat beater.**

PALETTE KNIFE—Hand tool with a thin blade and rounded tip used to pick up dough or spread icing; a narrow **spatula.**

PALLET—Low-set, portable stand on which supplies can be stacked to keep them off the floor.

PALMITIC ACID—Saturated **fatty acid** that occurs in many animal and plant triglycerides.

PALM OIL—Oil derived from the *Elaeis guineensis* plant; used in cooking and in margarine production.

PAMPHLET STITCHING—Binding folded sheets of a menu together with loops of thread that run from outside to inside, right through the seam.

PANCREAS—Gland containing the cells that secrete various digestive enzymes including insulin, the hormone that controls carbohydrate metabolism.

PANCREATIN—Digestive aid that contains enzymes derived from the pancreas of animals.

PAN FILE—Rack-and-slide assembly used to hold various sizes of hotel pans by their rims in a refrigerator or hot-food cabinet.

PAN FRYING—Cooking with a little fat in a hot uncovered skillet.

PANIER—Wickerware basket with a single long handle used to hold food.

PAN SCRAPER—Hand tool with a broad flat blade, useful for scraping waste material from griddle tops.

PANTOTHENIC ACID—B vitamin needed to metabolize fats and carbohydrates. Since it is found in all plant and animal tissues, deficiency is unlikely. Especially rich sources include eggs, organ meats, certain cereals and vegetables.

PANTOYLTAURINE—An acid that blocks utilization of **pantothenic acid,** thus causing dizziness, appetite loss, and irregular heartbeat.

PAPAIN—Enzyme derived from the **papaya** plant that breaks up the protein chains in meat and is used as a tenderizer.

PAPAW—Fruit from a tree related to the custard-apple. It has a mild flavor.

PAPAYA—Tropical fruit with a yellowish-orange color. It looks like a melon but is grown on trees. The flesh is used raw or cooked; the juice is used in exotic cocktails.

PAPER, BLOODPROOF—Strong, heavy paper coated with wax to prevent meat juice from seeping through.

PAPER FOLDING—Folding a large single sheet that is printed with the copy for a menu into several smaller pages. For example, a single 10 × 8 inch sheet can be folded in half to make two 5 × 8 inch sheets, which, if both sides are printed, makes four printed pages.

PAPER, FROZEN-FOOD—Special wax or plastic paper, usually **glassine,** used as the inner liner of packages for frozen foods. It is highly resistant to **cold cracking** and to the transmission of water vapor.

PAPER, GLASSINE—See **glassine.**

PAPER, MEAT-INTERLEAVING—Paper sheets that are placed between adjacent slices or cuts of meat to prevent discoloration and loss of juice.

PAPER PROFIT—Projected future profit that has not yet been realized.

PAPER SIZES—Menus can be printed on paper of various dimensions. Sometimes a large sheet is printed and then folded or cut to make several smaller pages. See **crown, demy, double crown, double demy, foolscap, imperial, medium,** and **royal sizes.**

PAPER TYPES, MENU—See **bond paper, book paper, bristol paper, coated paper, cover paper, index paper, tag paper,** and **text paper.**

PARA-AMINOBENZOIC ACID (PABA)—Vitamin of the B-complex that aids in the metabolism of proteins and in the formation of red blood cells. Deficiency has been linked to graying hair and high blood pressure. It is found in brewer's yeast, wheat germ, and yogurt; it is also partially synthesized by the body.

PARABEN, METHYL—A food preservative.

PARABEN, PROPYL—A food preservative.

PARAGONIMUS WESTERMANI—Parasite, a lung fluke, that causes **pulmonary paragonimiasis.**

PARASITE—Harmful organism that dwells in or on a host, drawing nutrients from it and thus weakening it.

PARATHORMONE—Hormone secreted by the parathyroid glands that controls the level of calcium in the body; oversecretion leads to calcium loss from the bones.

PARBOILING—Cooking food in boiling water until it is partially done; similar to **blanching,** but the item is in the water for a longer period of time.

PARCHING—Removing moisture with heat.

PARE—To remove peel, rind, or skin from vegetable or fruit, usually with a small knife known as a **paring knife.**

PARFAIT SPOON—**Iced-tea spoon.**

PARING KNIFE—Knife with a 2.5 to 3.5 inch blade used to peel fruits and vegetables.

PARISIENNE SCOOP—Instrument used to make melon balls from cantaloupe, honeydew, and the like.

PARMENTIER, ANTOINE-AUGUSTE (1737–1813)—French agronomist who wrote many works on food. One of his principal achievements was to introduce potatoes into the human food supply. Many potato dishes still bear his name.

PARSNIP—Root vegetable that is white, long, and thick. It can be served alone or as an ingredient in main dishes and soups.

PAR STOCK—Maximum amount of an item that should normally be on hand. When ordering new supplies, the amount ordered should be enough so that when it is added to existing inventory the total reaches the par level.

PARTIAL BLIND RECEIVING—Combination of **invoice receiving** and **blind receiving.** The receiving clerk gets a partially filled-out invoice or purchase order with the names of items listed but the amounts missing. He must count or weigh the items and complete the form.

PASS, COMPUTER—Complete machine run in batch processing of data.

PASSION FRUIT—Rounded purple-skinned fruit with yellowish flesh.

PASSIVE IMMUNITY—See **immunity, passive.**

PASTA—Paste made from hard wheat flour, rolled into various shapes and sizes. Popularized in Italy, pasta is high in carbohydrates and is often served with a sauce. The following are the most popular types.

Agnolotti: Turnover-shaped pasta that are filled with meat.

Ancini di pepe: Literally, peppercorns. Very small rectangular-shaped pasta used in soups.

Bocconcini: Literally, small mouthfuls. Tubular pasta one-half inch in diameter and one and a half inches long.

Bows: American egg pasta shaped like rounded bows.

Bucati: Literally, with a hole. Hollow pasta.

Bucatini: Hollow pasta similar to marcaroni but thinner.

Cannelloni: Large, hollow pasta served stuffed with cheese or meat fillings.

Capelli d'angelo: Literally, angel's hair. Very fine spaghetti-shaped pasta.

Capellini: Very thin spaghetti-shaped pasta, most often served in soups.

Cappeletti: Literally, little hats. Hat-shaped pasta served stuffed.

Cavatelli: Short, curled noodles.

Diali: Small, thimble-shaped pasta.

Elbow: Semicircular, hollow pasta in various sizes.

Farfalle: Literally, butterflies. Similar to American bows but not made of egg pasta.

Fettuccine: Literally, small ribbons. Wide spaghetti-shaped pasta.

Fusilli: Spaghetti twisted into corkscrew shapes.
Gemelli: Short spaghetti strands twisted together.
Giant shells: Large, grooved, shell-shaped pasta.
Gnocchi: Dumplings made from pasta dough.
Lasagne: Wide, flat pasta with rippled edges.
Linguine: Literally, small tongues. Narrow, thick spaghetti.
Macaroni: General term for tubular pasta.
Manicotti: Literally, small muff. Large, tubular pasta often
    served stuffed with meat or cheese fillings.
Orzo: Small rice-shaped pasta.
Pappardelli: Broad noodles.
Penne: Tubular pasta cut on a diagonal to resemble quills.
Rigatoni: Large, grooved pasta tubes.
Rotini: Wheel-shaped pasta.
Spaghetti: Solid, round, long, and thin pasta.
Tagliatelli: Similar to fettuccine but wider.
Tubetti: Small tubes, often used in soups.
Vermicelli: Literally, little worms. Very thin spaghetti.
Ziti: Literally, bridegrooms. Large, tubular-shaped macaroni.

PAST DUE—Payment has not been made within the time origi-
    nally agreed upon.

PASTEUP—Preliminary layout of the menu with text, photos,
    and other illustrations placed roughly where they should go, and
    with instructions provided for the printer.

PASTEURELLA TULARENSIS—Bacteria that cause **Tulare-
    mia.**

PASTEURIZATION—The use of heat to kill most of the bacteria
    in a product. Milk, for example, is pasteurized by heating it for
    30 minutes at 143°F (62°C) or for 15 seconds at 160°F (71°C).
    Some bacteria remain unless the product is totally sterilized.

PASTRY—Dough of flour, shortening, and water used for pie
    crusts, tarts, and the like. The term may also apply to all baked
    cakes, pies, and similar desserts.

PASTRY CRIMPER—Tool used to crimp the edges of pies, tarts,
    and so on. Also called a pincer.

PASTRY CUTTER—Instrument that comes in a variety of designs that is used to cut sheets of pastry dough into decorative shapes.

PASTRY KNIFE—Accessory to a vertical mixer consisting of a metal blade formed into a single loop. It is used to incorporate shortening into flour without overdeveloping the gluten.

PASTRY WHEEL—Small wooden wheel with a serrated edge that may be used to crimp the edges of pies and tarts.

PATHOGEN—Any microorganism that can cause disease.

PATHOGENIC—Able to cause disease.

PATTERN PRESS—Device with an embossed pattern used to mark the surface of a cake with a design that is then piped on with icing.

PAYBACK PERIOD—Time it takes for a piece of purchased equipment to earn or save enough money to pay for itself; calculated by dividing the total cost by the related income per year.

PAYDAY SPECIALS—Sales specials offered on days when a relatively large proportion of potential customers in the area get paid.

PAYSANNE, A LA—French; food prepared in country, farm, or peasant style.

PDQ's—Abbreviation for peeled, deveined, and quick-cooked shrimp.

PEACHES—Round, orange-yellow fruit with a large pit at the center. Used raw or in cooking in numerous ways.

PEAK DEMAND PERIOD—Period when energy use is at its highest. For foodservice establishments, this is normally during times of meal preparation.

PEAR—Fruit of the pear tree. Its distinctive shape results from a narrow neck and wider base. Pears may be eaten raw or cooked. They are not as popular as many other fruits in the United States, perhaps because of their gritty texture.

PEARLED BARLEY—Barley with the husks removed.

PEAS—Round seeds of a pod-bearing plant, available fresh, canned, dried, or frozen. They are served alone or in combination with other vegetables and foods.

PEBBLING—Embossing menu paper to give it a distinguished-looking rippled appearance.

PECTASE—Enzyme from citrus fruit pith that breaks pectin down to pectic acid.

PECTIN—Gel-like substance derived from citrus fruits and other plants that is used as a stabilizer and as the basis for jams and jellies. When combined with sugar and fruit juice acids, pectin forms a gel.

PECTIN, LOW-METHOXYL—Pectin from which methoxyl chemical groups have been removed. Since it can form a gel without sugar, it is used in low-calorie products.

PECUNIARY BENEFIT—Money value left from a business transaction after the costs have been deducted.

PEEL—Instrument used in bakeries that consists of a thin paddle with a broad blade and long handle; used to remove items from bake ovens.

PEELER—Piece of equipment that peels hard root vegetables with a lightweight spinning abrasive disc.

PEELING—Removing the skin of vegetables and fruits.

PEEL OVEN—Large bake oven in which loading and unloading is done with a **peel.** Steam injection may be used to give desired crispness to crusts.

PEKOE—Chinese black tea from young leaves.

PELLAGRA—Disease caused by insufficient **niacin.** Symptoms include skin inflammation and intestinal and mental disorders. If left untreated, pellagra can cause death.

PEMMICAN—High-fat, high-protein food concentrate prepared from fat and powdered meat pressed together into cakes.

PENTOSE—Any simple sugar in which each molecule has five carbon atoms, e.g., ribose.

PEPPER—Seasoning powder made by grinding the dried berries of the *piper nigrum*. Black pepper derives from grinding the whole berry; the milder white pepper is produced after the dark husks have been removed.

PEPPERCORNS—Berries of the *piper nigrum*, which are dried and ground to make pepper.

PEPPER MILL—Handheld device used at tableside to grind peppercorns into fresh pepper directly over food.

PEPPERS—Large hollow pods from **capsicum** plants. They may be served stuffed with meat and rice, sliced or diced fresh for salads, or used as a seasoning in many cooked dishes. Also called bell peppers, these are not related to **peppercorns.**

PEPSIN—Gastric enzyme that helps digest proteins.

PEPTIDE—Chemical chain of two or more amino acids of which proteins are formed.

PERCOLATOR—Coffeemaker in which water rises through a central column as it is heated, then sprays over the coffee grinds, extracting the flavor as it filters through back to the bottom of the pot.

PERFECT BINDING—Gluing the pages of a menu to the cover or to a special liner rather than stitching or stapling them together.

PERFECTING PRESS—Press that can print both sides of a menu sheet at the same time rather than separately.

PERFORATIONS—Holes in a package caused by piercing, chemical action, or other deterioration.

PERFRINGENS FOOD POISONING—Foodborne disease caused by the bacteria *Clostridium perfringens*. Symptoms include abdominal pain and diarrhea.

PERFUME—Fragrance or aroma of a wine.

PERICARP—Layer of cereal grain next to the outer husk; the source of bran.

PERIODIC INCOME—Revenue earned as a function of time periods, e.g., interest or rental income.

PERIPHERAL COMPUTER EQUIPMENT—Various hardware other than the computer itself required to do the work.

PERISHABLE—Any food item such as fresh fruit and bread that deteriorates quickly in storage and so is usually ordered every day.

PERLWEIN—German; a slightly sparkling wine.

PERMEABILITY—Allowing the transmission of gases and liquids, as in a container's packing material.

PERMIT—Certificate issued by the proper health authority that states that an establishment meets health standards and is authorized to serve food. May also refer to a certificate authorizing a person to handle food.

PERMIT REINSTATEMENT—See reinstatement of suspended permits.

PERMIT REVOCATION—See revocation of permit.

PERMIT SUSPENSION—See suspension of permit.

PEROXIDE NUMBER—Measure of the number of peroxides present in fat; it indicates how rancid a fat has become because of oxidation.

PERPETUAL INVENTORY CARD—Form on which a daily update of the balance of each item in the storeroom is recorded.

PERPETUAL INVENTORY MASTER RECORD—Single list of all items that have separate perpetual inventory cards, and the receipts, issues, and balances for each item.

PERSIAN MELONS—Large round melons grown in California that have pink flesh surrounded by a netted yellow skin.

PERSIMMON—Small orange or red fruit with a very tart taste, particularly when not fully ripe, caused by its large amount of tannin.

PERSONAL ACCOUNT—Credit arrangement between an establishment and an individual person, as opposed to another company.

PERSONAL PROPERTY—Assets that can be moved or consumed such as goods in a storeroom. Contrast **real property**.

PESTICIDE—Any chemical compound used to kill insects and other vermin.

PESTICIDE RESISTANCE—See **resistance, pesticide**.

PETIT-GRAIN OILS—**Essential oils** derived from the leaves or twigs of orange trees.

PETTY CASH FUND—Small amount of cash (often less than one hundred dollars) kept on hand for minor expenses that do not warrant a formal purchase order, such as office supplies or postage.

pH—Abbreviation for potential hydrogen, a 15-point acid-alkalinity scale in which 0 = extremely acid, 7 = neutral, and 14 = extremely alkaline.

PHAEOPHYTIN—Brownish-green chemical derived from chlorophyll and responsible for the color of cooked vegetables.

PHARYNGITIS—Inflammation of the throat caused by staphylococcal, streptococcal, or viral pathogens. Coughing can easily spread the responsible microorganisms to others, either directly or in food.

PHASEOLIN—One of the proteins in kidney beans.

PHASEOLUNATIN—Glucose-containing compound found in lima beans and other legumes.

pHB ESTER—Abbreviation for p-Hydroxybenzoic acid, a food preservative.

PHENOL OXIDASES—Enzymes in apples and potatoes that cause food to turn brown when slices are exposed to air.

PHENYLALANINE—One of the essential amino acids. The inherited inability to metabolize this amino acid is called **phenylketonuria**. Rich sources include legumes, meat, fish, and cheese.

PHENYLKETONURIA—Inherited inability to metabolize the amino acid **phenylalanine** completely. The toxic byproducts cause mental retardation during early growth. The only solution is a diet low in phenylalanine.

PHOSPHATASE TEST—Test of milk pasteurization. The milk enzyme phosphatase is destroyed at temperatures just above those required to destroy toxic bacteria, and their absence or presence indicates the extent of pasteurization.

PHOSPHATE—Group of atoms composed of one phosphorus and four oxygen atoms. Phosphates are involved in a number of bodily reactions, particularly those concerned with energy storage or release. See **adenosine triphosphate.**

PHOSPHATIDE—Any simple fat containing phosphoric acid. They are used as emulsifiers.

PHOSPHORIC ACID—Acid whose molecules contain phosphorus atoms. It is used in fruit-flavored drinks such as lemonade.

PHOSPHORUS—Mineral found in all human tissues, but especially bones and teeth. It is found in so many foods that deficiency is unlikely.

PHOTOENGRAVING—Letterpress printing of menus that uses a photographic plate given an acid bath to remove the nonprinting areas, in contrast to engraving a plate by hand.

PHOTOSYNTHESIS—Process by which green plants produce carbohydrates from carbon dioxide, water, and sunlight energy.

PHYLLOXERA—Plant lice, a variety of which is infamous for having destroyed much of Europe's vineyards in the nineteenth century.

PHYSICAL DEPRECIATION—Loss in the value of an asset over time caused solely by wear and tear, e.g., a restaurant oven wears out gradually from frequent use.

PHYSICAL INVENTORY—Count of each item physically on the premises.

PHYTIC ACID—Substance in cereal husks and certain legumes such as beans. It can combine with calcium and iron in the diet, rendering those two minerals unusable. Thus too much bran, which is derived from cereal husks, may lead to calcium or iron deficiency.

PIANO WIRE WHIP—Hand whip with very thin wire loops used to whip light materials.

PICA—Unit of measure of the length of a printed line and the depth of a printed area; each pica equals about 12 **points** or one sixth of an inch. Also, in people, an urge to eat bizarre things like paper or sand.

PICA TYPEWRITER—Typewriter in which there are 10 characters to each typed inch. See **copy measurement.**

PICKLE—To immerse vegetables such as cucumbers in a 5–10 percent brine solution. Pickling ferments the sugars into lactic acid.

PIE AND CAKE MARKER—Round metal frame supporting cutters that accurately mark portion sizes on the surface of a pie or cake.

PIECE—French; a cask with a volume of about 60 gallons.

PIE OR CAKE KNIFE—Knife with a triangular flat or offset blade for cutting and removing wedges of pie or cake.

PIE PLANT—**Rhubarb.**

PIERRE-A-FUSIL—French; sharp flinty taste characteristic of some extremely dry wines.

PIE TIN—Round pan, usually eight to ten inches in diameter, with shallow sloping walls.

PIGMENTS—Coloring agents in paint or **printing ink.**

PILFERAGE—Theft of items from an establishment, usually by employees.

PILFERPROOF SEAL—Seal that cannot be opened without damage. Damaged seals indicate tampering.

PILSNER GLASS—Beer glass with a short stem and a tall funnel-shaped bowl.

PIMIENTO—Fruit of the pepper family with a mild flavor and red color. Used to add color and flavor to a variety of dishes. Also spelled pimento.

PINEAPPLE—Edible tropical fruit with firm, juicy, yellow flesh encased in a football-sized rind that is tough and spiked. The juice and fruit are tasty; both can be used innumerable ways in food.

PINION—Tip of a poultry wing. Pinions have very little meat; they are used to flavor soups and stocks.

PIONEERING STAGE OF ADVERTISING—First stage of advertising; designed to make the public aware that a new establishment or product exists. See **competitive stage** and **retentive stage.**

PIPE—Oaken cask that holds 138 gallons when used for port and 110 gallons when used for Madeira wine.

PIQUANT—French; in white wine, a pleasantly acid or tart flavor; in food, a highly seasoned or spicy taste.

PIQUE—French; wine that is turning to vinegar and is no longer suitable for drinking.

PIQUETTE—French; an ordinary or cheap wine.

PIT—Stonelike seed at the center of fruits such as apricots and cherries. Although inedible when whole, an edible oil can be derived from them.

PITH—White, fibrous inner peel of citrus fruits; a good source of pectin.

PITTING—Small holes in a metal surface (as of a container) indicating corrosion.

PIVAL—Type of **multiple-dose poison.** It kills by anticoagulant action.

PIZZA OVEN—Specialized oven providing high bottom heat,

ideal for baking pizza crusts. Compartments are usually narrow and may be stacked several units high.

PIZZERIA—Foodservice establishment specializing in pizza.

PLAIN SWELLED RULE—Printed line often used in menu design that is thick in the middle and tapers off at both ends. See **rules.**

PLAIN TUBE—Nozzle with a plain round opening for cake-decorating bags or syringes; used to make dots, balls, lines, and to write with icing. Also called a round tube.

PLANK—Small finished hardwood board or slab on which meat or fish is cooked and served to impart flavor.

PLANNED-PROFIT METHOD—Method of establishing selling prices by figuring in a desired level of profit as well as all costs, and then calculating the price accordingly.

PLANTAIN—Edible tropical fruit resembling a large banana.

PLAT—French; plate of food. In reference to wine, flat or lifeless.

PLAT DU JOUR—French; specialty of the day.

PLATE FINISH—Menu paper with a hard, smooth surface.

PLATE FREEZER—**Blast freezer.**

PLATE WASTE—Food left on the plate by the customer. If a large proportion of customers leave a significant amount of a given item that must be thrown away, this can indicate that portion sizes are too large or that food quality is low.

PLATFORM SCALE—Weighing scale on a wheeled base. It can be wheeled out to the loading dock when needed. Goods are placed on the platform on top of the base.

PLEDGED ASSET—Asset set aside as collateral for a loan or for a purchase contract with a creditor.

PLUM—Small round edible fruit with smooth skin of varying colors, e.g. reddish, purplish. At the center is a hard pointed pit.

POACH—To cook food in lightly bubbling water in order to prevent overcooking.

POELE—Long-handled skillet with sloping sides used to toss foods. The term for something cooked in such a pan is *à la poêle.*

POINT—Measure of length in printing, used for menus. Each point equals about 1/72 of an inch or .0138 inch. Commonly used type sizes are 10 point to 14 point for normal print, and 18 point for headings.

POINT-OF-PURCHASE ADVERTISING—**Point-of-sale advertising.**

POINT-OF-SALE ADVERTISING—Advertising posted within an establishment for customers to see. For example, candy or tobacco ads can be posted on the cashier's counter.

POINT-OF-SALE TERMINAL—Computer terminal that performs the operations of a cash register and transmits and receives information over a channel.

POISSONIERE—French; an oblong pot with two loop handles used to poach fish.

POISSONNIER—French; chef who cooks fish.

POLISHED RICE—Rice that has been milled so that the husk and much of the nutritional content have been removed. Unless thiamine is added, for example, a diet high in polished rice can cause beriberi.

POLYMYXIN—Antibiotic used to control bacterial growth during brewing. It also has medicinal uses for humans.

POLYPEPTIDES—Protein molecules that are composed of long chains of amino acids.

POLYPHOSPHATES—Complex molecules, each of which consists of chains of phosphate units. As food additives, they improve the texture and quality of meat and other products.

POLYSACCHARIDES—Carbohydrates in which each molecule is composed of chains of monosaccharides, or simple sugars.

POLYUNSATURATED FATTY ACIDS—See **fatty acids, polyunsaturated.**

POMEGRANATE—Red-skinned, round fruit containing small, juicy, pulp and numerous tiny seeds. Eaten fresh or used to make a flavorful syrup (grenadine).

PONCEAU COLORS—Set of red food-coloring additives that are numbered. Red No. 1, for example, provides a maraschino cherry color.

PONY GLASS—Short-stemmed bar glass with a small tubular bowl that holds three quarters to one ounce of liqueur.

POONAC—Residue from coconut after oil has been pressed out.

POPULARITY INDEX—Figure reflecting how popular a given item is. It is calculated by dividing the number of items sold by the total number of guests served and multiplying by 100 percent.

PORCELAIN—Tableware made from fine quality clay that is vitrified and glazed, and then refired till the glaze forms a hard, glossy, transparent surface. Also called vitrified china.

PORK—The fresh meat of pigs. Pigs are usually slaughtered at five to six months. Quality pork has a soft gray-pink color, a fine grain, and white fat. The best pork cuts are from the loin, leg, and shoulder. Pork should be properly cooked to prevent **trichinosis.** Standard primal cuts are as follows:
Boston butt: Portion separated from the shoulder by a straight cut parallel to the breast side. The cut should have a slight amount of marbling.
Crown roast: An entire pork loin, usually served filled with mashed potatoes.
Ham hock: The ankle joint and its associated meat.
Jowl: Meat from the cheek and neck region; one source of bacon.
Pork fresh ham: Leg portion separated from the side by a straight cut perpendicular to the skin surface to a line parallel to the shank bones.
Pork loin: Back cut remaining after removal of the shoulder, ham, belly, and fat back. This cut yields the tenderloin, chops, cutlets, roasts, and ribs.
Pork shoulder: Portion separated from the side by a straight cut

perpendicular to skin surface. The pork shoulder yields the pork shoulder, fresh shoulder, butt, boneless shoulder butt, picnic pork, and shoulder steaks.

PORK GRADING—The four grades of pork, in order of descending quality, are U.S. #1, U.S. #2, U.S. #3, and Cull. See **meat grading** for grading criteria.

POROSITY—The condition of having pores, i.e., being permeable to the passage of gases or liquids.

PORTABLE UTILITY SCALE—Scale for weighing received goods. It looks similar to an ordinary bathroom scale.

PORTES-GREFFES—French; the American grapevine roots that are resistant to **Phylloxera.** They have been grafted onto many of Europe's vines as a consequence.

PORT GLASS—Small short-stemmed wine glass, about the size of a sherry glass but with a tulip-shaped bowl that holds two to three ounces.

PORTION—Measured serving size of a meat, fruit, or vegetable.

PORTION CONTROL—Establishment of standards for the size, weight, or number of each menu item that is to be served. Portion control not only treats customers fairly but also makes it easier to plan purchases and calculate profits.

PORTION-CONTROL MEASUREMENT—Use of weighing scales, dishes, paper cups, or ladles of known size to measure out accurately the standard size portion of each menu item offered.

PORTION COST—Cost per serving, derived by dividing total yield by portion size to determine the number of portions. The number of portions is then divided into the extended cost (total cost) to get the portion cost.

PORTION-COST MULTIPLIER—Index calculated by dividing the **cost factor** of an item by the number of portions per pound.

PORTION DIVIDER—Product of the **portion factor** and the yield percentage.

PORTION FACTOR—Number of portions per pound of food product, e.g., meat, calculated by dividing 16 ounces by the size in ounces of each portion.

PORTION SCALE—Small weighing device with a dial pointer calibrated in ounces used to apportion food accurately. Portion scales usually have a movable dial face that permits simple manual adjustment to allow for the weight of the vessel in which the food is placed.

PORTION SIZE—Weight or number of each menu item to be served to a single customer. The portion size should be controlled or standardized.

PORTION-SIZE DETERMINATION—Determination of what the standard portion size for a given item should be, based on observation of plate waste, customer comments, and what competitors offer.

POSITION REQUEST—Establishment's request to a periodical that its ads run in a certain place within an issue. See **guaranteed position.**

POST—To transfer financial changes resulting from business transactions from the journal to the ledger accounts.

POST-CHECKING—Check of the food on an order picked up by the waiter or waitress to make sure that all items have been listed on the sales check.

POSTDATE—To put a future date on a check or other document. The postdated check, for example, cannot be cashed until that date arrives.

POSTMIX—Carbonated soft drinks mixed on the premises with ingredients bought separately. It is less expensive than **premix.**

POTABLE—Safe to drink.

POT AND PAN BRUSH—See **gong brush.**

POTASH—Common name for potassium hydroxide and potassium carbonate. The latter can be converted into potassium bicarbonate, a leavening agent.

POTASSIUM—Mineral important for muscular and nervous function. It is found in most foods, although bananas and oranges are especially rich sources. Deficiency can directly affect the action of the heart. See **hypokalemia.**

POTASSIUM NITRATE—Food additive used in curing meat. The nitrate turns into **nitrite,** which gives the product a reddish color when it combines with the **myoglobin** of the meat. Also called saltpeter.

POTASSIUM SORBATE—Compound added to food to inhibit the growth of fungi such as molds and yeast.

POTATO—Tuberous root vegetable. The Irish or white potato is used the most. It is served baked, boiled, fried, processed into French fries or potato chips, or mixed with other foods.

POTENTIAL FOOD COST—Estimated or planned cost of a particular volume of food predicted to generate a given amount of income. The actual cost may well differ.

POTENTIALLY HAZARDOUS FOOD—Any food that is susceptible to invasion by disease-causing microorganisms and that will support their growth, e.g., meat, fish, poultry, eggs, and milk.

POT MARIGOLD—Flower with edible petals that may be used for seasoning. See **calendula.**

POT ROASTING—Method of cooking meat; it is browned, then cooked in a covered pot with only a little water. This combination of frying and steaming helps tenderize meat and keep it moist.

POT STILL—Fat-bellied liquor still with a long tapered neck. It must be refilled for each distillation, as opposed to the continuous or patent still.

POTTERY—Glazed clay product of better quality and durability than earthenware.

POULTRY—Domesticated species of birds, including chickens, ducks, geese, and turkeys, bred for their eggs or for the table.
Chicken—Domestic fowl **Gallus Gallus.** Chickens are high in

protein and vitamin B. It is among the most versatile of meats with innumerable methods of preparation. They are graded by age and size as regulated by law.

Broiler: Young bird that is four to six weeks old and weighs up to two and a half pounds. The French word for broilers is poussin. They are usually cooked whole and have little flavor or flesh.

Capon: Young castrated cock that has been fattened and weighs between six and ten pounds.

Cock: Mature male chicken with dark, tough meat.

Fryer: Bird that weighs as much as three and a half pounds with tender, tasty flesh. Fryers are also known as spring chickens.

Roaster: Bird that weighs three and a half to five pounds; roasters have the tastiest flesh.

Stewing hen: Female bird ranging in age from ten months to more than a year and a half old.

Duck: Swimming bird of which there are 60 to 70 species. Most domesticated ducks are descendants of the mallard or common wild duck of North America. The meat is darker and more tender than that of the chicken. In the United States, the Long Island duckling is the most favored.

Goose: Aquatic bird with dark, tender flesh and a gamey flavor. The goose is more fatty than chicken or turkey. The most common types are Embden, Toulouse, Chinese, and Canadian.

Turkey: Bird native to North America and one of our most valued table birds. The meat is lean and mildly flavored. The most popular breeds include the Bronze and the Bourbon Red. Turkeys average twelve to fourteen pounds.

POULTRY, DRESSED—Slaughtered poultry with the blood and feathers removed.

POULTRY GRADING—The four grades of poultry, in order of descending quality, are Grade AA, Grade A, Grade B, and Grade C. Quality is judged on fat, cleanness of the animal, shape, absence of pinfeathers, and the absence of such defects as torn skin, broken bones, and so on.

POULTRY NEEDLE—Long needle used to sew up the abdominal cavity of poultry after cleaning out the viscera. This gives the bird a neater appearance and helps to keep any stuffing in place.

POULTRY SAW—Power saw similar to meat saw but especially designed for cutting poultry. Instead of a movable carriage, the poultry saw has a stationary table. The operator stands at the right of the saw and uses both hands to guide the product through the blade.

POULTRY SEASONING—Special blends of herbs, seasonings, and spices used for flavoring poultry.

POULTRY SHEARS—Scissors in which one blade is serrated and one is not. Used to trim vegetables and meat as well as poultry.

POURRITURE NOBLE—French; so-called noble rot. It is the mold that grows on Sauterne grapes and gives the wine its characteristic flavor.

POUSSOIR—French; small machine used to stuff sausage meat into the casings.

POWER DICER—Device for cutting food into small cubes, used in conjunction with the vegetable-slicer attachment to vertical mixers.

POWER-DRIVE UNIT—Electric motor with a rotary output of 350 or 700 RPM used to operate food-processing equipment such as grinders, vegetable slicers, and any other accessory on a vertical mixer.

POWER RINSE—Tank in a dishwashing machine in which dishes are rinsed after washing by water pumped through a sprayer. Water temperature should be 180°F or higher.

PPM—Standard abbreviation for parts per million, an indication of how concentrated any one component is in a given medium.

PRECHECK—Sales check from **precheck machine** that provides the total of a sale as soon as the customer's order has been recorded. The food is then paid for before it is received.

PRECHECKING—Printing out the order on a cash register or other device and then using that printed slip to place the actual order.

PRECHECK MACHINE—Machine that automatically records the cost of an order as the customer's selection is punched in. The machines are used in the **machine system for recording sales.**

PRECIPITATE—Mass of solid substance that forms in a liquid due to some chemical action, e.g., the **lees** that form in wine.

PRECOCE—French; precocious, used to describe a wine that matures rapidly.

PRECONTROL SYSTEM—Method of determining food costs in advance so that selling prices can be established to achieve a desired level of profit. See **precosting.**

PRECOOL—To bring warm items to room temperature or below by placing them in pans of cold water before putting them into refrigerated storage. Precooling saves energy and is actually better for the quality of some foods.

PRECOSTING—Using sales forecasts and ingredient costs to calculate food costs for a given menu item in advance of sales. See **precontrol system.**

PREDETERMINED COST—Any cost calculated before it is actually incurred.

PREDICTIVE ACCOUNTING—Accounting technique in which costs are estimated in advance.

PREFLUSH MACHINE—Machine that removes most food and grease from dishes before they enter the dishwasher, thus preventing undue contamination of the wash solution. Also called prewash machine. See **prerinsing.**

PREMIER CRU—French; first growth, specifically from some of the best individual Bordeaux and Burgundy vineyards.

PREMIER JUS—French; high-quality fat derived from the kidneys of oxen and sheep.

PREMIUM—Amount of money added to the normal purchase price of an asset. The opposite of **discount.**

PREMIX—Carbonated soft drinks that have already been mixed before they are purchased by the establishment. Premix is more expensive than **post-mix.**

PREPAID INCOME—Income received before the goods or services from which the income is generated have been delivered.

PREPAY—To pay for goods or services before they are received or used.

PREPORTIONED FOOD—Foods, such as steaks, that have been separated into individual portions before storing. This enables the cook to remove just the right amounts to meet current orders.

PREPORTIONED FOOD INVENTORY CONTROL SHEET— Form on which **preportioned food** items can be listed, along with opening and closing inventories and the quantity sold.

PREPPING—Adding price marks or other labels to packages about to be sold at the retail level.

PRERINSING—Rinsing the larger, visible waste from dishes and utensils before they are placed in the dishwasher. Prerinsing helps prevent waste from clogging up the machine and keeps the dishwater cleaner.

PRESENT VALUE (PV)—Value in the present of an investment that will lead to a specific return in the future. PV tables reveal how much money must be invested now at a certain rate of interest for a set period of time to achieve a particular future goal.

PRESERVATIVES—Food additives that tend to inhibit the deterioration or spoilage of food. Some kill bacteria or yeast, others chemically inhibit the breakdown of food molecules.

PRESERVES—Fruit cooked in a thick sugar syrup. Placed in sealed jars, it can be stored (preserved) for a long time.

PRESET PRECHECK—The name, price of each item, and the total of the order are automatically recorded by the **precheck machine.**

PRESS—General term applied to any device used to extract juices from food.

PRESSURE COOKER—Device that cooks food by the application of steam at a pressure of 0 to 15 psi (pounds per square inch) at temperatures of 212°F to 250°F. Steam may be generated from a self-contained unit or from an outside source. Food is cooked faster than with boiling and with less loss of flavor, color, and nutrients. It is also more fuel-efficient than range-top cooking.

PRESSURE FRYER—Fry kettle with a tight-fitting lid that holds steam under pressure over the surface of the fat, thereby greatly reducing cooking time. The steam may come from the product being cooked or may be injected into the space under the lid.

PREVENTIVE MAINTENANCE—Maintenance to keep assets in good shape before something breaks down.

PRICE CONTRACT—Contract issued by a supplier to a buyer, that protects the buyer by guaranteeing him a set **unit cost** for goods regardless of how much he purchases (within certain stated limits). In return, the buyer promises to purchase that item only from that supplier.

PRICE DISCRIMINATION—Sale of the same item at different prices to different buyers. This may be legal (as when discounting volume sales) or illegal (as when restricting competition).

PRICE, ESCALATION—See **escalation price.**

PRICE LEADER—Item offered for sale with an especially low price, often temporarily, meant to attract customers into an establishment where it is hoped they will also buy other items at the regular prices.

PRICE LEADERSHIP—Price set by a dominant supplier that in turn is set at the same level by the minor suppliers, who do this rather than calculate their own from expenses and desired profit margins to avoid unwanted competition.

PRICE MAINTENANCE—Setting minimum prices for products' retail sale by a producer or wholesaler of those products.

PRICE MARGIN—Amount by which the selling price exceeds the direct costs to an establishment of the item sold.

PRICE STAMPING—Marking every package of received goods with its price upon receipt. This makes it easier to price inventories later.

PRICING-FACTOR METHOD—Method for establishing selling prices based on separating foods that require little or no preparation from those that require a lot, and then allocating labor, energy, and other costs accordingly.

PRICING POLICY—Guiding concepts used by managers to decide on prices. It may, for example, depend upon a set mark-up over costs.

PRICKLY PEAR—Exotic edible fruit of a type of cactus.

PRIMAL CUT—Wholesale cut of meat.

PRIMARY ACCOUNTS—Ledger accounts that contain overhead information on such costs as heating and lighting.

PRIMARY HOST—The creature, often human, in which a mature parasite lives; in particular those parasites that go through several definite stages, each in a different animal, during their growth to maturity. See **intermediate host.**

PRIMARY MARKET—Large central markets that set the price of a commodity and where supply and demand are largely controlled.

PRIMARY PACKAGE—First layer of packaging in actual contact with the product inside.

PRIME COST—The total of food costs and labor costs for a given item or set of items.

PRINTER, COMPUTER—Terminal that produces copies of the

computer-stored information by printing on paper. See **hard copy.**

PRINTING INK—Fluid used to produce printed images, as for menus. It is composed of solvents (vehicles), coloring agents (pigments), and drying compounds. The type of ink chosen depends heavily on the kind of menu paper to be used. For specialty inks, see these ink entries: **high gloss, metallic, moisture-set,** and **scuff-resistant.**

PRINTING, MENU—Process of transferring ink from a master plate to blank paper to make copies. See **letterpress, offset lithography,** and **gravure printing.**

PRINTOUT REQUISITION—Slip printed by a precheck cash register given to the preparation section to request that an order be filled.

PROCEEDS—Amount of money or other assets resulting from the sale of goods.

PROCESSOR, COMPUTER—Part of a computer whose circuits perform the arithmetic and logical operations requested by the program. Basically the same as the **central processing unit.**

PRODUCER GOODS—Items used to produce or manufacture other goods (e.g., flour and baking soda) rather than to satisfy human needs directly. Compare **consumer goods.**

PRODUCT COST—Expenses of raw materials and labor, as well as overhead, that go into the making of an item.

PRODUCTION CONTROL—Estimate of the number of each item that will be sold the next day; it is done to reduce unnecessary purchasing and production. See **anticipated sales.**

PRODUCTION PLANNING—To use **cover forecasting** and sales histories to decide in advance how many of each menu item should be prepared for a given day.

PRODUCTION SHEET—Written instructions to both the purchasing department and the kitchen to purchase and prepare the food items for any particular day.

PROENZYMES—Enzymes that are produced in inactive form that later become active, e.g., digestive enzymes.

PROFIT—Amount by which income exceeds costs.

PROFIT AND LOSS STATEMENT—Income statement.

PROGRAM, COMPUTER—Organized list of instructions for a computer needed to execute a given function or analysis properly.

PROGRAM EVALUATION AND REVIEW TECHNIQUE (PERT)—Technique to systematically evaluate and improve something over time, such as cost control methods, by considering various alternatives.

PROLAMINS—Proteins that are soluble in a 70–80 percent alcohol solution, but not in pure water or pure alcohol.

PROLINE—One of the nonessential amino acids.

PROMISSORY NOTE—Written and signed promise to pay, as made by a buyer to a seller.

PROMOTION—Any technique or method, such as advertising, that encourages sales or consumer acceptance.

PROMOTION EXPENSE—Cost of advertising a newly established business or a new activity at an already established business.

PROOF—Measurement of the alcoholic strength of a liquid with each degree representing .50 percent alcohol. Thus 86 proof represents 43 percent alcohol.

PROOF CABINET—Insulated cabinet that holds dough products at a controlled temperature and humidity to promote the fermentation process prior to baking. They may also be used to hold any hot food. Also called a proofer.

PROPERTY ACCOUNTABILITY—Responsibility for keeping track of small assets and other property that can be lost or stolen.

PROPHYLACTIC—Anything that helps prevent disease.

PROPIONIC ACID—Acid found naturally in milk that can be used as an additive in other foods to inhibit mold growth.

PROPYL GALLATE—Antioxidant food additive used to help preserve foods such as meat products and chewing gums.

PRORATE—To divide up a joint cost among different departments or products according to some plan.

PROTECTIVE COAT—Coating of paint or another substance to protect a surface against corrosion or weathering.

PROTEINS—One of the three principal food components in addition to **carbohydrates** and **fats.** Each protein is composed of a long chain of **amino acids,** of which there are twenty-two. The exact sequence and number of amino acids determine the nature of the protein. Some proteins serve as the building blocks of all living cell structures; others function as **enzymes.**

PROTEINS, CONJUGATED—Compounds in which each molecule is composed of both a protein and a nonprotein substance (e.g., a carbohydrate or a fat).

PROTEOLYSIS—Chemical breakdown of a protein into its constituent amino acids.

PROTHROMBIN—Protein in blood involved in coagulation.

PROTOCOL, COMPUTER—Agreement, between computer terminals about exactly how communications will be conducted, involving specifically what commands will be sent and how they will be acknowledged.

PROTOPLASM—Material of which all living cells are made.

PROTOZOA—Plural of **protozoan.**

PROTOZOAN—Microorganism composed of a single cell. Many of these one-celled creatures (e.g., amoebas) can cause disease.

PROVITAMIN—Substance that can be changed by the body into a vitamin. For example, carotene in carrots can be changed into vitamin A.

PRUNES—Dried plums. They are a natural laxative and a good source of vitamin A.

PSI—Pounds per square inch; a measurement of pressure.

PSYCHROMETER—Device for measuring relative humidity.

PSYCHROPHILIC MICROORGANISMS—Bacteria, yeasts, and molds that can grow at temperatures below freezing (about 13°F to 32°F), thus affecting food in cold storage. These bacteria grow even more readily in warmer temperatures of around 60°F. See **mesophiles.**

PTOMAINE—Poisonous compound, e.g., cadaverine, muscarine, and neurine, derived from decomposing proteins in deteriorating food.

PTOMAINE POISONING— Food poisoning that occurs when a person eats food containing **ptomaine** compounds. Many cases of food poisoning inaccurately attributed to ptomaines were actually caused by **staphylococci** bacteria. Deteriorated foods do not necessarily contain harmful ptomaines, although they may contain harmful bacteria.

PTYALIN—Enzyme in saliva that splits the starch molecules in food.

PUBLICITY—Newsworthy items of information given to the media and printed or broadcast free.

PUBLIC RELATIONS—Relationship between an establishment and its customers and other members of the public who come into contact with it. The relationship is strengthened by good service and sound advertising.

PUFFER—Type of **swell** caused by spoilage of the meat inside the can.

PULL DATE—Last day that a food item should be sold by a retailer. If it is sold after this date, the normal time the consumer holds it before final use might exceed the **shelf life.** After this date; the product can be expected to deteriorate and should be pulled from the shelves.

PULLED BREAD—Freshly baked bread with its crust removed.

PULMONARY PARAGONIMIASIS—Disease caused by the

paragonimus westermani parasite, a fluke that encysts in the lungs of its host. Contracted from eating improperly cooked crabs or crayfish, the disease causes lung damage, paroxysms of coughing, and even death.

PULPER—Machine that takes all kinds of waste material and breaks it down under water into small pieces. The water is then extracted and the particles are discharged into a container for easy removal. Nonpulpable material, such as cans and silver, are automatically rejected. This machine has the advantage of cleaning and deodorizing waste as well as reducing its volume.

PUMPING, BAROMETRIC—A package's **breathing**.

PUNCHEON—Large wine cask that holds 160 gallons.

PUNCHING, DOUGH—Folding dough over from its sides into the middle and literally punching it down during leavening to redistribute the yeast.

PUPA—Stage in the metamorphosis of some insects between the larvae and adult stages; characterized by a cocoon holding an essentially motionless immature insect.

PUPITRES—French; racks used to hold champagne bottles during the period when their sediment is shaken onto their corks for easy removal.

PURCHASE INVOICE STAMP—**Invoice stamp.**

PURCHASE ORDER—Form used to order supplies for the kitchen or bar. Copies go not only to the supplier but also to the receiving department and the accounting department.

PURCHASE ORDER SHEET—**Market quotation sheet.**

PURCHASE RECORDS—Purchase orders, contracts, vouchers, invoices, and other business records that verify purchases.

PURCHASE REQUEST—Form that the steward or other storeroom manager can use to inform the purchasing agent what goods and how many of each should be ordered.

PURCHASE SPECIFICATIONS—Description of the number, weight, size, and quality of food desired by an establishment.

PURCHASING AGENT—Person responsible for determining the needs of an establishment (from input provided by the various departments), comparing prices at different suppliers, and making the actual purchases.

PURCHASING DEPARTMENT—In larger establishments, department that is set up to order goods and to monitor the supply line until the goods are actually received.

PURCHASING POWER—Amount of a specific good or service that can be bought for a specific sum.

PURCHASING PROCEDURES—Standards and procedures by which specifications for the purchase of items are established. People who make the purchases should be supervised to ensure that they adhere to the procedures.

PUREE—Meat, vegetable, or fruit that is boiled, mashed into a pulp, pressed to a purée, and strained; may also refer to a soup containing purée.

PUREE PRESSER—Any one of several types of devices used for pressing through purées of meats or vegetables.

PURGATIVE—Substance causing the evacuation and cleansing of the bowels; a strong laxative.

PURGE—To force oxygen out of a container with a flow of nitrogen, which helps prevent infestation by aerobic bacteria or insects.

PURINES—Nitrogen-based compounds such as adenine and guanine that play a role in the formation of **nucleic acids.** Meats and fish contain some; there is little or none in cereals, fruits, and vegetables.

PUROTHIONINE—Protein found in wheat flour that can kill yeast and thus interfere with leavening.

PURVEYOR—Seller or vendor.

PYRENONE—Insecticide used to make materials such as paper resistant to insects.

PYRETHRUM—So-called natural pesticide that is useful both in killing houseflies and safe to use in foodservice establishments since it is nontoxic to humans.

PYREX—Glass that can withstand extreme changes in temperature and is thus useful for baking utensils as well as for serving food.

PYRIDOXINE—**Vitamin B$_6$**.

PYRIMIDINES—Compounds containing nitrogen (e.g., cytosine, thymine) that play a role in the formation of **nucleic acids.**

PYROGENS—Substances produced by bacteria that can cause fever if ingested with infected food or fluid. Although sterilization can kill the bacteria, the heat does not break down the pyrogens already produced.

PYRUVIC ACID—Substance produced in the body when glucose is broken down without oxygen, as can occur during vigorous exercise.

Q

QUALHEIM CUTTER—Food cutter that also dices, makes strips, and does other work that saves much preparation time.

QUALITATSWEIN—German; superior quality wine from certain designated regions of the country where strict quality controls are in effect.

QUALITY CONTROL—All procedures designed to ensure that products for sale are of satisfactory quality.

QUALITY OF MEAT—Texture and flavor of a cut of meat. One of the three characteristics checked in **meat grading.**

QUANTITY—See **minimum quantity level** and **maximum quantity limit.**

QUANTITY DISCOUNT—Discount provided by the seller when the buyer purchases a particular amount or more of the same item. See also **volume discount.**

QUARTER—To butcher an animal carcass into four major sections. Each includes one shoulder and part of the side meat.

QUARTER BOTTLE—Bottle of one fourth the standard size (25.6 ounces), or one that holds only 6.4 ounces.

QUARTZ OVEN—Small countertop unit that uses electric radiant heat on top and bottom to heat items as high as 750°F. It is useful for fast-cooking of small amounts of food. Also called an infrared oven.

QUATERNARY AMMONIUM—Active ingredient in many sanitizing compounds. It is not corrosive, unlike iodophors and chlorine compounds. Called quats for short.

QUENE—French; a cask used for burgundy that holds 120 gallons or 456 liters.

QUERCETIN—Pigment found in tea and onion skins and used as food coloring.

QUERCITRON—Yellow food-coloring additive derived from bark of the oak *Quercus tinctoria.*

QUICK-CHILL REFRIGERATOR—Refrigerator that rapidly cools cooked foods to a safe storage temperature.

QUILLAJA—Bark of the plant *Quillaja saponaria*; it is used in soft drinks to make them foam.

QUINCE—Hard-fleshed, apple-shaped fruit with a golden color. It contains large amounts of pectin and is therefore used in making preserves and jellies.

QUININE—Bitter flavoring agent used in tonic water and bitter-lemon drinks.

QUOTATION—Current price for a particular item as given (quoted) by a potential supplier.

QUOTATION-AND-ORDER   SHEET—**Market   Quotation Sheet.**

R

RABIOLE—Type of turnip.

RACE—French; literally means breed. Used to refer to a distinguished wine.

RACKING—Transferring wine or spirits from one container to another in order to remove wine from its sediment and to place it into a fresh clean cask.

RACK JOBBER—Wholesaler who supplies establishments with merchandise and display racks and then pays them a set percent of the resulting sales revenue.

RAD APPERTIZATION—Using radiation to reduce the amount of pathogenic bacteria in food to a safe level, but not to the point of **sterilization.**

RADIANT ENERGY—Movement of heat in waves through an available space, e.g., from white-hot broiler coils to the meat inside the broiler. See also **conduction** and **convection.**

RADIATION—See **radiant energy.**

RADIATION,   NUCLEAR—Ionizing   radiation   containing gamma and other rays. It can be used to sterilize food without making it radioactive. However, the radiation can alter some of the chemicals in the food (e.g., nitrites or flavors).

RADISH—Mustard-family vegetable used in salads, in relishes, or as a garnish. Young ones have the best flavor.

RAG CONTENT PAPER—**Cotton fiber content paper.**

RAISIN OIL—Oil derived from Muscat grape seeds that is added to raisins to keep them soft.

RAISINS—Dried grapes that are eaten plain or used in other dishes.

RAM—Mature male sheep.

RAMEKINS—Small, circular, individual China dishes in which sweet or savory custards are baked and served.

RAMPION—European plant with thick white roots used in salads.

RANCIDITY—Chemical breakdown of fats caused by oxidation resulting in spoilage.

RANDOM ACCESS MEMORY—Computer memory that is not organized in a strict historical sequence.

RANDOM ITEM STOREROOM INVENTORY—In addition to normal periodic inventories of all stocked items, certain high-cost or fast-moving items should be inventoried daily or weekly on a random basis, e.g., not all such items need be counted each time; a few can be selected for inventory one time and another set at another time.

RANGE—Equipment designed for cooking food in pots and pans on burners or heated plates on its surface, which is roughly waist high. Ranges may have a griddle surface and be combined with broilers and ovens.

RANGE, STOCK-POT—Low range about two feet in height with a high heat output and a surface large enough to accommodate one large stock pot.

RAPE—See **herbs**. Also, crushed grapes after the juice has been squeezed out.

RASHER OF BACON—Breakfast or lunch portion of bacon, usually three strips, broiled or fried.

RASPBERRY—Fruit resembling the blackberry, but usually reddish in color. It grows on low-lying bushes. Raspberries may be eaten raw or cooked into various types of jellies, syrups, and so on.

RATAFIA—Any liquor made by simple infusion rather than by distillation.

RATE-OF-RETURN PRICING—Setting the selling price so that the mark-up over cost provides a set return on the investment.

RATING—Credit standing of a potential customer.

RAW FOOD COST—Total dollar cost of food to be prepared.

RAW MATERIALS—Goods, such as flour and sugar, that are to be used as ingredients in an establishment's products.

REACH-IN STORAGE—Food storage in cabinets or upright coolers that require only that a person reach in through the opened door to obtain an item. Contrast **walk-in storage.**

REALIZED PROFIT—Profit that has actually been received, as opposed to a paper profit.

REAL PROPERTY—Land, the natural resources thereon, and the building. Synonomous with real estate. Contrast **personal property.**

REAM—Five hundred sheets of paper of the same size and quality, as for menus.

REBATE—Partial refund made to an establishment by a supplier if the establishment uses fewer supplies than originally billed.

RECEIPT, SALES—Written statement acknowledging that payment was received for goods or services delivered.

RECEIPT STUB—Portion of a sales check that is turned in to the cashier along with payment, validated by the cashier, and returned as proof that the cash was properly submitted.

RECEIVER—Employee with the responsibility of receiving and taking care of delivered goods.

RECEIVER'S SCALES—Weighing scales assigned by the food-service manager to the receiver so that he can weigh goods received from shippers and ensure that the proper amount has been delivered.

RECEIVING—Taking supplies or other assets into physical possession.

RECEIVING, BLIND—**Blind receiving.**

RECEIVING CLERK—Employee in charge of receiving goods and accounting for them.

RECEIVING CLERK'S DAILY REPORT—**Receiving sheet.**

RECEIVING DEPARTMENT—Section of an establishment whose job it is to ensure that all ordered merchandise actually arrives and is accounted for.

RECEIVING, PARTIAL BLIND—See **partial blind receiving.**

RECEIVING, PROCEDURES—Procedures that establish who is to receive goods, how, when, and where goods are to be received, and how they are to be accounted for.

RECEIVING REPORT SUMMARY—Monthly summary of the classes of foods received during that month and the total cost of each class.

RECEIVING SHEET—Form on which the receiving clerk lists and describes items as they are delivered, as well as noting the invoice number and the department to which the goods should be conveyed.

RECEIVING STAMP—Rubber stamp, usually with the date, used to mark the invoice that comes with goods received. The stamp impression includes a line where the receiver of goods signs his name, indicating that the shipment is acceptable.

RECHAUD—French; chafing dish mounted on a rolling cart (see **gueridon**) used to prepare special dishes and keep food warm.

RECIPE FORM—Form that lists for a given product the ingredients and amount of each, and also the price of each so that the cost per portion can easily be calculated.

RECOLTE—French; vintage.

RECOMMENDED DIETARY ALLOWANCE (RDA)—The RDA is a guide to the amounts of foods needed daily to ensure the adequate intake of needed nutrients. See also **minimum daily requirement** and **U.S. recommended daily allowance.**

RECONCILIATION OF MEAT TAGS—Form that lists meat tag numbers, names of the items, and the dates of receipt and issuing. Since meat tags are treated as requisitions, the purpose of the form is to verify the final disposition of the meat.

RECONSTITUTING OVEN—Equipment that can quickly defrost frozen foods without impairing their quality. Some models combine cycles of heat and refrigeration to reduce drying on the edges while gently thawing the center of the food. Other models, using infrared radiation, may reach temperatures as high as 850°F and are faster.

RECORD, COMPUTER—Any group of associated pieces of information; typically a logical unit, not necessarily a physical one.

RECOUP—To get back through sales the money invested in buying products or materials with which to make products.

RECOVERY VALUE—Income likely to be realized when a fixed asset is sold after its usefulness to an establishment has ended.

RECTIFYING—Changing the natural condition of an alcoholic spirit, e.g., adding sweetening, flavoring, or coloring.

RED CABBAGE—Cabbage with a dark-red color. It makes a decorative addition to fresh salads and can also be used cooked.

RED NO. 40—Red-coloring additive used in sausage, sodas, candy, and other desserts. Some studies show it causes cancer in mice.

RED SQUILL—**Single-dose poison** used for rats and mice. Humans vomit it up immediately, while rats and mice retain it; thus it is a safe poison for foodservice establishment use.

REDUCE SPIRITS—Lowering the alcoholic strength of a beverage by adding water.

REDUCING SUGAR—Sugar such as glucose that reduces certain reagents in chemical tests. Such sugars have nothing to do with calorie or weight reduction.

REDUCTION—Both reduction and its opposite, **oxidation,** take place during digestion and metabolism. It is a chemical process in which a substance loses oxygen or gains hydrogen. The term is also used in cooking, where it means the lessening of a volume of liquid by evaporation, particularly in sauces.

REEDED RULE—Set of fine parallel lines drawn very close together; used as embellishments in menu printing. See **rules.**

REEL OVEN—Mechanical oven in which food is cooked on trays that revolve in Ferris-wheel fashion. Food is loaded and unloaded one tray at a time through the oven's door.

REFINED CEREAL—Cereal that has been processed.

REFLECTOR OVEN—Oven that bounces heat off the oven's internal surfaces and onto the food being cooked, as opposed to exposing the food directly to the heat source.

REFRESH—To add a younger wine or spirit to an older one in the cask in order to enhance the latter.

REFRIGERANT—Freon or other gas used in the coils of a refrigerating unit to absorb and discharge heat as part of the refrigeration process.

REFRIGERATED STORAGE—Insulated and chilled storeroom for food. It must be kept at temperatures just above the freezing point (32°F). Contrast with **frozen storage.**

REFRIGERATED STOREROOM OVERLOADING—Putting too many items, or items that are too warm, in a refrigerated storeroom. Overloading may exceed the ability of the unit to cool. It can cause a rise in the overall storeroom temperature, which could help bacteria grow and possibly strain the refrigeration unit.

REFRIGERATOR, MOBILE—Lightweight refrigerator on wheels that may be moved easily from one location to another.

REFRIGERATOR, PASS-THROUGH—**Reach-in refrigerator** with doors front and back so that food may be loaded on the kitchen side and removed on the serving side.

REFRIGERATOR, REACH-IN—Refrigerator in which a door swings open or a drawer pulls out to allow food to be reached.

REFRIGERATOR, ROLL-IN—Refrigerator into which a wheeled rack of food may be rolled.

REFRIGERATOR, WALK-IN—Refrigerator large enough for a person to walk into.

REFUND—Return of part or all of the purchase price to the buyer.

REGISTER, COMPUTER—Hardware device in which computer bits or characters are stored.

REGULATORY PRODUCTS—**Dangerous articles.**

REHOBOAM—Oversize champagne bottle with a volume of six regular bottles, i.e., 156 ounces.

REINSTATEMENT OF SUSPENDED PERMIT—Cessation of the **suspension of permit** if an establishment corrects the conditions that led to the suspension.

REJECTABLE QUALITY LEVEL—Below a minimum level of acceptability and not fit for sale, e.g., burned baked goods.

RELATED COSTS—Costs of advertising and other sales activities, as opposed to the costs to produce goods.

RELATIVE HUMIDITY—The humidity actually present, as a percentage of the maximum humidity possible, given the existing air pressure and temperature in the space. Contrast **absolute humidity.**

RELATIVE SALES APPEAL—See **entree sales ratio.**

RELEASE AGENT—Fatty acids, wax, and any other substance coated on the surface of a can to prevent food from sticking.

REMITTANCE SLIP—Statement that accompanies a payment and identifies the debt for which the payment is intended.

REMUAGE—French; turning the bottles upside down during champagne production, then shaking and turning them slightly to settle the sediment on the cork for easy removal.

RENDER—To melt down fatty animal tissues in order to liquefy and extract fat from the connective tissues.

RENNET—A preparation of the stomach of animals that is used, usually in powder form, to coagulate fresh milk in the process of making junket or cheese.

RENNIN—Enzyme in gastric juice that clots milk; sometimes used as a substitute for **rennet.**

REORDER POINT—Point at which the stock on hand of a given item reaches the **minimum quantity level** and it is time to order more.

REPELLANT—Aversive chemical substance that makes insects tend to avoid an area. It may not kill them, however.

REPORT PROGRAM GENERATOR (RPG)—Computer language that produces material in a particular format, e.g., invoices and payroll.

REQUEST FOR CREDIT MEMORANDUM—Receiving-control form that lists shortages in quantity, nonconformance of the quality to specification, or any other discrepancy in order to request credit.

REQUIREMENT ANALYSIS, COMPUTER—Initial determination of a computer user's needs before the development of a computer system.

REQUISITION—Form that can be used by any department within an establishment to request supplies from the storeroom.

RESCALE—To change the size of an advertisement so that it fits into a larger or smaller space.

RESERVATION—Setting aside salable items, either physically or on paper, to fill a specific order. Also, advance request that a table or dining room be held for later use.

RESERVE—On wine labels, the word indicates mature quality.

Also, to request in advance that a table or dining room be held for later use.

RESERVOIR—A source (e.g., other animals or the soil) in which microorganisms can thrive when they are not infecting humans.

RESIDUAL SPRAY—Insecticide that leaves a surface residue strong enough to kill insects that come into contact with it for a period of time after spraying.

RESILIENCY—Ability of a material to absorb blows and other shocks without cracking or permanently changing shape.

RESILIENT FLOORING MATERIALS—Materials such as linoleum and vinyl tiles that can be used to cover floors because they possess **resiliency.**

RESINATED WINE—Usually Greek, this is a wine that has been stored in large jars pitched with tar. Such wines pick up a resinous flavor, which is then further enhanced by the addition of aromatic gums and spices.

RESISTANCE, PESTICIDE—Genetic immunity to a particular poison by some members of a population of pests. They survive and multiply, spreading this resistance to later generations.

RESPIRATORY TRACT INFECTION—Any infections of the throat, bronchial tubes, and lungs caused by streptococcal or staphylococcal bacteria or viruses. These microorganisms are easily spread to others or to food via coughing and sneezing.

RESPONSE, COMPUTER—A system's reaction to terminal input.

RESPONSE TIME—Period of time between computer terminal input and response.

RESTOCK—To replace food or other items issued from the storeroom with new purchases and receipts.

RESTRICTED-USE PESTICIDES—Pesticides that are so dangerous that only properly trained and certified persons should use them. Standards for their use are promulgated by the Federal Environmental Protection Agency (EPA). Contrast **general-use pesticides.**

RETAIL—Markets that purchase from wholesalers or brokers and then sell to users.

RETAIL METHOD OF INVENTORY—Evaluation of inventory according to the selling price rather than the purchase cost.

RETENTIVE STAGE OF ADVERTISING—Third and final stage of advertising, in which an establishment or product already enjoys a distinctive and favorable public image. Customers continue to patronize or use it because of its reputation and word-of-mouth advertising. See **pioneering stage** and **competitive stage.**

RETINOL EQUIVALENTS (RE)—Measurement of vitamin A content expressed in terms of the vitamin's activity on the retina of the eye. It is fairly new; one RE equals five of the older International Units (IU).

RETRIEVAL, COMPUTER—Extraction of information from a computer data base.

RETROGRADATION—Crystallization of the amylose in foods that contain starch gel. This alteration of structure occurs when foods such as bread and potatoes are stored more than briefly.

REUSING OF CHECKS—Way of cheating in which the server uses the same order check twice, collects from both customers, but turns in only one payment.

REVENUE—Money received by an establishment from its customers.

REVOCATION OF PERMIT—Permanent withdrawal of an establishment's permit to serve food. Such action by a health authority follows only severe or repeated violations of health standards. See also **suspension of permit.**

REVOLVING FUND—Fund in which money spent is repeatedly replaced to bring the total back up to a set level.

RHAMNOSE—Sugar that is only about a third as sweet as ordinary table sugar. It occurs as a **glycoside** in many plants and is eaten naturally, not used as a foodservice additive.

RHEOSTAT—Device that can control the amount of illumination emitted by a given set of lights.

RHINE WINE GLASS—Wine glass with a long stem, sometimes knurled, and a broad rounded bowl.

RHODOPSIN—Pigment composed of protein and vitamin A that is required for the rods in the eyes to function in dim light.

RHUBARB—Plant yielding edible leafy stalks that are most tender when young. It is used in sauces, sherbets, jellies, and pies. Rhubarb was originally called the "pie plant."

RIBBON—Beating egg yolks and sugar together until they form strips when dropped from a height.

RIBOFLAVIN—**Vitamin B$_2$.**

RIBONUCLEIC ACID (RNA)—Nucleic acids that function within the body to form new protein in part from the amino acids received through digestion.

RIBOSE—A type of sugar involved in a number of important biochemical reactions, e.g., in the formation of nucleic acids.

RICE—Starchy edible seeds of a cereal grass that grows in warm, moist climates. It is a staple in Asian and Indian diets. Also, to force through a sieve to form ricelike particles. See **ricer.**

RICE, BROWN—Rice that is still in the hull. It is high in nutrient content. Contrast **rice, polished.**

RICE, INSTANT—Convenience food consisting of rice that has been precooked, thus requiring only hot water to prepare it quickly for serving.

RICE PAPER—Thin edible paper made not from rice but from the pith of certain trees in Taiwan. It is sometimes used in baking cookies, and also used as a wrapper.

RICE, POLISHED—Rice with the hull removed; the usual way rice is sold. Polished rice loses its vitamin B and nicotinic acid content, although modern steaming methods allow the rice to retain most of its nutrients. Contrast **rice, brown.**

RICER—Mechanism with small holes through which boiled potato is pressed to give it a ricelike consistency.

RICE, WILD—Uncultured grain that grows naturally in swampy areas and is harvested by hand. Served unpolished.

RICHE—French; wine with fine flavor, bouquet and fullness of body.

RICK—Warehouse rack or framework on which barrels of liquor are stored for aging.

RICKETS—Softening and malformation of the bones of children caused by a lack of vitamin D, which is required for the body to use calcium.

RIDDLE—Large-holed sieve.

RIDDLING—American term for **remuage.**

RIFT VALLEY FEVER—Viral disease with influenzalike symptoms that infects cattle and sheep and can spread to those humans handling the carcasses, as when butchering meat.

RIGOR MORTIS—Temporary rigidity of muscle tissue beginning in the hours following the death of a creature. Meat eaten at this point would be tough, so normally it is hung in a cooler for several days until the period is past.

RING MOLD—Hollow circular container with a hole in the middle. It is used to mold foods like gelatins into a decorative ring shape.

RINSE THERMOMETER—Thermometer immersed in the water used to rinse dishes in order to be sure the proper temperature is maintained.

RIPENED CHEESE—Cheese developed over time through the action of enzymes and bacteria naturally present.

RIPENING—Holding meat for 10 to 14 days at specific temperatures and under controlled relative humidity to improve its quality. Also called aging.

RIPENING LAMPS—Ultraviolet lamps used to ripen fruits and vegetables quickly.

RIPPLE RIBBON TUBE—Nozzle for a cake-decorating bag or syringe with a flat curved opening, used to make ribbon shapes with icing.

RISER PANEL—Side of a paperboard box of items (e.g., candies) that pops up and contains advertising for the product inside.

ROAST-BEEF SLICER—Knife with a narrow round-tipped blade usually about 14 inches long used to slice cooked roast beef.

ROASTING—Dry-heat food preparation method whereby meats and vegetables are cooked in an uncovered pan in the oven in such a manner that the product is raised and will not cook in its own juices or fat. A trivet is frequently placed in the bottom of the pan, for example, to keep meats above their own juices.

ROASTING JACK—Mechanical device used to turn the spit during roasting of meat.

ROASTING PAN—Large rectangular pan with medium-high sides used to roast meats in the oven.

ROBE—Thin film of color seen in a clear glass once it has been emptied of a deeply colored red wine.

ROBUSTA—One of the two varieties of coffee beans. See **arabica.**

ROCK CRYSTAL—Top quality glassware. It is a potassium and lead silicate that is beautifully clear and shining.

RODENTICIDE—Substance poisonous to rodents such as rats and mice. See **multiple-dose poisons** and **single-dose poisons.**

RODENT—Small animal pest, such as a rat or mouse. Rodents carry a variety of human pathogens including typhus and **salmonellosis.**

ROE—Clump of fish eggs still surrounded by the ovarian membrane. Often served fried or broiled with bacon.

ROLLING PIN—Cylinder used in hand rolling of pastry dough.

ROLLOVER—Renewal of a short-term debt rather than paying it off.

ROLL WARMER—See **hot-food server.**

ROM—Computer acronym for read only memory. It is the digital memory that, after its initial programming by the manufacturer, can only be read and no longer written upon; thus it is a permanent memory.

ROMAN TYPE—Modern typeface that is suitable for printing menus. Each letter is highly legible, with good contrast between thin and thick lines and perfectly curved strokes. Bodoni type is an example. Contrast **italic type.**

ROOM SERVICE—Service provided in hotels and motels that allows guests to call the dining room or kitchen and have food and beverages delivered to their own rooms.

ROOM SERVICE CHARGE VOUCHER—Printed slip used to record the name and room number of a guest ordering through **room service.**

ROOT VEGETABLE—Vegetable whose roots are the main part eaten, e.g., carrots, turnips, and beets.

ROSE—Any pink wine. The **must** begins fermentation exactly as for red wines but is separated from the grapeskins earlier, thus acquiring less color and tannins from them.

ROSE-GOTTLIEB TEST—Test that reveals the amount of fat in a sample of milk.

ROSE HIPS—Fruit of roses; it is very rich in vitamin C.

ROSETTE IRON—Iron used to fry rosette pastry shells.

ROSETTES—Pastry or candy roses used in decorating cakes.

ROSE TUBE—Nozzle for a cake-decorating bag or syringe with an elongated teardrop-shaped opening that produces icing in petal shapes for decorative roses, carnations, or daisies. It may also be used for making ribbons, swags, bows, and streamers.

ROSSO—Italian; red. Used in reference to wine.

ROTARY BEATER—Kitchen utensil used to blend or beat liquid mixtures through the spinning action of its blades. Also called an eggbeater.

ROTARY OVEN—Oven in which food is cooked on trays that revolve in a horizontal plane around a central axis. There may be several different levels of trays.

ROTATING MENU—**Cyclical menu.**

ROTISSERIE—French; in classic cookery, the part of the kitchen that is especially equipped for the roasting of meats. The term also applies to a modern portable appliance used to roast meats on a spit.

ROTISSERIE BROILER—Broiler in which food is cooked on slowly rotating spits before gas flames or infrared heating units.

ROTWEIN—German; red table wine.

ROUGHAGE—See **fiber.**

ROUND, MEAT—Meat in the hindquarter, accounting for about 23 percent of the carcass.

ROUNDWORM—Parasitic nematode worm, so named because it is round in shape like the common earthworm. Contrast **flat-worm.**

ROUX—Thickening agent for stocks, soups, and sauces consisting of equal parts of butter and flour by weight, cooked together. It may be white, blonde, or brown, depending on the cooking time.

ROYAL SIZE—Printing paper for menus with each sheet measuring 20 × 25 inches (50.8 × 63.5 cm). See **paper sizes.**

RULE—Straight or curved line or lines used in printing to provide ornamentation to menus. See **ornamental rule, plain swelled rule,** and **reeded rule.**

RUSSIAN SERVICE—Serving system in which the waiter or waitress picks up large platters of food in the kitchen and brings them to the table where he or she divides the food among the diners.

RUSSIAN TEA—China tea served with lemon juice or lemon slices rather than cream.

RUTABAGA—Type of turnip that is quite large and has a yellowish color. Unlike the true turnip, the rutabaga's greens are not eaten.

RUTIN—Disaccharide sugar found in certain cereal grains such as buckwheat.

RYE—Small, dark cereal grain used to make rye and pumpernickel breads. Also used in the production of certain whiskeys.

S

SACCHARASES—Enzymes that split complex sugar molecules to liberate the fructose or glucose contained therein.

SACCHARIMETER—Device used to measure the purity of sugar.

SACCHARIN—Artifical sweetener that is about 550 times as sweet as plain sugar yet contains no calories. It is derived from coal tar.

SACCHAROMETER—Device that measures the sugar content in liquids such as wines. Also known as a mustimeter.

SACHET—Small cloth bag of spices that may be added to a stock.

SADDLE STITCH—To bind folded sheets of a menu together by stapling right through the seam, outside to inside. See **binding.**

SAFE TEMPERATURES—Any temperature outside the **temperature danger zone,** i.e., below 45°F or above 140°F.

SAFETY STOCK—Minimum amount of an item that an establishment must have on hand to function.

SAGO—Starch derived from palm tree pitch used as a thickener in pie fillings and puddings.

SALAD BAR—Wide range of salad materials in containers, displayed on a refrigerated counter for self-service by the customer.

SALAD DRESSING—Flavorful sauce applied to salads to enhance their appeal.

SALAD GARNISH—The decoration or "icing on the cake" of an otherwise plain salad, offering contrast in color, flavor, and texture as well as harmony with the rest of the salad.

SALAD GREENS—The following is a list of the most common salad greens.

Amaranth: Plant of over 50 varieties with a high protein content and a spinachlike flavor. It has rounded leaves with red splotches.

Arugula: Plant related to the mustard family. Arugula has small, dark-green notched leaves and a peppery flavor.

Belgium endive: Root of the chicory plant. Endive has pale yellow, boat-shaped leaves and a bitter flavor.

Bibb lettuce: Dark, crisp leaves with a delicate nutty flavor.

Borage: Plant with fuzzy leaves and a cucumber flavor. Borage grows wild in Europe.

Boston lettuce: Also known as butter lettuce, this salad green has a loose head with delicate, sweet leaves.

Chicory: Also known as curly leaf endive, this plant has curly leaves and a bitter taste.

Cress: Wild plant with green notched leaves and a peppery flavor. Also known as watercress.

Dandelion: Weed with leaves that have a tart flavor and are high in iron.

Endive: Salad green similar to chicory.

Escarole: Plant of the chicory family with broad, flat leaves and a slightly bitter taste.

Fiddlehead fern: Young shoots of ferns with a spiral shape and a nutty flavor.

Iceberg lettuce: Pale green leaves in a tight head. Iceberg has a crisp texture and a bland flavor.

Looseleaf: Group of lettuce including red leaf and green lettuce. Looseleaf lettuce has a mild, sweet flavor and tender leaves.

Mâche: Also known as lamb's lettuce, this is a wild green with small, round leaves that have a mild flavor.

Mustard greens: Plant of the mustard family with leaves that have a peppery flavor and a high vitamin A and B content.

Oyster plant: Gray-green leaves with a fresh oysterlike flavor. Also called salsify.

Radicchio: Plant of the chicory family with a compact head and red leaves. Radicchio has a tangy, bitter flavor.

Rape: Leaf plant with a mild flavor.

Romaine: Also known as cos, this lettuce has dark green, oval leaves with a pungent flavor.

Salad burnet: Plant with round, serrated leaves and a cucumber flavor.

Sorrel: Wild herb with a sour taste and a high vitamin C content. Types include mountain and french sorrel.

Spinach: Plant with bright green, medium-sized leaves and a mild, musky flavor.

Swiss chard: Plant of the beet family with leaves that have a mild flavor.

SALAMANDER—Small broiler, usually gas-fired, used to glaze or brown items. Also called backshelf broiler.

SALERATUS—Baking soda used to leaven flour.

SALES ALLOWANCE—Reduction in the selling price of goods because of damage, late delivery, discounts, rebates, and so on.

SALES ANALYSIS BOOK—Business record showing the sales tally of each item for a given day. The date, weather, and any other factor that might affect sales is also recorded.

SALES AND POTENTIAL COST ANALYSIS—Form on which past costs and past sales revenue are recorded so that potential future costs can be calculated.

SALES BREAKDOWN—Tally sheet for a given period that is automatically printed out by an electronic register.

SALES CHECK—Slip on which a waiter lists the items ordered by a customer, the price of each, and the total including tax.

SALES CHECK DUPLICATES—Second copies of sales checks. One copy can be given to the bar, for example, while the other goes to the kitchen, thus saving time for customers who order both food and beverages.

SALES CONTROL PROCEDURES—Procedures to ensure that items are correctly priced, the number of each sold recorded, and the resulting revenue collected and accounted for.

SALES DISCOUNT—Reduction in the selling price if the customer pays early or buys a given quantity or more of the same item.

SALES GOAL PER HOUR—Amount of sales volume per man hour of work (see **sales hour**) that management has designated as necessary to achieve a desired level of profit.

SALES HISTORY CARD—Form that records how many of each menu item were sold at each meal. This can be used in forecasting future needs.

SALES/HOUR—Index of productivity calculated by dividing the dollar value of all sales during a given period by the total man hours worked. This computation can be done for all employees as a total group or for each type of subgroup separately (e.g., busboys as well as waitresses).

SALES JOURNAL—Business record in which the amount of sales are initially recorded. Sales may also be classified by type.

SALES MIX—Total number of each item on the menu that is sold to all customers combined during a given period.

SALES PER EMPLOYEE—Indication of employee productivity calculated by dividing total sales revenues by the number of employees.

SALES PER SEAT—Index calculated by dividing net sales by the total number of customer seats in an establishment.

SALES PROJECTION—**Forecasting.**

SALES RECORD—Recording the number of portions sold by checking sales slips, in order to ascertain customer acceptance of menu items.

SALES RETURN—Purchased goods sent back by the buyer for some reason. The seller must deduct the income received or expected from his gross sales account.

SALES REVENUE—Total income from sales for a given period.

SALES SLIP—Form on which the order is taken from the customer.

SALES SUMMARY RECORD—Any form (e.g., a columnar journal sheet or an adding machine tape) on which the total sales of a given waiter for a given shift is itemized.

SALES TALLY SHEET—Sheet on which the various types of food or drinks sold are listed. As each is sold it is checked off and at the end of the day the exact number of each type sold can be tallied up.

SALES VOLUME—Total dollar value of all sales in a given period.

SALINOMETER—Device used to determine the concentration of salt within a solution.

SALMANAZAR—Champagne bottle with a volume of 270 to 312 ounces, that of 10 to 12 regular bottles.

SALMONELLA—One of the bacteria that commonly cause **salmonellosis,** a food poisoning. Cooking food long enough at high temperatures kills the bacteria.

SALMONELLA TYPHI—Salmonella bacteria that cause typhoid fever. They can be spread in numerous ways, e.g., through infected water supplies.

SALMONELLOSIS—Food poisoning caused by ingesting Salmonella bacteria. Symptoms appear within 12 to 24 hours and include nausea, gastrointestinal pain, vomiting and diarrhea. It can occasionally be fatal.

SALSIFY—Plant with long white roots that have a taste similar to oysters. Served as a vegetable, e.g., in soups or stews.

SALT GRINDER—Small mortar or mill used to grind rock salt into small granules. Also called égrugeoir; French.

SALTING TUB—Large bucket in which pieces of meat are placed to be cured in brine. The best ones are made of stone or cement and have a latticework frame that is placed on top of the meat to hold it under the surface of the brine. Also called saloir; French.

SALTPETER—See **potassium nitrate.**

SALT PORK—Salt-cured pork, usually the fatty sections of the back, belly and sides.

SALT-RISING BREADS—Breads made without yeast, with flour, milk, salt, shortening, sugar, and white cornmeal.

SALTS—Any compound derived from the interaction of an acid and an alkali.

SALT, TABLE—Pure salt is sodium chloride. Sodium-sensitive people may experience high blood pressure if salt is eaten to excess. See **sodium.** Commercially manufactured salt often contains added **iodine** to help prevent thyroid goiter problems.

SANGUINE—Sweet orange whose flesh has a blood-red color.

SANITARIAN—Public-health professional who inspects food-service establishments to enforce regulations and to educate their personnel in personal and professional hygiene.

SANITARY—Absence of all pathogens, poisons, and other harmful creatures or substances; thoroughly clean.

SANITARY ENGINEER—Engineer responsible for ensuring that water supply and sewage systems are constructed and run in a sanitary manner.

SANITATION—Process of creating a sanitary condition in an area.

SANITIZATION—Reduction in the number of pathogens on a surface to a safe level, but not necessarily eliminating them altogether.

SAP—Liquid substance from trees and other plants, e.g., the sap from sugar-maple trees is boiled to produce sugar and maple syrup.

SAPODILLA—Tree whose sap is used to make chicle, which is used to make chewing gums.

SAPONIFICATION—Process of separating the **glycerol** from the **fatty acids** in fats.

SAPONINS—Substances derived from plants used to produce foam in beverages and detergents.

SATURATED FATS—See **fatty acids, saturated.**

SATURATION ADVERTISING—Bombarding a locality or region with a large amount of ads in a short time, often through two or more media simultaneously.

SAUCE BOAT—Dinner-service vessel of porcelain or silver, usually oval shaped, that holds sauces and gravies. Some have double bottoms for heating. Also called saucière; French.

SAUCE PAN—Small pan with a single long handle that is usually three to six inches deep and holds 1.5 to 11.5 quarts. Used for stove-top cooking of materials that require whipping or stirring.

SAUCEPOT—Large round pot of medium depth with two loop handles that holds 8.5 to 60 quarts. It is used to cook materials that require constant whipping or stirring.

SAUCER—Stemmed wine glass with a broad shallow bowl, used for champagne and for certain desserts.

SAUCIER—French; person in charge of making sauces.

SAUMONIERE—Oblong pot used to poach whole fish of the size and shape of salmon. Also called a salmon kettle.

SAUSAGE SKIN—Membrane layer that encases many types of sausages. It is made from hog or sheep intestines.

SAUTE—French; to cook in shallow fat from 335° to 425°F (168° to 223°C).

SAUTE PAN—Round shallow pan with sloping sides and a long

handle used to quick-fry foods in small amounts of fat. Also called sauteuse; French.

SAUTOIR—French; large, round, shallow straight-walled pan with one long handle and sometimes an opposite loop handle. It is used to cook foods in shallow fat. Sizes range from 2.5 to 4.5 inches deep and 10 to 20 inches in diameter.

SAVARIN MOLD—Ring-shaped metal pan used to shape and bake a sweet cake called *savarin*.

SAVORIES—Seasoned snacks such as cheese straws and deviled shrimp.

SCALD—Brown, mushy patches that sometimes appear in stored apples. Also, to heat milk to a temperature just below the boiling point.

SCALE—Relationship of the size of an original to the size of its reproduction, i.e., it may be larger or smaller. Also, to remove the scales of a fish.

SCALE, BEAM—Weighing device that uses a counterbalance that slides on a beam marked off in pounds and ounces. This type of scale is very accurate over a wide range of weights.

SCALE, DIAL—Weighing device in which the weight of the item is shown by a dial and moving pointer.

SCALE, EVEN BALANCE—Device to weigh exact amounts of ingredients in a kitchen or bakery. It uses two opposing balance pans, and a sliding beam. A weight of the desired amount is placed in one pan and a quantity of food in the other. A pointer-dial shows whether the portion is over or under the needed weight.

SCALE, FAN—Scale for weighing small quantities of goods sold by weight. The weight and price are read out on a fan-shaped dial.

SCALE, RECEIVING—Scale of large capacity used to check the weight of goods as they are received. Goods are placed on the scale's flat balance pan.

SCALE TESTING—Checking the receiver's scales for accuracy on a periodic basis by using standardized weights.

SCALLION—Young-onion stalk. Scallions are used in cooking foods, salads, or served as appetizers. Also called green onion.

SCAMPI—Italian and French for a European lobster; in English it means large shrimp prepared with a butter and garlic sauce.

SCANTLING—Supports or wooden beams used to hold casks in a wine cellar.

SCATTER SHEET—Sheet on which the cumulative number of sales for each menu item during a given period is recorded.

SCHAUMWEIN—German; dry or sweet sparkling white wine.

SCHEDULE OF APPORTIONMENT—Accounting plan in which indirect costs are divided (apportioned) among two or more departments.

SCHEDULING—Management's decisions regarding the hours of duty for each employee so that adequate **staffing** can be maintained throughout the week.

SCLEROPROTEIN—Protein found in connective tissue such as tendons and skin as well as in hard substances such as bones, horns, and fingernails.

SCOOP—Rounded shovel-like utensil, made in various standard capacities, used to scoop flour, sugar, ice, and the like.

SCOOP, ICE CREAM—Bowl of various standard sizes mounted on a rigid handle with a thumb-operated bale, used to form and release balls of semisolid food such as ice cream. Scoops are numbered according to their size, the number referring to the servings yielded per quart. Also called dipper, disher.

Scoop number	Measure	Approximate weight
30	2 tbsp	1–1½ oz.
24	2⅔ tbsp	1½–1¾ oz.
20	3 tbsp	1¾–2 oz.
16	4 tbsp	2–2¼ oz.
12	5 tbsp	2¼–3 oz.
10	6 tbsp	4–5 oz.
6	10 tbsp	6 oz.

SCORE, BUTTER—Numerical rating given to butter based on a subjective judging of the butter's body, color, and salt content. The higher the score, the higher the grade awarded, e.g., a score of 93 equals Grade AA.

SCORE, PAPER—Crease that facilitates the folding of heavy paper, such as that used for menu covers.

SCORING—Preparation technique of making gashes with a knife before baking, as on ham or pie crust.

SCRAMBLE SYSTEM—Cafeteria in which each different type of food is laid out on a separate counter. The customer walks from counter to counter, choosing what he wishes. Contrast **straight line cafeteria.**

SCRAPING BLOCK—Block on which utensils are placed in order to remove solid waste from them. It should be set just above a garbage disposal or container.

SCRAP VALUE—Financial worth of a piece of equipment after its usefulness has ended and it is to be junked.

SCREENING—Inspecting all produced goods prior to sale to remove those of unacceptable quality.

SCREEN PROCESS PRINTING—Menu printing process in which a mesh of silk, metal, or synthetic fiber holds a stencil in place. Ink is forced through the screen and the image area of the stencil onto the paper.

SCUFF-RESISTANT INKS—Menu printing inks that stay bright and legible even when handled roughly and frequently. See **printing inks.**

SCUM—Layer of waste food material floating on the surface of a cooking liquid. In boiling stock, for example, the coagulated protein may rise to the surface and then congeal when the liquid is cooled.

SCURVY—Disease caused by insufficient amounts of vitamin C. Symptoms include soft and bleeding gums, bleeding beneath the skin, muscle weakness, and joint pain.

SCUTELLUM—Part of the germ in cereal grains that surrounds the embryo and provides a rich source of vitamins.

SEAFOOD FORK—Small fork used to eat small seafood items such as clams, oysters, or shrimp.

SEALED-BID PURCHASING—Purchasing procedure in which a large organization takes contract offers from several different suppliers, compares the sealed bids on a given day, and awards a long-term contract to the company with the best offer. Contrast **open-market purchasing.**

SEAR—To brown the outside of a meat with high heat prior to the main cooking, in order to contribute to overall color and to seal in juices.

SEASONAL BANQUET CONTRACT—Contract that covers all banquets planned by a group in a given season, rather than a separate contract for each.

SEASONAL FLUCTUATION—Changes in income or expenses related to the time of year. For example, fresh fruit costs more in the winter; income in resort areas goes up during the tourist season.

SEA URCHIN—Spiny round sea creature, of which the fleshy parts and roe can be eaten.

SEAWEED—Any of a variety of plants that grow in salt water. Some forms are not only edible, but contain a wide variety of vitamins and minerals, although they are low in protein. See **chondrus crispus.**

SEC—French; a dry wine, or when used with champagne a medium sweet one.

SECONDARY AUDIENCE—People who read a publication (and its advertisements) in addition to its purchaser, e.g., friends, visitors, or clientele in a physician's office.

SECONDARY MARKETS—Locations to which most of the products handled by the **primary market** will flow, and out of which they will be shipped to local markets.

SECONDARY SALES EFFECT—Effect that occurs when people are attracted by specials on the menu (e.g., two-for-one entrees or drinks) and then also buy other things at the regular price.

SECURED ACCOUNT—Credit account in which collateral is held to back up the amount borrowed.

SECURITY, COMPUTER—Prevention of access to a data base by those unauthorized to retrieve it.

SEDIMENT—Precipitate that forms in wines as they develop. It tends to settle on the bottom.

SEED HOLES—Tiny holes made in wooden containers by boring insects or worms.

SEKT—Dry or sweet white sparkling wine that is the German equivalent to champagne.

SELENIUM—Mineral required by the body in trace amounts. It plays a role in several functions, including antioxidation, many enzyme systems, cell integrity, and antibody production. Excessive amounts can be toxic. Food sources include organ meats, seafood, whole grains, and food grown in regions where the soil contains an abundance of the mineral.

SELF-CLOSING DOORS—Doors with a spring or other device that makes them close as soon as they are released. This helps prevent the entry of pests and reduces heat transfer in or out.

SELF-COVER—Menu cover made of paper that is the same as that used for the inside pages.

SELLER'S MARKET—Condition prevailing when demand exceeds supply. Sellers have more options and prices are generally higher. The opposite of **buyer's market.**

SELLING EXPENSES—Costs incurred as part of an establishment's sales effort, e.g., advertising.

SELLOUT TIME—The amount of time it takes for a given pre-prepared item to sell out during a meal period. If an item sells out quickly, the foodservice manager will know that more should be prepared next time. See **forecasting.**

SEMI A LA CARTE MENU—Menu that offers the basic meal (e.g., an entrée with salad and vegetable) for a single price and lists extra charges for such things as appetizers and desserts.

SEMICONVENIENCE KITCHEN—Kitchen equipped to handle both convenience items and those that must be made from scratch. Contrast **full production kitchen.**

SEMIVARIABLE EMPLOYEES—Those types of employees of whom the needed number varies slightly with large fluctuations in the volume of business, e.g., cooks. Contrast **variable employees** and **fixed employees.**

SENSIBLE HEAT—Warmth that can be sensed directly that is the result of an increase in temperature. Contrast **latent heat.**

SEPARATOR—Machine used in dairies for separating cream from milk.

SEPTICEMIA—Disease caused by pathogens circulating in the blood. Symptoms include chills, fever, and the spread of infection to other organs. Also called blood poisoning.

SEQUENCE, MENU—The order in which food items are listed on the menu.

SEQUENTIAL ACCESS—Retrieval of computer information in the order in which it was stored.

SERINE—One of the nonessential amino acids.

SEROSA—Membraneous lining of the body's large cavities that "holds" the organs, e.g., the intestinal lining.

SERUM CHOLESTEROL—Free cholesterol in the bloodstream.

SERVER— Any worker who serves food or drinks to customers, e.g., a waiter.

SERVICE—Set of utensils used to serve food at the table. Also, waiting a table.

SERVICE BAR—Any bar in which the server takes orders to the

bartender and brings drinks back to the customer. Contrast **cash bar.**

SERVICE CAPACITY—Potential of equipment (e.g., ovens or typewriters) to provide valuable service.

SERVICE COMPRIS—French; service included, i.e., a service charge is already included in the basic meal price. However, an additional tip is not inappropriate.

SERVICE LIFE—Period that an asset is expected to provide useful service to its owner. The depreciation rate is often based on this estimated number of years.

SERVICE PAN—See **counter pan.**

SERVICE PLATE—Round decorative plate, about 12 inches in diameter, used at the center of the cover, or place setting, at each seat of the dinner table. The appetizer or soup is placed with an underliner on top of the service plate, which is removed before the entree is brought in on its own dinner plate.

SERVICE STAND—Dining-room fixture in which the server's **mise en place** is kept, or everything needed to service tables, including tablecloths, napkins, plates, glasses, silver, ashtrays, salt and pepper shakers, spices, and sauces.

SERVING FORK—Larger version of the dinner fork, used to serve food at the table.

SERVING SPOON—Spoon with a large bowl, which may or may not be slotted, used to serve food at the table.

SERVING TONGS—Utensil for picking up and serving large pieces of food at the table.

SESAME SEED—Tiny seeds of the Asian sesame plant, used as a topping on bread rolls, crackers, and cookies.

SET—Process by which a liquid food solidifies, as a gelatin does as it cools.

SEVE—French; an aromatic or vigorous wine.

SHADOW TYPE—Menu printing type with a dark shaded area to

one side of each letter, giving the appearance of a three-dimensional figure casting a shadow. See **special type.**

SHALLOT—Bulb of an onionlike plant, used as a seasoning.

SHAPED PAN—Cake pan with a distinctive shape used to bake novelty cakes.

SHARPENING STEEL—Steel rod with a rough surface used to sharpen knives and give them an even edge. It is gripped by the handle and the grainy surface is repeatedly passed along the blade of the knife.

SHEET-FED PRESS—Printing press into which individual sheets of paper are fed one at a time. Contrast **web press.**

SHEET PAN—Rectangular pan with very shallow walls used for baking in the oven.

SHELF-DISPLAY DATE—Day a food item was put on display for sale. Although this does not reveal the **expiration date,** it does help in **stock rotation.**

SHELF LIFE—Amount of time that a given food can stay in storage and still remain in satisfactory condition, assuming that proper conditions of temperature and humidity are maintained.

SHELL—Drinking glass shaped like a tall plain cylinder.

SHELLFISH—Edible fish with shells; crustaceans or mollusks. Shellfish are high in protein, vitamin B, iodine, and mineral salts. The following are the more popular types.

Abalone: Marine snail found in the tropical waters of the world. In the U.S., abalone is found on the Pacific Coast. The mussel has a rubbery texture.

Alaskan king crab: Crab related to the hermit crab, found in waters of the Bering Sea. They grow as large as 24 pounds. Only the meat of the claws, legs, and shoulders is usually eaten.

American lobster: Also known as the Maine lobster, this shellfish is found from Canada to North Carolina. The average weight is one to five pounds. Any over three pounds is

called a jumbo lobster. The lobster harvest has declined
in recent years.

Blue crab: One of the most abundant crustaceans found in the
Atlantic from New Jersey to Florida. Blue crabs are sold
in hard shell or soft shell.

Clam: Bivalve shells encase the edible body, consisting of a
muscle and a neck. The most popular Atlantic species
include hard clams or quahogs (also called cherrystone),
surf clams, and soft shell clams. The Pacific Coast clams
include razor clams, butter clams, littleneck clams, and
geoducks.

Crayfish: Small, lobsterlike crustaceans particularly abundant
in Louisiana. There are over two dozen species, with the
red swamp crayfish being the most popular. Also called
crawfish.

Dungeness crab: Crab with a flattened body and a reddish,
spotted shell. This crab is most abundant on the Pacific
Coast.

Icelandic lobster: Imported species smaller than the American
lobster. It has tender white flesh and a red shell that does
not change color when cooked.

Mussel: Bivalve mollusk with dark blue shell. Mussels are
abundant on the New England coast. They are high in
protein and low in fat.

Oyster: Bivalve mollusk of the genus *crassostrea.* The most
popular species include the Pacific oyster, the European
oyster, the Atlantic oyster, and the Olympia oyster. Oysters are at their peak from October to May and are good
sources of iron, iodine, and calcium.

Prawn: European term for large shrimp.

Rock shrimp: Member of the shrimp family with a rigid shell
and flesh that is similar to lobster. Rock shrimp are abundant in Southwest Florida.

Scallop: Mollusk with fluted shell and sweet-flavored muscles.
Sea scallops are larger and less sweet than the bay scallops. They are most abundant from April to October.

Shrimp: Small, 10-legged crustacean with a thin shell. The
most popular varieties include the white shrimp, the pink
shrimp, and the brown shrimp. The Gulf and Pacific

coasts are the most abundant sources for shrimp, particularly from January to April.

Snow crab: Crustacean with long legs and a hard shell. They are abundant on the Pacific Coast and have a sweet, delicate flavor.

Softshell crab: Crabs that are molting or have lost their shells and have not yet grown larger ones. Crabs in this temporary condition are considered a delicacy, for the soft shell may be eaten as well as the crab.

Stone crab: Crab abundant on the West Coast of Florida, particularly from October to April. Stone crabs have very hard shells and pincers with black tips. Only the claws of the crab are eaten for their firm, sweet flesh.

SHERRY GLASS—Wine glass with a short stem, wide top, and deep bowl with slanting sides. It holds two to three ounces.

SHIELD-GRADE STAMP—Stamp in the shape of the federal shield used by the U.S. Department of Agriculture. It is used to certify the federal grade of a product.

SHIGELLA—Bacilli that cause **shigellosis.**

SHIGELLOSIS—Bacillary **dysentery,** a type of food poisoning caused by the ingestion of **shigella** bacteria. Symptoms include abdominal cramps, diarrhea, chills, and fever.

SHOPPER—Giveaway publication composed entirely of advertising printed on newsprint. Special sales or introductory offers from one or more establishments are usually included.

SHOPPER SYSTEM—Control technique, in which an outside person unknown to the regular employees comes into an establishment pretending to be a customer so that he can check for fraud or poor service by the employees.

SHORT DRINK—Slightly smaller than authorized portion served by a bartender to a large number of customers. The extra ounces can be sold later for his or her own profit.

SHORTENING—Soft fats, either animal or vegetable, that make batter smooth and creamy and the baked product crisp and flaky.

SHORT INVENTORY—See **inventory, short.**

SHORT-ORDER KITCHEN—Kitchen with minimal equipment that is set up mainly to handle a limited line of fast-food items, e.g., hamburgers, hot dogs, and french fries. Contrast **full production kitchen.**

SHORT-SHIPPED—When less goods are sent than the number or weight specified in the original order. In such cases, the receiver should issue a **credit memo** before accepting the shipment.

SHORT SLIP—Form that states that some or all of the merchandise ordered by an establishment was not received. They are therefore due a **credit memo.**

SHORT WEIGHT—When delivered goods weigh less than the amount ordered.

SHOT GLASS—Short, squat bar glass that is wider at the top than at the bottom and holds one to two ounces of liquor.

SHOWTHROUGH—When the print on one side of a sheet can be seen through the paper from the other side. Contrast **opacity.**

SHRINKAGE, MEAT—Decrease in the size of a meat cut after cooking. The amount depends on the type of meat, cut, amount of fat, and cooking temperatures.

SHUCK—To remove the meat from the shell of a mollusk such as a clam, oyster, or scallop.

SIALOGOGUE—Substance that stimulates secretion of saliva.

SIDE STITCHING—Binding separate sheets of a menu together by stapling or stitching along the back edge, front to back. See **binding.**

SIFT—Separating smaller from larger particles in a substance such as meal, or shaking a powder such as flour through a sieve to make it fluffy.

SIEVE—Round metal frame with a screen bottom used to **sift** flour or other dry ingredients.

SIFTING—Leaking of a finely ground product such as sugar through the seams or cracks in its container.

SIGNATURES—Set of menu pages formed by folding a single large sheet that was printed following **imposition.**

SIKES—English method of measuring the alcoholic strength of beverages.

SILENCE PAD—Sheet of felt or foam rubber placed between the table top and the tablecloth to act as a cushion in order to reduce the clatter of tableware and protect the table from mars, burns, and spills.

SILICA GEL—Sandlike compound that absorbs water and is used as a drying agent.

SILK SCREEN PRINTING—Former name for **screen process printing.**

SILVER—Trace amounts are used in coating nonpareils, the silver-colored beads that decorate cakes and candies; it is nontoxic in such small quantities.

SILVER BURNISHER—Machine that polishes silver by the action of agitating metal shot.

SILVER WASHER—Machine designed especially for the washing of flatware.

SIMMER—To cook food immersed in a liquid at a temperature of 185° to 205°F (85° to 96°C), just below a full boil.

SIMPLE SYRUP—Beverage sweetener consisting of equal amounts of sugar and water that have been boiled until the sugar dissolved. Used particularly in alcoholic beverages because sugar does not dissolve readily in alcohol.

SINGE—To pass a plucked bird over an open flame to burn off the pin feathers.

SINGLE-ACTING BAKING POWDER—Baking powder that releases carbon dioxide as soon as it is moistened. See **double acting baking powder.**

SINGLE CRUST—Pie that does not have a crust for its top or cover but only one for its base.

SINGLE-DOSE POISONS—Rodenticides that need to be ingested only once to cause death, which follows almost immediately. This type lacks the safety factor of **multiple-dose poisons.** Examples are ANTU, red squill, and zinc phosphide.

SINK, THREE-COMPARTMENT—Sink for dish washing that has three independent sections: for washing, for rinsing, and for sanitizing, either with chemicals or hot water.

SINK, TWO-COMPARTMENT—Sink for dish washing that has two independent sections: for washing and for sanitizing, either with chemicals or hot water.

SIPHON—Carafe of thick glass, often encased in wicker or metal, that holds water made effervescent with carbon dioxide gas under pressure. The water is discharged through a spout opened by a lever.

SITOLOGY—Scientific study of diet.

SITOSTEROL—Sterol that is most common in vegetable oil. It is chemically similar to cholesterol.

SIZING—Coating menu paper with some substance that allows it to resist absorbing spilled water or other liquids.

SIZZLING STEAK—Service on a heated heavy-gauge aluminum platter so that the steak and its juices sizzle as the platter is presented to the consumer.

SKELETAL MUSCLE—Muscle attached to the skeleton that is responsible for the voluntary movement of the body. In contrast to **smooth muscle,** these muscles are the principal source of salable meat.

SKEWER—Fairly long spike or spit of wood or metal on which pieces of food to be broiled or fried are laced. Also called brochette; French.

SKEWERING—Fastening foods onto a fairly long spike or spit for cooking or service.

SKID—Low wooden platform on which goods can be stacked that raises them slightly off the floor.

SKILLET—Shallow round pan made of heavy metal used for pan-broiling or frying.

SKIMMER—Flat perforated spoon used to skim solids from the surface of a liquid.

SKUNKY—Aroma of beer that has been ruined by excessive heat and light.

SLAWING MACHINE—Machine for rapidly shredding large volumes of cabbage or other vegetables.

SLICE THICKNESS REGULATOR—Control on a food slicer that determines the thickness of slices by changing the position of the gauge plate.

SLICING MACHINE—Machine for cutting food in slices of consistent thickness, from paper-thin up to three quarters of an inch. It consists of a motor-driven disc knife and a movable carriage tray that holds the food and moves it at a right angle across the spinning blade. The food rests against a gauge plate parallel to the blade that can be adjusted to control the thickness of the slices. Some models have a motor-driven carriage tray and a device that picks up and stacks the slices as they come off the blade. Also called a food slicer.

SLOGAN—Catchy, appealing phrase that identifies a product or establishment and distinguishes it in some way.

SLOTTED SPOON—Spoon with a perforated bowl used to lift solids from a liquid medium.

SLUSH—To clean the inside of a container by filling it partially with fluid, covering its opening, and then shaking it.

SMOKE—To hang meat or fish in a room filled with hardwood smoke. Natural chemicals such as phenols change the flavor and also help preserve the food.

SMOKE POINT—Temperature (usually over 160° C) at which cooking oils and fats begin to decompose and give off smoke.

SMOOTH MUSCLE—Muscle within the hollow inner organs, such as the stomach and intestines that is responsible for their involuntary movement. Although just as edible as **skeletal muscle,** the average consumer does not favor these meats (e.g., tripe, chitlins).

SMORGASBORD—Swedish buffet or arrangement of appetizers or full meals on a large table for self-service.

SMUT—Fungi that infest wheat.

SNACK—Small portion of food eaten at any time; a very light meal.

SNAIL—Slimy land mollusk that lives in a distinctive spiral shell. Certain species are edible after considerable cleaning and preparation. They are considered a delicacy, especially when they are called escargot (French).

SNEEZE GUARD—See **counter guard.**

SODIUM—Essential mineral required for proper functioning of the nervous system. One sodium atom is found in each molecule of table salt. Sodium, which is also present in other foods, such as shellfish, is believed to contribute to hypertension by increasing the amount of water in the blood, thus adding to the blood's pressure in the artery. See **salt, table.** Since contemporary diets often include an abundance of salt and sodium in all forms, excess is far more common than deficiency.

SODIUM BICARBONATE—Active ingredient in baking powder that releases carbon dioxide when mixed with acid powder and water. See **acid calcium phosphate.**

SODIUM BISULFITE—Additive used to bleach and preserve foods such as dried fruit and dried potatoes. It destroys much of the vitamin B_1 content.

SODIUM CHLORIDE—Ordinary **table salt.** Each molecule consists of an atom of **sodium** and an atom of chlorine.

SODIUM FLUORIDE—Chemical often used in foodservice establishments to kill cockroaches. Since it is a white powder resembling baking soda, great care is needed in its use. Cases have been reported in which sodium fluoride was accidentally mixed in food. Within several minutes the customers experienced vomiting, abdominal pains, diarrhea, and even convulsions.

SOFT-BALL STAGE—Temperature (238°F) to which sugar solution is cooked so that a bit of it dropped into chilled water congeals into a soft ball. Contrast **soft-crack stage.**

SOFT-CRACK STAGE—Temperature (270°F) to which sugar solution is cooked so that a bit of it dropped into chilled water forms a hard ball that becomes less brittle when removed from the cold water. Contrast **soft-ball stage.**

SOFTWARE—Programs and instructions for a computer or microprocessor system to perform a required function.

SOLANINE—Bitter glycoside found in potato sprouts. It can be toxic in large amounts.

SOMMELIER—French; wine steward, who discusses with customers the various wines to be served and is responsible for the wine cellar.

SORBET—French; sherbet flavored with a liqueur rather than a fruit syrup.

SORBIC ACID—Compound used to inhibit the growth of mold and yeast; it is nontoxic to humans.

SORBITOL—Alcohol derived from fructose and found in various fruits such as apricots and plums. Although it is only about half as sweet as table sugar, it has no ill effects on diabetics and does not cause tooth cavities; it is therefore often used to sweeten foods for diabetics, as well as other foods.

SORGHUM—Cereal used to make a sweet syrup; it may also be ground and added to crackers and some snack foods.

SOUP SPOON—Large oval spoon used to eat soup.

SOURCE PROGRAM—Computer program that must be translated into machine language prior to use.

SOUR CREAM—Cream that has been soured with lemon juice or vinegar; useful in cakes, salad dressing, dips, and the like.

SOUR GLASS—Bar glass with a short stem, narrow top, and deep bowl holding three to six ounces.

SOUR MASH—Process in which fresh yeast is combined with old working yeast from another fermentation and the mix is added to a new mash to induce fermentation. See **mash** and **sweet mash.**

SOUR MILK—Milk that has gone sour. It is a useful baking ingredient as the acid reacts with baking soda in the preparation of biscuits, cakes, doughnuts, and the like.

SOUSED—Pickled; see **pickle.**

SOW—Mature female swine.

SOXHLET—Device used to extract fats or other solids from solvents.

SOYBEAN—Vegetable bean that is high in protein, with no starch and little sugar. Considered a meat substitute and used as a meat extender. Available commercially in a cheeselike form called **tofu.** The oil can be used in cooking among other uses.

SOY SAUCE—Dark-brown salty condiment made from soy beans, corn syrup and salt. It is used to season Chinese and other foods.

SPACE—Area on a menu page not filled with print. See **letter-spacing** and **line spacing.**

SPACE SPOTS—Large series of small newspaper ads purchased under a single contract, normally with a quantity discount.

SPACE SPRAY—Aerosol insecticide that, sprayed into an enclosed space, floats in the air long enough to kill flying insects.

SPAN OF CONTROL—Number of employees for whom a given manager or supervisor is directly responsible.

SPARKLET—Small capsule containing liquid carbon dioxide, used to carbonate beverages.

SPATULA—Hand tool with a wide thin blade and a blunt tip used to scrape bowls or spread butter and icings. Spatulas with narrow blades are sometimes called palette knives.

SPECIAL ORDER—Request for items or supplies not ordinarily offered by the supplier. The cost of producing these special items can be separated from the cost of other items, and charged to the purchaser.

SPECIAL PROMOTIONS—Offering special items for sale or lowering the cost of items on a particular day such as a holiday or other particular event.

SPECIALTY OPERATIONS—Items offered by an establishment that cater to the particular background and preferences of the potential customers in the area. For example, it may offer Greek food in a neighborhood with a large Greek population.

SPECIAL TYPE—Any sort of menu-printing type beyond the ordinary ones found in normal books, magazines, and newspapers. These are used to draw attention. See **boldface type, decorated type, inline type, inline-shadow type, outline type,** and **shadow-type.**

SPECIFICATIONS—Exact descriptions of the quality and type of goods desired by an establishment. They are given to potential suppliers so that they may quote a price.

SPECIFICATIONS, FOOD—Description of the quality, weight, and age of meat or other products desired for purchase by an establishment.

SPECIFICATION SHEETS—Forms on which the requirements for an order of goods can be listed. Copies go to the supplier, the receiver, and the control office.

SPECIFIC DYNAMIC ACTION—Temporary increase in metabolism after eating.

SPECIFIC GRAVITY—Density of a substance (e.g., wine) expressed as the ratio of its weight to that of an equal volume of water.

SPEED DRIVE—Attachment that triples the speed of a vertical mixer used with the vegetable-slicer attachment.

SPICES—General term for a wide variety of aromatic seasonings. The following are among the more popular used today.

Allspice: Dried berry of the pimento tree, grown in the West Indies. It has a flavor similar to cinnamon, nutmeg, and cloves, and is used in pickling, stews, and preserved fruits.

Cardamom: Seeds from a plant of the ginger family. As seed or powder, it is used in pickling, curries, and in baked goods.

Celery Seed: Pungent seed from a plant related to garden celery. It is used in a great variety of dishes.

Chili powder: Blend of chili peppers, cumin seed, oregano, and garlic powder. It is used in chili, sauces, and stews.

Cinnamon: Bark from various trees of the laurel species. In powder or stick form, it is mostly used in baked goods, Middle Eastern cookery, and candies.

Clove: Dried flower bud of a small evergreen shrub. It is used to flavor ham, stocks, soups, and sweet dishes.

Coriander: Aromatic herb of the carrot family with a lemony sage flavor. It is used in pickling, liqueurs, and meat products.

Cumin: Plant of the parsley family. The seeds have a bitter flavor. Cumin is used in curry powder, liqueurs, cheeses, and breads.

Curry: Blend of 16 spices including turmeric, ginger, red pepper, cumin, and coriander. Curry powder is used in Indian cookery to flavor meat, fish, eggs, and chicken.

Fenugreek: Leguminous plant whose ground seeds are used in curry powder.

Ginger: Dried root of a plant native to the East and West Indies. Ginger has a sharp, warm flavor and is used with Chinese and other dishes, preserves, and baked goods.

Mace: Covering of the outer shell of nutmeg, dried and ground. Mace is used to flavor baked goods, spinach, and in pickling.

Mustard: Seeds of the mustard plant that are pulverized, mixed with water to form a paste, and used as a relish or condiment.

Nutmeg: Seed of a tropical tree native to the East and West Indies. The kernel of the plant is used with desserts and in some vegetable dishes.

Paprika: Hungarian red capsicum pepper that is powdered and used to flavor fish, shellfish, chicken, goulash, vegetables, and egg dishes.

Pepper: Seed-bearing fruit of the pepper plant *piper nigrum*. Black pepper is derived from the dried, small, immature berries while white pepper comes from the mature berries whose hulls have been removed. Pepper is used in meat, vegetable, fish, and egg dishes.

Poppy seeds: Tiny seeds of the poppy plant; used in breads, cookies, cakes, and noodle dishes.

Turmeric: Root of a plant of the ginger family. Turmeric has a strong, mustardy flavor. It is used in meat and egg dishes and in curry powder.

Vanilla: Mexican climbing orchid with seed pods that are dried, fermented, and used to flavor baked goods and other foods.

SPILLAGE ALLOWANCE—Portion of a liquor bottle's contents, e.g., one ounce, that is assumed will be lost accidentally; it is not figured into the calculation of drinks per bottle.

SPIRAL PEEL—Continuous strip of fruit peel (e.g., apple, lemon) about three eighths of an inch wide that is cut by beginning at the stem and working around the fruit to its bottom. May be used as a garnish.

SPIRAL WHIP—Vertical-mixer attachment, with wires in spiral formation, that is used to whip sponge-cake batter, incorporate flour, and whip light marshmallows. The formation of the wires directs the ingredients down around the outside edges of the bowl and up through the center.

SPIRILLA—Bacteria that are shaped like little spirals rather than rods or spheres. Contrast **bacilli** and **cocci.**

SPIRITS—Distilled alcoholic beverages.

SPIT—Long pointed rod on which meat is roasted, before or over a flame or other source of radiant heat while being slowly turned by hand or by a motor. Also called broche; French.

SPLASH COVER—Accessory to a vertical mixer consisting of a

plastic dome that fits over the top of the mixing bowl to prevent ingredients from splashing out.

SPLIT—Wine bottle one-fourth the regular size that holds 6 to 6.5 ounces.

SPLIT RING—A way of cheating an establishment at the cash register, i.e., an employee rings up the charge incorrectly on a mechanical register, rings up a partial correction so quickly that the customer does not note the amount on the first ring, and pockets the difference. For example, for a $3.95 charge he or she may ring up $1.75 and then twenty cents, pocketing the remaining two dollars of the payment.

SPLIT SHIFT—Daily work shift of two portions with a long break in between (e.g., 10 A.M.–2 P.M. and 4–8 P.M.) rather than one continuous work period (e.g., 9 A.M.–5 P.M.). Such a schedule can pose problems for some employees.

SPOILAGE—Loss of food's edibility because of chemical contamination, oxidation, the presence of harmful microorganisms, or any other breakdown of the food's components.

SPOILAGE REPORT—Form on which a storekeeper lists spoiled goods and the reasons for such spoilage. If the fault is the supplier's, the storekeeper can recommend a refund or a credit.

SPORE, BACTERIAL—Quiescent state in which bacteria develop thick walls and suspend most life functions. They can then survive extremes of cold or heat, so that, for example, pasteurization does not succeed in killing them, and can then germinate later under more favorable conditions.

SPOT CHECKS—Random or occasional monitoring of parts of any functioning system, e.g., the cost-control system, in order to ensure that employees are performing it correctly.

SPOT PRICE—Cost of goods available for sale and immediate delivery.

SPOT PURCHASE—Purchase of goods, usually with cash, for immediate delivery.

SPRINGER—Type of **swell** in a sealed can. The bulge disappears when pressed but springs out elsewhere.

SPRINGFORM PAN—Round baking pan with a bottom that can be separated from the sides. The two parts are held together by a spring clamp.

SPRING SWITCH—**Dead man control.**

SPRINKLER SYSTEM—System of water pipes and sprinkler valves installed in the ceiling that is automatically activated in case of a fire.

SPUMANTE—Italian: sparkling.

SQUAB—A young pigeon.

SQUASH, ACORN—Squash with a hard green or orange-green shell. The flesh is yellow-orange. It is often baked with butter and a brown-sugar coating.

STABILIZERS—Substances such as **agar-agar** that help stabilize emulsions.

STABLE EMULSION—An **emulsion** in which the two liquids do not readily separate out.

STACHYOSE—Complex sugar found in soy and some other beans in which each molecule is composed of four molecules of simpler sugars.

STAFFING—Management's decisions regarding the number of each type of employee it needs to handle the job. See also **scheduling.**

STAFFING CHART—Table used by management to estimate the number of each type of employee it will need to run an establishment, given different numbers of customers.

STAFF MEALS—**Employee meals.**

STAG—Male beef carcass that was castrated after maturity.

STAINLESS STEEL—Metal used extensively in foodservice fixtures and equipment. It has good appearance, durability, and resistance to corrosion. The stainless steel recommended for foodservices is No. 302, which contains 18 percent chromium, 8 percent nickel, and no more than .08 percent carbon, 2 percent manganese, 0.04 percent phosphorous, 0.03 percent sulfur, and one percent silicon.

STANDARD—Criterion or measure used to evaluate a quantity, quality, or volume.

STANDARD ADVERTISING REGISTER—Annual volume that lists ad agencies and the advertisers who employ them.

STANDARD COST ACCOUNTING—Accounting technique in which standard, regular costs are entered in the books during the accounting period. At the end of the period, any discrepancies with actual costs are taken into consideration.

STANDARD DRINK SIZES AND RECIPES—List of **standard recipes** for each type of drink and the size glass it should be served in.

STANDARD GRADE—Fourth highest grade out of eight grades of meat. See **meat grading.**

STANDARDIZED RECIPE—Formula, established by management, that gives a consistent, known quality and quantity of product.

STANDARD PLUCK—What is removed from a tea's branch tip, i.e., two leaves and a bud.

STANDARD PORTION SIZES—Form that lists the menu items offered by an establishment and the amount or weight of each considered to compose one serving.

STANDARD PRICE—Reasonable cost for goods purchased that can be realized through careful comparison shopping.

STANDARD RATE AND DATA SERVICE, INC. (SR&DS)—Company that publishes Business Publication Rates and Data, a directory of print and broadcast media, their circulations, and advertising rates.

STANDARD RECIPE—List of each ingredient and the amount

needed, along with the cooking procedures, to prepare a given menu item.

STANDARD SALES RECONCILIATION—Form on which is calculated the amount of liquor sold, the total dollar volume anticipated, the actual total, and the difference between these two sums. Any difference could reflect error (e.g., spillage) or pilferage.

STANDARD SALES VALUE PER BOTTLE—Amount of sales revenue possible when all the liquor in a given bottle is sold as individual drinks. It is calculated by multiplying the number of drinks per bottle by the selling price per drink.

STANDARDS OF FILL—Specifications regarding the proportion of space in a canned good that must be filled with actual product, as opposed to water or juice.

STANDARD YIELD—**Yield** resulting from the processing of a food item according to standard procedures. This should result over time in yields that are similar in size.

STANDBY EQUIPMENT—Ovens and other equipment that are required to handle an establishment's needs during peak periods but that often remain idle during slack periods.

STANDING ORDERS—Requests to suppliers to deliver a certain amount of perishable supplies each day. These orders remain in effect until changed, ensuring a continual supply without having to reorder each day.

STAPHYLOCOCCAL POISONING—Poisoning resulting from the ingestion of food that is infected with **staphylococci** bacteria. Within two to four hours after eating, symptoms of nausea, cramps, diarrhea, and vomiting appear. An absence of fever distinguishes this from many other kinds of food poisoning.

STAPHYLOCOCCI—**Cocci bacteria** that are massed together in clusters. They exist in the air and can be found on most objects.

STAPHYLOCOCCUS AUREUS—Type of **staphylococci** that can cause food poisoning.

STAPLES—Grocery items that can be kept in the storeroom. Contrast with **perishables.**

STARCH—Each starch molecule is composed of linked molecules of glucose. Starch is the principal carbohydrate in plant foods such as potatoes. It provides energy following digestion.

STARCH, ACID-MODIFIED—Starch paste to which acid has been added in order to make it more pliable for use in the production of gum drops and similar candies.

STARCH, PREGELATINIZED—Cooked and dried starch. It will mix better with other ingredients in packaged foods such as instant puddings.

STARTER CULTURE—Sample of bacteria used to initiate growth in a medium, as in milk to produce cheese or yogurt.

STAR TUBE—Nozzle with a star-shaped opening used on a cake-decorating bag or syringe to make decorations such as stars, shells, and rosettes.

STATEMENT OF ACCOUNT—Report from a creditor (e.g., an establishment) to a debtor (e.g., a customer) showing how much he or she still owes.

STATEMENT OF PROFIT AND LOSS—**Income statement.**

STATEMENT OF REVENUES AND EXPENDITURES—**Income statement.**

STATIONARY PHASE—Third phase in **bacterial growth,** characterized by a stabilization of the colony. The number of bacteria remains approximately constant.

STEAK KNIFE—Table knife with a sharp-edged blade, often serrated, used to cut steaks and chops.

STEAK MACHINE—See **Meat tenderizer, mechanical.**

STEAMER—Device that cooks food by the application of moist-heat steam at 0–15 psi. See also **pressure cooker** and **convection steamer.**

STEAM GENERATOR—Electric or gas-heated device that produces clean dry steam for use in pressure cookers.

STEAM-HEAT EXCHANGER—Device that uses heat from contaminated steam to generate clean steam for use in pressure cookers.

STEAMING—Cooking with steam, as in a pressure cooker.

STEAM-JACKETED KETTLE—Moist-heat cooking device consisting of a hemispherical inner vessel surrounded by an outer shell. Pressurized steam in the space between the inner and outer walls heats and cooks the food inside the kettle. Large quantities of liquid and semiliquid foods may be cooked without danger of scorching. Contents may be removed by tilting with some models, or drawn off through a drain valve. Large models may have electric stirrers and systems that inject cold water into the jacket for rapid cooling of the product after cooking.

STEARIC ACID—One of the **fatty acids** found in triglycerides in both animal and vegetable fats.

STEEL—See **sharpening steel.**

STEEP—To soak food in liquid somewhat below the boiling point to release color and or flavor, as is the case with tea soaking in water before service.

STEER—Castrated young beef animal.

STEPPED ENERGY COSTS—Energy expense that increases in steps as business activity increases. For example, ovens use more energy as more meals are cooked.

STERILE—Absence of all microorganisms and other life forms, whether harmful or not. Compare **sanitary.**

STERILIZATION, FOOD—Killing all the microorganisms in a food with heat, chemicals, or radiation.

STERILIZE—To eliminate microorganisms, such as bacteria, through intense heat, either by steam, dry heat, or boiling.

STEROIDS—Group of related compounds with strong effects on the body, e.g., sex hormones, vitamin D, and certain poisons.

STEROLS—Alcohols that have the same fundamental **steroid**

chemical structure as well as an additional oxygen and hydrogen atom, e.g., cholesterol.

STEWARD—Person in charge of storeroom security and operation. See **storekeeper.**

STEWARD SALES—Sales that are at cost, with no mark-up to produce profit; usually to employees.

STEWING—Method of cooking in which small cuts or cubes of meat, poultry, and vegetables are cooked in a little water with seasonings in a pot over a burner.

STILBOESTROL—Synthetic hormone used to stimulate growth, hence meat production in cattle.

STILL—Device in which a wine or fermented mash is heated so that alcohol evaporates, separates, and is recovered by condensation.

STILL WINE—Nonsparkling wine with no added alcohol or flavorings.

STIR—To mix food in a circular motion with a utensil in order to blend the ingredients and keep them from sticking.

STIR FRY—To cook food quickly in a pan at high heat with rapid tossing and stirring motions. The speed usually results in crisp textures and fresh tastes.

STOCK—Thin, flavorful liquids derived from simmering meat, fish, or poultry bones with vegetables and seasonings.

STOCK-IN-TRADE—Goods purchased by an establishment and held for resale.

STOCKLESS PURCHASING—Buying food items from a supplier who delivers only the amount actually needed by an establishment at that time. The supplier stores the rest of the stock on his premises, thus saving space in the establishment's storeroom.

STOCKOUT—Running out of a particular item in a stock of supplies.

STOCK POT—Large pot with high walls and loop handles that

holds 2.5 to 40 gallons. It is used to boil and simmer large quantities of liquids. There may be a drawoff tap at the bottom.

STOCK RECORD CARD—Card used to record the quantity of stocks on hand, the amounts received, and the amounts issued. Each item goes on a separate card.

STOCK ROTATION—Use of older goods of a given item before newer ones, placing recently received goods to the rear.

STOCKTAKING—Counting the number of each item in stock in the storeroom.

STONEWARE—Coarse clayware that has been vitrified and glazed. It is most suitable for heavy serving dishes and beverage containers.

STORAGE DEPARTMENT—Section of an establishment that not only maintains supplies in the storeroom but also keeps account of receipts, issues, losses, and balances on hand.

STORAGE LIFE—**Shelf life.**

STOREKEEPER—Person in charge of an establishment's storeroom(s). In smaller operations, he or she is responsible for ordering goods, receiving them, issuing them, and maintaining a running balance of the amounts on hand. See **steward.**

STOREROOM ARRANGEMENT—Plan of storage in which ideally each item has its own place, related items are kept near each other, and different items are kept apart. Items used up more quickly should be kept nearer the door.

STOREROOM INVENTORY DIFFERENCE—Difference between the number of items actually counted in the storeroom and the number that should be there according to the records. Such differences could reflect losses, thefts, or oversights in bookkeeping.

STOREROOM INVENTORY DIFFERENCE ADJUSTMENT—Adjustments in the receiving report summary or other records so that they reflect the correct number of goods in the storeroom according to the physical inventory.

STOREROOM ISSUE—Food or other items taken from the storerooms and delivered to the cooks or other production personnel.

STOREROOM LIQUOR CONTROL PROCEDURES—Procedures for putting all liquor purchases into a beverage storeroom upon receipt, keeping running balances of supplies on perpetual inventory cards, and issuing items only with proper requisitions.

STOREROOM OVER—More goods in the storeroom than indicated by the records; **total book issues** exceed **total actual issues**. The opposite of **storeroom short**.

STOREROOM PURCHASES—Purchases not intended for immediate use. They are placed in the storeroom and may be withdrawn later by requisition.

STOREROOM RECONCILIATION—Comparison of the amounts of goods that should be on hand according to the books with the amounts actually on hand according to a physical inventory, to determine if the storeroom is over or short.

STOREROOM ROTATION—See **stock rotation**.

STOREROOM SHORT—Less goods in the storeroom than indicated by the records; **total actual issues** exceed **total book issues**. The opposite of **storeroom over**.

STORING PROCEDURES—Procedures for placing goods in the storeroom, preserving them there, and maintaining a running balance of the number of each type of goods available.

STRAIGHT-LINE CAFETERIA—Cafeteria in which customers form a line and choose what they want as they walk past an array of foods. Contrast **scramble system**.

STRAIGHT WHISKEY—Distillation from fermented barley, corn, rye, or wheat. It is aged in charred oak barrels for two years or more. This spirit is available in four types, including bourbon, rye, corn, and bottled-in-bond whiskeys. See **liquors** and **liqueurs**.

STRAINER—Perforated metal bowl with a long handle, often with a hook for suspending across a pot. Used to drain liquids from solid foods, e.g., spaghetti. Also called a colander if it has a stand.

STRAINING BAG—Cloth bag used to filter liquid foods.

STRANGE WARE—Items that are accidentally shipped to the wrong purchaser.

STRAP CUTTER—Scissors-type device used by the receiving clerk to cut straps from packages.

STRAWBERRY—Reddish fruit that grows on small trailing plants close to the ground. The unique feature of this fruit is that its seeds are embedded on the surface rather than held within. Generally, smaller strawberries have a stronger flavor. They are often eaten raw, but can be used cooked or made into jellies, jams, and preserves.

STREPTOCOCCAL POISONING—Poisoning caused by food infected with streptococcal bacteria. Within 2 to 18 hours after eating, symptoms appear, including mild nausea (compared to that in **staphylococcal poisoning**), colic, and diarrhea.

STREPTOCOCCI—**Cocci** bacteria arranged in a form resembling a string of beads.

STREPTOCOCCUS PYOGENES—Bacterial strain that can produce hemolysins responsible for **hemolysis.**

STRONG CUTTING—Including a few pounds of cheap meat in a shipment of more expensive cuts and charging the higher price for all of it. Meat should be checked upon receipt to ensure the shipper has sent only the specified quality.

STRUCK FULL—Produce containers filled evenly to the top.

STRUVITE—Crystals of magnesium ammonium phosphate that sometimes form in canned seafoods such as tuna. Although it looks similar to glass fragments and may scare off some customers, it is harmless to eat.

SUBCLINICAL—Symptoms so slight that disease is suspected but a definite diagnosis is impossible.

SUBJECTIVE VALUE—Monetary value of an asset as decided

by management without an independent appraisal or assessment.

SUBLIMATION—Vaporization of a solid, when heated, directly into a gas without becoming liquid first. For example, solid carbon dioxide (dry ice) sublimates.

SUBROGATING—One creditor taking the place of another usually because the former pays the latter.

SUBSTITUTION—Supplier's sending a similar or equivalent item if an item ordered is not in stock.

SUBSTITUTION INVOICE—Form similar to an ordinary invoice used by the receiving clerk when goods arrive without an invoice.

SUBSTRATE—Chemical compound on which an enzyme has an effect, e.g., the enzyme sucrase works on the substrate sucrose.

SUCHAR—Activated carbon used to remove the color from solutions.

SUCRASE—Enzyme that splits **sucrose** into its component molecules fructose and glucose.

SUCROSE—Common table sugar, a natural sweetener. Each molecule contains one molecule of **glucose** and one of **fructose**. See **sugar.**

SUCROSE MONOSTEARATE (SMS)—An emulsifying agent.

SUET—Fat derived from oxen and sheep kidneys.

SUGAR—Class of carbohydrates extracted from sugar beets, sugar cane, sugar maple, honey, and various fruits. The following is a list of the more common types.
Brown sugar: Sugar that is unrefined or partly refined. It contains molasses and has a tendency to lump when dried.
Castor or superfine sugar: Finely granulated sugar.
Confectioner's sugar: Powdered sugar with added cornstarch to prevent lumping.
Confetti sugar: Sugar of fairly large crystals that is dyed for use as a decoration.

Corn sugar: Glucose derived from corn.

Cube or lump sugar: Sugar that has been moistened with sugar cane liquor and pressed into a mold.

Dextran: Sugar made up of connected fructose molecules. It is used in confections and as an additive.

Fructose: Sugar derived from honey and fruit.

Granulated sugar: Fully refined white sugar. This is the most commonly used type.

Invert sugar: Fructose and glucose mix derived from hydrolyzing sucrose.

Jaggery: Raw sugar with natural antioxidants that can be used as a preservative.

Mannose: Similar to glucose, with a different molecular structure.

Maple sugar: Very sweet, rich sugar made by evaporating the sap of the maple tree. It is twice as sweet as granulated white sugar.

Muscovado: Dark-brown sugar derived from cane.

Raffinade: Refined sugar of the highest quality.

Raffinose: Found in sugar-beet molasses.

Raw sugar: The unrefined, yellowish residue that remains after the molasses has been removed from the juice of the sugar cane. It contains 2–4 percent volume in impurities such as fibers and dirt.

SUGAR FREE—Any product that does not contain sucrose, common table sugar. It may have other artificial or natural sweeteners, however, such as **glucose** or fructose. See **sugar.**

SUGGESTIVE SELLING—Suggestions made by the server when the customer is not sure what to order.

SULFUR—Element present in certain amino acid molecules such as cystine and certain vitamins such as B_1. It is essential for life.

SULFUR DIOXIDE (SO_2)—Additive used as a food preservative.

SULFURED PRODUCTS—Foods (e.g., dried fruits) that have been treated with **sulfur dioxide.**

SULTANAS—Small seedless white grapes or the raisins made from them.

SUPERGLYCINERATED FATS—Fats in which each molecule has only one or two fatty acid molecules per molecule of glycerol, rather than the usual three; i.e., the fat contains more glycerol than normal. Such fats make good emulsifiers.

SUPPLEMENTARY COST—Overhead and other indirect costs in addition to the basic or direct cost that add to the purchase price.

SUPPLY—Amount of a particular item that producers have made available for purchase. See **demand.**

SUPREME—French; an especially fine cut of meat, piece of fish, or poultry breast.

SURFACTANT—Emulsifying substance, such as pectin, that keeps jellies or other substances soft by reducing the surface tensions between food ingredients.

SURFACTANT, DETERGENT—Substance in detergents that reduces water tension along the surface to be cleaned, thereby allowing the cleanser to penetrate more rapidly.

SUSPENSION OF PERMIT—Temporary withdrawal of the permit to serve food, issued by a health authority when an establishment fails to maintain standards or to comply with its directives. See also **revocation of permit.**

SWEAT—To heat food gently in butter in order to extract the flavor. Also, another name for perspiration.

SWEETBREADS—Organ or variety meat consisting of the thymus glands of calves or the pancreas; considered a delicacy.

SWEET CHOCOLATE—Blend of chocolate liquid, sweetening, and extra cocoa butter; also known as dark and semisweet chocolate; contains 40–65 percent sugar.

SWEET-DOUGH HOOK—Vertical-mixer attachment for kneading sweet doughs that are not high in gluten content.

SWEETENERS, NONNUTRITIVE—Compounds that taste

sweet (e.g., saccharin) but are not carbohydrates and supply no nutrition.

SWEETENERS, NUTRITIVE—Carbohydrate sugars, such as fructose, maltose, and sucrose, that taste sweet and have nutritive value. See **sugar.**

SWEET MASH—Method of using fresh yeast only to induce fermentation in the mash. See **mash** and **sour mash.**

SWELLS—Improperly sterilized canned goods in which live bacteria have generated gases and sometimes poisons. The gases expand the can with bulges at the ends. Sometimes the swell will not show unless the can is struck. See **flippers.**

SWIFT STABILITY TEST—Bubbling air through warmed fats and oils to determine their degree of chemical stability.

SWISS CHARD—See **chard, Swiss.**

SWIZZLE STICK—Small spear or decorative plastic stick used to hold the garnish in a cocktail. Can be used as a merchandising piece when tied in with the decor theme of the operation.

SYNERESIS—Process that causes separation of the fluid portion from jelly or other gels after they are cut.

SYNTHESIS, CHEMICAL—Process by which a complex chemical (e.g., a nonessential amino acid) is built up in the body from chemicals derived from digestion of food.

SYRINGE—Decorating instrument used instead of a cake-decorating bag with creams that are too heavy to be forced easily through a bag. It consists of a piston that forces the material out of the cylinder through a special type of tube.

SYRUP—Any solution of a liquid and glucose or other sugar.

T

TABLE D'HOTE—Complete meal, usually including dessert and beverage, offered for a single fixed price. The opposite of **à la carte.**

TABLESPOON—Unit of measure equal to three teaspoons or one half ounce.

TACHYPHAGIA—To eat too rapidly.

TAG PAPER—Strong, water-resistant paper that bends and folds well; ideal for menus. See **paper types.**

TAKADIASTASE—Group of commercially prepared enzymes that split starch into its sugary components.

TALLOW, RENDERED—Processed animal fat from which **oleo oil** can be separated. The oil is used in the manufacture of margarine.

TALLY SHEET—Sheet on which is recorded the cumulative number of sales during a given period for each menu item listed.

TAMARIND—Large brown pods that are the fruit of the tropical tamarind tree. They taste something like plums.

TAMMY—Fine cloth used to strain foods.

TAMPER-RESISTANT SEAL—**Pilferproof seal.**

TANGIBLE ASSET—Physical item of property, as opposed to an **intangible asset.**

TANK—Name given to any of several sections that make up a dishwashing machine.

TANKAGE—Parts left over after all usable portions have been removed from a slaughtered animal.

TANKARD—Straight tall beer vessel of heavy glass with a handle on the side.

TANNINS—Group of bitter **phenol** compounds found in such plant products as coffee, tea, and wine. Tannins tend to shrink or pucker the mucous membranes in the mouth. Wine tannins tend to drop out in the sediment as wines age, thus mellowing their flavor.

TAPE, COMPUTER—Magnetic ribbon, often of plastic, used for the storage of information in conjunction with computer input and output.

TAPEWORM—Parasitic worm of the **Cestode** type, so named because it is long and ribbonlike in shape.

TAPIOCA—Thickening agent made from the cassava plant; popular in puddings.

TARE WEIGHT—Weight of packaging materials, as opposed to the weight of the product inside. Both combined equal the **gross weight.**

TARGET PRICE—Base price that can be adjusted without warning if conditions agreed upon in the sales contract come to pass (e.g., a bonus for early delivery). Contrast with **firm price.**

TARO—Starch-rich root used as a food in the South Pacific. It is often pounded into a paste called poi.

TART—Acid or sharp taste, as when referring to wine.

TARTAR, CREAM OF—Another name for potassium hydrogen tartrate, one of the compounds in baking powder.

TARTARIC ACID—Acid found in grapes and other fruits. It is used to add acidity to jam and to release carbon dioxide in baking powder.

TARTAZINE—Yellow food color called Yellow No. 5.

TASTE BUDS—Small conelike projections, mainly on the tongue, that contain **taste receptors.** Each person has about 10,000 taste buds.

TASTE RECEPTORS—Microscopic cells that convert the chemicals of food into taste sensations. Every taste bud contains 15–20 receptors, each of which is specialized to respond mainly to salt, sour, sweet, or bitter qualities.

TASTE TESTING—A procedure used to decide which brand of foodstuffs to buy. It may be done within an establishment, when several staff members independently rate the varieties of a given item for taste. Rankings should be considered as well as cost factors when making a decision.

TASTE-VIN—French; a small silver cup used to examine and taste wine. It is often suspended from a chain about the neck of the sommelier or wine steward.

TAWNY—Pale color that port wines develop as they age in wooden casks and undergo repeated finings. See **fine.**

TEA—Beverage derived by steeping tea leaves in hot water. It is served hot or cold, with flavor and hue dependent upon the fermentation of the leaves. Varieties include **green, oolong, black,** and **pekoe.**

TEAR TESTING—One of the techniques used in **grain testing.** A menu sheet is torn by hand. If the tear forms easily and is straight, that is the direction of the grain. If the tear is ragged and turns to the side, that is not the direction of the grain.

TEASPOON—Medium-sized spoon with oval bowl used to stir tea and coffee and to eat some desserts. Also, a standard measure equaling one sixth of a fluid ounce. See also **tablespoon.**

TEMPERATURE DANGER ZONE—Range from about 45° to 140° F (7.2° to 60° C) in which most bacteria thrive. Thus, foods should not be stored at temperatures in that range for very long.

TEMPERATURE RECORD BOOK—Book or ledger in which the temperatures found in various parts of refrigerated areas can be recorded on a daily basis.

TENDERIZE—Use of an enzyme such as papain or an acid such as vinegar to make meat more tender by breaking up the tough connective tissue that holds meat fibers together.

TENDEROMETER—Device used to determine if peas are tender enough to be canned.

TERMINAL, COMPUTER—End point of a computer system where input is placed or output is gathered.

TERMINATION—End of an employee's service in the establishment, either through quitting or being fired.

TERMINATION INTERVIEW—Interview conducted when an employee quits or is fired. He or she is questioned by management to determine the reasons for departure, since if the consistent causes of turnover can be discovered it can be reduced.

TERMINATION INTERVIEW REPORT—Printed form on which a terminated employee's stated reasons for leaving are entered, along with statements by supervisors and any background information on the employee. A file of such reports makes possible a more objective evaluation of a turnover problem than a set of mental notes alone.

TERPENE—Main ingredient in citrus fruit oils, accounting for as much as 95 percent of the total. Since they tend to be bitter and relatively insoluble, they must be removed before the oil can be used in food.

TERPENELESS OILS—Citrus-fruit oils from which the relatively insoluble **terpenes** have been removed. The remaining oil is then useful as a food flavoring.

TERRINE—French; vegetable, meat, fish, or poultry pâté stored in an earthenware pot. Also, may refer to the earthenware pot itself.

TEST, PRODUCT—To check a sample of a product to see if it is of acceptable quality. It is more efficient than checking all of the items.

TETRACYCLINES—Group of **antibiotics** used to improve meat yield and help preserve fresh poultry and fish; they may be passed on in small amounts to those who eat the meat. Tetracyclines are also used as a drug in combatting disease; calcium intake, as in milk and milk products, interferes with the drug's absorption.

TEXT—Main material to be printed in a menu, as opposed to the **headings.**

TEXT PAPER—Colorful water-resistant paper that is useful in menus. It also has an attractive texture.. See **paper types.**

THAWING CABINET—Compartment in which food is thawed quickly and evenly to a 40°F temperature by heating. The temperature is then maintained by refrigeration.

THERM—Unit of heat measurement; one therm equals 100,000 **BTU's.**

THERMAL STRESS CRACKING (TSC)—**Crazing** caused by exposure to excessive temperatures, as in containers left too close to ovens.

THERMIZATION—In cheese production, using enough heat to kill some of the microorganisms in milk but not enough for complete pasteurization.

THERMODURIC—Usually harmless bacteria found in milk that can survive the temperatures at which pasteurization is done.

THERMOMETERS—Calibrated instruments to measure the temperature of foods as well as the temperatures in ovens, refrigerators, rooms, and so on.

THERMOPHYLE—Bacteria that thrive at temperatures above 131° F, can easily tolerate up to 176° F, and can survive even a certain amount of boiling.

THERMOPLASTICS—Plastics used for containers that can repeatedly soften with heat and harden with cold, thus changing shape as needed without breaking. Contrast **thermoset plastics.**

THERMOSET PLASTICS—Plastics used for containers that harden once exposed to heat and cannot be resoftened to change shape. Contrast **thermoplastics.**

THERMOSTAT—See **automatic kitchen thermostats.**

THIAMINASE—Fish enzyme that destroys **thiamine;** ingesting too much can cause thiamine deficiency.

THIAMINE—**Vitamin B$_1$.**

THREE-COMPARTMENT SINK—See **sink, three-compartment.**

THREONINE—One of the essential amino acids found in protein. Since it cannot be synthesized by the human body, it must be supplied by the diet. Rich sources include legumes, meat, and fish.

THROUGHPUT—Computer's rate of productivity.

THURICIDE—Strain of bacteria that has no ill effects on people but kills insects. It is used as a crop pesticide.

THYMINE—One of the **pyrimidines** found in **nucleic acids.**

THYROID GLAND—Gland in the neck that secretes hormones controlling metabolism and the rate of growth. Malabsorption or a deficiency of iodine in the diet causes the swelling in this gland known as goiter.

THYROXINE—Thyroid hormone derived from **iodine** and the amino acid **tyrosine.** Production depends on a supply of these two nutrients.

TIERCE—French; a wine cask that holds one third of a **pipe.**

TIER PANS—Set of cake pans of several diameters, used to make multilayered tier cakes.

TILL—Unit of fresh-produce measurement, about five to six quarts.

TILTING FRY PAN—Large flat-bottomed kettle, heated by gas or electricity, mounted in a sturdy framework with a mechanism that allows tilting of the kettle up to 90 degrees for easy removal of the contents. It is a versatile piece of equipment and may be used for braising, boiling, griddling, thawing, deep and shallow frying, as well as for holding foods hot. Also called a tilting skillet.

TIMBALE—Deep pastry crust or metal utensil that can be filled with food. The word itself means a kettledrum, which a timbale resembles.   •

TIME-AND-TEMPERATURE PRINCIPLE—**Potentially hazardous food** should be kept at temperatures above or below the **temperature danger zone** in order to prevent the growth of pathogens.

TIMER—See **automatic kitchen timers.**

TIME SHARING, COMPUTER—Carrying out two or more computer functions during a single time period.

TIME STAMPING—To stamp received goods with the date and exact hour of delivery. Making the time of delivery easily traceable encourages efficiency in the receiving department and speeds the process of getting goods into storage.

TIN—Metal often used as the inner lining of food cans because of its resistance to rust.

TINTOMETER—Device used to determine the chemicals present in food substances by comparing their colors (natural or in response to reagents) to a standardized set of colors.

TITLE—Having ownership (and normally possession) of personal property, e.g., automobiles or goods in the storeroom.

TOASTER, AUTOMATIC POPUP—Electric device that toasts bread, muffins, or buns to a preselected degree. The items are placed in slots, drop or are pushed down, and pop up when done. Some models can toast up to eight items at one time.

TOASTER, CONVEYER—Equipment for high-volume toast production. It carries a continuous supply of bread or buns between heating elements at a controlled speed.

TOASTING—Radiant direct heat application (as to bread) that results in surface browning.

TOCOPHEROL—**Vitamin E.**

TOFU—Soybean purée curdled with lemon juice or other acid into a gelatinous mass and cured. The resulting soft cakes are high in protein, but have little flavor if served alone. Also called bean curd.

TOLERANCE—Maximum amount of deviation from a specification that can be allowed. For example, pasteurized milk is permitted to have a certain amount of bacteria with a tolerance factor of a small amount more.

TOMATINE—Fungicide derived from the stems and leaves of tomatoes resistant to wilting.

TOMATO—Juicy round fruit that ripens from green to red. Tomatoes vary from cherry size to large orange size and can be used alone, in salads, or cooked in an endless variety of dishes.

TOM COLLINS GLASS—Bar glass shaped like a tall cylinder, usually holding around 12 ounces.

TONGS—Device for lifting items by gripping with two opposable jaws.

TOOTH—Property of menu paper that allows it to absorb ink well; related to the roughness of the paper surface.

"TORPEDO"—Slang for any rodent-killing **single-dose poison** mixed with bait and wrapped in paper.

TOTAL ACTUAL ISSUES—Total of all issues from the storeroom during a certain period, whether or not recorded in the business records (see **total book issues**). It is calculated by adding purchases during the period to opening inventory and then subtracting closing inventory.

TOTAL BOOK ISSUES—Total of all issues from the storeroom during a certain period, according to the business records. Contrast **total actual issues.**

TOXIC—Poisonous.

TOXICITY—Quality of being poisonous.

TOXICOGENIC—Having the ability to produce poisons, as many bacteria can do in food.

TOXINS—In relation to nutrition, toxins are the poisons produced by bacteria that cause food poisoning (e.g., botulism).

TRADE ACCOUNTS RECEIVABLE—Amounts owed to an establishment by credit customers for goods they have received.

TRADE DISCOUNT—Any discount other than one based on early payment, e.g., quantity discounts and discounts to retailers.

TRADEMARK (TM)—Distinctive name or symbol that identifies a producer's products. By law, no other producer can use that symbol.

TRADE PRICE—Price charged by wholesalers or producers to retailers, i.e., the **list price** minus the **trade discount.**

TRAGACANTH—Emulsifying gum derived from the shrub *Astragalus* and used as a thickener.

TRANSACTION—Any business dealing, such as a sale or purchase, that must be entered into an establishment's business records.

TRANSAMINATION—Process by which many nonessential amino acids are formed within the body.

TRANSFERS IN—Items ordered by the kitchen not from a supplier but from another department within an establishment, e.g., wine from the bar for cooking. The cost should be transferred to the using department.

TRANSFERS OUT—Items transferred from the kitchen to another department within an establishment, e.g., cream to the bar. The cost should be transferred to the using department.

TRANSPARENT INK—Any menu ink through which the underlying ink from a previous printing can be seen. Contrast **opaque ink.**

TRANSPORTATION ADVERTISING—Advertising posters in vehicles of transportation such as buses and subways.

TRANSPORTER—Insulated chest for holding and transporting hot or cold foods. Various sizes and designs are made for different types of loads. It is particularly useful for catering operations, where food may be prepared in one location to be served in another.

TRASH COMPACTOR—Hydraulically operated machine that reduces the volume of garbage and trash by compressing it into small packages, thereby lowering the cost of waste disposal as well as reducing odors, pests, and fire hazards.

TRAY DISPENSER—Device that presents trays to the customer at a convenient level by means of a spring-loaded or counterweight mechanism that continuously raises a stack of trays as each one is removed. It may be mounted on wheels to permit loading in the dishroom and easy movement to the service area.

TRAY RAIL—Surface on which the cafeteria customer may rest and move his tray while he makes selections. It usually consists of three or four stainless steel rails supported on stainless steel brackets. Alternatively, it may be a solid steel surface with longitudinal ridges. Also called tray slide.

TRAY SERVICE—Serving method in which dishes are assembled onto trays so that a complete meal can be taken to a person at once. This method is typical of hospitals, for instance.

TRAY STAND—Portable folding device used by the server to rest his or her tray while serving a table.

TREACLE—Dark molasseslike syrup made during sugar refining.

TREMATODE—Parasitic flatworm, e.g., the liver fluke.

TRICHINELLA SPIRALIS—Parasitic worm that causes **trichinosis** if infected pork or wild game is eaten.

TRICHINOSIS—Disease caused by eating improperly cooked pork or wild game that contains live cysts of the parasite *Trichinella spiralis*. Symptoms include abdominal pain and fever; stiff muscles occur because the worms burrow into muscle tissue. Adequate cooking kills the cysts and makes the meat safe.

TRIGLYCERIDES—Fat in which each molecule consists of one molecule of **glycerol** and three of **fatty acids**.

TRIMMING—Cutting the top, right, and bottom sides evenly

after the pages of a menu or pamphlet have been collated and stitched together. Also refers to removing excess fat from meat.

TRIPE—Stomach lining of beef; **smooth muscle.**

TRISODIUM PHOSPHATE—Cleaning compound that resembles cornmeal; it is toxic so it must always be labeled and kept away from food.

TRITICALE—Grain that results from the crossbreeding of rye with wheat.

TRIVET—Platform or holder on which fish are simmered to insure that they do not break up while cooking or when removed from the pan. Also, a stand or frame used to keep hot pots or dishes off a table surface.

TROPONIN—One of the proteins in edible muscle. It is less prevalent than actin or myosin.

TRUSS—To skewer or tie poultry legs and wings before roasting to insure proper shape for service.

TRUSSING NEEDLE—Needle used to tie the legs and wings of poultry or game close to the body, so that it retains its shape during cooking.

TRUTH-IN-MENU LEGISLATION—Legislation that makes it illegal for foodservice operators to use menu terms or symbols that misrepresent what customers will actually be served.

TRY OUT—To render oil from fat by cooking it.

TRYPSIN—A pancreatic enzyme that helps digest protein.

TRYPTOPHAN—One of the essential amino acids. Rich sources include legumes, nuts, meat, fish, and cheese.

TUBE BRUSH—Brush used to clean the wash-and-rinse tubes of the dish machine. It is usually furnished by the manufacturer of the machine.

TUBERIN—Main protein in potatoes.

TULAREMIA—Disease caused by the *Pasteurella tularensis* bacteria, which is spread by insects from rodents or wild rabbits to humans. Symptoms include headache, chills, and fever. Also called rabbit fever.

TULIP—Stemmed glass with a deep bowl shaped like a tulip blossom suitable for red or white wines or champagne.

TURBOTIERE—French; lozenge-shaped pot with a cover and removable metal grate designed to hold one whole turbot or similarly shaped fish during poaching.

TUREEN—French; a deep, broad, covered dish of porcelain or silver in which soup is served. Tureens are usually very ornate and elegantly designed. Also called a soupière.

TURNER—Utensil with a broad offset blade, sometimes with a chiselled edge, used to lift and turn items on a griddle, broiler, or range top.

TURNOVER—Number of times in a given period that assets such as merchandise are replaced (i.e., due to selling).

TURNOVER, FAT—Daily addition of new fat to the cooking supply without discarding the old, in order to keep it fresh and in good condition. This is cheaper than replacing the entire supply every day.

TURNOVER PER SEAT—Average number of customers in a given period (month, year, and so on) served by a single seat. It is calculated by dividing the total number of customers by the number of seats.

TURNOVER RATE, EMPLOYEE—Index of the number of staff members who have left an establishment's employ. It is calculated by dividing the number of separations during a month or year by the total number of employees on hand in the middle of the month or year, times 100 percent.

TWO-COMPARTMENT SINK—See **Sink, two-compartment.**

TYPE MIXING—Using two or more different typefaces in the printing of a menu. The occasional use of italics or boldface in addition to the regular type emphasizes certain words. Too much mixing, however, causes confusion.

TYRAMINE—Substance found in aged or fermented foods such as cheese, yogurt, soy sauce, and wine. If a person ingests tyramine while taking monoamine oxidase (MOA) inhibitors, which are drugs sometimes used to combat depression or hypertension, the interaction can force blood pressure up to dangerous levels.

TYROSINASE—Enzyme in potatoes responsible for the dark color that develops when raw potatoes are exposed to air; the enzyme converts **tyrosine** into dark pigment.

TYROSINE—Nonessential amino acid involved in the formation of hair and skin pigment.

U

UDO—California vegetable that is similar to asparagus.

ULLAGE—Air space in a wine bottle or cask resulting from evaporation or leakage. Such air may spoil the wine.

UNAUTHORIZED CHECKS—Sales checks brought in from outside the establishment by dishonest servers so that they can collect and keep the payments rather than turn them in.

UNDERCHARGING—Listing of only partial charges on a guest check by a bartender or waiter, who then collects full payment and pockets the difference.

UNDERCOUNTER DISHWASHER—Compact, lowstanding machine for washing, rinsing, and sanitizing tableware. It is used mostly in smaller foodservice operations such as snack bars and soda fountains.

UNDEREXTRACTED—Weak coffee flavor that occurs when

water is not in contact long enough with coffee grinds. Contrast **overextracted.**

UNDERLINER—Small plate on which another vessel is placed that holds soups, beverages, casseroles, appetizers, or desserts.

UNDERPACKAGING—Condition of packaging that provides inadequate protection of the contents against exposure or infestation, either because of the use of inferior materials or because the packaging was used improperly.

UNDERWRITERS' LABORATORIES (UL)—National laboratory that tests electrical equipment and awards its seal of approval only to those that meet its safety standards.

UNDULANT FEVER—**Brucellosis.**

UNESTERIFIED FATTY ACID (UFA)—Free **fatty acids** not attached to **glycerol.**

UNFAIR COMPETITION—Use by an establishment of illegal means to gain a larger share of the market to the detriment of its competitors. For example, one company may sell below cost to attract customers away from another one. Civil law suits or rulings by the Federal Trade Commission can put a stop to such actions.

UNIFORM SYSTEM OF ACCOUNTS FOR RESTAURANTS—System for setting up business accounts that is highly applicable to foodservice establishments. The system recommends which accounts should be opened and what they should include.

UNIFORM TASTE—The same item prepared at different times and by different people should always taste basically the same at the same restaurant. This helps build loyalty among customers who like the taste when they first try it. Using **standard recipes** can help create taste uniformity.

UNIT—Quantity in which a given item is normally sold, e.g., a pair, dozen, or gross.

UNIT COST—Cost of one unit of a given item. The unit cost is usually stated on the purchase invoice.

UNLOADING PLATFORM—Raised platform at the loading dock that is approximately the same height as the bed of trucks that deliver supplies.

UNSATURATED FATS—See **fats, unsaturated.**

UNSTABLE EMULSION—**Emulsion** in which the two liquids will not readily stay mixed.

UPGRADING—Unethical practice in which some suppliers grade their own food products higher than the items warrant so they can charge higher prices.

UPRIGHT BROILER—Top-heated gas or electric unit with a grid that slides out for loading. It may be mounted on an oven or be floor-mounted in tiers of two or three to conserve floor space. Some models are heated both above and below the grid. Also called heavy-duty broiler, hotel broiler.

UPRIGHT MIXER—See **vertical mixer.**

UPSET PRICE—Minimum price a seller is willing to accept for his goods.

UREA—Nitrogen-containing waste left from the utilization of protein. It is excreted in the urine.

URN—Container used to brew and keep beverages warm such as coffee. It has a spigot at the bottom for serving. Urns vary in size.

URN CUP—Cylindrical container with a one-gallon capacity. It has a cool handle and one-quart graduation marks to measure boiling water for brewing coffee.

USABLE HEAT—Amount of heat produced by a device (such as an oven) that is actually used for the purpose designed, i.e., cooking food. The rest is wasted through heat loss into the room, or through the roof, and so on.

U.S. CENTER FOR DISEASE CONTROL—Agency of the Public Health Service that investigates outbreaks of foodborne diseases.

U.S. EXTRA STANDARD or CHOICE—Second grade, or Grade B, of canned and frozen fruits and vegetables.

U.S. FANCY or EXTRA FANCY—Grades above U.S. No. 1, representing better than average quality of canned and frozen fruits and vegetables.

U.S. GRADE A or GRADE FANCY—First grade of canned and frozen fruits and vegetables.

U.S. NO. 1—Grade for fresh fruits and vegetables of high quality suitable for use in foodservice.

U.S. PUBLIC HEALTH SERVICE ORDINANCE AND CODE—Set of rules that regulate vending machines and their proper manufacture and maintenance.

U.S. RECOMMENDED DAILY ALLOWANCE (USRDA)—The FDA (**Food and Drug Administration**) develops a list indicating what the daily intake of each major nutrient should be. This list is then used as a guide by interested individuals, and in nutrition labeling on cereal packages and other foods.

UTILITY GRADE—Sixth out of eight grades of meat. See **meat grading.**

V

VACREATION—Removal of odors from cream by steam distillation.

VACUDRY—Process by which fruit is reduced to a 2–5 percent moisture content.

VACUUM MAKER—Small brewing unit that makes coffee by forcing boiling water up into an upper chamber where it comes in contact with the finely ground coffee and then filters down.

VACUUM SEAL—Seal strong enough to maintain a vacuum inside a container, prohibiting the entry of air, water vapor, or contaminants.

VALIDATION—Process of ensuring that the server picks up the proper order in the kitchen by comparing the original and duplicate checks. The total charges on each check and its duplicate should also be examined to make sure they agree.

VALINE—One of the essential amino acids in protein. Rich sources include legumes, nuts, fish, and cheese.

VALUE ADDED—See **added value.**

VALUE ANALYSIS—Analysis of what is needed compared to what is obtained, with value representing price divided into quality, or $V = Q/P$.

VANILLA—Fragrant seed pod from a tropical climbing orchid; extract derived from it is used to flavor cakes, ice cream, candy, drinks, and various other foods.

VANILLIN—The major flavoring ingredient in **vanilla.**

VAPOR BARRIER—Seal on insulation designed to keep out water vapor, which can condense and weaken the insulation's effectiveness.

VAPOR TRANSMISSION—Movement of a vapor, either of water or some other substance, into or through a material.

VARIABLE COSTS—Expenses that change as the volume of production and sales change.

VARIABLE EMPLOYEES—Employees who are needed on a changing basis depending on the amount of business, e.g., waitresses. Contrast **semivariable employees** and **fixed employees.**

VARIANCE, BUSINESS—Difference between the standard for a cost or performance and its actual outcome.

VARIETAL WINE—Wine named for the predominant grape variety used to make it, which must account for at least 51 percent of the total. Examples include cabernet sauvignon and catawba. Contrast **generic wine.**

VARIETY MEATS—Organ meats, including sweetbreads, brains, tongue, and liver.

VASQUE—Shallow round bowl of crystal, china, or silver, used to serve cold foods such as chaud-froids, mousses, fruits, or custards.

VAT—Large container used to ferment alcoholic beverages.

VEAL—Meat of a calf slaughtered between the ages of six and fourteen weeks. The finest veal is milk fed and the flesh has a creamy white or pinkish hue. The best comes from France, Holland, and Italy. American veal is usually older and stringier than prime veal. Veal is often larded because it is so lean it has a tendency to dry out. The more known cuts are as follows.
Breast: Portion of the foresaddle below the ribs.
Saddle cut: Back portions.
Veal hotel rack: Consists of seven ribs separated after the removal of the legs.
Veal leg, double: Portion of the hindsaddle remaining after the removal of the loin.
Veal loin, trimmed: Anterior portion of the hindsaddle remaining after removal of the legs.
Veal shoulder, unsplit: Portion including the large outside muscle system posterior to the elbow joint and ventral to the medial ridge of the blade bone.

VEAL AND CALF GRADING—U.S. Prime, U.S. Choice, U.S. Good, U.S. Standard, U.S. Utility. Grading criteria include conformation (shape), age, marbling, color, and texture.

VEGAN—Strict **vegetarian** who eats fruits and vegetables, but no meat or animal products, not even eggs, milk, or cheese.

VEGETABLE BRUSH—Small brush used to wash vegetables.

VEGETABLE BUTTERS—**Triglyceride** fats that occur naturally in various plants, e.g., cocoa butter in cocoa beans.

VEGETABLE PEELER, MECHANICAL—Device that removes the skins from potatoes and other vegetables by the abrasive action of the cylinder walls coated with a carborundum grit. As the vegetables are whirled about in the cylinder, a stream of water washes away the peels. Some hand trimming is usually needed to remove eyes and bits of peel in deep depressions. The machine comes in table- and floor-mounted models with capacities ranging from seven to sixty pounds. Also called a potato peeler.

VEGETABLE SLICER—Attachment to a vertical mixer that shreds, grates, or slices food. It consists of a rotary disc that cuts foods placed in a hopper. Interchangeable cutting discs perform a variety of functions.

VEGETARIAN—One who eats fruits and vegetables but no meat. Vegetarians may eat such animal products as milk, cheese, and eggs, however. See **vegans**.

VEGETATIVE—State in which a living cell (e.g., a bacterium or other microorganism) is involved in growth rather than reproduction.

VEHICLES—Fluid solvents that hold the pigments and drying substances in **printing ink**. It is one of the principal ingredients of the ink used in, e.g., menus.

VELLUM FINISH—Menu paper with a rough finish that absorbs ink well. See **tooth**.

VENDING SERVICE—Use of machines to dispense food.

VENDOR—Supplier; one who sells merchandise.

VENISON—Game meat from deer or reindeer.

VERJUICE—Juice derived from unripe fruits, e.g., apples or grapes; used in cooking.

VERMIFUGE—Any medicine that can kill parasitic worms in the intestine or at least drive them out.

VERMIN—Animal pests such as rats and insects that can contaminate food, cause disease, and otherwise bother humans.

VERTICAL CUTTER/MIXER (VCM)—Versatile high-speed food cutting and mixing machine consisting of a motor attached to the bottom of a mixing bowl that drives a set of cutting and mixing blades. Various types of interchangeable blades perform different functions such as mixing, chopping, blending, emulsifying, grating, grinding, mashing, blending, or homogenizing. Capacities range from 25 to 130 quarts. Blade speeds range from 1,750 to 3,500 rpm.

VERTICAL MIXER—Food mixer, floor or table mounted, with an overhead motor that drives a downward projecting shaft in a planetary motion, to which various types of mixing devices may be attached. The mixing bowl sits on a yoke that may be raised and lowered by hand or motor. There is usually a power take-off on the motor that can be used to drive accessories such as grinders or choppers. Bowl capacities range from 5 to 140 quarts, and motor horsepower from one sixth to five. Speeds vary from 55 to 318 rpm and may be controlled with a selector lever. Also called an upright mixer.

VESTIBULE—Partially refrigerated space that connects fully refrigerated areas to the general storeroom.

VESTIBULE BOX—Refrigerated storage unit in the **vestibule** for general groceries such as produce.

VICILIN—One of the proteins in peas and lentils.

VILLI, INTESTINAL—Small projections from the inner surface of the small intestine through which digested nutrients are absorbed into the bloodstream.

VINAIGRIER—French; small barrel of wood or earthenware in which vinegar is made.

VIN CUIT—Concentrated wine that can be blended with weaker ones to improve them.

VINEGAR—Fermentation of cider, wine, grain, and some fruits that results in a sour liquid containing **acetic acid.** Used in cooking for its flavor and preservative qualities. The following are the most popular types.
Balsamic: Mellow, reddish-brown Italian vinegar made from sweet wine.
Champagne: Sweet, slightly tart vinegar made from fermented champagne.
Cider vinegar: Strong, faintly apple-tasting vinegar.

Malt: Tart, strongly flavored vinegar made from grain and cider vinegar.

Raspberry: The acidulated syrup of raspberries. Raspberry vinegar has a mild, fruity taste.

White: Highly acidic, strongly flavored vinegar distilled from grains and used primarily in pickling.

VINICULTURE—Science and study of wine making.

VINIFERA—Grape species of most of the world's wines.

VINOSITY—Balance of a wine's body, bouquet, and flavor.

VINOUS—Relating to wines.

VINTAGE—Grape harvest and wine made in a given year; the year a wine is produced as noted on its label.

VIOLET BNP—Food-coloring additive with a violet hue.

VIRULENCE—Ability of a pathogen to overcome body defenses and produce disease.

VIRUS—Agent of infectious disease that is much smaller than a bacterium and is not even a complete cell. It is composed only of nucleic acids wrapped in a protein coat. Viruses can spread through food, water, or the air. Antibiotics are ineffective against them.

VISCOMETER—Device that measures the viscosity or density of fluids, e.g., syrup has a higher viscosity rating than water.

VISITS, RESTAURANT—Visits by cooks or other employees to other restaurants at an establishment's expense to study competing styles of operation.

VISUAL PURPLE—Common name for rhodopsin, the purplish pigment in the eyes derived from vitamin A and responsible for vision in dim light.

VITAMERS—Compounds that are chemically similar to various vitamins but with a less potent effect on the body.

VITAMIN—One of the main categories of nutrients contributing to the health and well-being of the body. Vitamins are received largely through diet. See the individual vitamins.

VITAMIN A—Required for growth, vision in dim light, healthy skin and mucous tissue, and proper immune-system functioning. Deficiency results in stunted growth, night blindness, and other eye and skin problems. Rich sources include carrots, egg yolks, liver, and dairy products. It is a fat-soluble vitamin (see **vitamins, fat-soluble**).

VITAMIN B_1—Required for proper carbohydrate metabolism, muscle coordination, and nerve tissue maintenance. Deficiency can cause **beriberi**. Rich sources include whole grains, cereals, and meat. It is a water-soluble vitamin (see **vitamins, water soluble**). Also called thiamine.

VITAMIN B_2—Required for the proper metabolism of protein, fat, and carbohydrates. Deficiency causes **ariboflavinosis**. Rich sources include whole grains, milk and milk products, green vegetables, and lean meat. It is a water-soluble vitamin (see **vitamins, water soluble**) and is also weakened by sunlight. Also called riboflavin.

VITAMIN B_3, B_4, B_5—No such vitamins exist.

VITAMIN B_6—Required for amino acid and nervous-system functioning. Deficiency, although rare, produces such symptoms as irritability and convulsions. Rich sources include meat, herring, whole grains, bananas, and potatoes. It is a water-soluble vitamin (see **vitamins, water-soluble**). Also called pyridoxine.

VITAMINS B_7, B_8, B_9, B_{10}, B_{11}—No such vitamins exist.

VITAMIN B_{12}—Required for red blood cell development, proper cell function, and maintenance of the nervous system. Deficiency affects almost all body tissues and may cause pernicious anemia and degeneration of the nervous system. Rich sources include organ meats, fish and shell-fish, milk and eggs. It is a water-soluble vitamin (see **vitamins, water-soluble**). Also called cobalamin.

VITAMIN C—Required for strong cell structure, healthy teeth and gums, and aids in the absorption of iron. Deficiency can cause easy bruising and scurvy. Rich sources include citrus fruits, potatoes, tomatoes, and green leafy vegetables. It is a water-soluble vitamin (see **vitamins, water-soluble**) . Also called ascorbic acid.

VITAMIN D—Required for the utilization of calcium. Deficiency causes rickets in children and contributes to osteomalacia and osteoporosis in adults. Rich sources include milk and milk products, fatty fish, and liver; the body produces its own vitamin D from sunlight. It is a fat-soluble vitamin (see **vitamins, fat-soluble**).

VITAMIN D$_2$—A **provitamin** for **vitamin D.** Also called calciferol or ergocalciferol.

VITAMIN D$_3$—A **provitamin** for **vitamin D.**

VITAMIN E—As an antioxidant, helps protect body tissues from aging and prolongs red blood cell life. Deficiency, although rare, can result in destruction of red blood cells and muscle degeneration. Rich sources include whole grain cereals, vegetable oils, eggs, liver, and peanuts. It is a fat-soluble vitamin (see **vitamins, fat-soluble**). Also called tocopherol.

VITAMIN H—Original name for **biotin.**

VITAMIN K—Required for proper clotting of the blood. Rich sources include green leafy vegetables, cereal grains; some is synthesized in the intestines. Deficiency, although rare, can cause hemorrhaging. Rich sources include green leafy vegetables and liver.

VITAMINS, FAT-SOLUBLE—Vitamins A, D, E, and K. They are stored in the body's fat tissues and thus persist in the body longer than the water-soluble vitamins.

VITAMINS, WATER-SOLUBLE—Vitamins of the B-complex and vitamin C. They are stored in body fluids (such as blood) and are more easily lost (e.g., in the urine) than the fat-soluble vitamins. They are also easily leached out by cooking.

VITELLIN—One of the main proteins in egg yolk, accounting for about 80 percent of the total.

VITICULTURE—Science and study of grape growing.

VITRIFIED CHINA—See **porcelain.**

VOLATILE—Liquid that evaporates readily, even at room temperature. Also, a liquid or some other substance that ignites readily at low temperatures, e.g., some solvents.

VOLUME DISCOUNT—Reduction in price granted by the seller when the buyer purchases a large number of goods in a series of purchases over a given time. Volume discounts differ from **quantity discounts,** which apply only to a single purchase.

VOTATOR—Machine that produces margarine by emulsifying fat and water.

VOUCHER—Any business form that authorizes a cash expenditure or that documents that cash has been spent, e.g., an invoice or bill.

VOUCHER CHECK—Check that includes information on discounts, the nature of goods received, and an invoice number, thus allowing it to serve as a **voucher.**

VOUCHER INDEX—Supplement to the **voucher register** that contains an alphabetized list of all the suppliers and other companies paid.

VOUCHER REGISTER—Record on which all expenses are listed along with related information such as the date and to whom it was paid.

W

WAFFLE IRON—Special mold made of cast iron used to make waffles. It consists of two opposing plates, usually of cast iron, embossed with matching designs.

WAGE-RATE STRUCTURE—Hierarchy of all the jobs in an establishment with the pay of each. A good structure usually provides incentives for continued service in terms of pay increases within the same job as a function of years spent there.

WAITER CHECKLIST—Form on which each waiter or waitress writes in the number of each guest check he has used and the amount collected for each.

WAITER SIGNATURE BOOK—Form on which each waiter or waitress signs for the numbered guest checks he has been issued.

WALK-IN STORAGE—Dry or refrigerated storage of food in its own room or rooms. One must enter the room to obtain an item. Contrast **reach-in storage.**

WALKOUTS—Customers who defraud the establishment by leaving without paying their checks.

WAREWASHING RACK—Square rack of plastic or steel used to hold materials to be sent through the dishwashing machine. Racks are made in various designs to hold plates, cups, glasses, or silverware.

WARFARIN—Type of **multiple-dose poison.** It kills through anticoagulant action.

WARRANTY—Written statement by a seller stating its responsibility for certain deficiencies in its products for a given time after purchase.

WASH—Fermented liquor that is ready to be distilled into whiskey.

WASH THERMOMETER—Thermometer that is immersed in the water of the dishwashing sink in order to ascertain its temperature and help maintain it at the proper level.

WASTE DISPOSAL—See **food waste disposal.**

WASTE PERCENTAGE—Ratio of the weight of unusable meat portions to the original total weight (see **AP weight**) times 100 percent. The higher the percentage, the worse the buy, all other factors being equal.

WATER-BASED SPRAYS—Insecticide sprays in which water is the solvent for the toxic compounds. These are preferred where oil could damage materials such as asphalt or rubber and create a fire hazard around ovens. See also **oil-based sprays.**

WATER CHESTNUT—Not a nut at all but an aquatic tuber that somewhat resembles a chestnut. They are used primarily in Chinese dishes.

WATERCRESS—Aquatic plant with long stems and thick leaves that is related to the mustard family. Its pungent leaves are used in salads or as a garnish.

WATER, DEMINERALIZED—Water from which the mineral salts have been removed by passing it over a bed of **ion-exchange resins.**

WATER HARDNESS—Tendency of water to precipitate soap, thereby preventing the formation of suds. The more minerals in water, the harder it is.

WATERMARK—Name or logo of the company that manufactured the menu paper, faintly pressed onto each sheet by the **dandy roll.**

WATERMELON—Very large log-shaped melon that may grow up to five feet long. It has a green rind, sweet red flesh, and plentiful seeds. The flesh is very flimsy and watery and is usually eaten raw, although it can be used in jellies and as a syrup.

WATER-MIXING VALVE—Plumbing device that combines the flow from the hot-water and cold-water valves so that the temperature of the combined flow can be manipulated by controlling the taps. Required in new foodservice establishments.

WAVE GUIDE—Part of a microwave oven that takes energy from the magnetron and directs it through a mixer into the oven cavity.

WEATHERSTRIPPING—Strips of insulating material around

doors, windows, and other openings to minimize heat loss in the winter and heat entry in the summer.

WEB—Continuous roll of paper used for menu printing in a **web press.**

WEB PRESS—Printing press into which a continuous roll of menu paper is fed. Once a sheet is printed, it is cut from the roll by the machine. Contrast **sheet-fed press.**

WEDGER—Special tool that rapidly cuts tomatoes, lemons, or other small fruits into uniform wedge shapes.

WEEKLY BANQUET SHEET—Summary of all the banquets to be held in the coming week at a given establishment. The relevant data is derived from the file of **banquet contract forms.**

WEEPERS—Bottles showing leakage through or around their corks.

WEIGHING—Using a scale to measure the weight of goods. It is important for the receiving clerk to measure the weights of received goods to ensure that they correspond with what was ordered and what the invoice states was delivered.

WELL—Hollow space left in a mold, or the space in a pastry shell to be filled with food.

WET SERVICE—Method for making tea by covering it with boiling water and allowing it to steep from three to five minutes.

WET WRAP—Wrapping meat or another product with cellophane that has been moistened with a sponge so that when the wrapping dries, it will form a tight seal.

WHEAT GERM—"Seed" portion of a wheat grain; it is only about 2 percent of the total but contains most of the nutrients.

WHEY—Liquid residue left after the casein and most of the fat have been removed from milk. Although casein is the main milk protein, lactalbumin and lactoglobulin proteins remain in the whey.

WHIP—To beat a mixture rapidly, which increases its volume and makes it "lighter" by the incorporation of air. Also, a utensil made of wire loops fitted into a handle, useful for stirring sauces, batters, and the like. Also called a whisk.

WHITE BLOOD CELLS—Blood cells that help the body resist infection. Also called leukocytes.

WHITE CHOCOLATE—Not really a chocolate, as it contains no chocolate liquid. It is made with vegetable fats instead of cocoa butter, and has added vegetable coloring and flavors.

WHOLESOME—Clean and in good condition; suitable for human use or consumption.

WIDOW—Single word left on the last line of a menu paragraph. Not a good practice, as it may go unnoticed and unread.

WINDFALL PROFIT—Unanticipated profit caused by factors an establishment cannot control. For example, a temporary detour may force a huge increase in potential customers to pass by the establishment, many of whom will stop and eat there.

WINE—Naturally fermented juice of ripe grapes, preferably freshly gathered and crushed at or near the place where they are harvested. Three factors govern the appreciation of wine: color, aroma, and taste. The best French reds and whites are deemed by most connoisseurs to be the finest in the world; German whites from the Rhine and Moselle districts have an unsurpassed lightness and fruitiness; Italian wines are hearty and earthy; Spain is famed for its sherry; the great variety of wines from the United States challenge the best wines of France.

WINE, FRANCE—France is geographically divided into 95 departments, all but two of which produce wines. The most important wine-producing regions and their wines are Gironde (Bordeaux), Côte d'Or (Burgundy), Marne (Champagne), Bas-Rhin and Haut-Rhin (Alsace), Sâone-et-Loire (Póuilly-Fuissé and Mâcon), and Rhône (Béaujolais).

The French government has adopted the Appellation d'Origine Controlée regulations strictly limiting the geographical boundaries of wine-producing districts, as well as the maximum amount that may be produced in that district. The following is an overview of the most important wine-producing regions in France.

Alsace: This region is famous for its rich, austere, dry white wines. The most famous Alsatian wines include muscat, pinot gris, pinot blanc, gerwürztraminer, traminer, and reisling.

Bordeaux: The Bordeaux region is divided into five major districts. The Médoc district produces elegant, tannic wines that are excellent with roasted and grilled meats. The grape variety principally used in this region is the cabernet sauvignon. The Graves district is also known for its use of the cabernet sauvignon grape to create resinous red wines. A number of aristocratic white wines, principally using semillon and sauvignon blanc grapes, are also produced in this district. The Sauternes district produces dessert wines with a thick honey color and taste. The wines are produced from the semillon and sauvignon blanc grapes. The Saint-Emilion district wines are mostly made of merlot grapes. They tend to be ruby, full wines. The Pomeral district produces full-bodied, sappy wines using mostly merlot grapes.

Burgundy: The wine regions of Burgundy include Beaujolais, Mâconnais, Région de Mercurey, Côte De Beaune, Côte De Nuits, and Chablis. The Beaujolais region is famous for its young, fresh, fruity wines made from the gamay grape. The Mâconnais region is particularly known for its white wines, especially the pouilly-fuissé. The other white and red wines from this region are largely carafe-type wines. The Région de Mercurey produces both red and white wines. These wines are quite good, though not of the quality of the Côte De Beaune. The Côte De Beaune is famous for its fruity, soft red wines and some excellent white wines including montrachet and mersault. The Côte De Nuits is famous for its strong, full-bodied pinot noir wines. Chablis is a little town in the department of Yonne that gives its name to a pale, dry, delicate white wine.

Champagne: This region is, of course, most famous for the production of champagne, a sparkling wine usually made from red pinot noir, pinot meunier, and white chardonnay wines. The Méthode Champenoise involves inducing a second fermentation in wines that releases carbon dioxide gas, thereby creating bubbles.

Rhône: The red Rhône wines are heady, robust wines, generally made from syrah, grenache, clairette, or bourboulene grape varieties. The most famous Rhône vineyard is Châteauneuf-du-Pape.

Sâone-et-Loire: The Loire Valley region produces red, white, rosé, and sparkling wines. The most popular Loire wines are white, including muscadet, pouilly-fumé, sancerre, and vouvray.

WINE, GERMANY—Germany ranks tenth among wine-producing countries, producing some of the world's great white wines. The most memorable wines are produced in the Rhine and Moselle valleys.

Baden: The Baden region produces both red and white wines. Weissherbst, a rosé wine made from the pinot noir grape, is produced here, as is Schillerwein, a highly esteemed claret.

Franconia: The white wines of Franconia are dry and full-bodied. They are mostly made using Müller, Thurgau and Silvaner grapes. The most outstanding vineyards are in Würzberg.

Moselle: These highly reputed wines are light, delicate, fruity, elegant, and dry. Most Moselle wines are low in alcohol, usually only about 8 to 10 percent. Piesporter, Braunberger, Zeltinger, Berukasteler, Doctor, and Wehliner Sonne Huhr are just a few of the most famous Moselle vineyards.

Nahe: The Nahe is a tributary of the Rhine and lies between the Moselle and Rhine valleys. These wines have a pronounced bouquet and combine the light freshness of the Moselle wines with the heartiness of the Rhein wines. The most notable wine-producing communes include Bade-Kreuznach, Munster, and Böckelheim.

Rheingau: The wines of the Rheingau are austere, fruity, and slightly hard. Popular Rheingau vineyards include Stein-

berger, Johannisberg, Rudesheimer, Hochheimer, and
Sonnenberg.

Rhein-Hessen: The Rhein-Hessen is the second largest wine-
producing region in Germany. These wines are softer and
fuller than those of the Rheingau. The. main wine-producing villages are Worms, Liebfrauenstift, Mettenheim,
Alsheim, Guntersblum, Oppenheim, Nierstein, and
Mayence.

Rheinpfalz: This is the largest wine-producing area in Germany, producing largely table wines that are earthy and
full-bodied. The most notable wine-producing communi-
ties in the Rheinpfalz include Bad Dürkheim and
Deidesheim.

WINE, ITALY—Wine is produced everywhere in Italy and the
Italians drink more wine than is consumed in any other country.
In fact, the ancient Romans are credited with having spread
vinification. Italy is largely known for producing good-quality,
abundant, and reasonably priced wines.

Apulia and Abruzzi: This area produces most of Italy's wines.
Aleatica grapes are used to produce a great deal of
Aleatica di Puglia, a dark, highly alcoholic wine. More
balanced wines are produced in Castel del Monte and
San Severo, including reds, whites, and rosés. Big, red,
long-aging wines are made in Santo Stefano and Torre
Quarto. Memorable whites produced in this region include Montepulciano d'Abruzzo and Trebbiano d'A-
bruzzo.

Campania and Basilicata: The most famous wine produced
here is Lacryma Christi, a golden, dry, aromatic white
wine. Other white wines produced here include the dry
Greco di Tufo and the almond-scented Fiano di Avellino.

Emilia-Romagna: Respectable wines from this region include
Gutturnio, a dry, full-bodied red wine made from barbera
and bonardo grapes, Sanrovese di Romagna, a smooth,
full-bodied red, and Trebiano di Romagna, a light, austere, white wine. The central area of Emilia-Romagna
uses a great deal of lambrusco grape varieties to produce a

lively, fizzy semidry red wine that has become quite popular in the United States.

Latium: This region is chiefly known for its white wines including Frascati, a fresh light white and Est! Est! Est!, a
straw-yellow, fruity and fresh white wine.

Lombardy: The most famous red wines are the Sassella, Gru-
mello, Inferno, and Valgella. These wines are made from
95 percent nebbiolo grapes. One of the most famous
white wines from this area is Lugana, a pleasant light
wine made from the trebbiano grape. The Riviera del
Gardu rosé, a light-red, soft, slightly bitter wine, is also
made in this area.

Piedmont: Piedmont produces the majority of Italy's most re-
gal red wines, equal in quality to those of France. They
tend to be rich, robust, and velvety. They are principally
made with Nebbiolo grapes. The most famous red wines
of this region are Barolo, Barbaresco, and Gattinara. Asti
wine, a sparkling wine made from the muscat grape, is
also produced in this region. This famous wine is sweet,
delicate, light and fresh.

Tuscany: Tuscany is the home of Chianti, Italy's quintessen-
tial wine. Chianti varies from deep and robust to light and
bright, depending on the producer. A number of grape
varieties can go into a Chianti. Principal grapes used include sangrovese, canaiolo nero, trebbiano tuscano and
malvasia del chianti.

Veneto: A number of well-known red wines are produced in
this region. Valpolicella, a fruity red wine blended from
corvina, rondinella, and Valpolicella grapes, is produced
here, as is the well-known white wine Soave. Soave is a
subtle, slightly bitter white wine that has grown in popularity in the United States.

WINE, SPAIN—Spain comes in third in world wine production.
The country is most distinguished for its production of sherry.
The bulk of Spanish wine is light, fresh table wine, though some
quality wines are exported.

Andalucia: The most southern province of Spain is world
renowned for its production of sherry. The Palomino

grape is the classic sherry grape used in Jerez. The best-known varieties of sherry include Fino, Amontillado, Manzanilla, and Oloroso.

Catalonia: The red wines of Catalonia have a solid reputation. Alella, north of Barcelona, produces light, dry table wines. Panadés produces reds and clarets. In the Bajo Panadés, cariñena, garnacha, and ull de llebre grapes are grown while the Alto Panadés produces chardonnay, sauvignon blanc, reisling, cabernet sauvignon and pinot noir grapes. A distinguished sparkling wine is produced around San Sadurni de Noya using the Méthode Champenoise.

Rioja: The red wines of the Rioja region are fruity, generous, and highly alcoholic. They are usually made with temprauillo, garnacha, tinta, graciano, and mazuelo grapes. The white wines are produced mainly from malvoisie grapes and are sweet and full-bodied.

Valdepeñas: La Mancha has a very large production of smooth, versatile, red and white wines. The whites, made from airen grapes, are dry and full-bodied. The reds are fruity and highly alcoholic.

WINE, UNITED STATES—American wines have so overtaken their counterparts, particularly in the medium to good grades, that even the French can no longer sneer at them. Indeed, California is now recognized as one of the world's premier wine-growing regions. Moreoever, with the successful planting of new French-American hybrid grapes in the East, dry European-style wines are being produced in the East as well. Most American wines are known by either a generic name such as rosé or by the grape name, a system that can create a great deal of confusion. The following is an overview of the main wine-producing areas of California and New York. Although space prohibits discussion of them here, it should be noted that other areas of the United States, particularly the Pacific Northwest, are producing memorable wines as well.

California: California has over 350 wineries. The Central valleys produce about three quarters of the wine in California, although the wines lack the intensity and distinctiveness of coast wines. The Guild Winery's Winemasters label makes excellent Chenin Blanc and Cabernet Sauvignon. D'Agostino Winery produces sound red wines, while Montevina Winery makes delightful Zinfandels, Sauvignon Blancs, and Cabernet Sauvignons. Gallo Winery in Modesto is the world's largest wine producer. None of them is really great. However, the winery does provide a quality product for everyday use. The best of the Gallo wines is the Chenin Blanc.

Monterey County, in the Central Coast of California, has the greatest number of acres planted with prime varietal grapes in the state. Monterey Vineyard produces notable white wines including Johannisberg Riesling, Gewürtztraminer, and Sauvignon Blanc. The Monterey Peninsula Winery makes excellent Ruby Cabernet and Gewurztraminer.

Santa Clara County is home of the well-known Almadén Winery, producer of consistent and inexpensive wines. The Johannisberg Riesling is fresh and fruity and the Chardonnays are dry and woody. Almadén also produces excellent Sauvignon Blanc, Blanc Fumé, and Merlot. Paul Masson Winery produces a strong line of proprietary wines as well as a substantial line of sparkling wines. The Pinnacles Selection is comprised of vintage-dated Monterey County appellation wines.

Sonoma Valley wines are growing in reputation and are beginning to rival those of Napa Valley. Sebastiani produces very ripe, full-bodied red wines. Particularly notable is the Barbera. The Gamay Beaujolais is fresh, fruity, and light. Souverain produces mostly 100 percent varietals. The whites are best, particularly the dry Chenin Blanc, the slightly sweet Johannisberg Riesling, and the flowery Chardonnays. The Simi Winery produces some very good red wines, including a rich Cabernet Sauvignon and an excellent Pinot Noir. J. Korbel & Sons, also found in Sonoma County, makes excellent sparkling wines.

Napa Valley is the best known of California's wine-producing regions. C. Mondavi & Sons produces some

excellent white wines, particularly the Chenin Blanc and
the Chardonnays. Beaulieu Vineyards has excellent Cabernet Sauvignons, rich and fruity Pinot Noirs and mellow, oaky Pinot Chardonnays. Inglenook, though no
longer a premium winery, still produces reliable, satisfactory wines, the best of which are the cask bottlings of
Cabernet Sauvignon and Pinot Noir. Beringer Vineyards
produces jug wines under the Los Hermanos label, as
well as other average wines under the Beringer Premium
label. The vineyard does produce some excellent Cabernet Sauvignons. The Louis M. Martini vineyard is best
known for its red wines, including a full-bodied Cabernet
Sauvignon and a fresh Zinfandel.

New York: New York is the second largest grape-growing state
in the United States. The finger lakes area of west central
New York is the site of a number of well-known wineries.
Taylor wines is the largest Eastern winery and the na-
tion's largest producer of sparkling wines. The best of
these is the slightly sweet Brut. Taylor also produces generic wines under the California Cellars label. These
wines are made from 100 percent California wines. Taylor Winery owns the Pleasant Valley Wine Company, famous for its Great Western sparkling wines. Gold Seal
Winery produces first rate sparkling wines, as well as a
strong line of Labrusca wines. Mogen David and Mani-
schewitz wineries, in the Chautauqua region of New
York, produce Kosher wines, largely made from Concord
grapes.

WINE BASKET—Cradle made of wire or straw used to hold a
wine bottle at the same angle in which it has been stored on a
wine rack, thus leaving its sediment undisturbed as it is brought
to the table.

WINE BROKER—Middleman between wine buyers and vineyard
owners. The wine broker buys in bulk from vineyard owners and
sells to wine dealers.

WINE COOLER—Ornamental bucket, often of silver, that holds

a bottle of wine surrounded by ice. It is used to cool wine at the table or in a stand beside the table. Also called an ice bucket.

WINE CRADLE—**Wine basket.**

WINTERIZATION—Refrigeration of edible oils in order to remove the glyceride compounds, such as **stearates,** that solidify at low temperatures.

WIRE BASKET—Almost-flat wire container used to hold a bottle of wine on its side. Also called wine basket.

WIRE LOOP—Vertical-mixer attachment made of heavy wire loops in a spherical arrangement. It is commonly used to whip light ingredients. Also called a whip.

WIRE WHIP, HEAVY-DUTY—Vertical-mixer attachment made of heavy wire loops that may be reinforced with a metal band. It is used for beating heavy ingredients.

WITH THE GRAIN—Folding printed menu paper along a line parallel to the paper's **grain.** Folding otherwise weakens the paper.

WOOD ALCOHOL—Common name for **methyl alcohol,** a poisonous fluid that sometimes gets mixed with drinking alcohol in the home production of alcoholic spirits. Ingestion can cause blindness, paralysis, and even death.

WORD—Data unit in computing that is standard for that system. For example, a unit of four bytes for a 32-bit system, or two bytes for a 16-bit system.

WORK-ASSIGNMENT SHEET—Form that supervisors use to instruct employees as to what menu items they are to prepare for a given meal, the number of each, and which recipe they should use.

WORKING CAPITAL—Amount of money used to finance current operations. It is calculated by subtracting current liabilities from current assets.

WORK-LOAD FORECASTING—Predicting the amount of work

each category of employee will need to perform, based on a forecast of covers and their preferences.

WORK-PRODUCTION STANDARDS—Established criteria of what an employee in a given position should accomplish. This could be measured for example in terms of units produced per day or sales dollars per hour.

WORK SIMPLIFICATION—Analyzing a job to find ways to save time and effort, thus increasing productivity.

X

XANTHINE—One of the **purine** compounds that does not play a role in nucleic acids.

XANTHINE OXIDASE—Enzyme found in animal liver and milk that oxidizes **xanthine** to uric acid.

XANTHOPHYLL—Yellow derivative of **carotene** that is found in all green leaves. Although related to carotene, xanthophyll has no vitamin A activity.

XANTHOPROTEIC TEST—Test for the presence of protein in a food substance.

XEROPHTHALMIA—Serious degeneration of the eyes caused by a major deficiency of vitamin A.

XYLITOL—Artificial sweetener used in chewing gum. It has been linked with cancer in laboratory animals.

XYLOSE—Plant sugar that is only about 40 percent as sweet as sucrose.

Y

YAM—Tropical plant that produces a vegetable similar to the sweet potato but juicier. Grown in the Southern United States.

YEARLING—Year-old animal that provides tender meat.

YEAST—Class of fungi. Some are useful, e.g., for leavening bread, for fermenting sugar into alcohol, or as a rich protein source. Others produce contaminants.

YEAST, COMPRESSED—**Yeast** plants packaged alive and ready for use and held in refrigeration until needed. It should never be used if stale, as recognized by its streaky appearance, slippery feel, and objectionable odor.

YEAST, DRY—**Yeast** plants made inactive through drying. Dry yeast does not require refrigeration. They require food, warmth, and moisture to reactivate.

YEAST EXTRACT—Water-soluble derivative of **yeast** used in food because of its plentiful B-complex vitamins and strong flavor.

YELLOW NO. 5, NO. 6—Two food-coloring additives used in gelatins, candies, and drinks. Many people are allergic to these particular agents.

YERBA MATE—South American tea made from the *Ilex paraguayensis* plant, which contains caffeine. Also called simply **maté.**

YIELD—Amount of meat available for sale after a portion has been cleaned of fat and bone, then cooked.

YIELD PERCENTAGE—Ratio of **yield** weight of meat to the original total weight (see **AP weight**) times 100 percent. The higher the yield percentage, the better the buy, other factors being equal.

YIELD TEST—Study to reveal the number of portions obtained from a quantity of food.

YOGURT—Milk that has been curdled with bacterial cultures until it is solid and creamy. It is often combined with sweeteners and fruit or other flavorings and is very nutritious.

YOLK INDEX—Index revealing the freshness of eggs; the higher the number, the fresher the eggs.

Z

ZEAXANTHIN—Natural yellow pigment in corn that is used as a food-coloring additive.

ZEIN—Protein in corn that is deficient in the amino acids lysine and tryptophan. Since both are essential amino acids, zein is a poor-quality protein.

Z-ENZYME—Enzyme that helps in the **catabolism** of amylose to maltose.

ZEST—Outer peel of citrus fruits, containing the color and oil sacs.

ZESTER—Small tool used to remove narrow strips of outer vegetable skin for decorative purposes in vegetable and salad preparation.

ZINC—Essential mineral required by several enzyme systems, and in the synthesis of nucleic acids and of protein. Best food sources include seafood, liver, eggs, and nuts. It is easily destroyed in cooking. Too much, however, can be toxic.

ZINC PHOSPHIDE—Type of **single-dose poison.**

ZOONOSIS—Any infectious disease in animals that can be spread to humans, e.g., **brucellosis.**

ZUCCHINI—Italian squash that is long, slender, and of delicate texture.

ZYGOSACCHAROMYCES—Yeasts that thrive in foods such as honey and chocolate candy, which have very high concentrations of sugar.

ZYMASE—Enzymes in yeast that perform the chemical changes involved in fermentation.

ZYMOSIS—Undesired fermentation, which can be controlled by the proper care of food.

ZYMOTACHEGRAPH—Device used to measure the carbon dioxide gas produced in dough by fermentation.